ADVANCES
IN
WRITING RESEARCH
VOLUME ONE

Children's Early Writing Development

Writing Research

Multidisciplinary Inquiries into the Nature of Writing

edited by Marcia Farr, University of Illinois at Chicago

Arthur N. Applebee, *Contexts for Learning to Write*

Lester Faigley, Roger Cherry, David Jolliffe, and Anna Skinner, *Assessing Writers' Knowledge and Processes of Composing*

Marcia Farr (ed.), *Advances in Writing Research, Volume One: Children's Early Writing Development*

Sarah W. Freedman (ed.), *The Acquisition of Written Language: Response and Revision*

IN PREPARATION

Carole Edelsky, *Writing in a Bilingual Program: Había Una Vez*

Robert Gundlach, *Children and Writing in American Education*

Martha L. King and Victor Rentel, *The Development of Meaning in Writing: Children 5– 10*

Judith Langer, *Children Reading and Writing: Structures and Strategies*

Anthony Petrosky (ed.), *Reading and Writing: Theory and Research*

Leo Ruth and Sandra Murphy, *Designing Writing Tasks for the Assessment of Writing*

David Smith, *Explorations in the Culture of Literacy*

Jana Staton, *Interactive Writing in Dialogue Journals: Linguistic, Social, and Cognitive Views*

Elizabeth Sulzby, *A Longitudinal Study of Emergent Writing and Reading in 5–6 Year Olds*

William Teale and Elizabeth Sulzby (eds.), *Emergent Literacy: Writing and Reading*

Stephen Witte, Keith Walters, Mary Trachsel, Roger Cherry, and Paul Meyer, *Literacy and Writing Assessment: Issues, Traditions, Directions*

Advances in Writing Research, Volume One:

Children's Early Writing Development

Marcia Farr, Editor
University of Illinois at Chicago

ABLEX PUBLISHING CORPORATION
NORWOOD, NEW JERSEY

Library of Congress Cataloging in Publication Data

Main entry under title:

Children's early writing development.

    (Advances in writing research ; v. 1)
    Includes bibliographies and index.
    1. Children—Writing. I. Farr, Marcia. II. Series.
LB1139.W7C47 1985   372.6   85-1353
ISBN 0-89391-179-8
ISSN 8756-1271

ABLEX Publishing Corporation
355 Chestnut Street
Norwood, New Jersey 07648

Contents

Writing Research

Multidisciplinary Inquiries into the Nature of Writing

Marcia Farr, series editor
University of Illinois at Chicago

PREFACE

This series of volumes presents the results of recent scholarly inquiry into the nature of writing. The research presented comes from a mix of disciplines, those which have emerged as significant within the last decade or so in the burgeoning field of writing research. These primarily include English education, linguistics, psychology, anthropology, and rhetoric. A note here on the distinction between field and discipline might be useful: a field can be a multidisciplinary entity focused on a set of significant questions about a central concern (e.g., American Studies), while a discipline usually shares theoretical and methodological approaches which may have a substantial tradition behind them. Writing research, then, is a field, if not yet a discipline.

The history of this particular field is unique. Much of the recent work in this field, and much that is being reported in this series, has been conceptualized and funded by the National Institute of Education. Following a planning conference in June 1977, a program of basic research on the teaching and learning of writing was developed and funded annually. The initial research funded under this program is now coming to fruition, providing both implications for educational improvement and directions for future research. This series is intended as one important outlet for these results.

Introduction

Marcia Farr

The primary focus in all five of the studies in this volume is on children at the beginning of learning to write.[1] They are part of a growing body of empirical research which has emerged within the last decade or two. This research complements the earlier focus on reading in the investigation of literacy by focusing primarily on writing. We increasingly are becoming aware from all this work that much literacy learning begins before formal literacy instruction. The first three studies in this volume (by Gundlach et al., Dyson, and Sulzby) explore what has come to be called emergent literacy (what children know of writing and reading before the onset of formal literacy instruction in school). The final two studies (by Greene and Sowers) are conducted in early elementary school classrooms; they explore emerging literacy capacities within the context of formal schooling.

Background

These studies, then, deal with literacy (and primarily with writing), development, and, to a lesser extent, schooling. Early studies of emergent literacy (Bissex, 1980; Clay, 1975; Ferreiro & Teberosky, 1982; Harste, Burke, & Woodward, 1981; Heath, 1981; Scollon & Scollon, 1981; Sulzby, 1981) broke new ground by demonstrating that children know much more about literacy before they can write and read in an adult, conventional sense than we had assumed. These researchers studied children from different countries, social classes, and racial and ethnic groups. They found that, although the specific kinds of knowledge about literacy that children from various backgrounds bring to the task of becoming literate may vary, practically all children in a highly literate society such as ours do bring knowledge about literacy to school with them. They do not begin as blank slates. Also, it has become increasingly clear that the knowledge they bring often clashes with the assumptions underlying current instruction, causing, at the least, confusion and possibly even interference in learning.

---

[1] I would like to acknowledge Robert Gundlach and Elizabeth Sulzby for their detailed comments on an earlier draft of this introduction. I would also like to thank Trika Smith-Burke and Michael Maltz for their helpful comments.

In addition to the above studies of emergent literacy before schooling, there have been a number of school-based studies which also address the question of children's literacy capacities. Elsewhere (Farr, 1984) I have provided a synthesis of three school-based studies (Graves, 1981; King & Rentel, 1981; Staton, 1982) which show that children (again from different backgrounds) have literacy capacities beyond what had been assumed. Moreover, they show that these capacities become more evident in classrooms which provide instructional frameworks that do not clash with children's emerging literacy. For example, literacy development is facilitated when literacy is treated as a means to an end rather than an end in itself (e.g., reading and writing become part of every learning activity in the classroom, rather than only subject areas in themselves). Also, instructional approaches which provide what has been termed scaffolding (Cazden, 1982) for the learner facilitate literacy development. In particular, the teacher and peer conferences studied in the Graves project and the dialogue journals studied by Staton both provide scaffolding in the form of questions which lead students to elaborate topics in their writing. Using literacy to communicate rather than simply to practice, and providing scaffolding which naturally extends learning, are key factors in the learning of writing in school.

The studies presented in this volume provide additional information both about the specific kinds of knowledge of literacy which children bring to school and about other ways in which we might build upon these capacities in school. In addition to the research-based knowledge which they add to a growing field, they also contribute significantly to our research "know-how." In a field which is multidisciplinary at base, questions of both methodology and theory are difficult and often unclear. These studies provide good examples of how to combine various methods and theoretical orientations to answer serious questions about the nature of literacy and its development. First, I will explore the methodological and theoretical bases upon which each study in this volume relies. Following that, I will provide an overview of the studies, and finally a conceptual framework in which we can consider in detail the knowledge the studies contribute to our understanding of children's early writing development.

Methodology and Theory

The study of literacy, and in particular writing, has burgeoned within the last 15 years, resulting in both an accumulation of research-based knowledge and a multidisciplinary array of methods for data gathering and analysis. These methods have come primarily from linguistics, psychology, and anthropology, often combined with intellectual frameworks from rhetoric. Each study in this volume combines methodology from two or more disciplines because the research questions asked require a variety of methodologies to be answered in any significant way. Specifically, observational methods adapted from anthropology are used by Gundlach et al., Greene, Sowers, and Dyson. Methods of linguistic analysis are used by Greene, Gundlach et al., Sulzby, and Dyson. Experimentally structured methods from psychology are used by Sulzby.

In terms of theory each of these studies also combines frameworks. Gundlach et al. use theoretical frameworks from sociolinguistics (for language functions and communicative competence), developmental psychology (the theory of Vygotsky), and clinical psychology (psychoanalytic theory as it informs emotional development). Dyson uses theoretical frameworks from linguistics (for language functions and language development) and psychology (the theory of Piaget). Sulzby uses theoretical frameworks from linguistics (for language development) and psychology (the theories of both Piaget and Vygotsky). Greene uses sociolinguistic theory (for language functions and communicative competence) and the developmental theory of Vygotsky. Finally, Sowers relies on developmental frameworks from Piaget and Vygotsky, as well as the general observational approach of anthropology.

Let us now return to the knowledge these studies bring to bear on our understanding of writing development. The various pieces of knowledge these studies provide are best understood within a conceptual framework, one which allows their results to be seen coherently, in relation to each other and to previous work in the field. I suggest a framework which consists of three views of writing: writing as language, writing growth as development, and writing as a varying entity in different contexts. Following an overview of the five studies, I will discuss each of these three views of writing and how each study contributes to our knowledge about each view.

Overview of Studies

Gundlach, McLane, Stott, and McNamee provide three case studies of preschool-aged children learning to write. The first case study is that of a 4-year-old boy who "experiments playfully" with written language in his home with his parents. The second case study is that of a 5-year-old girl whose writing is closely linked to her interactions with her 7-year-old sister and her mother; this case study also takes place in the home context. The third case study is that of three children: a 3-year-old boy, a 4-year-old girl, and a 5-year-old boy, who are in a preschool program in which children compose and dramatize their own narratives; this case study, unlike the first two, takes place within the preschool context. All three of the case studies provide rich descriptions, not only of the individual children who are beginning to learn to write, but also of the contexts in which the activity takes place. The notion of context in this study includes not only the physical setting or people involved in a given literacy event, but also the continuing relationship between the child and parents, siblings, and others. Because this study describes in detail individual children learning to write over the course of several months *and* a careful description of the contexts in which they do so, it contributes significantly to our knowledge in this area. Previous studies have done primarily one or the other, but not both.

Dyson provides case studies of three preschool girls learning to write in their kindergarten class. The descriptions of each child engaging in writing over the course of several months yield a picture of individual differences in development. Dyson focuses on the relationship between writing behaviors during the writing process and purposes for writing and individuality. She defines the latter as "a child's style of functioning, interests, and dominant intentions across a range of activities, including talk, socio-dramatic play, and drawing." This study departs significantly from previous work by investigating the interplay of three key factors in writing growth: the nature of the individual child, the nature of the situational context, and the nature of the writing system itself.

Sulzby explores children's developing understandings about written language before they are able to read and write conventionally. She provides the results of two studies with one group of kindergarteners. The first study is a general interview which elicits children's understandings about written language; the second study is an experimentally structured set of related reading and writing tasks. Overall, Sulzby selected tasks structured according to the paradigm of conversation, storytelling, dictation, and handwritten compositions (with rereading and editing of the written forms) in order to allow children to show distinctions they make between oral interactive language and monologic written language. This study contributes significantly to the field of emergent literacy in two ways: first, it combines an experimentally structured approach with more naturalistic observation, and second, it provides quite specific information about the concepts and capacities which children develop as they move toward literacy.

Greene investigates in detail the letters children write in an internal postal system in a bilingual elementary school in a large western metropolitan area. She chose to study these letters because they are functional (i.e., they are real communication to a real audience) and self-generated, rather than teacher-generated, writing. Her results show that letter writing allows children to draw more fully on their oral language competence than they can in most kinds of school writing. This is especially true for language functions: in most school writing children are asked only to inform, whereas in these letters they invite, apologize, brag, compliment, complain, and so forth. This study is an important addition to our understanding of children's writing for two reasons: first, it focuses on language function rather than just form, and second, it investigates a genre of writing other than the often-studied school theme.

Sowers reports on an observational, classroom-based study by Donald Graves, Lucy Calkins, and herself. This 3-year project started as an attempt to trace developmental patterns in children's writing in their natural classroom settings, but it evolved into a collaborative researcher-teacher effort which was a catalyst for change in writing instruction. Sowers' report of this process provides a detailed description of the context in which children grew as writers, with special attention to the writing conferences which were the heart of the instructional approach used by the teachers. As Sowers points out, at the beginning of the project context was seen as a backdrop to the research on writing development, but it became the central concern when it became clear that context was inextricably linked to the children's writing processes and growth. Sowers' careful description and analysis of context is a significant addition to the literature coming out of the well-known Graves project, and as such it adds important information to our growing understanding of children's actual capacities for writing in school.

In the following sections, I will discuss the three views of writing which I believe constitute the best framework within which the contributions of these five studies can be understood: writing as language, writing growth as development, and writing variation in context. Within each section I will start with a conceptual discussion of that view of writing and end with a description of how these particular studies add to our understanding of that view.

Writing as Language

The concept of linguistic competence introduced by Chomsky in 1965 still underlies much of our thinking about language. Essentially, linguistic competence is the abstract system of knowledge in the human mind which allows us both to produce and to understand our language. To Chomsky, the knowledge was that of an "ideal speaker-hearer" of English; what actually was spoken was linguistic performance, not competence. In contrast to competence, which was ideal, performance allowed for "error," or variation from the ideal. Sociolinguists such as Labov, Shuy, Gumperz, and Hymes pointed out that much variation in language use was not random, but patterned and predictable. Thus they argued that variation in speakers (e.g., sex, race, social class) as well as in the context of language use (e.g., in the classroom, at home, with peers or strangers) was actually part of linguistic competence. Hymes, in a significant paper (1971), created the term *communicative competence* to refer to the ability to use different forms of language appropriately in various contexts, thus connecting the social and cultural with the linguistic in a primary way. That is, communicative competence includes not only rules to generate the forms of one's language, but also rules for how to use those forms appropriately within the various contexts in one's culture.

Early studies of communicative competence (Bauman & Sherzer, 1974; Gumperz & Hymes, 1972) primarily focused on oral language. Even today, most linguists primarily study oral rather than written language, treating speaking as somehow more authentic than writing in the attempt to discern how language works. This may reflect the influence of Bloomfield, who earlier in this century asserted the primacy of oral language to turn linguists away from the exclusive study of historical documents, a practice which had previously dominated the field. Bloomfield's contention that writing was merely speech written down (1933) was necessary historically in the development of linguistics. However, it now seems appropriate, especially in view of the highly literate nature of our society, to include the forms and uses of writing in the study of language. Our model of communicative competence should include reading and writing as well as speaking and listening. Recently, some researchers, including those in this volume, have begun to do this (Florio & Clark, 1982; Gumperz, 1982; Heath, 1983; Scribner & Cole, 1981; Staton, 1982; Tannen, 1982).

Much of this recent work has explored the similarities and differences between speaking, listening, writing, and reading, following up the suggestion by Goody and Watt (1968) that literacy may have both cultural and cognitive consequences. Initially researchers began to describe "oral strategies" and "literate strategies" in the use of language; this work was based implicitly on definitions of oral language as typical casual conversation and written language as school-based essays, sometimes referred to as the British essayist tradition (Olson, 1977). Later, Tannen (1982) showed that a simple dichotomy between oral and written language does not exist in reality. Instead, language use in a literate society draws on aspects of both "orality" and "literacy" in complex ways. For example, oral strategies can be found in written language, and literate strategies can be found in oral language. Also, as Heath (1983) has shown, they are often overlapping and interwoven within a single speech or literacy event.

The research on oral and written language not only reinforces the inclusion of literacy in the conception of language, but also provides a context within which to study development. Oral language development seems to proceed on the basis of much practice in attempts to create meaning (in our culture, in interaction with adults). For example, babies have been shown to begin their acquisition of English by trying to communicate meaning, albeit without exactly-learned words and fully formed sentences (Halliday, 1977). With experience in speaking and listening, they learn increasingly sophisticated language forms, as well as how to use those forms appropriately in various contexts within their culture. We are now beginning to see that writing and reading also might best be learned in attempts to create meaning, especially if we view them as being as naturally a part of language as are speaking or listening. Moreover, it is now becoming clear that experience in one language process might affect development in another. For example, classroom activities such as sharing time, dramatic play, and listening to stories, which are often seen as oral language activities, apparently help children develop a sense of written language structures (Michaels & Collins, 1984).

Both emergent literacy research and research on oral and written language bring us to see language holistically, and language use as dynamic movement between oral and literate processes. Thus, children's language use can be seen as a movement, back and forth, between oral and written language structures and strategies as a way to develop communicative competence, rather than as a one-way developmental transition from oral to written language.

So far I have attempted to detail a model of communicative competence within which the studies in this volume might be viewed. Now I will discuss how these studies both support and contribute to this model. Their primary contribution is in illuminating the relationships among all the language processes, speaking, listening, reading, and writing. The first three studies, which focus on children who have not yet begun formal literacy instruction (first grade), show how literacy begins to develop while oral language is still being acquired. Gundlach et al., who studied the youngest children (most of them at home, before any schooling), emphasize the role of play in writing development, a factor which has been recognized as important in oral language development (Bruner, 1983). Dyson, citing extensive research on oral language acquisition from psycholinguistics, demonstrates the parallel role of individual variation in both oral language development and writing development. Sulzby illustrates how children use all their language capacities, both oral and written, to perform reading and writing tasks before they are reading and writing conventionally. The final two studies show how literacy development in school continues to parallel the patterns of oral language development. Greene's study reveals how the language functions defined in sociolinguistic research on oral language (e.g., complaining, inviting, insulting, apologizing) are found in the letter writing of elementary school children. Sowers' study of the "conferencing model" of teaching writing draws out in detail how the conferences follow a predictable routine which is like the mother/child interaction which has been studied, in our culture, during oral language acquisition.

In the next section I will discuss the second view of writing to which these studies contribute: writing growth as development. Again I will follow a conceptual discussion with a description of how these particular studies add to our understanding of this view.

Writing Growth as Development

When researchers began to study writing development, many of them looked not only to linguistics for a theory of language, but also to psychology for theories of development. Recent studies of child development have been based primarily on the theoretical framework of either Piaget or Vygotsky, or on a combination of the two. Although the two theories are distinct in important ways, they also share significant emphases. So, rather than being mutually exclusive as explanations of development in children, they can be viewed as complementary, each contributing part of the explanation for what happens in reality.

Piaget's theory, while originally used to study the acquisition of logical mathematical and physical knowledge, has recently been used to study the acquisition of written language (Ferreiro & Teberosky, 1982). One of the basic tenets of this theory is that the learner is an active constructor of knowledge and not simply a recipient of information from the world. Through interaction with the object of knowledge (e.g., a written language), the learner acquires knowledge, creating conceptualizations at each stage of development which increasingly approximate adult understanding. When new information conflicts with previous conceptualizations, the conflict is ultimately resolved by forming new conceptualizations which comprise the next stage of development. The stages of development are seen as psychogenetic ones, that is, they are constrained by a biological timetable. New information which conflicts with current assimilation schemes can only be used at certain points in development; at earlier points, it often appears to be ignored or distorted because it is assimilated into the child's current schemes. Also, behaviors which are seen by adults as "errors" at various stages of development are seen within the Piagetian framework as part of the developmental process. They are constructive errors which the child must create in order to reach the next stage of development.

Vygotsky's theory of development is also interactionist, but the interaction is not between the learner and the object of knowledge, as it is in a Piagetian framework, but between the learner and another person, usually an adult. Although Vygotsky saw the importance of a biological line of development, his contribution was that he saw another line, the cultural one, as equally, possibly even more, significant. His knowledge of dialectical materialism supported his view that

> in order to study development in children, one must begin with an understanding of the dialectical unity of two principally different lines (the biological and the cultural), to adequately study this process, then, an experimenter must study both components and the laws which govern their *interlacement* at each stage of development. (Vygotsky, 1978, p. 123)

Because he saw that historical and cultural contexts were ever shifting, and because these contexts were so integral to the learning process, his theory allowed for both individual and cultural variation. This view is distinctly different from that of Piaget, in which psychogenetic stages are seen as universal. To Vygotsky, each child uses signs and tools from his or her social context to construct knowledge at each stage of development. As these tools are manipulated, in interaction with others in the social context, what is first interpersonal later becomes intrapersonal. That is, children internalize what they learn first in interaction.

Each of the studies in this volume makes use of one or both of these theories. Gundlach et al. and Greene rely solely on a Vygotskian interpretation of development. Dyson relies, at least explicitly, only on Piaget. Both Sulzby's and Sowers' studies illustrate aspects of both Piagetian and Vygotskian theories of development.

Specifically, the study by Gundlach et al. explores the social context, primarily in the home, for the beginnings of writing development by preschool children. The context is defined not only physically and culturally, but also by including the relationships each child has with others. The interaction in these relationships is significant in the development of writing. In addition, the role of play in writing development, another important aspect of Vygotsky's theory, is shown to be highly significant. In Greene's study of the letter writing of elementary school children, the Vygotskian concept of social tools is illustrated. Greene sees the conventions of letter writing, especially those of this school's internal postal system, as tools which the children manipulate in order to progress in knowledge of written language.

Dyson's case studies of kindergarten children learning to write clearly exemplify the learner as a creator of concepts about written language, concepts which are reformed when a conflict arises between them and new information. Her detailed observations of each individual child interacting with the object of knowledge (the writing system) in the course of development shows her reliance on Piagetian theory. She departs, however, from a strictly Piagetian approach in her inclusion of the situational context (with such concerns as purpose for writing) as another aspect of the interaction which must be considered in any valid study of writing development.

Finally, both Sulzby and Sowers illustrate the Piagetian concept of the active learner while at the same time acknowledging the Vygotskian role of interaction with others in the learning process. Sulzby describes the conceptual nature of children's behaviors, both in performing reading and writing tasks and in their understandings about reading and writing. In this description she also sees how the child used interaction with the adult examiner as evidence for the child's concepts, including how they elicited and used adult support (e.g., the reliance by some children on a conversational style of language rather than a monologue style when dictating a story). Sowers sees the interaction in writing conferences about pieces of writing in progress as a classic case of scaffolding. The questions asked by a reader in the routine of the conference is the scaffolding which first enables young writers to perform with adult assistance. This is later internalized by them, enabling them to produce similar writing alone.

So far I have detailed two views of writing (writing as language and writing growth as development) as part of a framework within which to view the studies in this volume. In the final section of this introduction I will discuss a third view which is important in understanding children's writing development. This view entails seeing writing as a varying entity in different contexts.

Writing Variation in Context

Essentially, the terms literacy, writing, and reading are abstractions, constructs which we use to refer to *what people do with written language*. Such a broad definition, however, is not sufficient: people do many different things with written language. Moreover, many educators argue that people are literate at many different levels (e.g., technical decoding and encoding, or writing an eloquent essay as a response to literature). Thus, there are many different definitions of literacy and of writing in our society. In addition, there are many different uses to which these different kinds of writing are put. Consequently, we cannot refer to literacy as a single entity (one set of cognitive skills which learners can acquire). We must instead refer to a plurality of literacies, and variation in writing, if we are to reflect reality accurately.

This view of variation in writing parallels the variation in oral language that has been well documented by several decades of sociolinguistic research. This research has shown that, in addition to regional differences, there are both ethnic and social class differences in American English (Fasold, 1972; Labov, 1966, 1972; Wolfram, 1969, 1974; Wolfram & Christian, 1976; Wolfram, Christian, Potter, & Leap, 1979). If such variation is so abundant in oral language, and if we see writing, like speaking, as a natural reflection of language, then we would expect the variety in writing which research is in fact beginning to document (Farr Whiteman, 1981; Heath, 1983; Scribner & Cole, 1981).

What is crucial to all these studies of variation, in both oral and written language, is the social context in which the language is used. For example, the ethnic varieties of American English in the studies mentioned above are appropriate in certain contexts and not in others. Moreover, writing which is appropriate in one context is not appropriate in another. But how does one define context? This is not as simple as it may at first appear. Context cannot be defined simply as the particular group of people who are using the language. Nor can it simply be defined as a physical setting. As Erickson and Shultz (1981), combining their own definition with that of McDermott and Mehan, state

> Contexts can be thought of as not simply *given* in the physical setting—kitchen, living room, sidewalk in front of drug store—nor in combinations of persons

(two brothers, husband and wife, firemen). Rather, contexts are constituted by what people are doing and where and when they are doing it. As McDermott (1976a) puts it succinctly, contexts consist of mutually shared and ratified definitions of situations *and* in the social actions persons take on the basis of these definitions (Mehan et al., 1976). (Erickson & Shultz, 1981, p. 148)

Thus we can see that literacy, like oral language, is adapted to fit various contexts according to a notion of appropriateness and appropriateness is determined by language users according to their sense of context. In oral language use, context is sensed by what Gumperz (1982) has termed "contextualization cues," that is, verbal and nonverbal behavior such as changes in speech prosody or postural shifts which signal how messages are to be interpreted (other than literally). Contexts for language use, then, are always shifting and changing, and so, consequently, is our language and literacy use.

With this understanding of context and language variation, it is not difficult to go one step further to see why there is so much individual variation in oral and written language development. If the context is almost infinitely variable, and the language use within it ever shifting also, then each child learning language, and learning to be literate, experiences a unique variety of language and literacy events which help form his or her development. The total repertoire of literacy events within a given culture is theoretically available to each child, but the specific experiences which each child has, the preponderance of kinds or the order in which they occur, are probably unique for each child. Consequently, we would not expect, and research has not found, predictable stages of literacy development through which all children can be expected to pass.

The expectation that there might be predictable stages in development is an underlying assumption of Piaget's theory, which I have previously discussed in this introduction. His work does provide evidence for an internal line of development which may be psychogenetic, or constrained by a biological timetable. But his theory does not allow for the variation which is part of the reality of children learning language and literacy. Vygotsky's theory of development, while not negating an internal line of development, does allow for such variation; it attempts to combine the biological (internal) and the cultural (external) influences upon development. Because of this, Vygotsky's theory can be seen as more comprehensive, whereas Piaget's theory provides details about internal structuring in development more fully.

The studies in this volume, like other recent studies of children's early writing development, attest to the fact of individual variation in development. Indeed, individual variation in learning to write is more the rule than the exception. Dyson's study emphasizes this most strongly in its description of several different children with quite distinct learning styles, styles which can be understood only within the framework of each child's understandings and intentions. Dyson sees writing development as the result of a complex interplay of the individual child, the situational context, and the writing system itself, and explicitly draws the parallel to oral language development in this interplay. Because of the interplay of these factors, we expect individual differences in both writing and oral language development, and that is in fact what we find.

Gundlach et al. and Sowers also focus on individual children and their courses of development, but go further than the other studies in providing a rich description of the context in which the writing occurs. For Gundlach et al., this context (for most of the children) is that of the home, and they emphasize personal relationships with parents, peers, and siblings that partially constitute the definition of context. For Sowers, the context is that of the classroom, and more particularly, the writing conferences with teacher and peers in which the writing instruction primarily takes place.

Greene, like Sowers, focuses on the classroom context in which the writing takes place, providing a description of it through ethnographic observation. In addition, she provides a description of the linguistic context in which various language functions (complaining, inviting, etc.) occurred—the writing in the letters themselves. Through her presentation of individual children from the study, she illustrates how language functions vary in context.

Although Sulzby, combining Piagetian and Vygotskian frameworks, posits some general sequences through which the children in her study progress toward literacy, there is enough variation in their progress through these sequences to stop short of seeing them as discrete stages of development. Furthermore, Sulzby includes careful observation of the context in which the children read and write to explain differences in performance.

All five of these studies, then, attest not only to differences in both language use and development, but they also relate the fact of this variation to the ever variable context. In different ways, these studies provide further knowledge about variation in writing and how it is shaped by particular contexts, as well as further knowledge about what constitutes a literacy context.

Summary

In this introduction, I have placed the five studies within the context of the larger field of research on writing. I have emphasized how they contribute, on the one hand, to methodology and theory, and, on the other hand, to our understanding of children's writing development. For the latter, I have used a framework which views writing as language, writing growth as development, and writing variation in context. In the details, and in the focus on variation, we should not lose sight of the commonalities which exist across these and other studies of writing development. I hope that these commonalities (e.g., the language base of writing, individual differences in development as the rule rather than the exception, etc.) are apparent throughout this introduction. Some readers will want to hold them in mind as they read these reports. Each study, however, can stand on its own as well. Indeed, each provides a unique contribution to the field.

REFERENCES

Bauman, R. & Sherzer, J. (Eds.). (1974). *Explorations in the ethnography of speaking.* London: Cambridge University Press.

Bissex, G. (1980). *Gnys at work: A child learns to write and read.* Cambridge, MA: Harvard University Press.

Bloomfield, L. (1933). *Language.* New York: Holt, Rinehart and Winston.

Bruner, J. (1983). *Child's talk.* New York: Norton.

Cazden, C. (1982). Adult assistance to language development: Scaffolds, models and direct instruction. In R. Parker & F. Davis (Eds.), *Developing literacy: Young children's use of language.* Newark, DE: International Reading Association.

Clay, M. M. (1975). *What did I write? Beginning writing behaviour.* Exeter, NH: Heinemann Educational Books.

Erickson, F., & Shultz, J. (1981). When is a context? Some issues and methods in the analysis of social competence. In J. Green & C. Wallat (Eds.), *Ethnography and language in educational settings.* Norwood, NJ: Ablex.

Farr Whiteman, M. (Ed.). (1981). *Variation in writing: functional and linguistic-cultural differences.* Hillsdale, NJ: Erlbaum Associates.

Farr, M. (1984). Writing growth in young children: What we are learning from research. In C. Thaiss & C. Suhor (Eds.), *Talking and writing, K-12.* Urbana, IL: National Council of Teachers of English.

Fasold, R. (1972). *Tense marking in Black English: A linguistic and social analysis.* Washington, DC: Center for Applied Linguistics.

Ferreiro, E., & Teberosky, A. (1982). *Literacy before schooling* (translated from Spanish 1979). Exeter, NH: Heinemann Educational Books.

Florio, S., & Clark, C. M. (1982). What is writing for? Writing in the first weeks of school in a second-third grade classroom. In L. C. Wilkinson (Ed.), *Communication in the classroom.* New York: Academic Press.

Goody, J. & Watt, I. (1968). The consequences of literacy. In J. Goody (Ed.), *Literacy in traditional societies.* Cambridge: Cambridge University Press.

Graves, D. H. (1982). *A case study observing the development of primary children's composing, spelling and motor behavior during the writing process* (NIE-G-78-0174). Washington, DC: National Institute of Education. (Available through ERIC)

Gumperz, J. J. (1982). *Discourse strategies.* Cambridge: Cambridge University Press.

Gumperz, J., & Hymes, D. (Eds.). (1972). *Directions in sociolinguistics.* New York: Holt, Rinehart and Winston.

Halliday, M. A. K. (1977). *Learning how to mean: Explorations in the development of language.* New York: Elsevier North Holland.

Harste, J. C., Burke, C., & Woodward, V. (1981). *Children, their language and world: initial encounters with print* (NIE-G-70-0132). Washington, DC: National Institute of Education. (Available through ERIC)

Heath, S. B. (1981). Oral and literate traditions: Endless linkages. Moving between practice and research in writing. *Proceedings of the NIE-FIPSE grantee workshop.* Los Alamitos, CA: SWRL Research and Development.

Heath, S. B. (1983). *Ways with words: Language, life and work in communities and classrooms.* Cambridge: Cambridge University Press.

Hymes, D. (1971). Competence and performance in linguistic theory. In R. Huxley and E. Ingram (Eds.), *Language acquisition: Models and methods.* London: Academic Press.

King, M., & Rentel, V. (1981). *How children learn to write: A longitudinal study* (NIE-G-79-0137 and NIE-G-0039). Washington, DC: National Institute of Education. (Available through ERIC)

Labov, W. (1966). *The social stratification of English in New York City.* Washington, DC: Center for Applied Linguistics.

Labov, W. (1972). *Language in the inner city: Studies in the Black English Vernacular.* Philadelphia, PA: University of Pennsylvania Press.

McDermott, R. P. (with Gospodinoff, K.). (1976). Criteria for an ethnographically adequate description of activities and their contexts. Paper delivered at the Annual Meeting of the American Anthropological Association, Washington, DC, November 19.

Mehan, H., Cazden, C., Fisher, S., & Maroules, N. (1976). The social organization of classroom lessons (Technical report submitted to the Ford Foundation).

Michaels, S., & Collins, J. (1984). Oral discourse styles: Classroom interaction and the acquisition of literacy. In D. Tannen (Ed.), *Coherence in spoken and written discourse.* Norwood, NJ: Ablex.

Olson, D. (1977). From utterance to text: The bias of language in speech and writing. *Harvard Educational Review,* **47,** 257–281.

Scollon, R. & Scollon, S. B. (1981). *Narrative, literacy and face in interethnic communication.* Norwood, NJ: Ablex.

Scribner, S., & Cole, M. (1981). *The psychology of literacy.* Cambridge, MA: Harvard University Press.

Staton, J. (1982). *Analysis of dialogue journal writing as a communicative event* (NIE-G-80-0122). Washington, DC: National Institute of Education. (Available through ERIC)

Sulzby, E. (1981). *Kindergarteners begin to read their own compositions: Beginning readers' developing knowledges about written language.* (Final report to the Research Foundation of the National Council of Teachers of English). Evanston, IL: Northwestern University.

Tannen, D. (Ed.). (1982). *Spoken and written language: Exploring orality and literacy.* Norwood, NJ: Ablex.

Vygotsky, L. (1978). *Mind in society: The development of higher psychological processes.* Cambridge, MA: Harvard University Press.

Wolfram, W. A. (1969). *A sociolinguistic description of Detroit Negro speech.* Washington, DC: Center for Applied Linguistics.

Wolfram, W. (1974). *Sociolinguistic aspects of assimilation: Puerto Rican English in New York City*. Washington, DC: Center for Applied Linguistics.

Wolfram, W. & Christian, D. (1976). *Appalachian speech*. Washington, DC: Center for Applied Linguistics.

Wolfram, W., Christian, D., Potter, L., & Leap, W. (1979). Variability in the English of two Indian communities and its effects on reading and writing. Final report to the National Institute of Education (NIE-G-77-0006). (Available through ERIC)

1 The Social Foundations of Children's Early Writing Development

Robert Gundlach
Northwestern University

Joan B. McLane
Frances M. Stott
Gillian Dowley McNamee
Erikson Institute, Chicago

INTRODUCTION: STUDYING CHILDREN'S EARLY WRITING

In this chapter we consider the experience of a small number of preschool children in the earliest stages of learning to write. We present three cases studies: a study of the writing activities of a 4-year-old boy who, with considerable encouragement and support from his parents, experiments playfully in a number of ways with written language; a study of the rather different writing activities of a 5-year-old girl, with particular attention to her interactions in writing projects with her mother and her 7-year-old sister; and a study of the activities of a 3-year-old boy, a 4-year-old girl, and a 5-year-old boy who together participate in a preschool program in which children compose and dramatize their own narratives. If, as James Britton (1973) has remarked, teachers who aim to teach writing to even the youngest elementary school children "seek continually to reap a harvest they have not sown," (p. 12) our concern here is with that earlier period when the seeds are planted, the learning of writing begun.[1]

By studying the early writing experience of preschool children, we seek to extend a relatively new line of inquiry. Until quite recently, research on how children learn to write has been conceived as the study of how school-age children learn various parts of the language arts curriculum. In this research tradition, writing has been defined as a set of specific skills, and

---

[1]We are grateful to the Anne J. Richardson Fund and the General Service Foundation for support of various parts of this project.

the learning of writing has been regarded as the outcome of writing instruction. Since the mid-1970's, however, researchers alert to dramatic advances in theory and research on children's language acquisition have begun studying children's development of writing ability as a process analogous to the process of spoken language development. In this research, writing is characteristically given broader definition, encompassing the social and personal uses of writing, the various levels of form in written language, and the cognitive and behavioral processes of written composition. In this work, too, a more complex relationship is assumed between learning and instruction. Indeed, a central theme in recent studies by such researchers as Glenda Bissex, Donald Graves, Lucy Calkins, Susan Sowers, Marie Clay, Emilia Ferreiro, Yetta Goodman, Jerome Harste, Martha King, Anne Dyson, and Elizabeth Sulzby has been that learning to write involves more than being taught.

In developing this theme, a number of researchers have turned their attention to those children who begin incorporating written language into their play and into their social interactions well before they encounter formal instruction in either reading or writing. The pioneering work of this kind is Glenda Bissex's *GNYS AT WRK: A Child Learns to Write and Read* (1980). *GNYS AT WRK* is an extended case study of the writing and reading activities, especially those undertaken at home, of Bissex's son Paul, from the time Paul was 5-years-old until he turned 11. Bissex's point of departure is her interest in her son's curious spellings—among his first written messages are RUDF ("Are you deaf?"), and EFUKANOPNKAZIWILGEVUAKAN-OPNR ("If you can open cans, I will give you a can opener."). Like the preschool children studied by Charles Read (1975) and Carol Chomsky (1971), Bissex's son began writing before he had made much progress in learning to read, and thus his early spelling was based not on a comprehension of English orthography, but rather on a temporary rule system of his own making that he evidently derived from what he knew of the names of letters in the alphabet and from familiar bits of written language in his environment.

Bissex, following Read and Chomsky, examines her son's invented spellings in much the same way child language researchers have studied younger children's unconventional spoken language forms. She views invented spellings as evidence of learning-in-progress and as indications of the young child's capacity for developing, presumably at a nonconscious level, abstract linguistic principles that govern the structure of the language the child produces. Indeed, this parallel between the way a child acquires structural principles in speech and in writing is central to Bissex's analysis. In summarizing her view of Paul's strategy for learning how to read and write, she observes: "He took an active, problem-solving approach to print, as young children do in learning the rules of their spoken language" (p. 192).

Bissex expands the range of linguistic forms studied beyond spelling to include various aspects of text structure, but she concentrates throughout on the evidence she can muster for describing Paul's development of formal principles. In this respect her treatment of Paul's early writing follows in the tradition of Piagetian developmental studies, yielding an image of the child constructing, more or less on his own, a personal representation of the principles underlying the structure and functions of written language. Other recent research on young children's writing that emphasizes the child's cognitive construction of the system of written language includes studies by Clay (1975) and Ferreiro (1978).

Although Bissex, Read, Chomsky, Clay, and Ferreiro are themselves quite restrained in the interpretations they place on their findings, a number of educators have used evidence from their studies to argue that children can, and in supportive print environments do, learn the early lessons of literacy on their own, naturally, without aid of instructor or curriculum. Indeed, some suggest that the preschool child's interest in print and his subsequent spontaneous experiments with writing are properly understood as signs of the child's emergent literacy, much as the very young child's early attempts to combine words in speech may be understood as evidence of emergent grammatical knowledge.

In the past few years, this notion of the child's autonomous literacy learning has encountered sharp criticism, especially from ethnographers who study the social organization of literacy acquisition. Schieffelin and Cochran-Smith (1984) are especially succinct:

> The point we wish to stress is that the print interests of children in this community (or any community) do not emerge "naturally" at all. Rather, in this community they emerge out of a particular cultural orientation in which literacy is assumed and which organizes children's early print experiences in particular ways. (p. 6)

Research and theorizing instructed by this line of criticism have, in effect, expanded the unit of analysis in children's writing research from the child's text and his individual composing behavior to a frame that encompasses interaction between child and adult, interaction among children, and the reading and writing activity that a child may observe at home, in a day care center, or in a kindergarten classroom. This shift of focus from studying the child's solitary composing operations to investigating the social contexts of the child's early writing activities has not reduced the interest or even the mystery of the young child's composing processes, but it has led researchers to think more carefully about the role of adults and older siblings in the child's learning.

Thus researchers have begun to study the various ways adults collaborate with young children in reading and writing undertakings and to trace cultural patterns reflected in families' habits of including children in particular kinds of reading and writing activity. Research of this sort is ethnographic in aim and method, seeking to provide rich descriptions of the circumstances in which children conduct their early writing experiments and, in some cases, seeking also to provide comparative portraits of the literacy environments in the homes of children belonging to different cultural groups. Particularly noteworthy studies that aim to accomplish both goals are Heath (1982b), which examines the varying orientations to reading and writing provided to young children in families from different socioeconomic and ethnic groups in the United States, and Scollon and Scollon (1981), which compares the confident early reading and writing play of an American middle-class child with the more diffident literacy habits of older Athabaskan children in Fort Chipewyan in Alberta, Canada.

Complementing the comparative ethnographic studies undertaken by Heath and the Scollons are more narrowly focused microethnographic studies of the kind proposed by Cazden (1981) that examine in considerable detail the interactions between adult and child in the child's early reading and writing activity. In such studies, the adult is often viewed as a tutor, a collaborator who provides "scaffolding" in the form of verbal cues and manual assists and who thereby lends structure to the child's activity. Investigators pursuing this line of inquiry have drawn frequently on the theories of Lev Vygotsky (1962, 1978), positing that when a young child receives help in reading or writing from an adult or perhaps an older sibling, the child and his collaborator may be understood to inhabit the "zone of proximal development," the realm of activity in which the child must receive help if he is to succeed in what he is doing. The Vygotskian interpretation often imposed on microethnographic data of this sort is that when the child is provided with coaching and guidance from a more capable collaborator, he not only succeeds in performing the task at hand, but also encounters problem-solving strategies that he may eventually internalize and use on his own, thus advancing the level at which he can operate autonomously. A further assumption of this kind of research is that differences in the kind of collaboration provided by families in different social and cultural groups help to explain the different "literacy orientations" described in broader comparative ethnographic studies such as Heath's and the Scollons'.

These recent studies of the cultural and social contexts of children's early writing experience have raised many interesting questions but have provided few firm answers. Sketches and anecdotes of the sort presented by Heath and the Scollons do suggest interesting and significant cultural variation in the character of reading and writing activities in the families of preschool children, but little account has been taken so far of the possible changes in literacy habits over time within a particular family, or of the possible variation in the reading and writing practices of different families within a social or cultural group. And while microethnographic studies promise to provide detailed descriptions of the mechanics of adult-child interaction in brief reading and writing episodes, we have not yet begun to gather longitudinal data that might give us clear evidence whether, in fact, a particular child has indeed internalized the specific strategies for reading and writing demonstrated to him by an adult collaborator. For all of the limitations, then, of restricting the focus of her inquiry to the relatively autonomous activity of her son, Bissex's orderly and thorough longitudinal case study remains the richest portrait we have of an individual child's writing development.

The three studies we report here are attempts to place careful observations of an individual child's writing activity, observations much like those Bissex made of her son's early writing, in the broader social contexts to which recent ethnographic studies have called attention. If Bissex concentrated on the vertical dimension of Paul's young writing life, charting changes over time in his uses of writing and his formations of written language, these studies seek to supply a horizontal dimension, examining the context, and especially the human interaction in the context, of young children's early writing activity.

The first of the three studies reports on the writing activity of Jeremy, a 4-year-old who writes all the time. Much of his writing is what most adults would call "pretend writing," and so it may seem to Jeremy, although it is difficult to know. What is certain, however, is that Jeremy makes substantial use of the cultural materials of writing, both to please and entertain his parents and to make contact with them while he pleases and entertains himself. In this report we concentrate especially on the role Jeremy's parents play, both in supporting his writing activities and in contributing to his understanding of the nature of written language. The second study focuses on the early writing of 5-year-old Jill, examining the ways in which Jill's writing activities are structured or otherwise influenced by her mother and by Jill's 7-year-old sister Nina. Nina, we observe, often plays an influential role in Jill's writing projects, serving alternately as a model, a coach, a competitor, and a co-conspirator. The third study shifts the focus from writing at home to writing in a preschool program. Here we analyze several episodes in which young children compose fantasy narratives aloud for a teacher who transcribes them, and who then helps the children dramatize their narratives with their classmates. Drawing on Vygotskian developmental theory, we examine the ways this sort of preschool composing and dramatizing activity provides a social context, indeed virtually a small-scale culture, in which children not yet reading and writing independently may nonetheless be developing an understanding of the character and uses of written language. We will report the results of each study separately and will conclude by considering the implications of the three studies taken together.

CASE STUDY ONE: "I WROTE IT MYSELF"

Introduction

This case study of one child's writing activities explores the notion that for some children writing begins before school—and that by school age some children have already acquired understandings, ideas, and feelings about writing, as well as some specific writing skills. What resources are available to children who write at home? What contexts support and facilitate early writing? What activities serve, in Gundlach's (1982) phrase, as "bridges" to writing? One assumption that underlies this study is that if young children begin to write at home, parents must be involved in some way, as it is they who shape the context in which development takes place; in other words, writing does not just happen.

I began this study of 4-year-old Jeremy and his parents in order to find out something about the social context in which early writing develops.[2] My purpose was to describe the kinds of activities and interactions between Jeremy and his parents that involved writing, and the kind of support his parents provided for his early writing; I wanted to find out what Jeremy's parents were doing with and for Jeremy that might facilitate his early writing development.

In focusing on the social context in which early writing develops, I wanted to try to uncover and make explicit what I felt was largely missing (or left implicit) in Bissex's (1980) account of her son's writing development. Bissex describes "the drama of one child's coming into writing," and furnishes a detailed account of her son's invention of spelling and construction of knowledge about the forms and functions of writing. Bissex does not, however, provide much information about the support and "scaffolding" that she (and presumably her husband) provided for their son's early writing. Moreover, Bissex's account begins when her son Paul is 5-years-old. At five, Paul's writing development is already well underway and he is writing with invented spellings that are generally interpretable (at least by a sympathetic adult, of which more later). What happened *before* Paul was able to write "RUDF"?

When I explained my interests to Jeremy's mother, she expressed some skepticism about the notion that either she or her husband were doing anything to encourage or facilitate their son's writing; however, she did agree to observe and record Jeremy's writing activities as well as her (and her husband's) part in them. She did this intermittently between January and June, 1982.

---

[2]When we first formulated the results of this work, the individual investigator who carried out fieldwork also took responsibility for drafting a report (see Gundlach, McLane, McNamee, & Stott, 1983). When we accepted the invitation to prepare a report of all three studies for this volume, we decided that although we would revise each report extensively, we would preserve in each the first-person (singular) perspective of the original investigator. Let us note, then, that primary responsibility for "I Wrote It Myself" should be attributed to Joan B. McLane; primary responsibility for "Writing Under the Influence of Nina" to Frances M. Stott; and primary responsibility for "Writing Instruction Through Play in the Classroom" to Gillian Dowley McNamee. Robert Gundlach wrote the introduction and conclusion and served as a consultant to the whole of the project.

Jeremy was four in December 1981. He is an active, verbal, and engaging child. He was an only child until May 1982, when his baby sister was born. Jeremy's parents spend a lot of time with him, and invest a lot of energy in their shared time: there are many conversations and playful interactions. On the basis of the records supplied by his mother, supplemented by my own informal observations, Jeremy participates in an environment that Cazden (1981) would describe as language and literacy rich. The house is full of book and magazines, both parents read a lot for their own pleasure—and they read a lot to Jeremy. Both parents are writers, they talk about books and writers, and they often write at home. In this literary environment, Jeremy engages in a variety of activities which involve writing, reading, and/or narration, and his parents play an active part in many of them. He also watches "Sesame Street" daily.

Jeremy also has easy access to a variety of writing tools, including pencils, crayons, markers, paper (sheets and notebook), and his own typewriter, as well as magnetic letters. When I first observed Jeremy a month after his fourth birthday, he was doing "scribble writing" and was beginning to form individual letters. He could also recognize a few printed words. (Jeremy and his parents were chosen for this study because his parents were friends, and not because I had any reason to think that Jeremy's writing abilities were precocious or unusual.) According to his mother, Jeremy's writing skills were—and are—no better than those of his contemporaries. What is unusual, of course, is that both of Jeremy's parents are writers.

JEREMY'S WRITING ACTIVITIES

Jeremy's writing activities and interactions elude easy and orderly categorization. Most of the activities have an element of play—be it fantasy, drama, role-play, language play, or game playing, and there is often a playful approach to language itself. Many activities also have an element of dramatic performance, with Jeremy as performer and his parents as audience. Some of Jeremy's writing activities, however, appear to be directed toward mastering the new and challenging skill of writing itself.

In what follows, Jeremy's writing activities are arranged in rough categories that reflect what seems most salient about the activity: Pretend Play and Writing; Writing as Performance; and Writing Letters and Spelling Words. The categories are not neat, as many recorded incidents include more than one kind of writing activity. Indeed, the very fluidity of Jeremy's writing activities is an indication of how much they are a part of his ongoing daily activity.

The writing activities occurred over a 6-month period, begining when Jeremy was 4 years and 1 month of age. Most of the activities in the first category occurred in late January; those in the second category from late January to mid-June; and those in the third from early February to mid-June. Within categories, activities are presented chronologically. Jeremy's various writing activities seemed to have occurred in spurts. This may partly reflect his parents' interest and attention to record keeping, but it probably reflects Jeremy's changing interests and developing competence as well. Bissex also observed that her son's writing development occurred in spurts followed by periods of relative inactivity.

Pretend Play and Writing

Jeremy spends a great deal of time engaged in dramatic pretend play—alone, with friends, and with his parents. Sometimes this play includes writing as part of the action, sometimes this play also leads into writing activity, and sometimes writing serves as a playful extension of pretend play and fantasy.

"Police" (January 24th).   Jeremy asked his mother to play "police" with him. He was the police chief and she was the "police girl": she answered the phone and took a call about an escaped canary; Jeremy responded "I got to write this down," whereupon he laboriously wrote "O E" on one page of a shiny new notebook belonging to his mother. Jeremy's mother commented that his behavior in this episode was probably modelled on a TV show called "The Bloodhound Gang," and that the presence of her new and attractive notebook probably contributed to this bit of writing. She did not comment on the fact that she allowed Jeremy to use her new notebook —and more importantly, that she enthusiastically participated in her son's pretend play. In participating in Jeremy's play, she allowed him to take the lead in establishing the subject, and then proceeded to use her own imagination to extend and elaborate on it. That she did this suggests that she values and appreciates Jeremy's make-believe play, and that she enjoys playing *with* him in an imaginative way.

"Playing office" (January 26th).   The following episode was described by Jeremy's mother as a "morning drama" and recorded as a dialogue:

Jeremy:	(Going into the mother's study.) Can I play office?
Mother:	What do you want to do?
Jeremy:	(Pause) Write.
Mother:	Okay. (Gives him a piece of paper and a pencil.)
Jeremy:	I have to turn on this office thing. (Switches on the desk lamp.)
Mother:	What are you going to write?

Jeremy: O and this other letter. (Draws it in the air, then draws an O and upside down L on paper.) See?

Mother: I'm not sure what that letter that is.

Jeremy: It's a V. (Seems all done writing.)

Mother: What were you writing? Was it a message, or a story or something?

Jeremy: It was a story, but a very short one.

Mother: That's nice.

Jeremy: If you want me to keep going you have to roll it up. Let's put question marks all over it, and then we'll paste little pieces of paper on the question marks. Here are two lines going down. (Draws a cross.)

Mother: Here's a question mark. (Shows him how to make a question mark.)

Jeremy: Put question marks here and here and here and here and here...

Mother: (My showing how to make a question mark seems to have stopped his writing. Time to go to school.)

In this conversation, Jeremy's mother again took her cue from Jeremy, and again served as a willing and responsive participant in his pretend play —and his pretend writing. He defined the general subject ("playing office") and she provided access to the necessary materials. After Jeremy produced a small bit of writing, his mother provided him with alternative definitions for it ("a message" or "a story"). In doing this, she was instructing him about writing in general, and about his own writing. She was letting him know that writing has conventional forms such as messages and stories, and that a piece of writing should fit into one of these categories. With regard to Jeremy's own writing, she was suggesting that it *could* have such a form, and that it could be treated *as if* it had such a form. In modeling this non-literal approach to Jeremy's writing, his mother was indicating her willingness to "amplify" Jeremy's writing and pretend that it is more than it really is. And she is also letting him know that he can define his writing after the fact.

A writing game (January 31st).   In late January, Jeremy's mother described a variation of a game they often played. The basic game consisted of Jeremy's mother challenging him to do something before she counted to a certain number. For example, his mother would say "get into the bathtub before I count to four" or "pick up the toys before I get to 10", and so forth. One day, Jeremy made up his own version of the game. He told his mother she had to write down a word while he got dressed: "See if you can write the word 'pencil' before I put my shirt on." His mother reported that Jeremy looked around the room to find words for her to write, and tried to find long ones for the more complicated articles of clothing ("bear" was for his socks, and "Christmas Tree" was for his sweatshirt). Later in the same day Jeremy reversed the roles in this new version of the game when he wanted his father to come downstairs: "See if you can get downstairs before I write 'TO'," Jeremy called and then dashed into his room. A minute later he came out, having written "OT" (on the same piece of paper that his mother has used earlier). Jeremy was delighted: "I did it! See the letters? I wrote it myself!" His mother commented that his "triumph here was divided between winning the race and writing the letters."

Here, Jeremy took a ritualized, game-like routine previously established by his mother and used it for his own purposes—to structure a writing game and to take on the parental role with its overtones of discipline and control ("See if you can...before I..."). He initiated the game by taking over the directing role himself and by changing the content of the game, and eventually he took over the writing role in addition to the directing role. Again, we see Jeremy's parents willing to follow his lead and support his initiatives. In this instance they also supported his playing with a familiar, established routine, much as they also support his play with familiar established language routines such as nursery rhymes.

"Danger" (April 4).   This incident involves writing in the service of a fantasy. One morning in early April, Jeremy asked his mother to give him a piece of paper and a pencil and to tell him "the letters that spell 'danger'." His mother asked why and Jeremy replied that he wanted "to make a danger sign" to put on the door of his room. Then he told his mother an "involved and changing story" about various catastrophes that had happened in his room, which explained why there was a hole in his floor. After describing each catastrophe—"a bear tore my room up; a tree fell down; there's a monster up there"—he would say "Really, Mommy. Really, that's true."

His mother gave him a pencil and paper, and told him to start with D. His mother reported that he had "much trouble writing it, but I assured him it was a D. A was easy, N was shaky, and he absolutely refused to try G and insisted I write it for him. E was a breeze, and he asked me to do the R." Then they found some string and some tape and made a handle so the sign could hang on Jeremy's door, where it stayed for the rest of the day. Periodically, Jeremy would ask his mother if anybody had been in his room. "Nobody can go in here but me," he would say, "Because there's danger in there."

In this interaction, Jeremy's mother accepted his fantasy and helped him use writing to elaborate on it. When she helped him make the letters for the 'DANGER' sign, she also provided him with the kind of contingent, finely-tuned assistance described by Wood, Bruner, and Ross (1976) as "scaffolding." She provided Jeremy with a supportive framework that enabled him to complete a difficult and meaningful task. In scaffolding this writing activity, Jeremy's mother encouraged him to make as many of the letters as he could himself, but she also was willing to fill in the gaps by making the letters that Jeremy found too difficult to execute himself. Thus he was not overwhelmed or discouraged by demands too far outside his immediate capabilities and the task was kept manageable for him.

Pretend Writing, Pretend Reading and Language Play: Writing as Performance

Many of Jeremy's writing activities involve both pretend writing and pretend reading. The pretend readings often have the quality of dramatic performances, and often include play with words and written language forms. Jeremy clearly enjoys playing with language—with the sounds of letters and words, and with word rhythms, patterns, and rhymes. According to his mother, he likes to recite nursery rhymes correctly *and* with his own variations; he likes to rhyme words like "shoe" and "blue", as well as his own made up words. He also likes to make up songs and he often performs what his mother describes as "soft shoe routines" with a battered Uncle Sam hat and a collapsible cane. Indeed, much of Jeremy's pretend reading and word play has the quality of play acting and theatrical performance, with his parents serving as a responsive and enthusiastic audience.

Fairy tales and nursery rhymes (January 25th & 26th).   Jeremy's mother reported that one evening in late January he used his own typewriter to type what looked like a random assortment of letters, numbers, and symbols on both sides of a piece of paper. He described these bits of writing as "Goldilocks and Three Bears," "Snow White and the Three Dwarfs," "The Three Billy Goats Gruff," and "The Brementown Musicians." While typing these "stories," Jeremy took the paper out of the typewriter every few minutes and ran up and down the stairs to show each parent what he had added to the page. He was clearly very proud of himself, and at one point shouted with great glee, "I can read! I can write!" Several times he announced "I did it all myself! Nobody helped me!" Clearly, Jeremy delights in playing the role of a writer.

Jeremy continued this activity early the next morning, typing on both sides of another sheet of paper. This time, he said he had written "Mary had a little lamb." Jeremy's father "read" one side of the page as "Mary had a little lamb," whereupon Jeremy corrected him by taking the paper and reading it himself as: "Mary had a little–turn the page over–(which he did) lamb." This last activity involves pretend reading (by Jeremy and by his father) as well as pretend writing. (It also indicates that Jeremy has a sense of words as separate entities of print.)

Here, Jeremy used the titles of several familiar stories (and a nursery rhyme) to label and define his bits of writing. In this incident, Jeremy's father accepted his son's pretend writing of "Mary had a little lamb" in the playful spirit in which it was presented and gave it a pretend reading. Thus, Jeremy's father demonstrated his willingness to amplify Jeremy's writing and to act as if it were the "real thing."

"Old Mother Hubbard" (February 15th).   One morning in mid-February, Jeremy asked his mother to give him some paper and get out his typewriter. He announced that he was going "to type the whole alphabet with no mistakes." This grandiose plan suggests that Jeremy may have some magical notions about his writing competence, particularly when he uses his typewriter. His mother reported that when he made a mistake or missed a letter he got very angry. Soon he asked his mother to tell him the letters, so that he could type them. (He confused E and T, C and D, but was able to pick out the right letters on the typewriter keyboard.)

After getting to G, he was tired and frustrated, and announced he had finished. Then he said he had been writing a story. His mother asked him what the story was about.

> Jeremy: Nothing. It's a very short story.
> Mother: It's not about anything?
> Jeremy: Just Mother Goose nursery rhymes.
> Mother: Which nursery rhyme is your favorite?
> Jeremy: This is what I wrote. Old Mother Hubbard. But it's different.

Then Jeremy recited:

> Old Mother Hubbard went to the balloon store
> To get her poor child a balloon,
> But when she got there the store was all closed
> So she had to run away
> (pause to think of an ending)
> To Jack and the Beanstalk.

Jeremy and his mother both laughed at his version. She reported that Jeremy went on to make up "other silly rhymes" such as "Bobby Shaftoe went to sea, with a typewriter on his head!"

Jeremy began this activity with the idea of writing the alphabet, and the "very short story" was clearly an afterthought, a way of salvaging a frustrating situation. Jeremy's mother accepted his redefinition of the writing activity, and adjusted her role accordingly when she asked him about his "story." The definition of story is one that she had suggested to Jeremy in an earlier interaction ("playing office"); now he has offered it as his own. After he did this, his mother then asked him for further information and seemed reluctant to accept a story that was "not about anything." In doing this she "raised the ante" (Bruner, 1978) by expecting more of her child than she had earlier.

"The ABC News" (March 7th).   One Sunday afternoon, after dressing up in various costumes and pretending he was "a baby learning to fly", Jeremy wrote some letters and letter-like figures on an 8 x 10 piece of paper. He showed this to his mother and said "Now wait for the surprise." Then he held the paper in front of his face while he shouted:

Good evening ladies and gentlemen!
This is the ABC News!
Now we have lots of weather!

His mother reported that this produced "great laughter" on the part of both Jeremy and herself.

Shortly after this, while Jeremy's mother was putting things away, she picked up his typewriter, at which point Jeremy decided to type. He typed a single line of what looked like randomly chosen letters on three or four sheets of paper, and then told his mother that those were his "news schedules." Two of the items of news which he then read to her were "My study is full of alligators" and "The ice cube is melting all down and making my feet say 'bleech'."

In this eposide, Jeremy's pretend writing served as the central prop for a dramatic performance. This incident illustrates Jeremy's delight in using bits of his own pretend writing for dramatic verbal performances, as well as his mother's availability as a receptive audience.

A *"Book of Poems"* (March 13th).   One evening, Jeremy told his father that he wanted to make a book. His father gave him four 5 x 8 cards, and Jeremy typed a line of randomly chosen letters on one side of each card. He then took them to his father and asked him to staple them together into a book. His father asked him what he had written, and Jeremy replied "a surprise." (In reporting on this, his mother commented that this response usually "means that Jeremy doesn't have an answer.")

The next morning, Jeremy and his father listened to a radio program which included school children reading their own poetry. Jeremy than asked where his book was. His mother found it for him, and Jeremy asked both parents to come to the living room so that he could read his "Book of Poems" to them. He announced "Page one" and then gave what his mother described as "a garbled but still very recognizable version of a short poem about a Christmas tree." (The poem was unfamiliar to his parents who assumed Jeremy had heard it in nursery school.) "Page two" consisted of another Christmas poem. His mother observed that in reciting both poems "when he couldn't remember the words he tried to think of something that rhymed and kept up the sing-song metre." When his parents asked what was on page three, Jeremy turned to page three, peered at it, and then said "that's all for now." Jeremy's mother added that she and Jeremy's father "of course greatly applauded his poetry."

In this case, the book of poems seems to have originated as a "construct" or a "written object" (Britton, 1970) made for the pleasure of making something rather than for any specific communicative purpose (such as a pretend reading performance). Jeremy's mother reports that Jeremy has made similar little books, the pages of which are sometimes covered with letters, and sometimes left blank. These books are not necessarily "read." The radio program of children's poetry seems to have provided Jeremy with a definition for the book he had made earlier—and with the idea of using it as the central prop in a dramatic recitation for his parents. Here again we see Jeremy entertaining his parents with a literary performance—for which they are a responsive and appreciative audience.

"A drawing with rhymes" (March 12th).   Some of Jeremy's writings themselves (as opposed to his "readings" of them) show his playful and poetic interest in letters and words. At the time he was making books with lines of randomly-typed letters, he was also making "pictures of letters." These were large pieces of paper covered with letters drawn with crayons of different colors arranged in rows or patterns. Shortly before he produced the "book of poems," he made what he called a "drawing with rhymes."

On the paper were letters, scribbles, shapes, and pictures of faces and other objects, including the following:

(scribble)   O A O A A J

(strange shapes)   O   (a smiling stick figure
                                                            with curly hair
                                                            holding something)

                    bp

Jeremy explained to his mother that this drawing included the following rhymes:

"J" and "A"
"A O" and "A O" (read from right to left)
"O" and "toe" (the strange shape was a toe with a jagged toenail)
"b" and "p"
"Raggedy Andy holding candy" (the stick figure)

Thus, Jeremy has rhymed letters with each other, letters with pictures of objects, and pictures with other pictures.

"A poem" (July 13th).   Several months later, his mother reported that while playing in his room during nap time, Jeremy took three pieces of paper from a small (1-1/2 x 2) notebook and typed the following "poem":

Page 1:   "U U U U P"
Page 2:   JJ 1'"
Page 3:   J J J J J J

When he finished typing, he found his mother and asked if she wanted to hear his poem. She said she did, and Jeremy read it to her. (He explained that the small marks on Page two were "bullets making gun noises.") Jeremy then stapled the three pages together end to end. Jeremy's use of rhymes in this poem and in the "drawing with rhymes", as well as his pretend reading of his "book of poems" suggest that he has some notion of what a poem is, and that poems, as well as stories, news accounts, and signs, are writing forms that are potentially available to him.

These playful combinations of letters, words, scribbles, marks ("bullets making gun noises"), and representational drawings also indicate that for Jeremy, the activities of writing and drawing are sometimes closely linked. This is true for many children, as Gardner (1980), Gundlach (1982), Bissex (1980) and others have observed.

Writing Letters and Spelling Words

Along with these playful approaches to writing, Jeremy has shown a steady interest in mastering the skills of making letters, and more recently, in spelling words. Indeed, these interests can be seen in many of the incidents already discussed. In the activities described below, the primary focus seems to be on skill mastery, although there are often elements of play and of performance.

Writing letters (February 5th).   In early February, Jeremy's mother reported that he sometimes spent time writing specific letters of the alphabet, particularly the letters in his name. He did this at nursery school, at home, and outside in the snow. At such times, his interest seemed to lie in making the individual letters themselves, rather than in making them as part of some pretend story or pretend play episode. Jeremy's mother commented that these letters were "sideways or backwards or upside down" but that Jeremy "couldn't stand to be corrected." She added that there didn't seem to be "any framework or purpose" to these activities and that they were "just something that Jeremy did every once in a while—like deciding to play with Tinkertoys for a while, and then putting them away."

Jeremy's interest in writing letters continued. His mother reported that during a "long and boring plane ride" at the beginning of March, Jeremy got "tired of playing with his plastic cowboys and announced that he wanted to write for a while." He was given a sheet of airline stationary which he covered on both sides with rather shaky looking letters and letter-like shapes. When he finished, he read them to his mother, and then went on to another activity.

Jeremy also demonstrated his interest in making letters with his typewriter. In mid-February, as described above, he announced to his mother that he was going to "type the whole alphabet with no mistakes." After several mistakes (and omissions), which made him very angry, he stopped with the letter "G." Commenting on this attempt at writing the alphabet, Jeremy's mother observed that much of his writing "seems to be directed toward the act of writing itself, without any communication goal. This I think comes from watching "Sesame Street" and the "Electric Company," and learning the alphabet at school, and at home—where letters and sounds are taught in isolation, without any communication context. Jeremy is very interested in achievement per se, in mastering skills, and knows that mastering letters is very important and honorific. . . ."

This comment probably reflects a general adult view of young children's writing activities. Indeed, Jeremy does seem very interested in mastering writing skills. It seems to me, however, that most of Jeremy's writing activities, including writing the letters of the alphabet, *do* serve some communicative function for him; certainly they are one of the ways he communicates with his parents.

Spelling Words

Valentines (March 17th).   Sometimes in March, Jeremy began demonstrating an interest in spelling and writing words, as opposed to writing individual letters. For example, in honor of St. Patrick's Day, he made valentines. He found some leftover red paper hearts, which he glued onto pieces of white paper. He then asked his mother how to spell "Papa". She told him, letter by letter, and he wrote "PAPA", from right to left, on one of the valentines, which he then proudly presented to his father. He then wrote PAPA (from right to left) on two more valentines: one for his mother and one for himself.

Magnetic letters (March 29th).   In late March, his mother reported that Jeremy had been spending a lot of time playing with his magnetic letters, which were kept on the refrigerator door. He would ask his mother how to spell words and would arrange letters in alphabetical order (usually from right to left). Sometimes he arranged them in small groups of 3–7 letters and then asked his mother what they spelled. She would sound out "words" such as X-M-R-E-O-U-A or F-D-L-P-A, which Jeremy found very amusing. Rather than dismissing these words as nonsensical and unpronounceable, Jeremy's mother was willing to respond to his interest and curiosity in his terms—while, at the same time, providing him with instruction in sounding out letters. Not long after this, his mother observed that he "often asked how to spell words."

Copying

The Leonard Bernstein page (April 2nd and 3rd).   One evening in early April, while listening to a record of "Peter and the Wolf," Jeremy started looking through the album for "the book." He found a sheet that described the record, and announced to his mother that he was going to copy it on his typewriter. Without listening to the rest of the record, he went up to his room and typed out 'leonard bernstein com posar con con ctor" (Leonard Bernstein, composer, conducter). His mother said that he was "very proud" of this and called it his "Leonard Bernstein page."

The next morning he asked for his Leonard Bernstein page, which he said he was going to make part of a book, but that he needed three more sheets of paper. He then typed a line of what appeared to be randomly chosen letters and numbers on each sheet and then asked his mother to staple them together. After she had done this, Jeremy asked her to read "the book" to him. His mother began to "read" a story about "Jeremy listening to a record," but Jeremy protested "No, no, read what it *really* says." His mother read the type as "phonetically as she could, and Jeremy responded 'That's it! That's the way I wanted you to read it'!"

Jeremy's mother later commented that she thought Jeremy wasn't sure whether his randomly typed letters meant anything or not, and that he may have thought they were words like "Leonard Bernstein." She added that Jeremy may have supposed that whatever was typed into a typewriter would somehow magically become words.

Spelling Homework (May 4th).   One evening early in May, Jeremy announced to his mother that he was "going to do his homework." When she registered some surprise, he asked her what homework was. She said it was "work you bring home from school, like practicing spelling or numbers or finding out all about dinosaurs." He thought about this for a while, and then observed that "you also do homework at school but then you call it schoolwork." Then he said he wanted to "practice his spelling."

His mother suspected a "major bedtime stall" and said they would "do homework *in bed,* in pajamas." After Jeremy got ready for bed, his mother found him a piece of paper and a book on which to lean. He found a pink marker and a pale green crayon. The following dialogue ensued:

Mother: What word do you want to spell?
Jeremy: Ball.

Mother:	Okay. What letter do you think it starts with?
Jeremy:	B.
Mother:	Can you write a B?
Jeremy:	I'll write a small b. That's easier. (Writes b.)
Mother:	Very good. What do you think has an "ah" sound for the next letter?
Jeremy:	I?
Mother:	No.
Jeremy:	E?
Mother:	That does sound like it, but the letter you use for ball is A.
Jeremy:	(Writes a capital A.)
Mother:	Very good. Now what has the "LL" sound?
Jeremy:	(No hesitation.) L.
Mother:	Right! Can you write that?
Jeremy:	No. You do it. I did all these other letters. Now you have to do some.
Mother:	Alright. (She writes an L.) Now can you write another right next to it?
Jeremy:	Okay. (Writes an O.)
Mother:	That's not an L.
Jeremy:	(Laughs wickedly. Great delight at the trick he has played.)
Mother:	Do you want to read a story now?
Jeremy:	Yes.

In this instance, Jeremy's mother provided her son with assistance finely tuned to his understanding and ability to complete the task at hand. She *asked* him to sound out the first three letters (BAL), and then *told* him to add the final L (for which she offered no explanation). She knew that with some assistance Jeremy could figure out the first three letters, but that the final L was beyond his current understanding.

In these writing and spelling activities we can see that Jeremy's mother helps him with the mechanics of writing *when* he requests such help. When he does not, she does not expect or demand correctly formed letters or properly spelled words; rather, she is willing to accept his poorly formed letters and backwards spelling as adequate approximations. This kind of assistance seems to be sensitive to Jeremy's level of competence and to his level of confidence. His mother takes into account not only his observable level of skill or competence, but also his own sense of what he can manage. Such assistance seems likely to give Jeremy a feeling of control over the activity of writing.

Discussion

These, then, are some of the writing activities Jeremy engaged in over a 6-month period. To return to my original question: What do Jeremy's parents do to facilitate his early writing development? What kinds of parent-child interactions involve writing? What kinds of support or scaffolding for writing do his parents provide? And why might Jeremy want to write?

As the activities and interactions described should make clear, writing (and reading) are very much a part of the context of Jeremy's daily life, and for Jeremy they are very "natural" activities. A brief incident reported by Jeremy's mother illustrates how natural and spontaneous an activity writing can be for Jeremy. Just before going to school one morning in February, Jeremy asked his mother for a piece of paper from her desk to "write something." His mother gave him the paper and he scrunched down in the hall and scribbled on it. When he finished he said to his mother "Okay, now will you watch me do a somersault?" His mother asked him what he had written and he replied "An upside down letter N. Now watch me." Then Jeremy did a somersault. Like doing a somersault, writing is something to do—and a good way to gain his mother's interest, attention, and approval. Writing is natural in the sense that it is such an integral part of the social and cultural context that it seems spontaneous and unremarkable. But to say that Jeremy's writing seems natural and spontaneous does not mean that it is unimportant to his parents; on the contrary, his writing is noticed, valued, and delighted in. Jeremy's parents take great pride and delight in their son and his accomplishments, and his writing is one of the things that particularly delights them.

What Jeremy's parents do is, first of all, to participate in a strong, invested relationship with Jeremy. To this relationship they bring their interest in books, stories, poetry, fantasy, and pretend, as well as their own sense of themselves as readers and writers. Perhaps because both his parents are writers, Jeremy knows that writing is an important, valued, and prestigous adult activity. One incident reported by his mother indicated that Jeremy regards writing as a powerful means of expression. His mother noted that Jeremy had watched a TV show with the babysitter and later wanted to tell his mother about it. In telling her, Jeremy decided that spoken words weren't adequate to describe how strong the "Dukes of Hazzard" were. "I'll write down how strong they are!" This was followed by several seconds of frantic scribbling with pencil and notebook. "There! See!" Jeremy had made four pages of scribbles, none of it recognizable. Jeremy's mother asked him to tell her "in words how strong they are," to which he replied "Forty-ninety-eleven-zero!"

Within the context of this relationship, there are several specific things that Jeremy's parents do that may encourage and facilitate the development of his writing activities: they read to Jeremy; they encourage his pretend play, his fantasy stories, and his pretend writing and reading; and they assist him in his efforts to write and spell correctly. For his parents, it seems natural to do all of these things with Jeremy; activities that involve writing are *in* the relationship. Writing is part of the fabric of the relationship, and writing is one of the many activities in which the relationship is formed and through which it is expressed.

Reading to Jeremy

Reading is a pleasurable and valued family activity. Jeremy frequently asks to be read to, and he is read to often. Over the years, Jeremy's parents have read a rich variety of books to him—stories, fairy tales, and poetry. Sometimes reading to Jeremy has an "instructional" quality. For instance, while I was observing Jeremy and his family in mid-February, Jeremy got the *Sesame Street* magazine and sat in his father's lap. They looked at the magazine together and found a page with the letters of the alphabet, all of which Jeremy was able to identify in response to his father's questions. When his father asked for words that began with a "J" sound, Jeremy gave a number of examples. After this they found a page with several words such as "STOP" and "EXIT" printed as signs, and Jeremy identified all of them correctly. Jeremy seemed very pleased with his ability to recognize letters and words, and both father and son clearly enjoyed the interchange.

The importance of being read to has been emphasized by anthropologists and educators in discussing what they have variously described as "literacy socialization" (Heath, 1982b); a "literate orientation" (Scollon & Scollon, 1981); a "literacy set" (Holdaway, 1979); "naturally developed literacy" (Teale, 1982); or the "spectator role" (Britton, 1982). While he is being read to, Jeremy is learning that books are an important and readily-available source of pleasurable interaction with his parents, and he is developing "high expectations of print" (Holdaway, 1979). Jeremy is also learning to pay attention to language. He is learning about letters and words, and about the forms of written language such as stories and poems; he is learning to follow narratives, and to enjoy the patterns and juxtapositions of poetry; he is also learning "how to fictionalize anything and everything"— and to make himself, his "toys, household objects and foods the object of imaginative manipulation in the frame of a story" (Heath, 1982b).

Books for Jeremy are a rich source of stories and elaborate language, of ideas and fantasies, which he uses for his own purposes in his own fantasies, narratives, and pretend play. Jeremy's mother reported that Jeremy often tells stories to himself which are clearly derived from books. He often narrates long stories of hardships and rescues (particularly when he is in the bathtub). He uses a story-telling intonation and literary language such as "all but one has fled"; "they all ran away, save one who stayed"; and "'goodbye', he said, stepping into his boat." Recently, Joyce Carol Oates (1982), in discussing *her* development as a writer, observed that she had discovered "at the age of 3 or 4", that "telling stories...is a way of being told stories." For Jeremy, telling stories to himself may be one way he can take on the adult's role in the activity of story reading and make the activity of being read to his own.

Pretend Play

As we have seen, Jeremy's parents enjoy and encourage their son's pretend play activities. They often serve as a responsive and enthusiastic audience for his fantasy stories, and his pretend readings and playful recitations. There are a number of ways in which pretend play may be related to the development of early writing. Vygotsky, Piaget, Bruner, and others have commented on the relationship between pretend play (or symbolic or representational play) and the development of other forms of symbolic activity. Vygotsky (1978) has argued that the creation of an imaginary situation in pretend play marks "the first manifestation of the child's emancipation from situational constraints." As such, pretend play is an important step in the development of abstract, disembedded thinking. Vygotsky has also specifically linked the symbolic activity that is involved in both pretend play and writing: "symbolic representation in play is essentially a particular form of speech at an earlier stage, one which leads directly to written language" (p. 111).

There may be other, perhaps less direct, links between play and early writing. Bruner (personal communication) observed that "to play with something is to open it up for consideration." Play allows the child the freedom to use materials in a non-literal, hypothetical, "as if" manner, and this may be an important way of learning new ways of doing things. Cazden (1976) has also argued that play with language is important for the development of "metalinguistic awareness" which is "the ability to make language forms opaque and attend to them in and for themselves" (p. 603).

It may be that playing at and with writing—by scribbling, drawing, pretending to write and pretending to read, and by playing verbally with written forms—serves to open the activity of writing up for consideration and exploration. Exploring and manipulating the forms, processes, and uses of writing in a playful manner allows the young child great freedom and control; the child is free from the pressures and constraints of producing a correct answer or product. This freedom confers a sense of control because the writing is made, defined, and presented by the child in his or her own terms. (It is important, of course, that parents accept the child's writing more or less as presented by the child.)

That Jeremy's parents support and encourage his pretend play, as well as his pretend writing activities and his playful uses of language, apparently seems natural and unremarkable to them. Not all parents, however, do value play, and some parents, for example, equate fantastic stories with lies which are not acceptable (Heath, 1982b).

Scaffolding Early Writing

In reading to Jeremy, and in encouraging and facilitating his pretend play, his parents are providing him with a rich foundation for the development of writing. There are other more direct or specific ways in which Jeremy's parents support and facilitate his writing development.

At the most basic level, Jeremy's parents provide him with access to the necessary tools for writing. These materials are available to Jeremy so that he can write more or less whenever he wishes. Jeremy's mother assists him with his writing activities when he requests help, and yet she also accepts his often very rough approximations as he presents them. In general, she appears to be very responsive to Jeremy's ongoing interests and concerns. Like the effective preschool teachers described by Wood, McMahon, and Cranstoun, she serves as a "resource" for her child and often acts as "an extension of his own intentions" (1980). This kind of responsive assistance enables Jeremy to carry out activities that would otherwise be beyond him, while at the same time such assistance seems designed to allow him a sense of control over his expanding writing activities.

In scaffolding Jeremy's writing activities his mother also has her own "agenda." When she responds to Jeremy's initiatives, she often does so in ways that extend his knowledge and understanding about writing, offering suggestions and definitions and generally focusing and clarifying his writing activity. In the interaction centered around "playing office," we saw that Jeremy's mother first asked him to define what he had written, and then offered him two definitions ("a message" or "a story"). In so doing, she offered him instruction about conventional writing forms *and* suggested that his writing could be treated as if it had one of these forms. In telling Jeremy that he could act as if he had written a story, his mother may have been establishing her expectations that one day he *will* write a real story.

Her technique here seems similar to that employed by middle-class mothers in Wertsch, McNamee, McLane, and Budwig's (1980) study of assisted problem solving. In helping their children complete a model copying task, these mothers frequently made task demands slightly ahead of their child's immediate understanding and capacity, and then guided the child through the appropriate responses. This kind of assistance implies high expectations of the child and at the same time helps the child figure out strategies to meet them. Such assistance seems well designed to stretch and expand the child's knowledge and understanding of the activity under consideration.

An interesting aspect of the scaffolding provided by Jeremy's parents for his writing activities concerns their role as audience. As an audience, they are available, responsive, supportive, and appreciative. This is important because most of Jeremy's writings take on communicative meaning only in the context of immediate social interaction; a line of randomly typed letters *becomes* a nursery rhyme, a poem, or the "ABC News" when Jeremy pretends to read it as such to his parents. Thus, as interpretable communications, most of Jeremy's writings are almost entirely context dependent and it is his parents who supply the context by serving as audience. Without this contextual support Jeremy's writings would be hard to interpret and the activity of writing would probably be far less interesting and satisfying to him.

Jeremy's parents serve as audience not only for his dramatic readings and recitations, but also for other pieces of his writing, such as his page of handwritten letters, his poems, and his valentines. These various bits of writing, with their poorly formed letters and backwardly-spelled words, are received with enthusiasm and appreciation. In accepting Jeremy's rough approximations with pleasure, his parents respond to his early writing as many parents respond to their infants' babblings and early vocalizations. As Bruner (1974, 1975), Ryan (1974), Holdaway (1979) and others have pointed out, most parents accept all sorts of vocal approximations as adequate, interpretable utterances. In the *Foundations of Literacy* (1979), Holdaway argues that the kind of support for language learning that most parents provide—particularly the acceptance and reinforcement of rough approximations as adequate communications—could well serve as a "developmental model" for learning to read and to write.

Jeremy's writing, then, is supported by his parents in a variety of interrelated ways, both direct and indirect. Writing is part of Jeremy's relationship to his parents, and part of his ongoing daily activities, including his play. The support his parents provide helps to define writing as a natural, pleasurable, and worthwhile activity for Jeremy, an activity that he seems to feel is within his developing competence. At the moment, Jeremy appears to be developing "emergent" writing skills, and to be on his way to becoming a writer. It is impossible, however, to predict his future writing development. For one thing, he has yet to face school writing instruction, where the demands and expectations of his audience will no doubt be very different. It is also difficult to anticipate what meaning and importance writing may have for Jeremy in later years. It does seem clear, however, that at the moment writing is a significant activity in Jeremy's life.

CASE STUDY TWO: WRITING UNDER THE INFLUENCE OF NINA

Introduction

This is an observational study of some of the writing activities 5-year-old Jill engaged in at home, with particular attention to the ways in which her relationships with her family influenced the development of her written language. The focus will be on the influence of her sister Nina, who is 18 months older. While there has been increased interest recently in the study of the social contexts of children's early writing, this work has centered primarily on the role of adults. No one, as far as I know, has looked at the influence of siblings' interactions.

DEAR NICOLE,
I LIKE SCHOOL VERY MUCH. HOW ABOUT YOU.
      (picture of a winter scene)
WINTER REMINDS ME OF YOU.
                              LOVE JILL

This letter represents the first time Jill, 5 years and 10 months old, initiated an activity whose function is unique to writing in that it is normally used to communicate across distance and through time. The idea of sitting down at home and writing this particular piece was Jill's; she only asked her older sister and mother for some spellings. Jill was experimenting with the medium of written language, yet she brought many assumptions about writing to the task. For example, she employed many of the basic principles of writing, such as the ideas that print stands for something besides itself, that there are a limited number of written signs, and that print is arranged on a page in a particular way. She also seemed to have the notions that writing is alphabetic in nature, that words need to be spelled correctly, and that there are linguistic conventions to be observed in writing letters. How is it that Jill, without formal instruction, came to be able to accomplish something so complex?

Scribner and Cole (1981) conceptualize the achievement of literacy as not simply a matter of developing abstract skills, but as the use of reading and writing in the performance of the practices which constitute one's culture. Accepting this view of literacy, we can see that the child's social environment must play an extremely important role in influencing the development of his or her writing ability. Children develop competence in the sociocultural practice of writing through the internalization of social relationships, that is, children internalize the structure of the activities involving writing which they experience in their environment. This internalization presupposes an active role on the part of the child. Rather than simply observing other people writing and then copying that activity, the child must somehow act together with the other and share in the activity. The child then gradually internalizes specific means whereby he or she can ultimately appropriate written language and make it his or her own. The child begins to write because he or she has come to know about and value writing from these interactions with important people.

To say that Jill's writing developed out of earlier social interactions can be misleading. It was not just a matter of her mother or sister providing instruction or guidance, nor was it only a case of Jill's taking initiative and seeking to model herself after an available person. Interaction is more than two people involved at the moment—it encompasses their history and specific relationship with all of its permutations. It is the particular nature of the relationship which gives specific meaning to their joint activities (writing and otherwise). In order to consider what Jill brings to her writing interactions, I will attempt to discuss the psychological issues that are important to Jill at this time in her life. I will therefore employ psychoanalytic theory to explain the themes (e.g., competition, identification, cooperation) that appear to run through her interactions. I will not use psychoanalytic theory in an attempt to understand the *content* of Jill's written language, but rather to help explain the *process* by which a young child comes to write without formal instruction.

The following examples are of writing activities Jill engaged in during the 6 months preceding her letter to Nicole. The observations were made primarily by the girls' mother, and in some cases by the author. While the order is roughly chronological, it is not based on a developmental continuum. The two major categories are "Mother and Sister as Models" and "Jill and Nina Joined in Purpose". These categories are descriptive and were developed according to the ways in which Jill's relationships contributed to making written language significant for her.

Mother and Sister as Models

By the time Jill was 5-years-old, she had had ample opportunity to develop a "literate orientation" (Scollon & Scollon, 1981). Her parents had always read books, played word games, and engaged in many kinds of language activities with the girls. In addition, Jill's mother had always valued writing as a medium of expression for herself. Jill undoubtedly watched her mother write children's stories and her husband's social work reports, among other things. Nina, who had just begun second grade, often engaged in writing activities and delighted in practicing what she knew.

Given Jill's many experiences with written language and her observations of her mother and sister writing, how was she able to make use of these encounters to further her own written language? The following three examples illustrate ways in which her mother and sister functioned as models of cultural roles.

"A Halloween Story"

Jill asked her mother for a piece of cardboard and said, "I'm going to write a story." She sat down and "wrote" a tale of a witch flying through the sky and a black cat. Her production consisted of parallel horizontal lines of cursive scribble, letters, words (BK CAT KIRA; JILL), and pictures (a witch flying over a box representing the sky with the moon and stars in it; a 5-year-old's hieroglyphic).

As Jill was "writing" her story, she was telling it out loud. Yet she clearly did not want her mother to come too close, as her tale seemed to be disrupted when her mother did so. She didn't ask for any help and was unwilling to answer any questions about it. When Jill finished she asked her mother for a piece of tape and taped the story on the living room wall.

The immediate stimulus for this story was probably a similar Halloween story which Jill had heard at school. Her kindergarten teacher had a chart with the same combinations of pictures and words on display in front of the classroom. Even though Jill had this as a model and initiated the story at home on her own, there was still a profound influence that her mother undoubtedly exerted.

One way in which her mother regulated the writing activity was that she was available both to provide technical assistance (giving Jill the materials) and to receive the finished product. Perhaps more important, Jill's mother functioned as an object of identification. While Jill most certainly appreciated the value for her mother of writing in general, in this instance there was a more literal antecedant. When Jill was 4, her mother had written a children's book about a witch. Jill not only listened to the story many times, but was able to recite it with impressive accuracy. The origin of the story can be considered to be in the interaction with her mother, and gives texture to Vygotsky's famous dictum of how an interpersonal process is transformed into an intrapersonal one:

> Every function in the child's cultural development appears twice: first, on the social level, and later, on the individual level; first *between* people (interpsychological), and then *inside* the child (intrapsychological). This applies equally to voluntary attention, to logical memory, and to the formation of concepts. All the higher functions originate as actual relations between human individuals . (1978, p. 57)

First Jill participated with her mother by listening to the story; then she rehearsed it out loud. Finally, she used the memorized words as she talked to herself to guide her activity as she "wrote" her own story a year later.

Jill's Halloween story was important to her writing development as she was able to extract from all her previous experience and recreate a story of her own. In order to understand something of why she was motivated to do so, it is important to look at some of the unconscious issues involved in Jill's relationships. Based on psychoanalytic developmental psychology, it is assumed that the 5-year-old is in the stage where he or she is negotiating Oedipal issues. That is, the girl in this phase is thought to be more seductive with her father while identifying with her mother and competing for the father's attention. By taking on one of her mother's roles, Jill was able to successfully compete with her. In this framework, competition was the probable reason why Jill didn't want her mother directly involved in her story.

A related function for Jill in successfully writing a story on her own was that it enabled her to meet her need for control. As the youngest (by only 18 months) of two children, a central issue for Jill was forever being in the least powerful and independent position. As such, she was faced with having to compete with Nina, who was also identifying with their mother by taking over important activities. In this instance, mother and Nina were not writing stories, so Jill could be both powerful and independent. Only once she had completed an "acceptable" product, was she able to present it to the world. This may also account for the fact that Jill historically (including the chronologically later example of her letter to Nicole) had few invented spellings. Unlike many young writers (see Bissex, 1980; Read, 1975), Jill had a strong desire to spell correctly. If Jill's need to be more adultlike in her writing is a function of sibling rivalry, perhaps it is the case that investigators of invented spellings have looked primarily at first or only children.

"Keeping Up With Nina"

Nina was making a book called "Types of Plants" in which each page had a picture and label of a different plant. Jill asked her mother if she too could make a "book," and her mother stapled several pages together for her. Jill's text had the appearance of a book, parallel horizontal lines of letters and symbols. There were isolated words interspersed: MOM, JILL, KRA ꭾ꘡ (Karen, a beloved babysitter). She incorporated many of the same symbols she used in her pictures of that era (a star, tree, and person).

There was no joining of purpose between Jill and Nina in this activity; rather they each worked independently. Jill tried to be a part of Nina's activity, but could not. For example, Nina would ask her mother a question about classifying the plants (which even she barely understood); Jill would attempt to ask a similar question and then become upset when it didn't work. Jill became unusually demanding of her mother's attention, complained a lot, and broke into tears.

Once again, Jill's mother's influence was at work. Bookmaking was perceived by both girls as a valuable activity, and their mother's interest in horticulture (she was taking a course in it at the time) set the topic. Jill was taking the immediate culture of her family and making it serve her own purposes, one of which again included identifying with her mother.

Nina's role in this activity added a new dimension because her influence was more direct: she had the idea of making a book, which was something Jill could aspire to. However, what Nina was doing with her book, developing a rudimentary system of classifying plants, was too difficult for Jill. Jill therefore adapted what she knew to the new form of bookmaking: she drew familiar pictures and made isolated letters and a list of names that she had written before.

Things did not go well for Jill during this writing activity. She experienced far more conflict while making her book than during her other writing occasions (with or without Nina). She experienced many more frustrations during the process and was not as pleased with her product (which also wasn't as good as others of that period). In order to understand why this experience was problematic for Jill, it is important to try to capture something of the meaning of it for her. While she simply may have been irritable that day, a real possibility is that she was feeling stymied in her attempts to identify with her mother and compete for her father. While this is a somewhat elusive concept, the child's identification can be seen as the creation of a unique individual through shared activities. For Jill, however, sharing in activities with, and trying to be like her mother, is complicated by having an older, more competent sister. She is often, as was mentioned earlier, faced with having to compete with Nina, as well as being third in line to her father.

The primary motivation for Jill in this activity seems to have been to keep up with Nina. Bookmaking was obviously a highly-charged, positive way to make contact with her mother, please her, and be like her. Yet, Jill was faced with someone who could do it "better," and was therefore made keenly aware of her own limitations. Her conflict centered around her strong need to identify with her mother on the one hand, and the danger and pitfalls of competing with Nina on the other. It is probably not a coincidence that Jill omitted Nina's name from her list of important people (it is also interesting that Dad was not included; this may be evidence that the story was written *for* Dad).

From the standpoint of Jill's psychological development, the situation may have been a healthy means to act out her frustrations. The interaction was not optimal for Jill's writing development, however, in that she could not successfully negotiate her sibling rivalry issues. Because she did not feel a sense of mastery, Jill was unable, in this instance, to appropriate written language as an effective tool for herself. Rather, her attempt at modeling herself after Nina was comparatively unsuccessful. Thus, while Nina did offer a specific writing form which Jill was able to adopt, it was a problematic learning experience, and how much Jill gained in terms of the development of her writing ability is questionable.

In the preceding example Nina served as a role model Jill was motivated to copy, perhaps because of competitive feelings. The following is an example of an attempt by Nina to influence Jill more directly.

"I amn't going to do it"

For some time, Jill had been using the word "amn't." One day she used it in conversation with Nina. Nina told her it was wrong and that she shouldn't use it. Jill insisted that she *could* use it if she wanted to. She launched some discussion of the word "ain't" to prove her point. Jill was adamant. Nina was annoyed. Finally Nina shouted, "Jill, don't use it. It *disturbs* me."

A few days later, Jill again used the word "amn't." Nina again called her on it: "Jill, that's not *correct*." Jill insisted, "I don't care." Nina told her that if she continued to use "amn't" in the second grade, the kids would make fun of her. Jill would not give an inch on her right to use that word. Finally in exasperation, Nina screamed at her, "Jill, if you keep saying that, no one will want to marry you!"

This was followed by a less heated sisterly discussion about the desirability (or lack thereof) of marriage.

In this example Jill insisted on controlling the rules of her language and was not yet ready to accept the culturally-agreed-upon usage—at least not as presented by Nina. Nina's admonition that "no one will want to marry you" vividly illustrates the recurring Oedipal theme. Rather than being outdone, however, Jill came out of this exchange with an increased sense of autonomy as well as good feelings about herself. While Nina was unsucessful as a role model in this instance, Jill's language learning was not hampered as she was well aware of the incorrectness of her word. In fact, her feelings of control over her language in this situation might well have led to her being more receptive in later interactive situations in which she could move toward making writing her own. It is important to keep in mind that Jill *does* want to be like her sister and mother, but must preserve her own identity at the same time. Far more frequently than not, Jill turns to her sister for writing and other cultural conventions.

Jill and Nina Joined in Purpose

In the "bookmaking" example cited above, Nina's influence on Jill was rather indirect; she served largely as a model and the girls worked independently. While they were both writing for the same reason, to please and identify with their mother, they were cast in an adversarial position. There were other instances in which Nina played a far more direct and less conflicted role in the development of Jill's writing. The following two examples illustrate how Nina regulated the *degree of difficulty* of the tasks, rather than just influencing the *occurrence* of a writing activity. In the bookmaking activity, Nina regulated the occurrence of Jill's writing simply by having the idea. The form of "books," however, and the process of bookmaking, were not new to Jill. Her finished product was also not any more fully developed than others she had made. In the following circumstances, Nina's involvement resulted in Jill's accomplishing more sophisticated or difficult pieces than she would have on her own.

"A Magic Potion"

Each girl had a sheet of paper and they were talking about making a list of ingredients for a "magic potion." Nina wrote and spelled out loud, and Jill wrote the following:

POCION UNGRINE PEPER, HAIR + HONEY + e GARLIK

In this example, Nina functioned in an authoritative role much as a teacher. She had the idea, arranged for the materials, provided a model, and "spelled" words for Jill. (The invented spellings were Nina's—once again likely perceived by Jill as more correct than her own could be.) However, the quality of the interaction was very different from that of the book-making activity. Earlier that day Nina and Jill had actually concocted a "magic potion." Because the experience grew out of earlier mutual play, and because it was not conflicted by competitive dynamics, the girls were able to enjoy working and talking together.

This interactive event also differed from those involving adults in a very important way. Nina was engaged in an activity that was pleasurable and meaningful to both herself and Jill. In that sense she and Jill had a "shared agenda." For both girls this writing activity was an extension of their earlier play. In mixing and then recording the ingredients, the girls were controlling or influencing the environment in ways not possible in other contexts. The experience shared the "paradoxical" quality of pretend play (Bateson, 1972; Vygotsky, 1978) in that it was both pretend and real at the same time. This quality allowed the girls to feel that they had created their *own* meaning while involved in an activity that had a social, objective meaning (e.g., cooking, making shopping lists).

As a consequence of the girls' *mutual involvement,* Jill's written product was more sophisticated than her earlier work. While she had made lists of names before, they were always of the same familiar people. In the potion list, each word (some of which Jill contributed) was purposeful and decided upon consciously. Thus, the mutuality which enhanced Jill's sense of control over her writing enabled her to produce something she would not have been able to without Nina's help.

"Writing To Make The Time Go By"

The girls had been talking about a brand of vitamins called "Flintstones" all morning. Their father then went out to the store and was going to buy some. He was gone a long time and the girls began to write notes. Nina wrote: "Dad put the flinsones on the table." Jill (with Nina's help with spelling) wrote:

DAD DO YOU HAVE THE FLINST
ONES?

Once again the writing activity for Jill can be seen as an outgrowth of social interaction. They were mutually involved in discussing and playing with the "Flintstone" vitamins all morning. The girls were also joined in purpose in that they were becoming impatient waiting for their father. The primary motivation for both girls' notes seems to have been to express (and perhaps objectify) their impatience. While both notes served the same function, their level of sophistication was different. The notes differed in syntax; Nina's had an instrumental purpose, and indeed, she taped it on the door where her father would be sure to see it. Jill's note was less communicative in the sense that it was not as much a message as an expression of hope for the vitamins.

As in the preceding example, this writing experience was a highly successful and unconflicted one for Jill. It enabled her to allay her impatience while waiting, and once again the written product was richer due to Nina's influence. She discovered that writing was something she could to "to make the time go by"; she incorporated the word "Flintstones"; she used a question mark; and she experienced another form of writing (the note) used to communicate to others (as was her letter to Nicole, which was written soon after).

A Special Case Of Joint Purpose: Jill And Nina As Co-Conspirators

The preceding examples (with the exception of Jill's use of the word "amn't") have all been activities in which writing was the primary medium. The purposes for writing letters, stories, books, lists, and notes were those served by the enduring aspects of writing; they communicate across distance and through time, or record information. In all of these activities Jill was, to some degree or other, attempting to adopt the adult practice of writing and/or struggling with her own mastery of the written word. The following two examples present situations in which writing is secondary. The functions of these episodes are primarily served through other symbol systems; speaking, drawing, and play. What is of interest in these examples is that writing *is* included, when it is not essential to the task.

"Some Scatological Musings"

Jill and Nina were in a room alone. Amid *much* hilarity Jill, with Nina's help (dictating and spelling) produced the following pages.

Page One: JILL DANIELS
PIS + PIS
NOW DID YOU
THINK OF LOOK
ING AT THIS
SECR
ET   ROBERT
PAGE   GOING
PEE.

At the bottom of the page is a flower with a penis and a boy with an elongated penis urinating.

Page Two:

JILL DANIELS
ROBERT
PIS + PIS
NOW TAKE A LOOK AT TN

Page Three:

JILL DANIELS
KIRA (crossed out)
BUTT
ROBERT

There are several pictures of what appear to be penises.

Page Four:

PI
KIS SING
LOVE ING
e H

At the top of the page is a picture of a sun. At the side of the page is a boy crying and urinating.

This is a powerful example of the two girls banding together in order to deal with unconscious issues and their feelings toward a difficult neighbor. Robert, who is 7-years-old and lives down the street, appears to have serious emotional and learning problems. The girls are almost always angry with Robert for one reason or another.

Scatological musings are common for children of this age in that they help the child develop control or mastery over his or her feelings. In this case the girls were most likely defending against Oedipal feelings by berating and making fun of males, and by treating the penis as a liability rather than as an asset. The words and pictures served to both satisfy their voyeuristic impulses as well as to defend against underlying anxieties. The purpose was to be offensive both in the sense of being revolting and in the sense of making an attack (Maria Piers, personal communication). The objects of the attacks were probably powerful adults *and* Robert, who so often upset them with his unpredictable behavior.

While saying the words undoubtedly gave the girls great pleasure and served as sublimation, their scatology also took the form of drawings and written words. Re-enacting the scatology in other symbolic mediums served to further distance the sublimation. Writing and drawing allowed the girls to be able to both see and look away, thus enabling them to maintain feelings of control. Two things are interesting about the nature of the interaction and of each girl's contribution. First of all it was Jill who did all of the drawing and writing; Nina only provided spelling and some dictating. Nina was having Jill do "the dirty work." This may have been the case because Nina was exerting her power as the older sibling; or another possibility is that as a child more into the latency stage, Nina was more concerned with social conventions.

A second aspect worth considering in this example is the relationship between the drawings and writing. The drawings were all done by Jill; the words, though recorded by Jill, were essentially Nina's contribution. While the drawings might have been merely illustrations to the text, it is likely that if she were alone, Jill would have created her meaning only through drawing "dirty" pictures. One can speculate that for Nina, the catharsis was in the written word, while the pleasure for Jill was in drawing. Support for this line of reasoning comes from Gardner (1980). He states that the child who has not yet learned to read or to write with some fluency is not yet ready to "marshall her literary resources and to express significant messages with her pen...and so until the task of writing has been mastered," Gardner continues, "the system of drawing is the only one sufficiently elaborated to permit expression of inner life" (p. 155). Yet Jill did, as an extension of Nina, write the words, and as a result produced a more sophisticated piece than any of her other work of that time.

The last example is of a "Spying Game" that the girls and their friends played over a period of several months, culminating about the time Jill wrote the letter to Nicole "on her own."

"The Spying Game"

Summer: Jeannie, a playmate about 2 years older than Nina, introduced the game of "spying" last summer. Several children were playing—Jeannie (entering fourth grade); Nina, Georgie, and Kira (all entering second grade); and Jill (entering kindergarten). Jeannie had the idea of a "spying club." She organized the activity and set the rules. All the children met together in a group, made plans to sneak about the immediate neighborhood, observe peoples' activity, record their observations (each was supplied with paper and pencil), then return to a meeting spot and compile their findings. The only problem was that Jill wanted to play, but she couldn't write. So Jeannie said that Jill could either accompany one of the others and help them spy or she could go out on her own and come back and tell someone who could write her "spy." There was much discussion of who should go with who, where they should spy, and where the meeting place would be. Whistles were distributed for some sort of signaling purpose. The game caught. It was played with intensity and enormous enjoyment.

Some days after the game had been initiated, Jeannie and Nina decided that there should be a test to join the club. The two of them set about meeting to devise such a test. Jill was worried—how could she get in the club if she couldn't write to pass the test? Nina was pretty rigid ("Well then you can't be in the club'') but Jeannie prevailed in her decision that there should be *two tests,* one for those who could write and one for those who couldn't. She found out what Jill could do—"Jill can write her name, right? Well, then something like that will be her test.''

Winter: Nina and Jill continued to play a modified version of The Spying Game. Usually this took the form of each of them writing down something they had "spied" on their own sheets of paper (e.g., DAD IS TALKING TO MOM). While Nina usually provided spellings, the content was often jointly arrived at.

Spring: Mother was folding clothes on Jill's bed. Jill pulled a slip of paper out of her desk, and with Mother's help with spelling (and obviously pleased with her accomplishment), wrote:

MOM IS
FOLDING
CLOTH
ES

In the "Spying Game," writing, though significant, was but one element of a complex activity. The game undoubtedly met the school-aged children's need for camaraderie and explicit rule-governed play. But more important, this game can be seen as the children's realization in play form of tendencies that cannot be immediately gratified (Vygotsky, 1978). Spying is a magnificent way in which to gain power over people; they have no secrets you cannot discover. For children, who are continually striving to gain control and feel effective in an adult world, spying affords the wonderful opportunity to turn the tables and discover "what *they* are up to!"

In a further consideration of the "Spying Game" it is interesting to speculate about why writing was incorporated into the game. It may be that the school-aged children had some notion that individuals who control the medium of writing have more power (Gundlach, 1982). The children also had some recognition of the enduring aspects of writing and its potential for capturing and savoring experiences. When asked what the writing was for, Nina's response was "So we don't forget."

The influences of the "Spying Game" on Jill were many and complex. Obviously the whole notion of "spying" was as meaningful to Jill as to the others and she thoroughly enjoyed being a member of the older group. In some ways Jeannie, the oldest child, functioned as an adult for Jill. She structured the situation so that Jill could participate as fully as possible. First, she suggested that Jill could either accompany someone or dictate her "spy" to someone who could write. Then, unlike Nina, who was acting as the "upholder of the cultural standard" (or, as an older sibling), Jeannie suggested an alternative literacy test that Jill could "pass."

Nina's influence in the "Spying Game," over the course of the winter, was much as it was in the examples of "The Magic Potion" and "Make the time go by.'' Jill and Nina were joined in purpose; as an outgrowth of their play they began to write, and in so doing discovered a new means to work out their cognitive and affective needs. Again, as a consequence of their mutual involvement, Jill developed a more sophisticated use for writing. Nina also served in somewhat of an authoritative role in that she supplied the spellings.

Finally, in the spring, Jill wrote her own ''spy.'' While she did this independently of Nina, it is interesting that she transferred Nina's authoritative role to her mother, who was both the object of the ''spy'' and the provider of the spellings. One possibility for this was that Jill was feeling guilty for ''spying'' and needed to let her mother know what they were up to—for her approval, because secrets are a heavy burden. Unlike the scatology, however, the Spying Game never had the same quality of doing the forbidden. While the children's voyeuristic tendencies were undoubtedly involved in the game, the overriding need seemed to be for a means of group identification. In looking at adults and sharing that information, the children became a community. It seems that Jill's pleasure came from feeling like an effective member of that community. It may be that asking her mother for spellings was a reflection of the fact that Jill needed technical assistance and no one else was around.

The ''Spying Game'' does illustrate one way in which early literacy is developed through social relationships. Through mutual participation in a very meaningful game, Jill experienced an activity which involved writing. Over a period of time, and with additional support from Nina, she was able to come to the point when she wanted to conduct this activity for herself. While she was still somewhat dependent on her mother, she was now in control in that she initiated the situation (''spying'') and chose the symbol system (writing). It is quite likely that Jill came to write her letter to Nicole in a similar fashion.

Conclusion

The development of Jill's writing can thus be seen as originating in the relationships she had with her family. On one level her parents provide an environment which is replete with the artifacts of literacy, and they clearly value reading and writing as relevant aspects of their lives. They engage in countless language activities *with* their daughters, provide materials and assistance, and are an encouraging and appreciative audience for all of the girls' attempts at mastering written language (including the most remote of approximations). In these ''substantive'' ways, Jill is put in touch with the forms, processes, and functions of written language in her family in particular, and in society in general (Teale, 1982).

On a deeper level, Jill's interactions with her family around literacy *motivated* her to learn to write; they served to forge links between Jill's internal psychological forces and writing. Still in the Oedipal phase of development at age 5, she primarily sees her parents only as they relate to her own self. The challenge of this phase lies in the recognition that one's self is not invariably part of every human equation (Basch, 1975, 1977, 1980). The child needs to successfully master her anxieties and come to grips with her separation in the sense of accepting realistic limitations to her power. Writing, for Jill, is one way in which she can both hold on to, and at the same time separate from, her mother. Through sharing in activities and eventually taking them on as her own, Jill identifies with her mother.

What of the role of an older sibling in the development of early writing? Having considered the range of writing activities Jill engaged in "under Nina's influence," it appears that the presence of a sibling at home is a force to be acknowledged. Nina's influence does not always serve to facilitate or move Jill's writing development forward. If the girls are cast in an adversarial position where they are competing for the same role, Jill is generally frustrated. Nina's considerable edge over Jill in writing deprives Jill of the power and pleasure she can experience from writing on other occasions.

More often than not, Nina's influence is extremely beneficial to the development of Jill's written language. At these times, Nina's collaboration helps to "stretch" Jill's writing, much in the manner Vygotsky (1978) speaks of in his discussion of the instructional area he calls the "zone of proximal development." This is the distance between what the child can accomplish alone (the level of actual development) and what the child can do when helped by a more competent adult or peer (the level of potential development). It is important, however, to distinguish between the role of an adult and that of a more capable peer. Each time Nina's influence was positive, her role was not primarily instructive, but rather the girls were joined in purpose and engaged in mutual *play*.

For Vygotsky, play, like instruction, is a major source of development —indeed play *leads* development.

> play creates a zone of proximal development of the child. In play a child always behaves beyond his average age, above his daily behavior; in play it is as though he were a head taller than himself. (1978, p. 102)

Just as play leads Jill's writing development, so does Nina. As Nina and Jill play together, they project themselves into the adult activities of their culture and rehearse their future roles. Play also enables the girls to master their various conflicts, wishes, and fears. Thus, through mutual needs, the girls share an agenda when they play. Because Nina is sufficiently older, and because she has had more school experience critical to literacy (first and second grades), she is considerably further along in her writing development.

As a writer who has already experienced some of the uses of writing, Nina, sometimes unwittingly, serves to induce or entice Jill into writing. Nina usually provides the idea and the wherewithal to write. By being "carried along" in the context of play, Jill can participate in writing to her current ability and expand her competence without experiencing frustration or defeat.

In addition to regulating the occurrence and frequency of writing in their play, Nina enables Jill to experience new forms (lists, notes, etc.) of writing. Most important, through their collaborative efforts, Jill learns new and significant uses for writing. While concocting a "magic potion," for example, Jill learns a new way to represent the ingredients and learns that a list is something you can consult later. By experiencing writing as another symbolic medium with which to express the potent themes involved in scatology or "spying," Jill advances in her skill as a young writer. Thus, Nina's influence is not that she "teaches" Jill how to write, but through mutual involvement they use writing to create shared meanings.

CASE STUDY THREE: WRITING INSTRUCTION THROUGH PLAY IN THE CLASSROOM

Introduction

Our discussion of writing development now turns to the classroom arena. In this setting, storytelling interactions between preschool children and their teacher will be examined. The activities consist of children individually composing narratives aloud with their teacher writing down their words; later, the teacher reads each story for the class to dramatize during a formal group time. Using Vygotsky's theory of development, two meanings to "social origins" of literacy skills are explored. In one sense, writing can be said to have origins in the interaction between the child who wishes to compose a story and the teacher who helps him or her put it on paper. In the role of scribe, the teacher can organize the conversation so that the child, in responding to questions, develops a fuller narrative than he or she might without help and prompting. What the child and teacher accomplish together, the child will eventually be able to accomplish alone. In the meantime, child and teacher inhabit a zone of proximal development.

Writing ability may have social origins in another sense: the child's motive or impetus for composing a story seems to be derived from the social world of the classroom. Initially, the idea of composing narratives to be written down comes from the teacher. Very quickly, however, the children begin to make use of the stories and their dramatizations to inform one another of social preferences and private fantasies. The storyteller asks someone to be his friend by giving him or her a role in his story. As in other play situations, the child, thus supported, is free to express fears, concerns, and to propose solutions. The stories, when shared, form part of the fabric of their relationships with one another. The teacher, along with the children, participates in the building of a small scale culture where story ideas are shared, redefined, created anew, and connected to ongoing experiences.

This study explores the hypothesis that the foundations of literacy can be established for preschool children through such one-on-one dialogues with a teacher and large group interactions with peers. Case studies will analyze what children learn about writing when writing helps them make more effective contact with one another, and when writing serves a meaningful function in play.

Play and Writing in the Preschool Classroom

It's 9:15 a.m.: 24 preschool children and their three teachers are halfway through the first hour of free choice activity time in their classroom. Three children are putting babies to bed in the doll corner, others are building a zoo in the block corner, and some are making crowns and superhero capes out of construction paper at the art table. There is a group making pizza at the playdough table, and a few boys are digging tunnels and caves for dinosaurs at the sand table. In the center of this busy play a 4-year-old girl, Melissa, has just finished dictating the following story to one of the teachers:

> Once upon a time there was Cinderella. The stepmother said "Clean the floor." Then the stepmother said "Clean the windows." Then she did it. Then the stepmother said, "If you have a dress to wear, you can go to the ball." Then Cinderella said, "Thank you." Then the stepmother said, "I have to go to the ball quick, Cinderella." Then Cinderella ran upstairs to her mice and she said "Mice, can you mend my dress pretty so I can go to the ball?" Then the mice said "Hurrah, hurrah!" Then her dress was all done. Then Cinderella wear it. Then she said, "Wait for me. I have a dress to go to the ball." The end.

Eight other children patiently wait their turn to dictate a story. In this classroom, the activity of storywriting competes with the doll corner, art table, and block corner for the interest and attention of the children. Day after day, children opt to forfeit play time for the opportunity to compose a story which will later be dramatized with the rest of their classmates at group time.

The teacher in this classroom is fortunate because this set of activities provides her with the opportunity for intimate contact with individual children. She finds out what they are thinking about and has a built-in opportunity to guide the logic of the child's thinking with questions to help them clarify their ideas with more precise wording and grammar. The children can find out about written language as their own ideas, word-for-word, are transposed into written form which will remain fixed on the paper for teachers, parents, and friends to read at any time thereafter.

The dictation of each story (expeditiously limited to one page) can take anywhere from 4 to 10 minutes. During the dictation process, the flow of the child's thinking must adapt to the speed of the teacher's capacity to write. As an observer it is impressive to see the children's patience and enthusiasm sustained throughout what initially appears to be a laborious and time-consuming process. I questioned: Why were children (boys and girls alike) so eager to move toward the teacher and a relationship that offered such rich teaching opportunities for the teacher but which was surely not as satisfying to the children as other available play activities? Why was this kind of storytelling as compelling as (and sometimes more compelling than) playing Cinderella, Darth Vader, or mother, sisters, and baby in the doll corner and block corner?

The head teacher in this classroom, Vivian Paley, points out that she did not always have such rich storytelling going on in her classroom. In *Wally's Stories* (1981), she recounts that story dictation had always been an activity she made available to her classes of kindergarten children, but only a handful of children (usually girls) occasionally enjoyed telling stories over the course of the year. One day, however, after more than 20 years of teaching, she discovered a prolific connection: the relationship of storytelling to story dramatization for the young child.

> The first time I asked Wally if he wanted to write a story he looked surprised. "You didn't teach me how to write yet," he said.
>
> "You just tell me the story, Wally. I'll write the words."
>
> "What should I tell about?'
>
> "You like dinosaurs. You could tell about dinosaurs."
>
> He dictated this story.
>
> The dinosaur smashed down the city and the people got mad and put him in jail.
>
> "Is that the end?" I asked. "Did he get out?"
>
> He promised he would be good so they let him go home and his mother was waiting.
>
> We acted out the story immediately for one reason—I felt sorry for Wally. He had been on the time-out chair twice that day, and his sadness stayed with me. I wanted to do something nice for him, and I was sure it would please him if we acted out his story.
>
> It made Wally very happy, and a flurry of story writing began that continued and grew all year. The boys dictated as many stories as the girls, and we acted out each story the day it was written if we could.
>
> Before, we had never acted out these stories. We had dramatized every other kind of printed word—fairy tales, story books, poems, songs—but it had always seemed enough just to write the children's words. Obviously it was not;

the words did not sufficiently represent the action, which needed to be shared. For this alone, the children would give up play time, as it was a true extension of play. (*Wally's Stories,* 1981, pp. 11–12)

Paley had discovered a set of activities in which instruction can join hands with the forces of children's play; where adult and child, teacher and class are aligned in joint purpose—using written words to better understand one another. This discovery suggests one solution to an ongoing conflict between educators and psychologists. On the one hand there have been those who believe in play and in respecting the child's rhythms and unfolding of development. Within this school of thought, adults play a more passive, non-intrusive role in the child's learning so that the child can take an active role in determining the nature of the day-to-day development of thinking. At the other extreme are those who endorse an active role for the adult in the developmental process of young children and who favor a more passive, receptive role for the child. Particularly in the area of learning to read and write, there is widespread belief that literacy skills are mastered primarily through didactic instruction, in the innumerable subskills that go into the writing process; for example, children practice writing and reciting the letters of the alphabet, tracing them, copying small words and then larger words onto sheets of paper, and eventually copying them into preformed sentences which similarly get copied into notebooks as a means of learning to write sentences. Educational efforts in this tradition have assumed that literacy equals the sum of the individual mechanical skills that go into putting words on paper. Their opponents however, would argue that the skills approach ignores the most vital aspect of writing—that writing is a means of communicating: a meaning-making and meaning-sharing activity among people.

Both approaches have proved dissatisfying because they presuppose an all-or-nothing role for one of the participants in the teaching-learning situation; and yet both points of view are right in a limited sense. There is a need for adult instruction in the process and there is a need for children to have opportunities to play with the forms and functions of written language, just as they have had such opportunities in learning to speak. But what would play with written language look like for young children? This is where the significance of Paley's approach lies—the stories become the children's scripts for the kinds of play situations they might enact in other areas of the room, but it quickly becomes evident to them that at times the stories as play are a much more powerful and satisfying communication tool.

Upon examining a selection of stories from this class of children, it can be seen that they use the stories in many ways: they make wishes, speculate on what life is like, mark special occasions (e.g., a Chinese New Year story), welcome a friend back to school, and express anxieties brought from home. Through the stories teachers and peers may enter the storyteller's world, seeing it through the child's wishes, ideas, and fantasies. Stories become the children's way of telling those around them how they think at the time they are trying to figure out what they do think.

Melissa. Melissa's Cinderella story provides us with a good example of writing instruction intertwined in a child's play. Melissa takes one of the favorite heroines of the 3 and 4-year-old girls, Cinderella, and uses the familiar details of Cinderella's life to fashion her own life, with modifications of course. Melissa is 4 and came to this classroom at the age of 3 not speaking a word of English. She is an outgoing and friendly child and enjoys coming to school. As Paley discovered with other non-English speaking children, dramatization of stories contains a powerful incentive to speak:

> the lure of becoming a character in a story proved stronger than their resistance to public speaking. This attraction seems almost magical. If the child's belief in magic is based on the assurance of being changed into something else in the future, then dramatics is the immediate representation of this idea.

> Play provides a similar opportunity but lacks the powerful certainty of outcome. The printed story, whether by an adult or a child, promises dependability. The soldier will always kill the witch; the lost child will invariably find his parents; everyone will live happily ever after.

> Stories have yet another magical quality: fully developed sentences borrowed from someone else. The dialogue can change a child from inarticulate embarrasment to confidence, as if by a magic wand. The only task required is to memorize the words. With enough practice, anyone can do this, because the practice is part of the reward. (*Wally's Stories,* 1981, pp. 121–122)

The story of Cinderella held just this sort of magical sway over Melissa. She had a record that narrated the story of Cinderella which she brought to school, and she and any number of other children could be found off in a corner listening to it over and over again, singing the songs, and saying the words with the narrator. Becoming Cinderella over and over again transformed Melissa into a fluent, English-speaking child in a matter of months. This year, Melissa is one of the most regular storytellers in the class and she is the narrator and scriptwriter for her fantasies of Cinderella.

Melissa's Cinderella story as reported above is a story about her friendship with a new Chinese-American girl, Sara, who joined the class this year. This is evident in the dialogue between Melissa and her teacher. Melissa begins her story with the ritualized story form, "Once upon a time there was Cinderella". After the teacher writes this, Melissa says "That says Sara. I'll be the stepmother." Giving her best friend the role of Cinderella is a nice gift and gesture to someone who means a lot to her. The pleasure however, does not go entirely to Sara, for Melissa has a need to assume the upper hand at times in the relationship and have her friend conform to her wishes.

And so in the early part of the story, Melissa utilizes her rich store of commands to direct the activities of Cinderella.

While Melissa dictates this story to the teacher, Sara is sitting at the table next to them involved in her own forms of play that acknowledge and reciprocate the terms of the friendship. Half way through the dictation of the story, Sara interrupts and shows the teacher a picture she has been drawing:

Sara: Look Mrs. Paley.
Mrs. Paley: Pretty colors, Sara, what an interesting design.
Sara: I'm gonna make Wonder Woman bracelets for Melissa and me.
Mrs. Paley: Good idea.

As the story comes to a close, we see Melissa acknowledge the social purpose of this writing exercise. Her teacher says "Now do you want me to read the whole story back to you?" Melissa promptly says "No, I want to play Wonder Woman with Sara now." Melissa makes it clear that getting on to the next episode of play with Sara, now through the script of Wonder Woman, is the most pressing business at hand.

The child's agenda has been to fashion a satisfying play situation with her friend which the rights of authorship give her. The writing down of her script however has provided the teacher with many "teaching opportunities". For example, when the child says "Once upon a time there was Cinderella. That says Sara," to Melissa this is a statement of what she envisions as the story begins to be dramatized—Sara being created as Cinderella. The teacher interprets Melissa's intention, and shows her how the logistics of Sara becoming Cinderella can be handled in this story script: the teacher writes "Sara" next to Melissa's word, "Cinderella". As the dictation continues and the stepmother is introduced, the teacher pauses to show Melissa how she writes "Melissa" by that word to signal that this is the part that she wants to play. Melissa shows us that she has only the vaguest conception of what the adult is putting down on the paper when she says, "How about Sara?" The teacher again shows her the configuration of letters that represent Sara's name. Thus the child is made aware of the nature of the writing process. Over the course of the year these 3-, 4-, and 5-year-olds will have hundreds of such experiences where the written symbol system is equated with their own words. The child will gradually digest the fact that these symbols are in fact reliable and predictable, and that their meanings stay on the page.

Still educators might ask, what is the child learning about reading and writing if the teacher is doing the writing and reading? Maybe young children are practicing logic and clear expression, but what are they learning about the processes themselves? How will children learn to write letters, words, and sentences from merely dictating and dramatizing stories? Until recently, American and European educators and psychologists have accounted for children's development as a function of either environmental input (i.e., adult instruction and guidance), or children's maturation or self-initiated activities and discoveries. In the last 20 years, however, new translations of the work of Vygotsky (1962, 1978, 1981) have offered an alternative theory, one that accounts for development as a function of the interaction between adults and children working together in activities; indeed, Vygotskian developmental theory unites child's play with adult instruction.

Vygotsky believes, as do other developmental psychologists, that development is cumulative. Achievements at each stage are built up through integration and reorganization of earlier developments while behaviors of an earlier stage often look very different from their mature counterparts in a later stage. Vygotsky differs from other psychologists in that he pointed to the significant others in a child's environment as determining the course of the reorganization of a child's thinking from one stage of development to the next. Using Vygotsky's theory, Bruner (1978) gives us an example, in his analysis of how children learn to speak, of the importance of adults in shaping human development. He points out that language development does not begin when the child utters his first word between the age of 1 and 2, but that the foundations of oral language have been laid down in human interactions from the time of birth. He points out that oral language does not emerge only by maturation nor because the infant receives training in sounds, syllables, and words in any direct or formal way. Bruner demonstrates that mothers and infants play hundreds of games during the first 12 months of life which give the infant an excellent foundation in dialogue. In other words, without actually communicating with words the infant has learned many things about making his needs and intentions known to another. The foundations for oral communication have been laid in a set of activities that do not immediately resemble actual talking.

Using Vygotsky's theory of development, we are exploring the hypothesis that learning to read and write is governed by similar developmental principles. Adults and children can participate in meaningful activities that involve the written word but do not require the child himself to have mastered writing or reading. It is the contention here that the activities of storytelling and story dramatization provide the child with exposure to the fundamental aspects of the writing process. In addition, these activities strongly motivate him both to master the mechanics of written language and to become increasingly more effective in expressing himself and understanding others' written messages. Several storytelling and dramatization interactions between Paley and the children in her class will be analyzed in detail through the framework of Vygotsky's theory to highlight the significance of the developments taking place. We will see how these activities of storytelling and dramatization fulfill both the adult's need to provide the prereading child with a firm foundation in language and literature, while fulfilling the child's need to develop the means to express him/herself more effectively in order to be understood—all through interaction in a child's zone of proximal development.

Case Studies

In Paley's classroom, the children have free choice activity time for the first part of the morning during which time the teacher is available for writing down the children's stories. Halfway through the morning, the children come together as a group to sing a song, have announcements and discussions, and to dramatize the stories written that morning. The children and teacher sit in a circle, the center of which is their stage. Sometimes the children have specified classmates who they wish to play a designated role in their story. If they have not, the teacher calls on the children from the edge of the circle one after another to play roles. The teacher is the scribe in the story dictation process, and director and narrator of the dramatizations.

Nathaniel. On arriving at school, Nathaniel, a 3-year-old child, wants to tell the teacher a story that he has heard at home: "The Fox and the Crow". His telling of the story seems quite sophisticated for his age:

> Once there was a crow and he had a
> tasty piece of cheese in his mouth.
> The fox came and then the crow opened
> his mouth and the cheese fell in the
> fox's mouth. The fox jumped and ran
> with the cheese.

He begins by telling the teacher that his story only has two characters. This reflects the child's having internalized the teacher's comments on "the characters" in children's stories over the past 4 months in many different contexts. The child can now use this concept to organize his narrative of a simple story. The following dialogue provides a detailed picture of the teacher's role as scribe and how the child benefits from watching and participating in the process of transposing his spoken words into writing.

Teacher	Child
	1. Once there was a crow and he had a tasty piece of cheese in his mouth.
2. Once*—there was a crow—and he had—a tasty piece—of—cheese—in—his—mouth.	
	3. I know (inaudible) be the fox.

4. You want to be the fox, all right.
You may. Look what I'll do,
Nathaniel. I'll put your name right
by the fox. Who would you like to
be the crow? (three second pause)

5. If the fox were the (inaudible)
————and he jumped around with
the cheese. (five second pause)

6. I didn't get all of that. Once there
was a crow and he had a tasty
piece of cheese in his mouth. Now.

7. and then the fox came—he...and
he...

8. Okay, wait, we'll do it slowly.
Then—

9. um...yeah

10. the fox...

11. and...

12. came...

13. and then, the, and then the crow
opened his mouth and, and the
cheese fell into, the fox's mouth.

14. Okay, now wait. Stop for one
moment. And then the crow—
opened—his mouth and—the
cheese—fell in—the fox's mouth.

15. And the fox jumped around with
the cheese.

16. The fox—jumped—and ran—
with—the chese.

---

*Dashes after a word in the teacher's utterances indicate a small pause as she writes down
that word or phrase. Blank lines indicate inaudible utterances.

As often happens with young children, Nathaniel gets carried away
with the excitement of his ideas and tells his story so quickly that the teacher
has to ask him to slow down so that her writing can keep pace with the dictation. This becomes a powerful teaching moment in the Vygotskian sense:
the child experiences the frustrations and limitations of the writing process
with an adult who tries to help the child hold onto the idea until it can be
recorded. The child sees over and over again how each word he utters gets
represented by a series of letters, and with repeated use, words and letters
become familiar to him. The teacher's repetition of each word as she writes
plus her rereading of phrases, sentences, and eventually the whole story reinforces awareness of the child's words now represented by this elaborate
symbol system.

The dramatization of this story affords the teacher opportunities to
work on concept building and language development with the whole class.
As the teacher begins to narrate the story so the children can act it out, she
asks "What's a crow?" Nathaniel replies: "A thing that flies." The teacher
presses on, "What is it that flies? What do we call it?" Nathaniel says "a
crow." The teacher proceeds to answer her own question by replying with
an acknowledging tone of voice, "It's a kind of bird," upon which a child
excitedly said "My daddy has a rubber crow at his office!"

This exchange between teacher and group provided everyone with the
same frame of reference for understanding the part of the crow in this story.

If Nathaniel and the other children do not know what a crow is, the story and subsequent actions would be meaningless.

The necessity of words making sense was further illustrated when it came time to act out the cheese falling from the crow's hand into the fox's mouth. Michael was playing the part of the crow and stood on a chair to represent his being in a tree. Nathaniel chose to be the fox. The dramatization went as follows:

Teacher	Child
"Once there was a crow and he had a tasty piece of cheese in his mouth." (Pause)	(Michael pretends to put cheese in his mouth.)
There, wasn't that nice the way Michael did that? He showed you he's picking up the cheese.	
"Then the fox came." (Pause)	(Nathaniel stomps over toward the chair and stops about 3 feet away)
And the crow opened his mouth, and the chee..." Open your mouth.	
"...and the cheese fell in the fox's mouth."	
(To Nathaniel:) Put your mouth under his so that it will fall in. Nathaniel look. If I were doing it, I would...	(Nathaniel, who is still three feet away from the chair, starts to sit on the floor)
(no no, you stand up. I would	
put my mouth like this: (she demonstrates)	
so the cheese falls from his mouth into my mouth. Okay? You do that. There. Now.	
"The fox came and the crow opened his mouth and the cheese fell in the fox's mouth."	
There, now we got it!	
"The fox jumped and ran with the cheese."	

The teacher thus helped the children to experience the precise meaning of the words in every detail of their gestures. The children experienced word meanings and the logical necessity of one event following another behaviorally and in relation to other people before they had to experience the meanings from words alone as adults do.

In contrast to Nathaniel's retelling of the fox and the crow story is one of his own original stories. This story, which has a structure more common to 3-year-olds, was told several days after the fox and the crow story.

> Once there was a zoo.
> A lion came and eated it up.
> Then the gorilla came and spanked him.
> Then came Superman.
> Then Spiderman came.
> Then Batman came.
> Then a piece of spaghetti came.
> Then a piece of pizza came.
> Then came a giant house.
> Then a tree came.
> Then a pencil came.
> Then a huge person came.

This story unfolds with a series of free associations that have no particular relationship to one another. The story takes shape as Nathaniel tells it and as he thinks of something else right on the spot. The child comes to the teacher with the urge to tell a story—to express something. He does not necessarily have an idea of what the story is going to be about or an idea to guide the relating of one event to the next. This kind of storytelling reflects a primitive level of story structure in which events have no overall relationship to one another. Nathaniel's retelling of the fox and crow story is clearly more developed than his own original story. However, it must be noted that the value and enjoyment of more primitive-level stories for the child and the group can be as high as for a more well-formulated story. Nathaniel's stories are slapstick comedies for the 3- and 4-year-olds which they love to act out.

Nathaniel is a child with great imagination, energy, and a passion for experimenting and repeating an activity over and over again until he grasps the idea. During the fall when he went outdoors to the playground he would run to the jungle gym, climb on the first rung, jump off, run away, run back, climb on the first rung, jump off, over and over again, day after day, and then one day he went up to the second rung. He is one child who tells stories every single day and uses them as almost daily exercises in practicing an idea and trying out a slightly different angle to the plot each time. He has now retold his fox and crow story with several variations in the ending as well as telling different versions of his own spaghetti and monster stories. He is a determined child who works at something until he gets it. He is struggling (at his own choosing!) to figure out what a story is and how to make something happen in his stories, but he cannot yet generate a real story plot of his own.

Arthur.   Arthur, 5-years-old, is a full 2 years older than Nathaniel, but he too has a style of learning in which he repeats an activity or a theme insistently until he masters it. In this case, Arthur had a clear concept of what a story was but he was stuck on a particular feeling that he used story-telling to express. He had been telling stories about a kitty cat who was intimidated by a monster for several weeks. Arthur consistently chose to play the part of the kitty cat when his stories were acted out. One morning his story revealed a breakthrough in his struggle that he could share with the teacher and later on with the class:

> A monster came. Then the kitty cat came. The kitty cat scratched the monster up. Then the kitty cat ran in the house.

When it was time to dramatize Arthur's story, the teacher introduced it as follows:

Teacher	Children
Arthur's Story. Oh, Arthur did tell a fine story. This is not the usual story that Arthur has been telling. He's surprising us with a new ending.	
Okay, Jason will be the monster and Arthur is the kitty cat.	
"A monster came."	
Jason, come right in the middle. Stand here.	
"Then a kitty cat came."	
Now watch what Arthur does.	
What did his kitty cat do in all his other stories? (Pause) Do you remember?	I remember. He scratch people.
Not his kitty cats, no. Not his kitty cats. That was in Kate's story.	I remember. They ran in the house.
They ran inside, alright. But now listen to what the kitty cat does this time.	
"Then the kitty cat scratched the monster up." Just pretend.	
"Then the kitty cat ran in his house."	
That's the first time the kitty cat's gotten the best of the monster!	

In this instance the child used the daily storytelling opportunity to give voice to an internal struggle he was going through represented by the cat continually being overpowered by a monster. Finally, he felt strong enough to stand up to the monster, and this internal growth was witnessed and experienced by his teacher and peers through the previous stories and the present one.

Patsy. The storytelling and dramatization by Patsy, a 4-year-old, represents another unique case study in the use of storytelling for communicating. This story was dictated to the research investigator and not the teacher. I spent several mornings visiting the classroom in order to get to know the children, and I often found Patsy sitting beside me and wanting to talk. She constantly wanted me to pick her up and carry her around. I told her that she was too heavy and that I particularly wanted to sit at the story table and listen to children's stories that they were telling the teacher. She sat on my lap and listened with me for a while and then said "I want to tell you a story." I told her I would like to hear it and that I would write it down just as the teacher would.

Patsy had written only three stories in nursery school (as opposed to every other child who had written a dozen or more). She wrote two in October with the assistant teacher, and one in November with the head teacher when there was no other teacher present. At that time she felt a great need to acknowledge a scary event that had just taken place in the city; a man climbed up the side of the John Hancock building (Patsy lives in a tall building near the John Hancock building). Her story from that occasion reads:

Somebody's climbing on the bridge.
It's the Billy Goats Gruff.
Spiderman is climbing the John Hancock.

The teacher explained that Patsy tends to avoid her and does not seek attention from the teachers. She is the sixth child in a family of nine children. Her parents are very energetic and involved with their children; Patsy's mother brings her to and from school each day and there is, as can be imagined, a great deal of hurrying and directing that the mother has to do to get the children to school and home at different times. Patsy is withdrawn from the teachers and sometimes from the rest of the class. She seems to be going through a temporary loss of footing in her world with the arrival of a new baby in the family, followed by the move to a new house, and the often confusing logistics of getting to and from school. The teacher senses that the child sees her as someone like her mother: a woman who takes care of a large number of children, is always making plans for the group, directing activities, organizing the day. She showed that she felt the need for maternal attention when she approached me—a woman without responsibilities or connections to this group of children. When I expressed my interest in stories to her, she realized that this was an activity where she would get my complete individual attention and thus her storytelling seemed to function primarily as a means of having emotional contact with an adult.

The story that she told was immature for her age; it was a distracted, discontinuous stream of consciousness:

> A big bad wolf and a man died and there was play dough in there—in the ice cream jar. And there was more play dough coming (We were sitting at the play dough table). It's coming from the ice cream jar toward our house. And all the cheese melted and it was so soggy out with snow on it and there was a typewriter. And there was a muppet show with all muppets.

Patsy's story portrayed a sense of her loneliness and sadness to me, and later to the group when it was dramatized. The teacher, realizing the importance of the fact that Patsy had told her story to me, asked me to direct its dramatization. The uniqueness of this story is displayed by the fact that it does not lend itself to being acted out. The two characters lay on the floor dead listening to the fragmented images.

Patsy's story points out the significance of the adult who receives the child's story and writes it down for him or her. The adult participating in the storytelling and dramatization is not arbitrary and dispensible. The storytelling process needs an adult and child involved in an ongoing emotional relationship.

Conclusion. The case studies presented here illustrate how storytelling and dramatization come out of the texture of daily living in this classroom. The social context of storytelling and dramatizations is critical to understanding the texts produced and shared. The children's needs and motives are intimately tied to the daily life of the group. Researchers need to know something about the life and context that is the occasion for the story if they are to understand one powerful context for early written language learning.

The social origins of literacy have been evident in two ways in this discussion. First, the children's commitment to storytelling when the teacher provided dramatization time exemplifies Vygotsky's theory (1962) that "The primary function of speech, in both children and adults, is communication—social contact. The earliest speech of the child is therefore essentially social" (p. 19). In the preschool setting described, children used gestures and words, oral and written, as a means of defining themselves and reaching out to those with whom they now share a life. The way their gestures and words were received, responded to, expanded upon, and revised in the daily forum of play activities provided the blueprint for each child's current unfolding development of thinking.

For Vygotsky, thinking (including the thinking involved in writing and reading) is fundamentally dialogic in nature:

the sign (words, gestures, pictures) initially is a means of social interaction and only later becomes a means of behavior for the individual. . . . In general, we could say that the relations among higher mental functions were at some earlier time actual relations among people. I shall relate to people as people relate to me. . . . The word's first function is its' social function, and if we want to trace how it functions in the behavior of an individual, we must consider how it is used to function in social behavior. . . . Relations among mental functions genetically must be linked to the real relations among people. Regulation of others' behavior by means of the word gradually leads to the development of verbalized behavior of the people themselves. (1981, pp. 158–159)

The storytelling and dramatization activities reported here demonstrate how writing can function as a relationship among people as well as a representation of relationships. The children start out focusing on themselves in the midst of their first experience in the larger society outside of the family setting. They need to secure their footing in this new setting while being assured that their place in the family has not changed. Then they must find out what other children think being 3- and 4-years-old is all about. Their stories reflect these primary concerns and may eventually serve to help manage them.

The second aspect of the social origins of literacy is evident in the reading and writing processes themselves, ever-present throughout the activities. The teacher initially assumes the responsibility for transposing the child's spoken language onto paper and shapes his or her thinking to the conventions and expectations of written language. Story material must follow a logical sequence of events, pronouns must have a clear reference, and obscure meanings need to be further explained. Vygotsky shows us that the process of questioning a child during story dictation, and the prompting and comments during dramatization play a key role in developing the child's awareness both of the demands of written communications and the thinking/editing functions he will someday carry out on his own. For now, the child remains an unknowing apprentice to the trade of writing and reading. He will learn the process of communication through written language while being immersed in compelling and meaningful relationships that are mediated by the written word.

CONCLUSION: THE SOCIAL CHARACTER OF CHILDREN'S EARLY WRITING ACTIVITY

Believing, with Vygotsky, that "human learning presupposes a specific social nature and a process by which children grow into the intellectual life of those around them" (Vygotsky, 1978, p. 88), we set out in these case studies to look for social contexts for children's initial experiments in written language, and indeed we found them. We found, for example, children encountering models of writers: a mother and father who write books, an older sister who writes at school, neighborhood children who write "spy" notes, and a teacher who transcribes stories that children compose aloud. In the situations we examined, children often came upon writers with whom to identify; they were also able to observe writing behavior they could imitate. We found, furthermore, that often the writers were willing to allow young non-writers to join them in writing activities and were also willing, sometimes eager, to help non-writers begin to learn how to manage writing for themselves. Sometimes the older, more capable writer staged a writing activity for the young non-writer, as in the storytelling projects organized by Paley or the modified "literacy test" proposed for 5-year-old Jill by the leader of the neighborhood spy club. In other instances, the young child initiated the writing activity, with the older and more capable writer helping the child succeed in what he or she had set out to do; thus did Jeremy's mother sustain him in his composing of the word DANGER, a difficult task for him at the time he undertook it.

We also observed the more experienced writer—parent, older sibling, preschool teacher—in the role of appreciative audience, encouraging more than helping during the process of composition and then responding to the product of the child's labor. The demands of the audience varied. Jeremy's parents, for example, freely accepted the pretense and fantasy in which he often situated his writing activities. They were also flexible about accepting Jeremy's interpretations of his own written texts, which to an adult reader were undecipherable. The children who composed stories in Paley's classroom, on the other hand, found themselves working in circumstances that required some linguistic coherence in their texts, and accordingly their teacher slowed them down as they composed so that a usable record could be made of their words. Although we did not observe sustained direct instruction in the cases reported here, there is no reason to suppose that direct instruction in writing is not part of some preschool children's early writing experience. Snow (1983), for example, presents a transcript of a conversation in which a mother tries to keep her 31-month-old son on track as she attempts to teach him to spell his name.

The case studies we have presented do not allow us to move beyond identifying some of the types of interaction in children's early writing activity to an analysis of which sort of interaction contributes most fully or efficiently to a child's development of writing ability. Nor do these observations yield reliable information about cultural patterns in such interactions, since the children we observed do not live in a very broad range of cultural settings and, furthermore, were not selected or studied in such a way as would permit generalizations about even a single group. What these studies do make very clear, however, is that the interactions during what Heath (1982a) has called "literacy events" between young children and older, more capable writers do not, at least in the cases presented here, occur as isolated episodes; rather, literacy events are embedded in the continuities of interaction that constitute longer-term relationships. It was in the context of relationships with parents, siblings, preschool teachers, and neighborhood friends that the children we observed engaged in their early experiments with writing. It was in the course of participating in those relationships—maintaining, expanding, and redefining the power relations in them—that Jeremy, Jill, Nathaniel, and the others found reasons for trying to write, for accepting help when it was offered, for seeking help when it wasn't offered, or for rejecting help altogether.

By drawing attention to enduring relationships which define the social contexts of some children's early writing activities, we do not mean to discount the significance of the cognitive operations, many of them unconscious, that any young child growing up in a literate society performs in building a personal understanding of the system of written language. Nor do we mean to underestimate the significance of the developmental constraints, whether linguistic, cognitive, or physiological, on the progress a young child can make in learning various uses, forms, and processes of writing. But we do wish to call into question the conception of early writing development that presents a picture of the autonomous child encountering a rich print environment and, on his own and in ways mysterious to the adults around him, reinventing the system of written language he has inherited. We wish to replace this image with a picture of a child experimenting with written language as a way of participating in important human relationships, and of a child receiving help with, and clues about, the forms, uses, and processes of writing from the people with whom the child shares these relationships. To put the point another way, the people in a child's life and not merely the print in the child's environment constitute the child's chief resource in learning the early lessons of writing. People, at least the people we observed in the lives of the children we studied here, provide the child with reasons to write, technical and emotional support (or challenge) during the process, and responses once the writing is done. They do this in various ways, from subtle collaboration to stern admonition, and with varying resources and motives of their own. And of course different children react in different ways, according perhaps to the child's interest in writing itself, but also, to judge from the studies we have reported here, according to the child's evolving roles in particular human relationships in which the use of written language holds either a temporary or enduring place.

If, as we suggest in the phrasing of our title, these relationships are properly regarded as the social foundations of children's early writing development, it is because such relationships provide children with their first contact with one, two, or perhaps several distinct communities of readers and writers—distinct groups of people who use written language in their daily lives, and who in their literacy practices draw on a shared knowledge of written language forms and uses. This shared knowledge includes, of course, a knowledge of the conventions of print normally associated with basic literacy in a given language: a system of orthography, a system of punctuation, standard text formats, and common discourse features. But, following Hymes (1973, 1974; see also Gumperz, 1968; Heath, 1981; Szwed, 1981), we can further specify a distinct community of readers and writers as a particular group of people drawn into common literacy practices, whether by vocational necessity, educational experience, family habit or tradition, political or social activity, participation in religious institutions, or some other form of personal, social, or business activity involving the use of written language. Members of such communities share an understanding of particular purposes for reading and writing and a knowledge of particular and perhaps specialized conventions, both textual and interactive, for easing written communication and for marking especially important written messages or valued verbal constructions. Shared, too, are attitudes toward the significance of an individual's skill and care in observing the community's conventions (on this point see Hymes, 1973, p. 65).

We recognize that this general sketch of the concept of communities of readers and writers does not carry the matter very far. It needs, for one thing, some qualification of the sense conveyed above of the coherence of any group of people for whom written language serves commonly understood purposes; people vary enormously in the extent to which they observe the conventions that organize any particular group's way of doing things, and because people use written language to communicate across time and space, one might expect diffuse internal organization of even particularly well-defined communities. Yet even a diffuse community is organized by a set of understandings or rules governing the distribution of roles, responsibilities, privilege, and power; an adequate characterization of a community of readers and writers would certainly have to attend to these arrangements. An adequate characterization would have to take into account, too, the possibility that its members may participate in several such communities, and hence the individual's repertoire of ways of reading and writing may be assembled from experience and perhaps instruction acquired in several different arenas of written language use.

For all its limitations, however, our brief definition does put us in a position to consider two important questions about children's early writing development: first, how do children initially come into contact with various communities of readers and writers? And second, how do specific aspects of the common literacy knowledge and practice of a particular community of readers and writers become accessible, and interesting, to children just beginning to read and write?

The studies we have reported in this chapter underscore the relevance of such questions to the study of children's early writing development, but suggest only a few clues to possible answers. We can begin with the premise that children not yet literate come into contact with the literacy practices of a particular community of readers and writers as they participate in relationships with literate people. To come into contact with a community is not, of course, to be provided with a full display of its practices and special knowledge. But then the readers and writers in some young children's social worlds are not unmindful of their role in initiating the child into particular uses of literacy. In some of the cases we have examined, adults and older children adapt the character of particular literacy practices to accommodate a young child's inexperience and immaturity; in other cases, the adult or older child seems to expect the child to accommodate himself to a particular writing activity as it is normally defined. And yet it should be noted that in both kinds of activity the children we observed seemed quite eager to learn, motivated at least in part, we suspect, by the prospect of acquiring the abilities and assuming the social roles of adults or older children they admire and seek to emulate.

We have observed, too, that play is the characteristic medium of the young child's apprenticeship in communities of readers and writers. This is hardly surprising, for, as Bruner, Jolly, and Sylva (1976) have noted, play is "the principal business of childhood, the vehicle of improvisation and combination"; and further: "What appears to be at stake in play is the opportunity for assembling and disassembling behavior sequences for skilled action" (pp. 15, 20). Thus we observed Jeremy, Jill, Melissa, Nathaniel, Arthur, and Patsy, none of whom yet commands the knowledge or skill expected of a full participant in any community of readers and writers, playing in various ways with the tools and materials of writing, the structures and formats of written language, and the social and cultural roles of writers and readers.

But how much does such early written language play contribute to the long-term development of writing ability? No one, as far as we know, has studied the matter, but we assume that the answer varies considerably from case to case: learning to write, in our view, is best understood as one thread in the narrative of an individual life, not as a uniform process superimposed on the particulars of an individual's experience. And of course it should be noted that there is no compelling reason to suppose that early playful writing experience is absolutely crucial in learning to write. It is conceivable that a child could meet formal writing instruction, or could decide to teach himself to write, having had no prior experience with writing. It is conceivable, too, that such a child's learning from that point forward could be entirely workmanlike and not playful in the least. But in places where literacy has a role in both public and family life, it is reasonable to assume that many children do incorporate written language and the act of writing into their play before anyone sets out to teach them to write, and it is an open question whether this experience provides a child with the beginnings of what in time will become enduring knowledge, skills, attitudes, and sensibilities. In any given instance, the answer to that question no doubt depends in part on the specific kind and amount of cognitive work a particular child undertakes (for the most part unconsciously) during the course of his playful explorations—that is, on the specific character of the inference-making and system-building performed by the child's "learning brain" (Smith, 1982). Certainly the answer depends as well on the writing opportunities and instruction the child encounters in school, and of course on what the child makes of those opportunities and that instruction. Finally, the answer must also depend on the ways in which a child's life remains connected to the lives of other people, both in school and out, with whom the child continues to discover a need, or perhaps a desire, to take up company in the uses of written language.

REFERENCES

Applebee, A. N. (1984). *Contexts for learning to write: Studies of secondary school instruction.* Norwood, NJ: Ablex.

Basch, M. F. (1975). Toward a theory that encompasses depressions: A revision of existing causal hypotheses in psychoanalysis. In E. J. Anthony & T. Benedek (Eds.), *Depression and human existence.* Boston: Little, Brown.

Basch, M. F. (1977). *Developmental psychology and explanatory theory in psychoanalysis. The annual of psychoanalysis.* New York: International Universities Press.

Basch, M. F. (1980). *Doing psychotherapy.* New York: Basic Books.

Bateson, G. (1972). *Steps to an ecology of mind.* New York: Ballantine Books.

Bissex, G. L. (1980). *GNYS AT WRK: A child learns to write and read.* Cambridge, MA: Harvard University Press.

Britton, J. N. (1970). *Language and learning.* Harmondsworth, Middlesex, England: Penguin Books.

Britton, J.N. (1973). Preface. Connie and Harold Rosen, *The language of primary school children.* Harmondsworth, Middlesex, England: Penguin Books.

Britton, J. N. (1982). Spectator role and the beginning of writing. In M. Nystrand (Ed.), *What writers know: The language, process, and structure of written discourse.* New York: Academic Press.

Bruner, J. S. (1974/1975). From communication to language—a psychological perspective. *Cognition, 3,* 255–287.

Bruner, J. S., Jolly, A., & Sylva, K. (1976). *Play: Its role in development and evolution.* Harmondsworth, Middlesex, England: Penguin Books.

Cazden, C. B. (1976). Play with language and metalinguistic awareness. In J.S. Bruner, A. Jolly, & K. Sylva (Eds.), *Play: Its role in development and evolution.* Harmondsworth, Middlesex, England: Penguin Books.

Cazden, C. B. (1981). *Literacy in school contexts.* Paper presented for the International Symposium on New Perspectives on the Processes of Reading and Writing, Mexico City, July 1–4.

Chomsky, C. (1971). Write first, read later. *Childhood Education, 47,* 296–299.

Clay, M. M. (1975). *What did I write?* Exeter, NH: Heinemann.

Ferreiro, E. (1978). What is written in a written sentence? A developmental answer. *Journal of Education, 160,* 25–39.

Gardner, H. G. (1980). *Artful scribbles: The significance of children's drawings.* New York: Basic Books.

Gumperz, J. (1968). The speech community. *International Encyclopedia of the Social Sciences.* New York: Macmillan.

Gundlach, R. (1982). Children as writers: The beginnings of learning to write. In M. Nystrand (Ed.), *What writers know: The language, process, and structure of written discourse.* New York: Academic Press.

Gundlach, R., McLane, J. B., McNamee, G. D., & Stott, F. M. (1983). *Perspectives on children's early writing development* (Erikson Institute Working Papers on Children's Writing Development). Chicago: Erikson Institute.

Heath, S. B. (1981). Toward an ethnohistory of writing in American education. In M. F. Whiteman (Ed.), *Variation in writing: Functional and linguistic-cultural differences.* Hillsdale, NJ: Erlbaum.

Heath, S. B. (1982a). Protean shapes in literacy events: Ever-shifting oral and literate traditions. In D. Tannen (Ed.), *Spoken and written language.* Norwood, NJ: Ablex.

Heath, S. B. (1982b). What no bedtime story means. *Language in Society, 11,* 49–76.

Holdaway, D. (1979). *The foundations of literacy.* Gosford, NSW, Australia: Ashton Scholastic.

Hymes, D. (1973). Speech and language: On the origins and foundations of inequality among speakers. *Proceedings of the American Academy of Arts and Sciences, 102*(3), 45–72.

Hymes, D. (1974). *Foundations in sociolinguistics.* Philadelphia, PA: University of Pennsylvania Press.

Oates, J. C. (1982). *The making of a writer.* New York Times Book Review (July 11, 1982).

Paley, V. (1981). *Wally's stories.* Cambridge, MA: Harvard University Press.

Read, C. (1975). *Children's categorization of speech sounds in English.* Urbana, IL: National Council of Teachers of English.

Ryan, J. (1974). Early language development: Towards a communicational analysis. In M. P. H. Richards (Ed.), *A child's integration into a social world.* Cambridge: Cambridge University Press.

Schieffelin, B. B., & Cochran-Smith, M. (1984). Learning to read culturally: Literacy before schooling. In H. Goelman, A. Oberg, & F. Smith (Eds.), *Awakening to literacy.* Exeter, NH: Heinemann.

Scollon, R., & Scollon, S. B. K. (1981). *Narrative, literacy, and face in interethnic communication.* Norwood, NJ: Ablex.

Scribner, S., & Cole, M. (1981). *The psychology of literacy.* Cambridge, MA: Harvard University Press.

Smith, F. (1982). *Writing and the writer.* New York: Holt, Rhinhart, and Winston.

Snow, C. E. (1983). Literacy and language: Relationships during the preschool years. *Harvard Educational Review, 53*(2), 165–189.

Szwed, J. F. (1981). The ethnography of literacy. In M. F. Whiteman (Ed.), *Variation in writing: Functional and linguistic-cultural differences.* Hillsdale, NJ: Erlbaum.

Teale, W. H. (1982). Toward a theory of how children learn to read and write natur-
    ally. *Language Arts, 59*(6), 555–570.
Vygotsky, L. S. (1962). *Thought and language.* Cambridge, MA: MIT Press.
Vygotsky, L. S. (1978). *Mind in society.* Cambridge, MA: Harvard University Press.
Vygotsky, L. S. (1981). The genesis of higher mental functions. In J. V. Wertsch
    (Ed.), *The concept of activity in Soviet psychology.* Armonk, NY: M. E.
    Sharpe.
Wertsch, J. V., McNamee, G. D., McLane, J. B., & Budwig, N. A. (1980). The
    adult-child dyad as a problem-solving system. *Child Development, 51.*
Wood, D., Bruner, J. S., & Ross, G. (1976). The role of tutoring in problem-solving.
    Journal of Child Psychology and Psychiatry, 17, 89–100.
Wood, D., McMahon, L., & Cranstoun, Y. (1980). *Working with under fives.* Ypsi-
    lanti, MI: The High/Scope Press.

2 Individual Differences in Emerging Writing

Anne Haas Dyson
University of Georgia

Vivi, a kindergartener, performs admirably in her language arts lesson; she identifies, without error, the objects in her workbook that "begin with the letter *C*." Later, at the writing center, Vivi writes her aunt's name, Carrie: RIDPR.

Vivi's friend Rachel sits next to her at the writing center. Rachel monitors her work closely, crossing out and starting over at each error. Finally, she completes a list of names to give "to my mommy so she'll know all of my friends' names that was over here": Linda, Viviana, Mrs. Dyson. In contrast, on another day, Rachel quickly forms a string of 13 characters (AuVnetvvnRanc), which she reads, "I got a lot of sisters."

These observations of Rachel and Vivi suggest the difficulties facing researchers interested in chronicling "stages" of written language development. First, written language, like oral language, is "a complex of interconnecting systems," including syntactic, semantic, and discourse rule systems (Nelson & Nelson, 1978, p. 225); children do not display their knowledge of these systems in neat sequential order, but in clumps which the researcher (not the child) must separate into neatly organized categories. Second, and again like oral language, written language is not an independent entity but is subject to the demands of the situation. Like a kaleidoscope, its parts are ever newly arranged, newly revealed. And, of course, the person controlling the kaleidoscope has his or her own intentions and style, his or her own sense of what's interesting. Third, and *un*like oral language, written language has both a graphic and a linguistic dimension. This dual nature of the writing system initially eludes young children. Children may, therefore, operate outside the very definition of written language assumed by adult researchers; they may not attempt to convey a particular message through an alphabetic (graphic/linguistic) system (Dyson, 1982, 1983).

In sum, the nature of the individual child, the nature of the situational context, and the complex nature of the writing system itself all interact in written language growth, just as they do in oral language growth (Nelson,

1981). The interplay of these factors suggests that individual differences are to be expected in writing development. Focusing particularly on oral rather than written language, Nelson has argued strongly for the recognition of variation in development:

> Because functional contexts are correlated with frequency of particular [linguistic] forms and constructions and because different children are exposed differentially to various types of contexts, different children will begin to put different parts of the language system together initially, and the course of acquisition will look different for different children. (p. 183)

By intensive comparative study of individual children, we can gain insight into the complex, interrelated variables involved in development (Stake, 1978). To elaborate, researchers interested in writing development have focused on diverse aspects of early writing, for example, the mastery of the graphic conventions of written language (Clay, 1975) and the discovery of the alphabetic nature of the symbol system (Ferreiro & Teberosky, 1982). Analyses of individual children writing will increase our understanding of how these varied facets are interrelated as children acquire written language. Through such study, we may find an illumination of the nature of the written language task and of the varied paths children may take as they develop within the diverse writing contexts available to them.

The purpose of this chapter, then, is to portray learning to write as the result of the interaction of child, system, and context by examining in detail the writing of three kindergarteners. Specifically, I will answer these questions:

1. What is the nature of each child's writing behavior? I include here specific characteristics of (a) the written products themselves, such as evident directionality and conventionality of letter forms; (b) the content of messages the child formulates; and (c) the procedures the child uses to relate oral and written language.
2. What are the purposes for which each child writes?
3. Is there a relationship between a child's writing purposes and writing behaviors? If so, what is the nature of that relationship?
4. Is there a relationship between individuality and writing behaviors? If so, what is the nature of that relationship? By individuality, I refer to a child's style of functioning, interests, and dominant intentions across a range of activities, including talk, sociodramatic play, and drawing.

The data reported here were gathered in a participant observation project which focused on young children's verbal and nonverbal (including graphic) behavior during the writing process. The use of participant observation methodology reflects the study's theoretical assumptions, that is, this investigation was based on a view of children as active constructors of knowledge. As researcher, I aimed to understand early writing (i.e., writing which occurred before formal instruction in the school context began) from the point of view of the children—from within the framework of each child's understandings and intentions. (For a clear discussion of this research approach see Bussis, Chittenden, & Amarel, 1978.) I was interested in the reasoning, and the motivational reasons, behind the children's varying writing behaviors.

BACKGROUND

The Complexity of the Medium

The complexity of the written language system is reflected in the diverse perspectives of the early literacy literature. Researchers have focused on children uncovering written language's

1. perceptual features: what it looks like (e.g., Clay, 1975);
2. symbolic nature: the relationship between print and the formal aspects of speech (e.g., Ferreiro, 1978, 1980; Ferreiro & Teberosky, 1982);
3. structural characteristics: the conventions that determine how connected discourse is put together, as in the structural features of stories (e.g., Applebee, 1978), or the cohesive features that link together sentences to form texts (e.g., King & Rentel, 1979);
4. discursive procedures: the processes through which a dynamic experience is transformed into an explicit, ordered, and linear format (e.g., Cook-Gumperz & Gumperz, 1981) and, conversely, by which a linear display is transformed, through both graphic and language cues, into an understood experience (e.g., Clay, 1979);
5. sociocognitive nature: how meaning conveyed in print relates to the knowledge of both the writer and the reader; that is, that sustained written language, to a greater degree than conversational oral language, must be interpreted independently from the context of a specific or personal situation (e.g., Cook-Gumperz & Gumperz, 1981; Donaldson, 1978; Wells, 1981); and
6. functional capacities: the uses of written language (e.g., Goodman, 1980).

The literature on early writing provides us with general descriptions of development. Researchers describe children as progressing in the direction of mastering the conventional system, following expected developmental principles articulated by Piaget (Piaget & Inhelder, 1969) and Werner (1948) (e.g., beginning in a global and approximate way, actively searching for patterns, differentiating out features of the written language system). However, researchers are only beginning to provide the finely-detailed portraits of child writers which allow us to understand how these diverse aspects of written language work together. To illustrate how the differing aspects of the written language symbol system may be woven together and also how variation in growth can occur, I will turn here to the literature on individual differences in symbolic growth.

Variation in Symbolic Development

In Werner and Kaplan's (1963) model of symbol use, any symbolic act involves the symbol itself, the symbol's referent, the person producing this symbol, and an intended recipient. With development, these four entities become increasingly differentiated or distanced from one another and also linked or integrated in new ways. Building on Werner and Kaplan's ideas, Wolf and Gardner (1979, p. 127) point out that, in early symbolic growth, children may concentrate on different aspects of this symbolic process: "... each component in the symbolic equation may be highlighted or neglected; the challenge of symbolization may be apprehended in diverse ways by different individuals." They are conducting a longitudinal study of early symbolic development (from 1 year of age) in nine children, examining child behavior across varied symbolic media (language, symbolic play, music, movement, two- and three- dimensional materials, and number). They have tentatively identified two styles of early symbolization. Wolf and Gardner refer to these patterned variations as differences in "cognitive styles," or in ways children use symbols at their particular levels of development. One group of children, "patterners," focused on the physical world and their first vocabularies consisted of a high proportion of object names. In painting and block building, they focused on physical aspects of the materials, such as how the paints mixed. Their symbolic activity tended to depend on the physical properties of the symbolic material so that, for instance, a red round shape would be referred to as an "apple." In contrast, "dramatists'" language contained a high proportion of proper names and social expressions. These children tended to use painting and block building to communicate with others. Their symbolic use of painting and blocks did not rely heavily on properties of objects, so a red round shape could be a "person," a "fish," or whatever the child wished.

Similar differences between more socially-oriented and object-oriented styles have been noted in the area of language development, particularly by Nelson (1973) and Peters (1977). For example, Nelson studied the first words of 18 children from approximately 1 to 2½ years of age. She found particular children, whom she referred to as "referential," whose first words consisted largely of object names (nouns) and others, whom she referred to as "expressive," whose vocabularies were more varied and included a large proportion of social routines ("Stop it," "I want it."). Nelson's referential children were similar to Wolf and Gardner's patterners, and her expressive children were similar to their dramatists.

In a review of the research on individual differences, particularly in oral language development, Nelson (1981) stresses that most children no doubt fall between the extremes of different styles; further, children may exhibit different styles of using language in different situations. Nonetheless, as she points out, studying children who are extremely different in style does illuminate the nature of the system to be learned—in the case of language, its lexicon, syntax, and pragmatic functions. Here it is relevant to raise the question, what might lead children to approach a system in different ways?

The Influence of Child Intentions

Varied factors may account for individual differences, including individual makeup, the factor Wolf and Gardner (1979) appear to stress. Nelson (1981), however, emphasizes the influence of children's differing conceptions of language's use. To elaborate, the social contexts within which children are exposed to language may influence what they think language is for (what functions or intentions it serves) and thus how they approach language parts (content). For example, children who are exposed to language in relatively more social contexts may view it as essentially a pragmatic medium and thus acquire proportionately more social routines. Those who are exposed to language in relatively more cognitive contexts (e.g., looking at books) may view it as primarily referential and thus acquire proportionately more object labels. Most children mix styles, varying how they speak across different contexts.

Franklin (1963, p. 48), discussing nonverbal forms of symbolic media, also emphasizes the importance of considering child intention and purpose in order to understand development:

We may say that species-specific growth tendencies and universally present opportunities for interaction with the environment underlie the emergence of the symbolic function and the general trends of its development. At the same time . . . in any given situation, many factors interact to determine the final outcome, the particular representation. In addition to basic competencies, we must consider the individual's purposes. What does the person want, consciously or otherwise, to 'say'? Is his intent explicitly communicative vis-a-vis another person, or not?

Turning specifically to written language growth, the argument being developed here is this. As the child actively seeks to understand how written language works, he or she will begin to master its diverse aspects. Because of common developmental principles governing cognitive development and because of the inherent nature of the medium being learned (written language), we can expect similarities in development. However, we can expect differences as well. First, the variation of written language across contexts may affect both the nature of the writing the child is exposed to and the child's own production of print. Second, there may also be differences in children's performance styles (as Wolf & Gardner (1979) suggest) and in their dominant interests; these differences, too, would influence how and why children explore writing. In brief, although all children progress toward the conventional model, variation in development may occur because of differences in the intentions of individual children, which in turn are influenced by situational context and individual makeup. Our symbols serve our intentions and our goals (Werner & Kaplan, 1963).

The literature on early writing development reflects a predominant interest in how children encode messages before they master conventional spellings. In the next section, I will discuss two seminal early writing studies, Clay (1975) and Ferreiro (1980). I will note how each work might be expanded upon or clarified by a consideration of the child's intentions or purposes in using print.

Examining Early Writing

Clay (1975) has provided the most detailed description of how early scribblings become progressively more print-like. She analyzed writing samples spontaneously produced both in the home and in school by New Zealand children between the ages of 4:10 and 7:10 years. She did not find any evidence of a set sequence or "stages" in writing development, but she did identify two general principles governing the learning-to-write process: (a) the initial writing products are gross approximations to be refined later: letter-like forms, invented words, and make-believe sentences; and (b) individual letters and words are first known in a very specific way; for example, Jenny writes her name as *Jehhy* and does not acknowledge *Jenny* as her name.

In her study of the progressive refinement of these early approximations, Clay identifies certain principles that children appear to discover. The most critical of these are the *sign* concept: letters and letter-like shapes carry some unknown message; and the *message* concept: messages the child speaks can be written down. Other principles reflect children's increasing "perceptual awareness of those customs used in written language" (p. 2);

for example, children discover the *recursive* nature of print (that the same basic forms recur repeatedly) and its *directional* orientation.

Clay describes the young writer as progressing from the creation of unknown messages through the use of signs (e.g., letters and letter-like forms) to the formulation of *intended* spoken messages and the subsequent search for specific signs to fit those messages. The process Clay describes is one in which the child's message—his intended communication—begins to control the writing process. A central concept in this growth is *message quality*. Although Clay does not explicitly define that term, from her analysis I infer that message quality refers to the child's ability to independently *formulate a meaning* and to then *encode that meaning* in conventional or near-conventional print.

In her work, Clay analyzes children's written products. But describing the message quality of a child's written products would appear to require an examination of the nonverbal and verbal behaviors surrounding the writing. How can one know what message a child intended—if any—without observing and listening to the child? Did the child formulate a spoken message he or she intended to convey, or did the child copy a message displayed in the environment? Did the child attempt to make orthographic matches between spoken and written language? I am suggesting here a need to place the child's developing control over the perceptual aspects of print within a finely-detailed analysis of individual children's intentions as they form letters and letter-like forms on their paper. Such an analysis might reveal particular patterns or paths in writing growth that are related to child writers' varying intentions.

Beyond the concern with children's developing control over written language conventions, recent research has centered as well on the child's developing notions of the written language symbol system; on the relationship between oral meanings and graphic symbols. For example, Ferreiro (1980) examined a group of 30 children between the ages of 3 and 6 years in Mexico City. She interviewed them regularly over a 2-year period. During the interviews, she asked each child to perform particular reading and writing tasks. She found that, regardless of social class, children initially hypothesized a concrete and direct relationship between graphic features and their referents. For example, Marianna, a 4-year-old, asked for four letters to write her own name, seven letters to write her mother's name (which has 2 syllables), and "as much as a thousand" to write her father's name (which also has only 2 syllables)—someone as big as her daddy should certainly have many more letters than someone as small as herself! At this early stage, children believed that only referents for concrete objects (the names of people and things) were actually written in a written sentence, although one read the "complete" sentence. Thus, when asked to read the printed sentence "Delfino vendio tres gatitos" ("Delfino sold three little cats"), 5-year-old Javier identified Delfino as the first word and the three remaining words as the three little cats. At a later point in development, the children's writing and reading behaviors reflected an understanding that a relationship exists between print and the formal characteristics of oral language.

In analyzing Ferreiro's work, it is important to note that she provided the children with the message to be produced; she told them what word or sentence to write. As she was interested in the relationship between oral and written language, the origin of the particular message to be written was secondary. Thus, she painted a picture of the developing child writer analyzing the written language symbol system in progressively more fine-grained ways.

Ferreiro's work provides a fascinating analysis of children's evolving mental construction of written language. Yet, her data do not allow us to see how children use and reason about written language as they incorporate it into their daily lives; the data lack the intentional framework within which a symbol system forms. In this regard, McDermott and Hood (1982, p. 234), building on the ideas of Cole and Traupmann (1981), describe experimental procedures as creating "constraints independent of the involvements and concerns of the people under analysis, and . . . rob [bing the children] of many of the normally available resources for organizing their own behavior."

Thus, my aim in this chapter is to examine the spontaneous writing of individual children. Although clearly influenced by the work of Clay and Ferreiro, I will focus greater attention on each child's intentional framework, on what the child intended to accomplish through writing. The physical context or setting for each child's writing was the same, a writing center in a kindergarten classroom. The individual child, however, decided on the nature of the writing activity (e.g., letter-writing versus list-making). In this sense, the activity context was structured by the children themselves, based on their own intentions and understandings regarding the writing task.

Focusing particularly on three case study children, I will examine differences in the nature of their writing (including characteristics of their products and their encoding or symbolizing system) and in how their writing varied across types of writing activities. In addition, I will place the description of each child's writing within a portrait of the child as an individual. This analysis will yield findings regarding the nature of early preconventional writing (as opposed to conventional, adult-like writing) and the relationship between the characteristics of that writing and the child's individuality (style of functioning, interests, and dominant intentions).

METHOD

In this study, I examined early writing by becoming a participant observer in a kindergarten classroom. I established a writing center, asking the children simply to write; they wrote according to how they defined the writing task. I considered this provision for child- (as opposed to researcher-) initiated and structured writing critical. As discussed in the above section, each child's interpretation of the writing task (i.e., what the child intends to do) shapes the resulting oral and graphic activity.

Site and Participants

The site was a self-contained, public school kindergarten located in a southwestern city. The classroom teacher followed the district's kindergarten curriculum, which did not include any formal instruction in reading and writing at the beginning of the school year.

The classroom selected was naturally-integrated and balanced socially, ethnically, and academically. Of the 22 child participants, 10 were female, 12 were male. Twelve children were Anglo, six were Hispanic, four were black. At the beginning of this study, the mean age of the children was 5 years, 7 months, with a range from 5 years, 1 month to 5 years, 11 months.

From this classroom of children, five were chosen for case study investigation after 15 days of observation. I selected five whom I judged (a) to reflect the classroom's range of developmental writing levels as determined by particular assessment procedures, and (b) to discuss willingly their writing with me.

Data Collection Procedures

I gathered data for this study daily for a 3-month period during the first half of the school year. The data were collected primarily in the morning, between 8:45 and 10:30, during the children's "center" or free-choice period.

Data collection proceeded through three overlapping phases. Each phase is briefly described in the following sections.

Phase one (Weeks 1–3): Preliminary observation/initial assessment. During this phase, I observed and interacted with the children as they worked in their centers. My role as participant was that of an interested, nonthreatening adult (see Corsaro, 1981, for a detailed discussion of strategies for field entry in participant observation studies). I adopted what Corsaro (1981, p. 118) refers to as "reactive" field entry strategy. Rather than directing or monitoring the children's activities, I followed their leads. For example, I responded to their requests for attention (e.g., "Know what?"). I acknowledged, but did not actively respond, to the children's attempts to involve me in situations requiring adult discipline.

Also during the first phase, I assessed the children's writing behaviors in order to identify possible case study children. To this end, I asked each child individually to "come over and write with me" and, then, to "tell me what you wrote." Each child wrote a minimum of two times and a maximum of five, with each occasion occurring on separate days. The exact number of writing sessions was determined by my judgment that: (a) the child appeared comfortable with me and, thus, I had confidence that the writing could be considered a reasonable reflection of his/her writing behaviors; and (b) the child wrote in consistent styles. For example, if the child wrote in cursive-like script in the first session, and then wrote conventionally-spelled words in the second session, I repeated the assessment sessions until no new writing behaviors were introduced.

I categorized the children into different types of child writers, basing the categorization on my analysis of their written products and their explanations of their writing. The analysis was dependent on two variables: level of linguistic organization and message quality (cf. Clay's [1975] rating scale for early writing).

The first step was to identify the highest level of linguistic organization evident in each child's written products. I then sorted each child's (the 22 sets of) written products according to these levels (i.e., into four groups of children whose highest level of linguistic organization was intermingled letters and letter-like forms, letters, words, or word phrases, respectively).

The next step was to sort the products, within each of the four levels of linguistic organization, according to perceived similarity in message quality. I defined message quality (a term borrowed from Clay, 1975) as the child's control over:

1. the formulation of meaning (i.e., Did the child freely formulate the message? Or, were all messages copied? Were all messages confined to the child's known words [words the child could easily spell]?) and;
2. the system for transcribing that meaning (i.e., Did the child evidence systematic procedures for connecting specific meanings to specific print? How conventional were these procedures? Could someone else read the child's message?)

On the basis of these analyses, I formulated descriptive categories which characterized each message quality group within each level of linguistic organization. For example, of the children whose products contained only letters, certain ones perceived themselves as having written letters, while others perceived themselves as having written specific words, but there was no orthographic similarity between those words and the written letters; of the children whose products did contain words, certain children wrote only a small set of known, conventionally-spelled words, while others wrote an unspecified set of words using an identifiable (if unconventional) system. I did not make claims as to the children's "developmental writing level" on the basis of this categorization. Again, the purpose of this initial assessment was simply to aid in the selection of five case study children. I chose Ashley, Tracy, Rachel, Vivi, and Freddy, who reflected the classroom's range of types of child writers.

Phase two (Weeks 3–11): Writing center observations/interactions. This was the major data collection period. During this phase, I placed primary emphasis on gathering data on the case study children. Secondary emphasis was placed on gathering data on any child who chose to come to the writing center.

I collected five types of data: audio recordings of the children's spontaneous talk at the center, audio recordings of the children's responses to my interventions into the writing process, handwritten observational notes, the children's written products, and daily log entries on perceived trends in both the writing of the class as a whole and in all 22 individual children.

1. *Spontaneous talk:* During the observational period, I sat at the writing center with the children. I placed a battery-operated tape-recorder either on the floor or on the edge of the table behind the box containing the children's papers. I placed a unidirectional microphone in the middle of the table. The microphone was directed at a case study child if one was present. If not, I directed the microphone at another participant who served as the focal child for that recorded session.

2. *Interventions:* At certain times in the writing center observations, I intervened with questions. I attempted to limit interventions in order to minimize my influence on the children's writing processes. However, understanding the children's reasoning required certain interventions. The nature of the questions asked depended upon the particular behaviors being observed. For example, in the following interaction my objective was to clarify the child's potentially significant statement:

   C: (Child has just drawn a dinosaur.) I'm gonna' write three more things.
      (Child makes letter-like forms.)
   Dy: What are you writing?
   C: The dinosaur.
   Dy: (I am unsure as to whether child is writing the words *the dinosaur* or if the dinosaur is the topic of the writing.) Did you say that says "the dinosaur"?
   C: This gonna' be the dinosaur's name (writing〜〜)...I don't know what it says. (That is, the child has written about the dinosaur's unknown name—the child has not written *the dinosaur*.)

3. *Observational notes:* As the focal child wrote, I took brief notes on writing behaviors.

4. *Written products:* Each child had a folder for completed papers. The folders were kept in a box at the writing center. I collected papers (with the exception of "notes" written to others) so that they could be examined as part of the data analysis. Since the chil-

dren used the writing center only during "center time"—and since I was always there during that time—I collected or viewed all papers produced during the 3-month period.

5. *Daily log:* I made daily entries in a journal. The entries dealt with the writing trends of both individual children and the class as a whole.

Phase three (Weeks 11-12): Completion of the case studies. In this phase, I gathered information about the case study children from both different types and sources of data. I informally assessed the children's knowledge of particular characteristics of written language: alphabet, sound/symbol association, and voice/print match (Clay, 1979). In addition, I interviewed the children individually about their perceptions of both what was required to learn to write and the reasons for writing. Finally, I interviewed the children's parents regarding the children's early and current interest in, and experiences with, print.

These data were gathered in Phase Three to avoid any influence these procedures might have had on the children's classroom writing behaviors, and to avoid changing the children's perceptions of my role. Again, I was curious participant in a child-structured situation—not a teacher-figure who routinely requested the completion of particular tasks.

(I note here that one additional source of data—observations of the case study children in situations other than the writing center—occurred continuously from Phase One on.)

In analyzing the case studies, I compared the Phase Two data with these additional sources of information. The comparison yielded support for the observed behavior patterns and the inferences made regarding individual children's definition of, and reasons for, writing.

DATA ANALYSIS

Categories of Analysis

At the end of the 11th week of observation, I had recorded approximately 36 hours of spontaneous talk, collected approximately 500 written products, made 112 observations of focal children, and written notations on 377 child visits to the writing center.

The analysis procedure was inductive. I began by organizing the data into analytic categories. Since I was interested in both the children's verbal and nonverbal behaviors during writing, my categories referred to both the writing process in general, and the functions of the accompanying talk in particular. The identification process was one of classifying and reclassifying data under different organizers (see Corsaro, 1979, p. 319). I initially based the analysis on the data collected during the first two weeks of the post-assessment observational period (Phase Two). However, the resulting categories were continually modified and refined during the construction of the case studies.

The goal of this qualitative analysis was not exact measurement and coding of variables to be statistically related. Rather, the goal was to detect categories and patterns of behavior which would yield a comprehensive description and interpretation of the children's behaviors. (For a discussion of differences between qualitative and quantitative analyses see Eisner, 1981; and McCutcheon, 1981).

The writing process categories. The first task was to organize the data into units upon which to base the analysis. The basic unit of analysis was the writing event. I based the definition of a writing event upon the handwritten and transcribed records of the focal children's observation sessions. A writing event was defined as encompassing any verbal and nonverbal behaviors:

1. *immediately preceding, and related to, the act of writing;* sample behaviors include drawing; discussing a planned letter, word, or phrase with peers; orally rehearsing that planned unit;
2. *occurring after the child has begun the physical writing act;* sample behaviors (beyond forming letters) include soliciting help, verbally monitoring letters as they are formed, rereading sentence or word written, and drawing; and
3. *immediately following, and related to, the writing act;* sample behaviors include reading the product, naming the letters written, soliciting approval. (writing event definition adapted from Graves' [1973] definition of a writing episode)

The end of a writing event was marked by the child leaving the center, or the child changing the purpose or topic of a graphic activity (most typically by stopping writing and beginning drawing on an unrelated topic).

The writing event was the framework for defining aspects or components of the writing process, the second step of category generation. I began by segmenting similar sections of the writing events. I based this segmentation on initial recognition of similar types of behaviors which occurred in each event. The four resulting writing event components were not linear segments, but overlapping, recursive aspects of the event which could be combined in alternate ways. The components were:

1. Message Formulation: devising the message(s) to be conveyed in print;

2. Message Encoding: using strategies to convert formulated message(s) into print;

3. Mechanical Formation: physically placing letters or letter-like forms on paper (i.e., handwriting); and, if Message Formulation and Encoding were not present,

4. Message Decoding: using strategies for translating an unknown message which had already been written (cf. Clay's [1975] *What Did I Write?*).

The relationship between these four components embodies the previously-defined concept of message quality: the child's control over the message to be expressed and the system for expressing that message.

The third phase of the category generation procedure involved the isolation of properties which characterized each component. The analysis process involved comparing similar components of the writing events and composing descriptors to specify distinguishing characteristics or properties. To illustrate, the Message Formulation components differed in the specificity of the message. There were two alternate child behaviors defining the property *specifity:* specifying only the topic of the message, or specifying the exact words contained in the message.

By this point, I had identified three hierarchically-organized categories—the event, the components, and the properties—for studying the children's writing. Using the same basic analysis procedure, I identified the writing purposes which appeared to guide the children's writing events, and the resulting forms of their written products. Writing purposes, properties of the components, and forms of the written products are given in Figure 1. These data analysis categories describe this group of children's writing behaviors.

WRITING PURPOSES

1. To write (i.e., no clearly identifiable purpose exists beyond this, e.g., "I'm gonna' do it how my Mama does it.")

2. To create a message (i.e., the meaning of the message is unknown to the child, e.g., "What does this say?")

3. To produce or to practice conventional symbols (e.g., the *ABC*'s, displayed written language) without concern for a referent

4. To detail or accurately represent a drawn object (e.g., the *S* on Superman's shirt)

5. To label objects or people drawn or located in the environment

6. To make a particular type of written object (e.g., a book, a list, a letter) without concern for a message

7. To organize and record information (e.g., to write a list of friends)

8. To investigate the relationship between oral and written language without concern for a particular referent

9. To express directly feelings or experiences of oneself or others (i.e., direct quotations, as in writing the talk of a drawn character), and

10. To communicate a particular message to a particular audience

Figure 1. The writing process categories.

WRITING PROCESS COMPONENTS

Message Formulation (Formulation of actual message to be written)

1. Level of *specificity*
    (a) the topic of the message is specified (e.g., "It's about my puppy.")
    (b) the actual wording of the message is specified (e.g., "This is gonna' say, 'My puppy eats too much.'")
2. Level of *coherence*
    (a) no apparent relationship exists between the message and graphics previously drawn or written on the page (e.g., a list of unrelated words)
    (b) message is related in some identifiable, thematic way to other (but not all) graphics on the page
    (c) entire product (including written and/or drawn graphics) produces a coherent whole
3. Level of *linguistic organization* (adapted from Clay, 1975)
    (a) word
    (b) any two- or three-word phrase
    (c) any simple sentence consisting of 3 or more words
    (d) a group of 2 or more sentences

Message Encoding

1. *Segmented* oral message
    (a) not applicable (i.e., one word message[s] not segmented into smaller units)
    (b) no segmenting exists
    (c) message is segmented into phrases, words, syllables, or sounds (i.e., a deliberate pause of ½ second or more exists between units)
2. *Systematized* procedures for encoding segments (i.e., procedures for independently selecting particular letters to represent particular oral language segments)
    (a) no orthographic systematizing exists; child may (i) use cursive-like script, (ii) select, in an apparently random fashion, letters or letter-like forms (from the child's pool of known forms) to be written, (iii) request entire message be encoded by another; child then copies message
    (b) some systematic, orthographic procedure or combination of procedures are used; child may[a] (i) rearrange a fixed subset of the alphabet (e.g., child's name), (ii) use a personal (unconventional) syllable-based strategy (i.e., writing a certain number of letters per syllable), (iii) use a letter-name strategy, (iv) use personal or conventional system of sound/symbol correspondences, (v) request spelling of a segment from another,[b] (vi) base spelling on visual recall, (vii) consult a reference (e.g., a word list)
    (c) a combination of systematic and nonsystematic procedures

Mechanical Formation

1. *Conventionality* of symbols
    (a) cursive-like script
    (b) letter-like forms
    (c) intermingling of letters and letter-like forms
    (d) letters
2. *Discreteness* of symbols
    (a) connected symbols
    (b) unconnected symbols
    (c) mixed
3. *Ease and efficiency* of production
    (a) each stroke is slowly drawn
    (b) some strokes are slowly drawn
    (c) letters or letter-like forms are fluently produced
4. *Spatial arrangement* (adapted from Clay, 1975)
    (a) no evidence of conventional directional pattern
    (b) part of the conventional directional pattern is in evidence: either "start top left," or "move left to right," or "return down left"
    (c) reversal of the conventional directional pattern (right to left and/or return down right)
    (d) conventional directional pattern
    (e) conventional directional pattern and spaces between words
    (f) extensive text without any unconventionalities of arrangement and spacing of text

Figure 1 (continued) *(continued)*

Message Decoding

1. *Segmented* written message
   - (a) not applicable (i.e., one word message not segmented into smaller units)
   - (b) no segmenting exists
   - (c) the written text is segmented (i.e., particular portions of the text are focused on to be decoded into particular oral phrases, words, syllables, or sounds)
2. *Systematized* procedures for decoding segments
   - (a) no systematic orthographic procedure is used for decoding text; child may (i) engage in apparent fantasy behavior, (ii) request entire message be decoded by another
   - (b) some systematic orthographic procedure or combination of procedures are used; child may (i) request decoding of text segment from another, (ii) use situational context as the basis for decoding, (iii) use a syllable-based decoding system (i.e., matching a number of oral syllables to the perceived number of segments in text), (iv) use a letter-name strategy (i.e., decode a word containing that letter name), (v) use a personal or conventional system of sound/symbol correspondences, (vi) base decoding on visual recall of (a similar) word

FORMS OF THE WRITTEN PRODUCT

1. A graphic product or a section of a graphic product (drawing and writing intermingled on a page)
2. A label or caption for a drawing (writing located in close proximity to the referents)
3. A list (single words arranged vertically)
4. The alphabet
5. A card (small paper attached to a present or an envelope containing addressee's name)
6. A letter (a product which included the names of the addressee and the sender)
7. An envelope (a paper folded around a letter which included, at the least, the name of the addressee)
8. A book (a multipaged product containing writing)

---

[a] No developmental order is implied here.

[b] A message must contain more than one word before the distinction between requesting as a systematic and as a nonsystematic procedure becomes meaningful.

Figure 1 (continued)

Language functions. After the preceding analysis of writing behaviors, I focused specifically on the children's language. I categorized the children's spontaneous utterances, basing the initial category system on the work of Halliday (1973) and Tough (1977). These functions were modified, deleted, and added to in order to accurately describe the collected data. The resulting classification system is two-tiered, with five major functions and the accompanying strategies used to effect each function. The language functions and strategies, which should not be viewed as mutually exclusive categories, are given in Figure 2.

Writing event types. To this point, I have described the formulation of categories for distinguishing child behaviors occurring within each writing event. The final stage of category generation involved comparing whole events; that is, I asked, what types of writing events can be identified? Analysis of the five sets of case study data led to the identification of 10 different event types. The varied types of events resulted from the children's varied purposes for writing.

LANGUAGE FUNCTIONS

1. *Representational* language: language which serves to give information about events and situations (real or imagined, past or present). The strategies used to carry out this function are:

   (a) *labeling,* e.g.,

   That's my middle name. (Child has written <u>MOKILHJK</u>.)

   (b) *elaborating* or detailing, e.g.,

   This is a box that goes like that and see, when somebody goes in it a skeleton will pop out and eat it. (Child has drawn several objects on her paper.)

   (c) *associating* or comparing with earlier experiences, e.g.,

   (Child has just written the word *present.*) You know what? My Grandma has a present for me in the bathroom. I can't look at it 'cuz it's a—I wanna' be surprised.

   (d) *reporting* an action or event, e.g.,

   (Child has drawn a picture of a girl standing beside a house.) She's locked out.

   (e) *narrating* a series of actions or events, e.g.,

   (Child is talking as she draws.) She [the girl in the picture] was swinging on the branch. She was swinging on the branch...and her Mama told her not to swing on the branch and she did and her Mama said she'll knock down her playhouse and she knocked down the house and the house just got small....

   (f) *dramatizing* or acting out a series of actions, e.g.,

   (Child is talking as she draws.) "Sister, open up the door! (Child knocks twice on table.) You dummy. Sister, you better come and open this door or else I'm gonna' throw this pumpkin shell on your head."

   (g) *reasoning,* e.g.,

   (Child is speaking to an adult who has been unable to read child's writing.) You can't read it 'cuz all these letters so teeny-weeny. Right? That's how they put it in the newspaper. Real tiny, don't they?

2. *Directive* language: language which serves to direct the actions of self and/or others. The strategies used to carry out this function are:

   (a) *monitoring* (strategy through which ongoing actions appear to be controlled and directed), e.g., (Child is copying someone's name.)...an *r,* and then...and then...and then—and then a *e.*

   (b) *planning* (strategy through which future actions appear to be controlled and directed), e.g., Now I'm gonna' write inside my book...I'm gonna' write a picture in the front of it.

   (c) *encoding* (strategy through which words or phrases are transferred from the oral to the written language channel; the child pronounces sounds, letters, syllables, or the word/ phrase itself), e.g.,

Child's Language	Text
H-B	HB
H-B...O...	O added
HBO, HBO Box	Vivi drew a box around *HBO:* HBO (*HBO Box* was Vivi's term for Home Box Office television.)

   (d) *decoding* (strategy through which sounds, syllables, words, phrases or propositions are transferred from the written to the oral language channel; the child matches oral letter names, syllables, words, phrases, or propositions to either some segment of the written text or to the entire text), e.g.,

   (Child is reading text; arrows indicate where the child points as she reads.)

Text:	Rudolph	the	Red-	Nosed	Reindeer
	↑	↑	↑	↑	↑
Child:	"Ru	dolph	the	Red	Nosed"

   (continued)

Figure 2.   Language functions and strategies.

(e) *accessing* (strategy used to seek or to retrieve letters or words from memory; in written language situations, this strategy involves rereading) e.g.,

(Child is writing the *ABC*'s.)

Child Language	Text
A	A
Now, *B*.	B
A-B (Rereading)	
A-B-C	C

(f) *instructing* (strategy used to convey information perceived as required or needed by someone else; language to "teach") e.g.,

(Child is telling another how to "make people.") Let me show you how to make 'em. Let me show you how to make people how I like 'em. See? I like 'em like this. This is how you make 'em. (Child draws.) Make it curl like that, OK? (Child waits and watches.) See?

(g) *requesting,* e.g.,

I need a red [marker].

3. *Heuristic* language: language which serves to seek information, to learn about or to explore reality. In reference to written language in particular, heuristic language may be used to seek information regarding encoding, decoding, or mechanically producing print (i.e., handwriting); the print being focused on could be letters, words, phrases, or propositions (although the child may not know what linguistic unit is being focused on).

Strategies include:

(a) *seeking confirmation,* e.g.,

What's that, a *P*?

My God! I've been trying to make a little *e*'s 'cuz I can't make little *e*'s good...and→ then like that?

(b) *seeking fact,* e.g.,

How do you spell *Christmas*?

What does this say?

(c) *seeking demonstration,* e.g.,

How do you make a *J*?

(d) *seeking to test,* e.g.,

(Child has written her mother's name, a word she frequently writes.) What does this say?

4. *Personal language:* language used to express one's feelings and attitudes.

Examples are:

I'm gonna' write my last name again. I like it.

That makes me mad.

Three strategies specifically identified which serve this function are:

(a) *evaluating others,* e.g.,

You made it very, very pretty.

You done it wrong again.

(b) *evaluating self,* e.g.,

I'm gonna' write a better *2*...Yuch! Can't write no *2*.

Oh my God! I done it wrong.

(c) *playing with language,* e.g.,

I got a puppy named Bobo...My puppy is Slobo...My puppy named Klobo.

5. *Interactional language:* language used to initiate, maintain, and terminate social relationships. No division into strategies was done. Examples of this function are:

Know what I'm doing?

This one's for my mother, and I'll give you one tomorrow. I promise.

Figure 2 (continued)

To identify these types, I coded all writing events of each case study child for both the writing process categories and the oral language functions. To guide this analysis, I devised the worksheet shown in Figure 3. After coding the events, I sorted the completed worksheets according to dominant writing purposes and then wrote descriptors of each resulting group or writing event type.

WORKSHEET

Child's name *Viviana*
Writing event # *4*
Observation session # *4*

WRITING EVENT

PURPOSE *Investigation* - *Process* ⑤   LANGUAGE FUNCTIONS[a]
COMPONENTS

Message Formulation   present ✓
                               absent ___

1. Level of specificity   *b*   *Directive: decoding*
2. Level of coherence   *b*   *(occurred simultaneously*
3. Level of linguistic organization *b*   *w/ Message Decoding)*

Message Encoding   present ✓   *Directive: encoding*
                               absent ___

1. Segmented oral message   *c*
2. Systematized   *b, ii*

Mechanical Formation

1. Conventionality   *c* b   *Directive: monitoring*
2. Discreteness   *b*
3. Ease & efficiency of production *c*
4. Spatial Arrangement   *b*

Message Decoding   present ✓   *Directive: decoding*
                               absent ___

1. Segmented written message   *c*
2. Systematized   *b, iii*

FORM *Graphic product -*
      intermingled writing & drawing

---

[a]Language Function categories associated with each component were entered in this column.

[b]Refer to Figures 1 and 2 for assistance in interpreting letters used to code each property (e.g., the *c* here referred to the child's use of conventional letter symbols).

Figure 3. Worksheet used to analyze and code writing events of each case study child.

The following chart depicts (a) the purpose and typical components of each writing event type; (b) the number of children who wrote in that manner at least once in the observational period; and (c) the names of the case study children whose analyses illustrated the event type.

Writing Event Type Purpose	Components	Number of Children Who Used Type	Case Study Children Who Used Type
A To label or to provide a caption for object(s), person(s), or event(s)	Message Formulation Message Encoding Mechanical Formation	17	All
B To detail or accurately represent a drawn object (e.g., a stop sign)	Mechanical Formation	5	Ashley Freddy
C To produce a message (meaning of message unknown to child writer)	Mechanical Formation Message Decoding	10	Ashley Rachel
D To produce a particular written product (typically a letter) without concern for a particular message	Message Formulation (limited to names of addressee and sender) Message Encoding Mechanical Formation	7	Ashley Rachel Vivi
E To produce conventional symbols (e.g., the alphabet)	Mechanical Formation	18	All
F To write	Mechanical Formation	14	Ashley Tracy Rachel Vivi
G To communicate a particular message to a particular audience	Message Formulation Message Encoding Mechanical Formation	5	Rachel Vivi
H To express or dramatize feelings of self or others	Message Formulation Message Encoding Mechanical Formation	6	Rachel Vivi
I To organize and record information (e.g., a list of friends)	Message Formulation Message Encoding Mechanical Formation	2	Rachel
J To investigate the relationship between oral and written language without concern for a particular referent	Message Formulation Message Encoding Mechanical Formation Message Decoding	3	Vivi

Note: Total number of children = 22

As the chart indicates, the most common types of writing in this classroom were Event Type E, writing to produce conventional symbols, particularly the alphabet; Type A, writing to label familiar people and objects, most typically, people's names; and Type F, writing to simply produce visually appropriate (e.g., linear, letter-like) script. The case studies illustrate both the variety of strategies the children used to effect these purposes and the range of conventionality evident in the resulting products.

Case Studies

The writing process and language function categories provided the organizational scheme for identifying themes and patterns in early writing. I compared the dominant purposes for which individual children wrote and the ways in which each structured the writing task. Looking within the confines of each child's writing, I asked if there was a relationship between the child's individuality and the nature of his or her writing behavior.

Although it is the variations in writing behavior among the case study children which are of the greatest interest here, there were notable similarities. As the previous chart indicated, all of the children appeared to write to produce conventional or appropriate-appearing forms and, in addition, all attempted to write names. I will return to the potential significance of this behavior in the Discussion section of this chapter.

At this point I wish to focus in detail on three of the case studies: Tracy, Rachel, and Vivi. I have chosen these three because to the casual observer—indeed to a teacher or researcher interested in children's mastery of traditional academic skills—they would appear to be at similar levels. All three children could easily form manuscript letters. They could also write their own names and that of at least one other family member. Tracy and Vivi knew the names of all the alphabet letters, while Rachel knew the majority of them. In addition, Rachel and Tracy could produce "the letter that begins" a particular word for approximately half the initial consonants, and Vivi could produce all of them. All three children were performing satisfactorily in the kindergarten language arts program, based on the Lippincott (Boston Educational Research Company, 1974) readiness program, which stresses such skills as the recognition of basic shapes, colors, and positions in space; direction following; and learning the names, sounds, and formations of each alphabet letter. Yet, when we consider each child's spontaneous writing—the purposes for which they wrote and the resulting processes—striking differences emerge.

In the next sections, I will present detailed portraits of each child. Each portrait begins with a brief description of the child's interests and interactive style, both at home and at school. I next describe the child's writing behaviors, beginning with those reported by the child's parents and, then, moving to those observed at school. Finally, I discuss the writing of all case study children against the background of literature on writing development and individual differences presented earlier in this chapter.

TRACY

Tracy, a Hispanic female, was 5 years and 5 months at the beginning of this study. A monolingual English speaker, Tracy was a quiet child. That reticence, combined with her tiny physical build, could be misleading. Although not physically aggressive, when angered, Tracy chose to hit, rather than to yell or call the teacher. As her peer Hubert remarked (after having received a firm, well-deserved shove), "She's a tough little thing."

Tracy was readily accepted as a play partner by both boys and girls. Somewhat of a loner, she had no particularly close friends; she appeared to choose centers without considering who her play partners would be.

Not surprisingly, Tracy was the only girl who regularly chose to work in the male-dominated big-block center. In addition, she regularly worked in the puzzles-and-games center and at the drawing/writing center, where she commonly drew houses and people.[1] She preferred such manipulative and constructive activities over, for example, dramatizing in the housekeeping center.

My observations of Tracy's behavior in school were complemented by the information offered by Tracy's mother, a secretary, and her stepfather, a student at the local community college. They described her as interested in real-life rather than pretend activities. As Tracy's mother explained, Tracy did not enjoy dramatic play. In fact, "I can't even get her to sit and watch TV...She always likes to be doing something—like trying to write or read."

As Tracy's parents talked with me, Tracy "did": she played with the dog, pulled up a few flowers in the backyard, put on a paper-bag costume and "spooked" everyone, rummaged through a box containing her old school papers, and rough-housed with her stepfather (hereafter referred to as "father").

Tracy: Writing at Home

Tracy's parents were eager to share information about their daughter's early reading and writing behaviors. Tracy's mother felt that Tracy's day care center experiences had had an impact on her early interest in writing:

---

[1]As described in the Method section, I established a writing center, inviting the children to come write whenever and however they wished. The children, however, came to draw as well as to write. Thus, the center, by the children's design rather than my own, became the drawing/writing center. This center is hereafter referred to as the "writing center."

She's been in preschool since she was 2. And in that school, they started coloring and—I think she was 3 or 4 when she first started to write.

I asked if the day care program had been very structured:

Yes. I think she learned a lot there. . . . It started them early on academics.

Tracy's mother showed me some samples of Tracy's work at day care; they were similar to the following:

Both parents agreed that Tracy began to write by scribbling, which Tracy called "writing," moved to producing letters and then to writing words. The first word she attempted was her own name. The following attempts at name writing were evident in Tracy's products (ages 3 to 5):

1. $\dagger$
2. $\dagger Tr Tr \wedge D\, D\, D\, \supset y$
3. $\dagger \vee \wedge D \supset \mu$
4. $Tr D \supset y$
5. $Tracy$

Her next words were family names: her mother's name, Sonya, her father's name, Pete, and her 8-year-old brother's name, Thomas.

Cursive-like writing was a late occurrence; it began after Tracy could already write a few words. Its appearance was related to her mother's work:

(Mom) When I was working on my shorthand a few months ago, she'd sit down and want to write too. So, I'd give her a paper and she'd make wavy lines. She's been doing this for at least 6 months.

Both parents agreed that asking questions was a major learning strategy for Tracy:

(Mom) Lots of times she'll bring books to me and ask, "What does this spell?"

(Dad) Or, she'll write with letters and ask, "What does this spell?" She wants to know if it's a word. I tell her it's nothing.

(Mom) She's always been interested in signs. There's a sign at the end of the street here: *Stop Ahead.* She asked me what it said. Now everytime we go by it, she says, "Stop ahead."

I asked how Tracy learned everyone's name. In her parents' response, another strategy was mentioned: observing.

(Dad) Tracy asked me, "How do you spell your name?"

(Mom) She asked for *Sonya* too. She just saw Thomas's, I guess, on his papers. She writes them, and pretty soon she has them by memory.

Tracy's mother felt that Tracy had learned a great deal from observing Thomas write and read:

Thomas helps her. She tries to do what he does. I know that's what's helped her develop in all areas. She has come along a lot quicker than Thomas has done. And it's that she's watched him.

I asked if Tracy showed an interest in reading too:

(Dad) Yes. She's always after me to read to her. She wants to read big books . . . I would be studying [and] she'd go get a big book so that she could read like me.

(Mom). . .Sometimes when I'm reading [his school reading book] with Thomas, she gets jealous and wants to read too. So, she gets a book and starts rattling away. She can't read, but she makes up stories.

Tracy's parents' description of Tracy as a young writer, as with their comments about her interests, complemented my own observations. A careful observer of others, Tracy was primarily concerned with learning the names of people and objects. In the next section I will examine in detail the nature of Tracy's school writing.

Tracy: School Writing

Tracy visited the writing center for 27 observation sessions and engaged in 24 writing events. Writing Event Type A predominated in Tracy's data (19 of the 24 events were Type A). In Type A, the child wrote labels for people, objects, and events. For Tracy, even one letter or one number could function as a referent, as the following excerpts reveal:

Tracy's Verbal Label:	Product
I'm going to write my number [i.e., the number of her apartment door].	*A*
My next door neighbor's is *B*.	*B*
That's how old my brother is.	*8*
That's how old I am.	*5*
That's my mother's name.	*Sonya*

The excerpts also illustrate that Tracy tended to orally label her written products so that their personal meaning would become explicit to an audience. In reference to Sonya, for example, Tracy consistently said, "That's my mother's name"—not, "That's *Sonya*; she's my mother." Similarly, she wrote Sonya—not, My mother's name is Sonya. The following excerpts, which occurred in the production of Figure 4, further illustrate this phenomenon:[2]

Language	Language Function	Comment
I can make my brother's name.	Personal/Directive: planning	Tracy wrote *Thomas.*
That's my brother's name.	Representational: labeling	
I'm gonna' write his G name too.	Directive: planning	Tracy wrote her last name, G. She then wrote her complete name: Tracy G.
That's my name.	Representational: labeling	

To this point, I have focused on Tracy's predominant purpose for writing (i.e., labeling) and on how written and oral language reflected that purpose in Event Type A. Because of Tracy's primary use of that process, the analysis will now focus on the components of that process.

Unlike the children in the classroom who often wrote unknown messages (Clay's [1975] *What Did I Write?* phenomenon), Tracy was in charge of forming her own messages and encoding them. Regarding message forming, Tracy appeared to view written graphics as conveying a specific message —a label. To encode that message, Tracy understood that one must produce specific letters in a particular order. To do so, Tracy appeared to memorize

---

[2]Conventions for the transcriptions are found in this chapter's appendix.

Figure 4.   Sample of Tracy's name-writing.

letters and their spatial arrangement. She seemed to recall letter patterns,
rather than simply shapes, as she wrote words in both upper- and lower-case
letters (SONYA and Sonya). During the course of the observation period or
Phase Two, Tracy learned several labels:

In an initial observation   In a later observation
Tracy wrote: Tracy wrote:

Tohaw   *Thomas*
(observation session #3)   (observation session #4)

PMTa	*Pete*
(observation session #7)	(observation session #23)
MSO	*M ℰ 0* [an apartment number]
(observation session #3)	(observation session #6)

By the end of the observation period, Tracy had written the following words independently: Tracy G (her last name), Thomas, Pete, Sonya, yes, no, and Santa.

Tracy, however, wrote many more words than this. The adult-dependent encoding procedure she regularly used was to request spellings, particularly object labels. The labels requested were typically for well-known objects and/or objects in the immediate environment. This request procedure is illustrated in the following excerpt:

Language	Language Function	Comment
Tr: That's my name: my last name and my first name.	Representational: labeling	
Oh!	Personal	
I got pen on my hand—	Representational: reporting	
How do you spell *pen*?	Heuristic: seeking fact	Tracy was directing her requests to me.
Vi: Here's the colors.	Interactional	Vivi was handing the colors to a peer.
Tr: How do you spell *color*?...	Heuristic: seeking fact	
You already spelled *Santa Claus;* now I want...uh... let me see, *toy—present*!	Heuristic: seeking fact	
You know what?	Interactional	
My grandma has a present for me in the bathroom. I can't look at it 'cuz it's a—I wanna' be surprised.	Representational: associating	

This latter excerpt again suggests Tracy's use of oral language to give the full meaning of the written graphics. Thus, present is, to borrow an Ashton-Warner (1963) phrase, a "key word"—it has a meaning in Tracy's life, and she tells me about that meaning with oral language. A similar event took place when Tracy announced that she had moved to a new house—and then promptly asked me, "How do you write house?"

Of course, as we have seen, not all the words Tracy requested were "key words"; often they were casual, what-do-I-see-now affairs. Whatever their origin, Tracy saved all the words she requested (i.e., she kept the slips of paper on which I wrote her words). She stuck some of the words into her pocket so that she could "write 'em at home"; others she kept in her writing folder. She frequently questioned me regarding the identity of these writing-folder words:

Language	Language Function	Comment
		At Tracy's request, I had just written *swimming pool* on a slip of paper that already contained *Mom* and *Valentine*. Tracy was unsure which word was which.
Tr: That's *Valentine*?	Heuristic: seeking confirmation	
Dy: Yeah...That's *Mom;* that's *Valentine;* and that's *swimming pool*.		
Tr: That's *Valentine;* that's *Mom*...	Directive: decoding	
That's *Mom*?	Heuristic: seeking confirmation	

Words, then, were important entities for Tracy. The form of the product in which those words were placed did not appear important: she did not create written objects in the form of notes, letters, or books. Indeed, even when all of her peers at the center were writing "notes" to each other, Tracy continued to produce pieces containing pictures and words without any particular form.

In all her writing events, Tracy consistently and easily produced conventional, unconnected letters in an appropriate directional pattern. She never wrote in a cursive-like style.

In sum, for Tracy, writing appeared to involve the creation of a visual image which served as a referent's label. There was no observed attempt at written communication with a particular audience, just as there were no attempts at written communication with a specific other reported by Tracy's parents. Tracy would, though, orally identify and elaborate upon those referents for interested others. The component properties of Tracy's writing processes were relatively conventional. In Message Formulation, she specified the precise wording of her message. In Encoding and Formation, this "take charge" approach continued: Tracy sought to produce the pre-planned word's correctly-sequenced letters by either requesting spellings from another or by visually recalling the specifics.

Although I am only speculating, Tracy's performance on the voice-print match task appeared to reflect a view of writing as a graphic representation of particular objects. Further, she appeared to assume that what one said orally or "read" did not relate in a linear, segmented way to what was written (cf. Ferreiro, 1978), for example:

Dyson: (reading print) This says, *The toy was broken.*
          You read it, Tracy.
Tracy: Toy's broken.
Dyson: Where do you think *toy* might be?
Tracy: (looking puzzled, points to final section of line [-*ken*])
Dyson: Can you point to the words as you read it?
Tracy: I can make a line under it.
Dyson: OK. So, what does this say?
Tracy: Toy broken.

The next case study, Rachel, evidenced control over a greater range of messages to be expressed in writing, although she had varying control over the system for actually getting them into print. For Rachel, writing was not tied to concrete referents. Rather, it was a system for expressing meanings, meanings which she first represented through talk. Writing was primarily a form of communication.

RACHEL

Rachel, a black female, was 5 years, 3 months at the beginning of this study. It is difficult to distinguish between certain developmental and dialect features of young children's speech; for example, the so-called double negative is apparently used by all young children at a stage of language development, and it is also a feature of particular adult dialects (Wolfram, 1979). A comparison of Rachel's speech with her peers indicated that Rachel spoke Standard English—a great deal of Standard English. (She may, though, have evidenced certain behaviors associated with Black culture, such as a reference to two black friends as "sisters".)

Rachel's major topic of conversation was relationships (e.g., "Do you like me?", "Theresa's my friend."). Even her imaginative narratives focused on relationships, particularly family relationships.

Rachel's conversational style was honest and direct. Both her concern with relationships and her directness are illustrated in this revealing telephone conversation with me:

Dyson: (answering telephone) Hello.
Rachel: I done it myself! (Rachel is referring to dialing the telephone.)
Dyson: Well, you sure did—Rachel?
Rachel: You got a husband?
Dyson: Mm mmm.
Rachel: Oh good. Then you're not lonely now. I've got a sister and a mother and a father...I fight with my sister [Julie]. Listen: (Rachel yells away from telephone) YOU STOP IT, JULIE.

Rachel seldom played alone; she was readily accepted by both girls and boys as a play partner. In addition, she was a member of a small group of girls who regularly sought each other's company: Courtney, Linda, Sance, Vivi, and Rachel.

Not surprisingly, Rachel preferred the writing, housekeeping, and library centers (the latter used for playing school). Her choice of centers was dependent on the availability of seating (i.e., Was there room for one more?) and, at times, on the urgings of a friend who desired her company at an already-chosen center.

At the writing center, Rachel's drawings frequently took shape within elaborate narrations. These narrations, as illustrated in the following excerpt, centered on the dramatic interplay between family members:

Language	Language Function	Comment
She was swinging on the branch. She was swinging on the branch... And her mama told her not to swing on the branch and she did and her mama said she'll knock down her playhouse and she knocked down the house and the house just got this small ...And then she got out of her house and they just had a little bitty door...And she had to get through a teeny, teeny old door.	Representational: narrating	Rachel was drawing as she told this story (see Figure 5).

Figure 5. "And then she got out of her house and they just had a little bitty door..."

As with Tracy, my observations of Rachel's school behaviors were complemented by the information gained from Rachel's home interview. I interviewed Rachel's mother, a journalism student at the local community college, before she left for her morning class. Rachel's father, a draftsman, was at work; he was also a student at the community college, preparing for an engineering major.

Rachel's mother reported that Rachel's major interest was in dramatic, imaginative play. She often played with her 7-year-old sister, Julie:

> They are pretty elaborate in their play (laughs). One's the mom and one's the dad. And they fight and whip the kids. In the bath tub they make a lot of noise pretending to do something.

And, as I will discuss in the next section, Rachel's mother explained that Rachel's writing often took form within the context of her play.

Rachel: Writing at Home

Rachel's mother, like Tracy's parents, described Rachel's first writing as "scribbling." She (mother) had not encouraged this activity:

> I didn't have much patience with that. I remember I used to do that [pretend to write by making linear cursive-like or letter-like forms] when I was a kid, and I remember Julie did that. But I guess I tried to get her to do something that made sense: "Why don't you learn your *ABC*'s instead of doing that?" That's just the way I am.

Unlike Tracy, Rachel had not attended a day care center. But Rachel's mother, like Tracy's, attributed Rachel's knowledge of written language to direct instruction:

> I haven't worked—this'll be my first time working. So all the time they were growing up I was at home with 'em [and had time to work with them]. . . . I started her writing probably—she was about 3,3 and a half. I started showing her how to make an *A* and letting her just do that. Because at the same time, I was teaching Julie, and I had to do something with Rachel that she was interested in. I couldn't just leave her out, and I didn't want to either. So, at about 3, 3 and a half, she started scribbling and trying to make *A*'s.

Rachel's mother also worked with alphabet flash cards:

> Rachel was probably about 3—Julie, she *knew* all of 'em when she was 3. She could recognize 'em. Rachel's always been a little bit slow. . . . I didn't push them, but I tried to be available for when they wanted to do those things.

Despite her mother's efforts, Rachel continued to prefer "scribbling":

> Rachel mainly scribbles. . . . She [scribble-writes] when they play store, doctor, and all that.

Rachel approached reading in the same quasi- or make-believe manner in which she approached writing:

> She likes for me to read stories to her, and, um, she has to wait a long time sometimes. Last night I was studying, and she wanted me to read this story to her—I'd already read it to her three times. It's a first grade book with two-word sentences, so I told her to read it. So, she went and read it to her dolls. . . . They already know the book 'cause I've read it, so they'll go and try to read it over to their dolls or read it over to me sometimes—you know, tell the story.

As reported by her mother, then, Rachel's home writing behaviors were very different from those of Tracy. Rather than displaying a dominant interest in learning conventionally-spelled names, Rachel appeared most interested in making functional use of writing in her play. A seemingly-related contrast can be seen in their respective question-asking behaviors. While Tracy's parents described her as a questioner, Rachel's mother reported that Rachel was just beginning to ask questions about print. Most of these questions were about reading than writing:

> Like if she sees something in the newspaper or on a box or something, she'll ask, "What does that say?" She probably just started doing that this year. . . . Rachel doesn't ask for spellings—not much. Julie's always asking that. Rachel mainly scribbles; sometimes she asks for a word, and she copies it.

A final contrast between the two girls can be seen in their reported relationships with their respective older sibling. While Tracy's parents felt that Tracy had benefitted from observing Thomas, Rachel's mother felt that Julie had not helped Rachel learn:

> Julie knows a lot more than Rachel does. She just likes to learn—she doesn't really teach Rachel that much.

In sum, Rachel's mother provided information which will serve to validate and illuminate the observational data. Rachel was sensitive to the meanings which writing could convey; she used those meanings in her play (e.g., prescription-writing, list-making). However, Rachel was just beginning to seek out information regarding the specific conventions of the system used to express those meanings. As will be seen, the major difference between the observational and the interview data is Rachel's mother's suggestion that Rachel may be "slow," an hypothesis not suggested by the observational data. In the next section I consider Rachel's school writing events.

Rachel: School Writing

Rachel engaged in 40 writing events in 25 visits to the center. In comparison to Tracy, Rachel wrote for a variety of purposes and, thus, engaged in a variety of writing event types. While she did write labels (Event Type A), the only names she could spell independently were Julie, her sister, and Vivi, her friend. In all, 14 of her 40 writing events were classified as Type A, but the quantitative data are misleading. To elaborate, while Tracy would write lists of from 5 to 10 words, Rachel would typically write but one word (in addition to her own name) and that word would not be related in any thematic sense to other graphics on the page. Thus, Rachel spent a relatively small portion of her writing time labeling.

Nonetheless, in school, Rachel was attentive to the print in her environment, particularly people's names. This interest is illustrated in the following excerpt, which occurred during the production of Figure 6.

Language	Comment
	Rachel wrote *BlRi;* this word is not *bird*. As Rachel explained,
This [pointing to *B*] goes in Brian's name... This [pointing to *l*] goes in my name...This [R] goes in my name ...This [i] goes in Brian's name.	

Figure 6. "This goes in Brian's name...This goes in
my name...This goes in my name...This
goes in Brian's name."

Like Tracy, Rachel also requested words. But unlike Tracy, Rachel
had specific, personal reasons for the words she requested—not just any
word would do. The following requests (categorized as Heuristic: seeking
facts) are illustrative:

How do you write [last name]? 'Cause I want to write my last name:
(repeats last name twice).

How do you spell *Judy*?...That's my mommy's name.

How do you spell *Twana*? 'Cause I don't know. She's my sister [friend]—only
4 years old.

The request for Twana illustrates Rachel's concern with meeting established standards (i.e., conventions) and her critical stance toward her
own abilities. Rachel's self-evaluation was evident in her writing of both
names and letters:

Language	Language Function	Comment
		Rachel had intended to copy *Dyson;* after *Dy,* however, she began to copy her own name, producing *Dysel.*
Uh Uh. I looked at my name.	Personal	
I'm mad...Shoot.		
I keep on messing up.	Personal: evaluating self	
		Rachel had been copying her *ABC*'s. She put *S* in the wrong place.
Oh my God.	Personal	
I done it wrong.	Personal: evaluating self	
		Rachel tried it again —this time she had difficulty with her *N:И*.
I'm messing up I'm leaving.	Personal: evaluating self	

Thus, similar to Tracy, Rachel did attempt to write conventional symbols (letters and words) and was concerned with the correctness of her work. When producing labels, she formed conventional, unconnected letters in an appropriate directional pattern. But, while all of Tracy's written messages were labels for particular things, persons, or events, Rachel's writing could function as does talk itself—to create new meanings. Rachel's letters were liberated from concrete entities, free to organize experiences, express feelings, and reach out to others.

In all, 15 of Rachel's 40 writing events involved messages which were more than simple labels. These events included: Event Type D (production of a written object), G (communication of a particular message to a particular audience), H (representation of orally-expressed feelings or experiences), and I (list-making). The quantitative information suggests that these events occupied a minority of Rachel's writing time, but this is not correct. For, while the previously-discussed Type A events took a relatively small amount of time, each of these events could involve an entire observation session (approximately 30 minutes); none took less than 10 minutes.

I will begin the discussion of these events with Type D (the production of a written object). In these events Rachel produced "notes," which were also referred to as "letters" or "presents." These objects were intended for a specific person. They involved a combination of drawing and conventional writing, but never cursive-like script, which Rachel did not regard as "real" writing. Although Rachel gave the completed objects to an intended recipient, the basic purpose of Type D events was not to communicate a particular message. Rather, it was to create a form (an object) within which a more skilled writer might communicate a particular message. Instead of such a message, Rachel included a standard graphic: a picture of the addressee. The following excerpt illustrates Event Type D:

Language	Language Function	Comment
		Rachel had just drawn a picture of Courtney. Now she added the names:
Courtney, how do you write your name?	Heuristic: seeking facts	Rachel Courtney
Now I wanna' make an envelope. I'm making an envelope. I'm gonna' make a envelope for her You hafta' have glue.	Directive: planning	Rachel folded her note. She then folded paper around her note. Rachel glued the outer paper together to form an envelope:
I'm gonna' write her name on the envelope ...'cuz you have to have the name on.	Directive: planning	Courtney
Now write *Rachel*.	Directive: planning	After writing Courtney's name, Rachel turned the envelope over; she then wrote her own name in the upper left-hand corner:
Where's Courtney: She waiting for her letter? She can come. Where's she hiding?	Heuristic	Rachel
I just remembered I'm suppose' to make a card on this. I have to go get my scissors.	Directive: planning	
. . .		

A card on this thing—
on the paper, so she'll
know—write her name
on here.

And Rachel added the
card, the finishing touch
(see Figure 7).

Go get Courtney.   Directive:
                                requesting

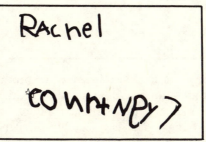

Figure 7.   The envelope for Rachel's
                letter to Courtney.

In the preceding event, Rachel established the rules for making letters.
When her peers began to make letters, they were expected to make them
"correctly":

Language	Language Function	Comment
		Vivi announced that she was going to make a note for Rachel, who was concerned that Vivi draw her appropriately.
Ra: Let me show you how to make 'em. Let me show you how to make people how I like 'em... See? I like this. This is how you make 'em.	Directive: instructing	Rachel drew a girl.
. . .		Then Vivi began to draw.
Let me see, Vivi.	Directive: requesting	
You did that much much OK...	Personal: evaluating others	

Now, make the hair like this. Make it curl like that, OK?	Directive: instructing	
. . .		
See? Now don't that look pretty?	Personal: evaluating others	
Vi: Yeah.	Interactional	
Ra: You need to make an envelope.	Directive: instructing	
Like this. Look.		And so Rachel continued until the letter was completed in the appropriate manner.

In Event Type G, Rachel also intended to produce an object. In this type, however, that intention was dominated by the desire to use that object to convey a specific message to a particular audience. Again, befitting the skills of this very young—and very sociable—writer, the communication took place through writing plus talking and drawing, as illustrated in the following excerpt (see Figure 8):

Language	Language Function	Comment
(to Dyson) I'm gonna' tear this [paper] out for you. And I'm gonna' give you a happy face 'cuz you been very good today.	Directive: planning Representational: reasoning	
How do you write *Mrs.*—Is that your real name, *Mrs. Dyson*?	Heuristic: seeking fact	I wrote my name, which Rachel copied. She then added a happy face and handed the "note" (Rachel's term) to me.
(to Dyson) You did good in school today. Let me give you a check plus ($\nu +$). That means you're a very good girl. Here.	Interactional	

In Type D, Rachel demonstrated an understanding that writing could function, as could oral language, to initiate and maintain social relationships —as a basis for interaction. In Type G, Rachel used writing, along with drawing and talking, to fulfill an additional function of oral language—to communicate a specific message. In Event Type H, Rachel used writing to represent language itself.

Figure 8. Sample of a note from Rachel to me.

To elaborate, in Type H, Rachel was not using writing to label; rather, she was using written language to represent her own talk. However, her strong sense of her own limitations as a writer, and her equally strong desire to be seen as competent, may have made her reluctant to use writing in this way. Consider, for example, the following excerpt (see Figure 9):

Language	Language Function	Comment
		Rachel had just written *Kenya* and *Twana,* friends' names. (Rachel often referred to these friends as "sisters.")
I made her [Twana's] name. I got a lot of sisters.	Representational: reporting	
(to Dyson) You have try to spell this without asking me.	Directive: requesting	Rachel wrote line A.
I already know what it spells.	Representational: reporting	
It says...um, "I got a lot of sisters." (Rachel points to sections of print as she reads)...	Directive: decoding	
You can't read it 'cuz all these letters are so teeny weeny, right? That's how they put it in the newspaper. Real tiny, don't they? Like this. You can't read it, but I can.	Representational: reasoning	

Figure 9. "I got a lot of sisters."

In another event, Rachel used print to express the words of the characters in an oral narrative. She thus captured her characters' interaction in text and could have shared that interaction with a reader—if only she had not used the "teeny-weeny" writing method:

Language	Language Function	Comment
		Rachel had been drawing the picture in Figure 10 as she narrated a story.
Ra: "Sister, open up the door!	Representational: dramatizing	

[Rachel knocks
twice on table.]
You dummy. Sister,
you better come
and open this door
or else I'm gonna'
throw this pumpkin
shell on your head."

That's what it's gonna' be saying.	Directive: planning	
		Rachel wrote line A in Figure 10.
(to Dyson) Come here. You have to try to read this, Mrs. Dyson. If you can't, you have to try to guess. This is a note right here.	Directive: requesting	
		Rachel used the word "note" to refer to any writing with a message.
Dy: Let's see if I can read it...um—		
Ra: It says, "Open the door, Sister. Open, open, open, else I'm gonna' throw this pumpkin shell right on your head."	Directive: decoding	

Rachel later explained that she wrote little "'cuz I wanted you to try to guess." The reader should note that Rachel used conventional letter forms in both these events; she appeared to "fix" the situations so that she would be immune from the criticism, "That's not real writing." This approach to writing necessitated the use of oral language to give the full meaning of the written text.

These Type H events emphasize Rachel's apparent desire to use written language, as she uses oral language, for legitimate purposes; in addition, they emphasize her equally apparent awareness of her own limitations. Bearing in mind these characteristics of Rachel, Event Type I is significant because it represents a type of event in which Rachel could rely soley on written langauge to fulfill a legitimate, adult-like writing function.

Figure 10. "Open the door, sister. Open, open,
open, else I'm gonna' throw this pumpkin
on your head."

In Type I, written language functioned as a label, but a label with an
overriding purpose—to organize and record information, as illustrated in
the following excerpt:

Language	Language Function	Comment
		Rachel had been writing the names of everyone at the writing center on a small piece of paper. She copied the names from each child's writing folder.
I've got Linda, Viviana, and Mrs. Dyson, but not my name...	Representational: reporting	
I'm gonna' put my name on here...I'm gonna' give this to my mommy so she'll know all of my friends' names that was over here.	Directive: planning Representational: reasoning	

The analysis of Event Types D, G, H, and I demonstrate that, for Rachel, labeling was not the only meaningful function of writing. In addition, writing could function as: (a) talk itself to communicate one's personal feelings and experiences and to transmit specific messages to particular audiences, and (b) a clerical tool to organize and record useful information.

In sum, Rachel's symbol producing processes—talking, drawing, and writing—all reflected a people-oriented, purposeful disposition. While Tracy primarily wrote labels, Rachel was motivated by more diverse purposes: no long lists of unrelated words for her, but rather, lists of peers, notes to friends, dialogues for stories, and personal statements.

Oral language (talk) was an integral part of Rachel's writing events; it functioned as it had for Tracy. The thematic content of the written product frequently evolved in the talk preceding writing. Talk was also used to elaborate on the full meaning of that product. Further, oral language was used as a tool to seek information perceived as needed, to assist self in the encoding of words, and, finally, to distance self from work (i.e., to express evaluations of completed products).

In contrast to Tracy, however, Rachel's writing appeared to be more than just graphics supplemented by drawings and talk. Her writing events, especially those categorized Event Type H, indicated that Rachel attempted to transfer her talk to print. This inference was supported by Rachel's performance on the voice-print match task. While it was not a simple activity for her, she did complete the task correctly:

Dyson: (reading without pointing) This says, *The toy was broken.* Your turn to read it.
Rachel: (reading and pointing correctly) *The toy was broken.*
Dyson: Where's *toy*?
Rachel: It's the whole word—right here. *The toy was broken,* see? *The toy was broken.*
Dyson: Where's just *toy*?
Rachel: *The toy* (reading and printing). This is the word *toy* (pointing to the correct word).

Rachel's writing event components varied in their degree of refinement (conventionality). While she could write in a manner similar to Tracy's conventional one, Rachel would also produce letters with no apparent orthographic similarity to their meaning. This occurred when Rachel intended to communicate a specific propositional message, as opposed to a single word. To fulfill such intentions, Rachel adopted a personal system for encoding messages. This type of writing was even more dependent on oral language (than her conventionally-spelled labels) if its meaning was to be shared with others.

The observational data indicated that Rachel was demanding of both herself and others (i.e., she felt standards must be met). This critical attitude may have been related to the previously-discussed home literacy lessons reported by her mother.

The next case study, like Rachel, could use writing as a form of talk. But, while Rachel was primarily interested in the *meanings* which written language can create, Vivi was interested in the *means* by which talk becomes print.

VIVI

Vivi, a black female, was 5 years, 3 months at the beginning of this study. Syntactically, Vivi's speech did not differ notably from that of her 5-year-old peers, although, as previously noted, it is difficult to distinguish developmental and dialect features in young children's speech. Vivi's speech did contain phonological features of nonstandard Black dialect, including weakening of final consonants, simplification of consonant clusters, and *l*-lessness (Wolfram & Fasold, 1974).

In comparison to the other case study children, Vivi was moderately talkative. Rather than Tracy's reticence or Rachel's conversations, Vivi's most distinctive verbal behavior was to break into song, typically pop songs (her favorite being "Looking for Love in All the Wrong Places") or her own creations (Vivi could set the letters *D-O-G* to a five-minute melody).

Vivi was a sociable, pleasant child—affectionate with adults (prone to giving hugs and declarations of "I love you"), mild-mannered with peers. In the event of a disagreement, Vivi would give in to her peer's wishes, rather than escalate the fight.

Vivi was accepted by both boys and girls as a play partner. In addition, like Rachel, she was a member of the small group of girls who typically played together: Courtney, Linda, Sance, Vivi, and Rachel.

Despite her sociality, Vivi engaged in a variety of both solitary and group activities. Each week, she regularly visited the library center, where she "read" or invented text, the puzzle center, and the writing center. In all solitary activities, Vivi persisted with the task until its completion. Like Tracy, and in contrast to Rachel, Vivi would not abandon a solitary activity for a more social one.

At the writing center, Vivi could pursue what were for her essentially solitary activities—writing and drawing—in the company of friends. Vivi's visits were unusual in that she wrote more frequently than she drew (she drew in 26 sessions; she wrote in 28).

Vivi's drawing papers appeared splattered with drawn objects. The drawn objects were not thematically related, but existed as single entities amidst splotches of letters. Although flowers, houses, and people were frequently drawn, a vast assortment of small objects appeared on Vivi's papers, including, for example, a sausage, dice, one tooth (with a cavity), a washeteria, a small bunny with large feet, and a rainbow. Occasionally, the produced objects were neither defined nor clearly definable.

The disorganized nature of Vivi's products belies the resolve with which she worked. Vivi approached the drawing task with apparent confidence, enthusiasm, and satisfaction, seemingly involved in the process itself. These characteristics are reflected in the following excerpt:

Language	Language Function	Comment
Vi: This is something.	Representational: labeling	Vivi was drawing an unidentified object (object A in Figure 11).
I need black.	Directive: requesting	
It's gonna' go all the way around...	Directive: monitoring	Vivi was now drawing object B.
I'm making something. This is a lollipop.	Representational: labeling	
Look at this lollipop.	Interactional	
. . .		
A *c* and a *o* . . .	Directive: monitoring	Vivi drew a *c*, an *o*, and then colored them in (see object C).
One more thing I'm gonna' do...	Directive: planning	
I'm making a spooky house...		Vivi was drawing object D.
Look.	Interactional	
I'm mixing this color up with this...	Directive: monitoring	

The preceding event also illustrates typical patterns of Vivi's oral language use. Her talk was very similar to Tracy's. Both Vivi and Tracy planned and labeled each individual object produced. (In contrast, Rachel's objects had a role within an overriding narrative.) Both girls also made frequent use of other-directed language as they sought an approving audience for their work. The most significant difference between Vivi's drawing and Tracy's was Vivi's frequent use of self-directing monitoring language (i.e., her comments on the ongoing process). Her language was inseparable from the planning, the doing, and the completion (the labeling) of the product.

In addition, the event reveals that Vivi's products were not required to be representative of anything. Further, the completed product need not match the plan. For example, in the planned production of the spooky house (object D in Figure 11), Vivi's involvement in the process (the curving

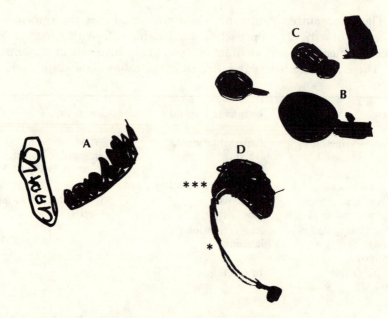

**Figure 11.   Sample of Vivi's drawing. *A green, curving line.
***A mixture of green and black colors.**

of the green line, the "mixing" of the black with the green) served to free
that process from the plan; the completed object is not a spooky house.

Vivi's process-oriented approach contrasts with the other case study
children's—particularly Rachel's—product-oriented approach. A corollary
contrast with Rachel lies in their differing attitudes towards their own work.
While Rachel characteristically evaluated her drawings against particular
standards, Vivi was accepting of her final products. Vivi was only once
observed to negatively evaluate her drawing. In that event, Vivi remarked
that her drawn heart "ain't no good." Vivi simply tried it again: "There,
that looks pretty."

My observations of Vivi were complemented by the information
shared by her mother. I talked with her mother in an employee's lounge at a
large university dormitory, where she worked as a food services supervisor.
Vivi's father worked for the Internal Revenue Service.

Vivi's mother conveyed great pride in Vivi, whom she regarded as an
independent child who liked to learn and who "catch [es] on fast":

> She know her phone number. She know my sister's phone number. She can
> dial anybody's number, 'cept long distance 'cause I won't give it to her. But
> she'll try it if you let her. . . . Her teacher sent a guide home with all the kids'
> names, and she picked out Rachel's phone number, and she called her one
> night too.

Vivi's mother also described Vivi as a "leader" who tried to teach her same-age cousins such skills as tying their shoes and writing their names.

In contrast to Vivi's observed school behavior, her mother reported that Vivi was very talkative. This verbosity may have been related to Vivi's having no siblings and no age-mates in her apartment complex:

> [Vivi's father and Vivi pick] me up at work at 7:00. And she'll talk from the time I get home. And I'll tell her, "Vivi, please." And she'll have a book and she'll wanna' write this. And I'll try to spend some time with her....and I'll say, "Oh, radio—I've got a radio." And she'll say, "Mom, I'm not a radio." She talks, talks, talks. She don't know when to stop.

Vivi: Writing at Home

As is suggested by the preceding excerpt, Vivi's generally confident and independent nature was reflected in her home writing behaviors. Like Tracy, Vivi had attended a day care center and, like Tracy's mother, Vivi's mother credited the center for Vivi's ability to write, particularly for her knowledge of letters and letter sounds:

> I had to work, so she went to a nursery school. And they teach her a lot like that: her colors, her numbers, and her letters....for about a year until she could go to kindergarten.

But Vivi's mother also had an effect on Vivi's writing progress. As did Tracy and Rachel's parents, Vivi's mother reported that Vivi had begun writing by scribbling at about 3 and a half:

> That's how she start out, going like that 〰〰〰 . "Mama, read this for me," and I'd tell her "Vivi, it's not anything....This is how you spell my name."

Vivi's early writing was more similar to Tracy's than to Rachel's, as her greatest interest was in name writing:

> And now she'll write *Reba* [Vivi's mother's name]. And she'll write *Kay* [Vivi's aunt] and *Kim* [Vivi's second cousin]. She'll try to spell *Sean*. She wants to spell *Shannon*, but it's kinda' long—but she keep trying. She'll say, "Shannon, how do you spell your name?" And she'll tell her, and she'll write it down.

Another frequent current activity was copying: "She can get a book and copy just exactly what the book has."

Vivi appeared to be as interested in reading as she was in writing. She read both signs and books:

We'll go to the mall and see something on a building, and she'll say, "What do that spell?", and I'll tell her, and next time we go by it she'll say [the word]: "Is that what that spells?". And she'll be right....

She have all kind of books at home....If she got it memorized, she can do real good.

Finally, Vivi's mother reported that Vivi had a great interest in the mail. Before she had started working, Vivi's mother often wrote letters. Vivi observed and expressed interest in writing at those times. Sometimes Vivi's mother would mail Vivi a card just so she'd get a letter. Vivi would "walk around with that card for days."

As with all the case studies, the interview data serves to complement and illuminate the observational data, suggesting hypotheses for Vivi's observed writing behaviors within the school context. To begin, Vivi was used to playing alone, which may explain her willingness to engage in and her concentration upon solitary activities, particularly writing. Further, Vivi's mother conveyed great pride in Vivi, whom she regarded as "quick" and as a "leader." She was excited about Vivi's interest in writing and reading; she could detail Vivi's accomplishments.

At home, Vivi showed interest in spelling names of people and, to a lesser degree, object names. Although Vivi was primarily interested in name-writing, she was also aware of the communicative function of writing and expressed interest and pleasure in letters. Both her awareness of the communicative function of writing and her interest in name-writing are evident in the following description of Vivi's school writing.

Vivi: Writing in School

Vivi visited the writing center 34 times and engaged in 39 writing events. Like Rachel, and in contrast to Tracy, Vivi used writing for a wide variety of purposes and, thus, engaged in a variety of writing event types, including writing labels (Type A), producing notes (Type D), and representing orally expressed feelings and experiences (Type H). Also like Rachel, Vivi demonstrated an understanding of writing as language. But, while Rachel tried to make this understanding functional, Vivi tried to make it transparent—she grappled with the precise nature of the oral-written connection. Thus, Vivi's analysis introduces Writing Event Type J: writing to investigate the relationship between oral and written language.

In this discussion, I will focus primarily on Event Type A, which predominated in the case study data accumulated from all five children, and Event Type J, which predominated in Vivi's writing data. The description of Type A serves to (a) detail the consistent characteristics of Vivi's writing event components (Message Formulation, Encoding, Mechanical Formation), and (b) to highlight differences between the familiar Event Type A and the newly introduced Type J.

In Type A, the child wrote labels for people, objects, or events. In such events, Vivi, like Tracy and Rachel, was in control of the writing process. But, while Tracy and Rachel could write a fixed set of labels (i.e., family members' names), Vivi's confidence and competence extended beyond the independent production and labeling of a limited number of words. Although she could recall and write particular letter patterns (e.g., Reba, her mother's name), Vivi had systematic strategies available for encoding any word—the limit was unknown.

In her encoding strategies, Vivi's self-directed language served as a bridge from the oral to the written "name." There appeared to be two predominant types of strategies: (a) syllable-based, writing one-to-four letters for each syllable or word part; and (b) letter-name based, listening for the letter-name sound in the spoken word. These two strategies could operate simultaneously. Vivi would write the name of any letter she could hear—but she would also include other letters (often R's and P's) to "complete" the syllable. These strategies are illustrated in the following event:

Language	Language Function	Comment
		See Figure 12. Vivi had just drawn a house.
house...ouse, house, house, house, house...	Directive: encoding	Vivi was speaking softly.
		Vivi wrote RPOPH (see Figure 12A).
Dy: How do you know how many letters to put there?		
Vi: Five...See, there's 2, and there's 3, and that's 5. There's 5 letters.		
Dy: Oh.		
Vi: huh ou	Directive: encoding	Vivi wrote POR.
...		
That's house, house. That's huh (pointing to RPOPH) ou (pointing to POR)...house... hou...huh (pointing to RPOPH) ouse (pointing to POR) house...house		

(to Dyson) That's a house (pointing to drawn house)...	Representational: labeling	
		Vivi then drew a person watching television.
Put a p...P...	Directive: encoding	
This pen don't work. (Vi. gets a new pen; she than changes the P to an R.)	Representational: reporting	
peeeee...	Directive: encoding	Vivi added POP.
peeee po, peeee po, peeee po...peeee po...		Vivi added O.
peep o...peep o		Vivi added POH. Text now looked (see Figure 12): RPOP OPOH
peep...peep (pointing to RPOP) o (pointing to OPOH)		
(to Dyson) peepo' (pointing to letters written)	Directive: decoding	
Dy: Am I a peepo'? Vi: Yes! Peepo'. Dy: Oooohhh. ...		
Vi: H-O...H-B ...O... HBO, HBO Box	Directive: encoding	Vivi wrote HBO. Vivi drew a box around HBO. HBO Box was Vivi's term for Home Box Office Television.

Only four of Vivi's writing process events were classified as As. Despite this small number (relative to those of Tracy and Rachel), Vivi actually did frequently write labels or "names" of objects. However, the majority ($n = 20$) of these name-writing events were classified as Js.

In Event Type A, Vivi moved systematically from formulated message (label) to encoding and mechanical formation. In Event Type J, this linear flow from oral to written language was disrupted. Vivi could move, not only from formulated message to encoding, but also from mechanical formation to decoding/formulating a message. In J, Vivi was process- rather than product-oriented. She appeared to explore the writing process itself: she

Figure 12. Vivi's written labels for the drawings: *house, peepo'*, and *HBO Box*.

segmented both oral and written language, making adjustments on both ends, searching for precise matches of text and talk. In this search, Vivi did not work towards one culminating product. Rather, she produced patches of words across the page. Figure 13 exemplifies a typical resulting product. The following excerpt illustrates the process Vivi used to write just part of that product:

Language	Language Function	Comment
H-O-R-B...	Directive: monitoring	Vivi wrote HORB.
A singer.	Directive: decoding	
(to Dyson) Did you know my mama was a singer?	Interactional	
. . .		
H-R-P-B—	Directive: monitoring	Vivi wrote HR. PB
Oh. That's the same as that.	Representational: reporting	Vivi noted the similarity between the latter two groups of letters.
Dy: Did you mean to do that?		
Vi: Uh uh [No].		
It says, My mama is a singer. (Vivi is moving her finger, trying to match the spoken words to the text HR. PB	Directive: decoding	

Now Vivi uses both the earlier written HORB and HR. She PB reads:) *Mama isa sin ger		* HR
		  ↑PB HO RB
		    ↖ ↑ ↑
		"Mama isa sin ger."
		(Arrows indicate which letters Vivi pointed to as she spoke.)

(Vivi tries it again:) **Mama is a singer.		** HR HO RB
		  ↑PB
		   ↖ ↑ ↑
		"Mama is a singer."
		(Vivi now wrote PR RH RY.)

(Vivi reads her new text:) Mama is a baby-sitter...***Mama isa baby --		*** PR RH RY ↑ ↑ ↑ "Mama isa baby--"
(Vivi adds PQ.) ****Mamma isa baby sitter.		**** PR RH RY PQ ↑ ↑ ↑ ↑ "Mama isa baby sitter."
(to Dy.) I know how to make a heart.	Representational: reporting	

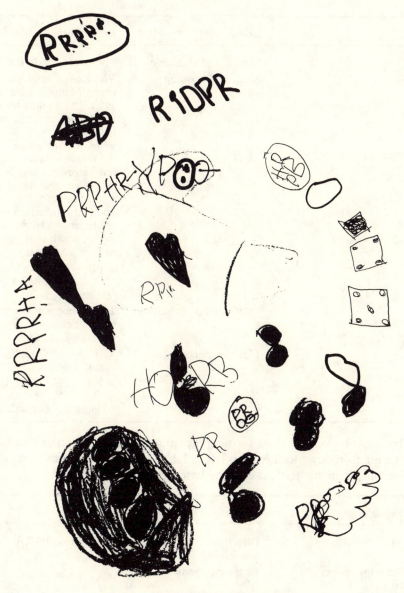

Figure 13. Sample of Vivi's writing.

In this event, Vivi appeared to be using primarily the syllable-based strategy: writing one-to-four letters for each syllable or word part. However, it's clear that this strategy does not always govern the letters that appear; Vivi may write, decode, and then use the syllable strategy to justify or rectify that encoding. Vivi's production of "Mama is a baby sitter" illustrates such a sequence of components:

Component	Description
Mechanical Formation	Vivi wrote PR RH RY.
Message Decoding	Vivi looked at text and read "Mama is a baby sitter." (Vivi may have had this sentence in mind before she began to write. My inference that the message came after, not before, writing is based on her hesitation *after,* not before, the physical production of the letters.) Vivi attempted to match oral and written language: PR RH RY ↑ ↑ ↑ "Mama isa baby."
(Message Formulation)	This component occurred simultaneously with Message Decoding.
Message Encoding	Vivi added PQ and read again: PR RH RY PQ ↑ ↑ ↑ ↑ "Mama isa baby sitter."

That same movement from forming the letters to decoding can be seen in the excerpts to follow. Rather than the syllable-based strategy, however, these excerpts highlight Vivi's use of the letter-name based strategy.

Language	Language Function	Comment
P-A-R-A, N-B	Directive: monitoring	Vivi wrote PARA NB.
That's my cousin's name.	Representational: labeling	

*Deb by	Directive: decoding	* PARA NB
		    ↑ ↑
		  "Deb by"

N (as writes N) ...	Directive: monitoring	Vivi wrote PE VN.
Then...Then (running finger under word)...then	Directive: decoding	

. . . H-N- N...H	Directive: monitoring	Vivi wrote HNiN.
. . . Dy: Tell me about this. Vi: Wait...H-N ...N...(Vivi is renaming letters written.)	Directive: decoding	Vivi repeated the names, as though deciding what word she could hear in them.

Absent from this discussion of Vivi's encoding/decoding strategies is any reference to requesting words, a strategy used by both Rachel and Tracy. This absence may have been due to Vivi's "I'll-do-it-my-way-you-do-it-yours" approach to writing. She clearly expressed the opinion that two spellings can exist for one word—and one word can exist in two ways. Thus, she was aware, for example, that I might spell a word differently than she did; she was even aware that my spelling was no doubt the one more widely used. But such awareness caused no lack of confidence:

(Vivi had just written *BMNSP*, which she labeled as *Peter*.)
Dyson: This is how I write *Peter*.
Vivi: Write it on here (Vivi hands me a paper listing her requested words.)
Dyson: (I write *Peter*.) How come we don't spell Peter the same way?
Vivi: I don't know—'cuz I spell *Peter B*—(turning to Sance) You wanna' know how? Put *B* on it...*B*...*M*...*B-M-N*...*S*...*P*.

Here is another example:

(Vivi had written *BUTTRS*.)
Vivi: *Cu pie* (reading)
Dyson: What does *Cupie* begin with?
Vivi: *Q*...(Vivi writes *QP*.) That's another way to write *Cupie*.

Vivi's hypotheses regarding the flexibility of our spelling system appear logical. Vivi's letter-name strategy worked perfectly well to produce many of the "words" she knew, for example, *HBO, PTA, IRS* (where Vivi's aunt and father worked), and *HEB* (a regional grocery store chain). Further, she knew that her own name could be spelled and pronounced in two different ways: *Viviana* (her mother's spelling, and *VEVE* (her father's spelling), both of which could be read as "Viviana" or "Vivi."

Despite this flexible attitude toward spelling, Vivi did request words, although she seldom copied them. Like Tracy, she requested names of known objects, actions, and people (music, sing, cookies, cakes, pies); objects in the immediate environment (pencil, colors, paper, book); seasonal objects (Christmas tree, Easter, Valentine's Day); and objects whose labels had been requested by a peer ("I want that too. Give me everything what she got.").

These words were additional data for Vivi's investigation of written language. She not only questioned me regarding the identity of whole words, as Tracy had done, she examined each using one of two familiar study techniques. One method was to rapidly whisper the word and the letters of the word to herself, for example:

dog dog dog gah d o jjjj—gggggg

The second method was to match written words to oral syllables. This second method led to questions regarding my own competency as a speller, for example:

Text: *my birthday cake*
      ↑   ↑   ↑   ↑
Vivi: *my birth   day cake"* (Vivi points to an empty space, eyeing me suspiciously. She tries the next word—)
Text: *book   stasher*
      ↑   ↑   ↑
Vivi: *"Book stash   er"* (Vivi again, with a disapproving glance, points to empty space.)

Vivi did not always use the letter-name and syllable-based encoding/decoding procedures. As with Rachel, strategy depended upon purpose. For example, Vivi's usual approach to communicating a particular message to a particular audience (Event Type G) was to use "curspid" (cursive): ‿‿‿‿‿ ; an oral rendition of the precise message followed ("This says, 'I love you.'"), a behavior similar to Rachel's translation of teeny-weeny writing. However, in one Type G event, Vivi combined a variety of strategies to produce the lengthiest, most coherent, and most conventional piece written by any of the case study children. Because of its significance, I am including a lengthy excerpt (see Figure 14):

Language	Language Function	Comment
(To Dyson) Look at your flower. That's for Courtney, that's for Linda, and that's for you (pointing to each of the three flowers in turn).	Interactional	Vivi had just drawn the flowers in Figure 14.
(to Linda) Look. Look at yours, Linda. Look at your flower.	Interactional	

I'm gonna' write names on 'em too.	Directive: planning	
B A-N-B-D	Directive: monitoring	
...flower, a flower (elongated)	Directive: decoding	
a flower for...	Directive: planning	
Let me see...	Directive: monitoring	Vivi consulted her list of requested words and located Mrs. Dyson.
M-R-S-D-U-S...S-O—	Directive: monitoring	
(to Dyson) What's this, a H?	Heuristic: seeking confirmation	
(Dyson: N) Oh,	Interactional	
...N...	Directive: monitoring	
Miss Dyson... flower for Mrs. Dys on, flower for Mrs. Dyson (Vivi is speaking softly, staring intently at page, pointing with both finger and voice.) Dyson, Dyson, ...Dyson	Directive: decoding	
(to Dyson) How do you spell Mrs.?	Heuristic: seeking fact	
(Dyson: This is Mrs., [pointing to Mrs.].)		
flower...Mrs. (speaking softly, partly inaudibly) Mrs. Dyson, Dyson, Dy son	Directive: decoding	
(to Dyson) How do you spell Dys?	Heuristic: seeking fact	
(Dyson: Like this [pointing to Dys].)		
Oh...	Interactional	Vivi now began to copy Linda from Linda's writing folder.
L-I-N-B-A	Directive: monitoring	
...And what about Courtney—	Directive: planning	
Oh, hers [her name] is too long.	Personal	
...		
Flower for Mrs. Dyson and for Linda too... for—	Directive: accessing	
(to Dyson.) How do you spell for?	Heuristic: seeking fact	I spelled for, which Vivi copied.
...		

F-O-R-rah...	Directive: monitoring	
for Linda (pointing to words), for Linda—	Directive: accessing	
(to Dyson) How do you spell too?	Heuristic: seeking fact	I spelled too, which Vivi copied.
t-o-o	Directive: monitoring	
There!	Personal	

Figure 14.   "Flower for Mrs. Dyson and for Linda too."

The pride and, also, the relief in Vivi's "There" was unmistakable. Although the presence of known names (Linda, Mrs. Dyson) eased message segmentation, this was a difficult, complex task. It involved continuous rereadings— rereadings to decide which part of the message had been written, where those parts were located, and which part to write now. (Note the initial missing of both *for*s and the absence of *and* and one *for* in the final product.) This complexity and difficulty suggests why "curspid" was Vivi's preferred method in Type G events.

The fact that Vivi did produce this relatively advanced (i.e., conventional) piece indicates that the prevalent Event Type J was not the only manner of writing available to her—it was her choice. Like Rachel, Vivi understood that (a) writing was language and (b) writing shared talk's purposes. Thus, in the previous event, Vivi moved from purposeful talk to purposeful writing. But, while Rachel concentrated on adapting the process to meet diverse purposes, Vivi chose to concentrate on analyzing the process, ignoring—but not ignorant of—purpose.

In sum, Vivi's written products varied greatly in degree of refinement (conventionality). The grossest approximations of writing were the wavy ("curspid") lines. She could also produce single, conventionally-spelled words, as did Tracy and Rachel. Most frequently, she produced words through systematic (although unconventional) encoding procedures. Her most refined writing consisted of a combination of conventionally-spelled words and those formed according to her personal, but systematic, procedures.

Like Tracy and Rachel, Vivi could preplan the individual words she intended to write; she could produce conventional and near-conventional spellings. Further, like Rachel, she did not confine her independently-produced work to her small repertoire of known, conventionally-spelled words, nor did she appear to associate writing solely with concrete referents. However, when Rachel expanded beyond labeling, she lost control over a system for producing conventional written messages. Vivi tackled this system itself, often abandoning control over or concern for the message. Talk frequently permeated Vivi's writing process, directing her efforts to connect oral and written language. Talk provided more *means* than *meaning* in Vivi's writing.

With this detailing of Vivi's writing, I have completed the portraits of three young writers. A comparison of their writing behaviors allows insight into the complexity of learning to write and the varied directions individual children may take. I will discuss this learning process in the next section.

DISCUSSION

In this chapter I have described the writing behaviors of three young children, including in that description an account of the purposes which guided and variably affected their behaviors. I have also linked each child's dominant purposes for writing to the themes, patterns, and intentions which defined her as an individual. In so doing, my goal has been to illuminate the complex and variable nature of learning to write. In this section, I will compare the children's behaviors both to each other's and to those described in the literature.

Similarities across Children

All case study children, including the two not discussed in this chapter, demonstrated an awareness of the graphic aspects of print, such as linearity, directionality, and the combination and permutation of letters or letterlike forms (for a discussion of Ashley and Freddy, see Dyson, 1981). In considering the information provided by the children's parents, it was clear that the children all began writing in a similar way—by exploring the nature of writing's form, by "scribbling." The parents' reports were consistent with the literature on early writing, which suggests that both writing and drawing originate in scribbling (Dyson, 1982). Between the ages of 3 and 6, children's controlled scribbling gradually develops into recognizable objects which they name (Brittain, 1979) and, similarly, the scribbling gradually acquires the characteristics of print, including linearity, horizontal orientation, and the arrangement of letter-like forms, which children may read (by inventing a text) or request that others read (Clay, 1975; Hildreth, 1936).

In addition to the evidenced understandings of writing's form, all children displayed an understanding of writing's labeling function. Parents noted that the writing of their child's own and others' names was a typical focus of early writing. Here again, the children's behavior was consistent with the literature. Children's first conventionally written words are typically the names of familiar people (Durkin, 1966; Stine, 1980). The writing of names may serve an important developmental function (Dyson, 1982; Ferreiro & Teberosky, 1982). In order to write, children must become aware that their transparent tool, language, can become a graphic object (Vygotsky, 1962). Names, then, allow children access to language as a graphic, visible object of reflection. In fact, children may initially view writing as the forming of letters for particular people or objects, which are then read as the names of those objects; in their view, the reader may extend or elaborate upon the written names (Ferreiro, 1978; Ferreiro & Teberosky, 1982). The children in this study used talk to suggest or to elaborate upon the meaning of their own written labels.

Differences across Children

Beyond the grasp of writing's perceptual features and a certain interest in written names, the differences between the children were more striking than the similarities. The children appeared to have different intentions with regard to written language and different ways of approaching writing, approaches which made sense when each child was viewed within the context of her own unique interests and style of functioning. I refer again here to the child in control of the written language kaleidoscope, arranging the parts to suit her own sense of what's interesting and what's appropriate.

To oversimplify, yet clarify, from both parent and observational data for the three children discussed in-depth here, there emerged a picture of

Tracy as a constructionist, Rachel as both a pragmatist and dramatist, and Vivi as an eager investigator. Tracy was concerned with acquiring the labels for particular persons and objects. The suggestion might reasonably be made that Tracy was at an earlier developmental stage in that she appeared to view writing as the producing of names. Yet, Tracy's interests in drawing and in constructive play were to "build" particular entities. Her interest in words as entities was consistent with that drawing and play style.

In contrast, Rachel did not write words for words' sake alone. She wrote for a variety of purposes. Typically, these purposes involved the communication of a message, a message which Rachel formulated in the narrating, dramatizing, and interactional talk preceding writing. Rachel's interest in using writing for communication is also consistent with observational data and parental information, both of which portrayed Rachel as a pragmatist and a dramatist.

In certain ways, Rachel might be seen as a less skilled writer than Tracy. She could write fewer conventionally-spelled words. She did not know as many letter names. Further, she wrote more often in unconventional ways (i.e., her "teeny-weeny" writing technique). Yet, in other ways, Rachel was a more skilled writer. She wrote for a wider range of purposes. And, relative to Tracy, she demonstrated a clearer understanding of the relationship between oral and written language.

Finally, Vivi, in all her activities, appeared process-oriented. Although she was interested in labels and in communicating with others through writing, her major interest was in understanding how the system worked. In certain ways, Vivi might be judged less skilled than Tracy. She could produce a smaller number of conventionally-written words. Like Rachel, her products varied greatly in degree of conventionality. She might also be judged less skilled than Rachel as she did not write as frequently for conventional writing purposes. But, in other ways, Vivi was the most sophisticated of the three girls. Like Rachel, she varied her writing process to meet her writing purpose. And, not only did she understand that a relationship existed between oral and written language, she was intent on figuring out the exact nature of that relationship. She appeared to be uncovering the nature of our alphabetic writing code. This study of young kindergarteners' writing, then, documents the variability and individuality in early literacy and thus complements the work of Bissex (1980), Bussis et al. (1979), and Clay (1975, 1977, 1979).

Early Writing as Symbol Development

The kindergarteners' writing, in both the similarities and differences noted across children, also complements the literature on earlier occurring symbol development. For example, in all areas of symbol development, children typically explore the basic properties of the vehicular material before using that material to symbolize. In the currently reported study, the frequently observed Event Type F (writing with no apparent concern for a particular message) was, in effect, an exploration of writing's form and similar to the early "scribbling" reported by the children's parents. It was also reminiscent of Weir's (1962) description of her child's language play and Kellogg's (1970) and Smith's (1979) descriptions of children's early exploration of drawing. Further, in all areas of symbol development, there are reported differences in children's use of varied symbolic materials (language, blocks, drawings), a phenomenon discussed in this chapter's review of related research. Certainly the observed children made contrasting uses of written graphics.

The differences in use of symbolic materials have been associated with different forms of resulting products (e.g., speech, block constructions, drawn pictures). These differences in use may also lead to different routes to symbolic competence (Nelson, 1981; Wolf & Gardner, 1979). For example, Wolf and Gardner have illustrated how "patterners," children whose early symbolic play typically leads to atemporal configurations, and "dramatists," whose play is strongly narrational, may progress differently. They describe a patterner, whose constructions with blocks and other toys became increasingly complex and articulate. Between 24 and 30 months, the child's constructions became sufficiently detailed to suggest particular characters and events; the child's construction skills thus supported the development of the previously neglected narrational skills. In contrast, Wolf and Gardner describe a dramatist, whose narrations became increasingly imaginative and rich. Between 24 and 30 months, this child's narratives began to require props and, thus, to support the development of the child's ability to represent objects' attributes.

I am suggesting here comparisons between the varied writing behaviors of the three observed kindergarteners and the variations described in the symbol development literature. In Wolf and Gardner's terms, Tracy appeared to be a patterner, Rachel a dramatist, while Vivi was less easily categorized, although she appeared to be more patterner than dramatist. However, I am not suggesting that there are particular types of child writers or preset paths children follow in learning written language. There are not sufficient data across varied symbolic tasks, nor are there the necessary longitudinal data on individual children. I do not know if the observed differences are the result of cognitive styles or environmental input. Nor do I know the ultimate developmental implications of the observed differences. Furthermore, it should be noted that evidence from symbol development in other areas suggests that most children are not easily typecast as to style of symbolizing (Nelson, 1981). Nonetheless, from the children's displayed differences, certain implications are clear. I will turn to these implications in the next section.

Implications for Research and Practice

First, investigations of young children's writing must focus on all aspects of the writing process. To elaborate, adult writers would no doubt agree that writing involves the representation of a message through an alphabetic code for a particular purpose. Yet, examinations of early writing have tended to focus on children's mastery of writing's perceptual features (Clay, 1975) and of the encoding system, specifically children's invented spellings (e.g., Chomsky, 1975; Read, 1975). The cited studies were seminal investigations which called attention to the activeness of the young child in·solving the written language puzzle. Yet, there has as yet been little focus on children's intentions, on the nature of self-initiated written messages, and on the purposes which writing serves in children's lives. (An exception is Bissex's [1980] study of her son's written language.) This narrow focus in written language appears comparable to language acquisition research, which initially focused on children's grasps of the syntactical structures of written language (e.g., Brown, Cazden, & Bellugi, 1969), with little emphasis placed on the meaning and intentions of young children.

There is a need, therefore, for research which focuses on the writing system as a whole. In this chapter, I have offered a scheme for viewing holistically young children's early writing. I have suggested that we view writing as involving recursive and overlapping components: Message Formulation, Encoding, Mechanical Formation, and Decoding components that evolve as children fulfill varied writing purposes. We may ask, then, what types of messages does the individual child attempt to communicate, if any? What procedures does the child use to encode those messages or to get those thoughts in print? How conventional does the child's product appear? For what purposes does the child write; in other words, what role in the child's life does writing play? Do the child's messages, encoding strategies, or forming and arranging of letters change with writing purposes? How does the child's use of more familiar ways of representing ideas, such as talk and drawing, interrelate with the use of writing?

A second and related implication of this study is that children can appear more or less skilled, depending upon which aspect of the written language system we are focusing on, a point which I attempted to show through my analysis of Tracy's, Rachel's, and Vivi's writing: Tracy could produce the largest number of conventionally-spelled words; Rachel wrote for the greatest number of purposes; Vivi was the most sophisticated in her analysis of the encoding system. Thus, as we change our lens from encoding strategies to, for example, writing functions, a different view of a child's competence may emerge. For learning to write, as learning other symbolic systems, involves a unique child coming to understand a distinctive system, within the particular contexts of his or her life.

As Nelson (1981) has suggested in regard to individual variations in oral language development, the variability of individual children allows us insight into both the nature of the writing system itself and the process of learning to write. Individual children's patternings of the writing act highlight varied aspects of the intricate writing web. As children learn about the writing system, adult observers learn as well. For example, in the current study, the five case study children demonstrated that many factors are involved in the writing process besides written language knowledge or skill, including individual style of functioning, risk-taking ability, and the particular purposes for which one has chosen to write. (For a discussion of Freddy, the case study child who appeared the least willing to take risks in various areas, not only in writing, see Dyson, 1981.)

The concept of individual differences has implications for practice as well as for research. Learning to write involves coming to understand how written graphics function as a symbol system (i.e., what kinds of messages can be encoded, how can they be encoded, what forms does the symbolic vehicle take) and, also, how writing functions in society. Individual children may focus on varied aspects of this writing act. Thus, the concept of individual differences implies the importance of careful observation so that teachers may understand children as unique individuals with particular styles of writing and of learning to write.

Teachers who aim to build upon children's writing strategies observe their children, noting the purposes for which children write and the manner in which individuals approach the task. They aim to expand children's awareness of writing's functions by incorporating written language into daily classroom life. In addition, they listen to their children, noting the messages each wishes to express and helping them to write those messages. While they seek to expand children's encoding strategies, sensitive teachers respect the difficulty of the writing task and the validity of different ways of getting thoughts in print, including dictating, recalling, "sounding-it-out," "looking-it-up," or just skirting the issue and ⌇⌇⌇.

Both researchers and teachers, then, benefit from focusing on the individual child, the child who is in control of the kaleidoscope we call written language. As we observe children arrange and rearrange its pieces, we gain new understanding of the intricacies of written language and of the learning child as well.

REFERENCES

Applebee, A. (1978). *The child's concept of story*. Chicago, IL: University of Chicago Press.
Ashton-Warner, S. (1963). *Teacher*. New York: Simon and Schuster.
Bissex, G. (1980). *Gyns at wrk: A child learns to write and read*. Cambridge, MA: Harvard University Press.

Bloom, L., Lightbown, P., & Hood, L. (1975). *Structure and variation in child language.* Monographs of the Society for Research in Child Development, 40.

Boston Educational Research Company. (1971). *Beginning to read, write, and listen.* Philadelphia, PA: Lippincott.

Boston Educational Research Company. (1974). *Beginning readiness kit.* Philadelphia: Lippincott.

Brittain, W. L. (1979). *Creativity, art, and the young child.* New York: Macmillan.

Brown, R., Cazden, C., & Bellugi, U. (1969). The child's grammar from I to III. In J. P. Hill (Ed.), *Minnesota symposium on child psychology* (Vol. 2). Minneapolis, MN: University of Minnesota Press.

Bussis, A. M., Chittenden, E., & Amarel, M. (1978). Collaborative research. In S. Madeja (Ed.), *The teaching process and the arts and aesthetics* (Third yearbook on research in arts and aesthetics education). St. Louis, MO: CEMREL.

Chomsky, C. (1975). *How sister got into the grog. Early Years, 6,* 36–39.

Clay, M. (1975). *What did I write?* Auckland, Australia: Heinemann.

Clay, M. (1977). Exploring with a pencil. *Theory into Practice, 16,* 334–341.

Clay, M. (1979). *Reading: The patterning of complex behavior.* Auckland, Australia: Heinemann.

Cole, M., & Traupmann, K. (1981). Comparative cognitive research: Learning from a learning disabled child. In W. A. Collins (Ed.), *Minnesota symposium on child psychology* (Vol. 14). Hillsdale, NJ: Lawrence Erlbaum Associates.

Cook-Gumperz, J., & Gumperz, J. (1981). From oral to written culture: The transition to literacy. In M. F. Whiteman (Ed.), *Variation in writing.* Hillsdale, NJ: Lawrence Erlbaum Associates.

Corsaro, W. A. (1979). "We're friends, right?": Children's use of access rituals in a nursery school. *Language in Society, 8,* 315–336.

Corsaro, W. A. (1981). Entering the child's world: Research strategies for field entry and data collection in a preschool setting. In J. Green & C. Wallat (Eds.), *Ethnography and language in educational settings.* Norwood, NJ: Ablex.

Donaldson, M. (1978). *Children's minds.* New York: Norton.

Durkin, D. (1966). *Children who read early: Two longitudinal studies.* New York: Teacher's College Press.

Dyson, A. Haas. (1981). *A case study examination of the role of oral language in the writing processes of kindergarteners.* Unpublished doctoral dissertation, The University of Texas at Austin.

Dyson, A. Haas. (1982). The emergence of visible language: Interrelationships between drawing and early writing. *Visible Language 16,* 360–381.

Dyson, A. Haas. (1983). The role of oral language in early writing processes. *Research in the Teaching of English, 17,* 1–30.

Eisner, E. (1981). On the differences between scientific and artistic approaches to qualitative research. *Educational Researcher, 10,* 5–9.

Ferreiro, E. (1978). What is written in a written sentence? A developmental answer. *Journal of Education, 160,* 25–39.

Ferreiro, E. (1980). *The relationship between oral and written language: The children's viewpoints.* Paper presented at the meeting of the International Reading Association preconvention, St. Louis.

Ferreiro, E., & Teberosky, A. (1982). *Literacy before schooling.* Exeter, NH: Heinemann.

Franklin, M. (1973). Nonverbal representation in young children: A cognitive perspective. *Young Children, 29,* 33–52.

Goodman, Y. (1980). The roots of literacy. In M. Douglass (Ed.), *Claremont reading conference* (44th yearbook). Claremont, CA: Claremont Graduate School.

Graves, D. (1973). *Children's writing: Research directions and hypotheses based upon an examination of the writing processes of seven-year-old children.* Unpublished doctoral dissertation, State University of New York at Buffalo.

Halliday, M. A. K. (1973). *Explorations in the functions of language.* London: Edward Arnold.

Hildreth, G. (1936). Developmental sequences in name writing. *Child Development, 7,* 291–302.

Kellogg, R. (1970). *Analyzing children's art.* Palo Alto, CA: National Press Books.

King, M. L., & Rentel, V. (1979). Toward a theory of early writing development. *Research in the Teaching of English, 13,* 243–253.

McCutcheon, G. (1981). On the interpretation of classroom observations. *Educational Researcher, 10,* 5–10.

McDermott, R. P., & Hood, L. (1982). Institutionalized psychology and the ethnography of schooling. In P. Gilmore & A. Glatthorn (Eds.), *Children in and out of school: Ethnography and education.* Washington, DC: Center for Applied Linguistics.

Nelson, K. (1973). Structure and strategy in learning to talk. *Monographs of the Society for Research in Child Development, 38.*

Nelson, K. (1981). Individual differences in language development: Implications for development and language. *Developmental Psychology, 17,* 170–187.

Nelson, K. E., & Nelson, K. (1978). Cognitive pendulums and their linguistic realization. In K. E. Nelson (Ed.), *Children's language* (Vol. 2). New York: Gardner.

Peters, A. M. (1977). Language learning strategies: Does the whole equal the sum of the parts? *Language, 63,* 560–573.

Piaget, J., & Inhelder, B. (1969). *The psychology of the child.* New York: Basic Books.

Read, C. (1975). *Children's categorization of speech sounds in English.* Urbana, IL: National Council of Teachers of English.

Smith, N. R. (1979). How a picture means. In H. Gardner & D. Wolf (Eds.), *Early symbolization.* San Francisco: CA: Jossey-Bass.

Stake, R. E. (1978). The case study method in social inquiry. *Educational Researcher, 7,* 5–8.

Stine, S. (1980). Beginning reading—naturally. In M. Douglass (Ed.), *Claremont reading conference* (44th yearbook). Claremont, CA: Claremont Graduate School.

Tough, J. (1977). *The development of meaning.* New York: John Wiley & Sons.

Vygotsky, L. S. (1962). *Thought and language.* Cambridge, MA: MIT Press. (Originally published, 1934.)

Vygotsky, L. S. (1978). *Mind and society.* Translation edited by M. Cole, V. John-Steiner, S. Scribner, & E. Souberman. Cambridge: Harvard University Press.

Weir, R. H. (1962). *Language in the crib.* The Hague: Mouton.

Wells, G. (1981). *Learning through interaction: The study of language development* (Vol. 1). Cambridge: Cambridge University Press.

Werner, H. (1948). *Comparative psychology of mental development.* New York: International Universities Press.

Werner, H., & Kaplan, B. (1963). *Symbol formation: An organismic–developmental approach to language and the expression of thought.* New York: John Wiley & Sons.

Wolf, D., & Gardner, H. (1979). Style and sequence in early symbolic play. In N. Smith & M. Franklin (Eds.), *Symbolic functioning in childhood.* Hillsdale, NJ: Lawrence Erlbaum Associates.

Wolfram, W. (1979). *Speech pathology and dialect differences.* Washington, DC: Center for Applied Linguistics.

Wolfram, W., & Fasold, R. W. (1974). *Social dialects in American English.* Englewood Cliffs, NJ: Prentice Hall.

APPENDIX

Transcript Conventions

The following conventions are used in the presentations of transcripts:

Speakers

Dy: Dyson
Tr: Tracy
Ra: Rachel
Vi: Vivi

( ): notes, usually about nonverbal information
[ ]: explanatory information inserted into quotations by me, rather than by the speaker
N - O: letters spelled by the speaker
. . . : generally, speaker pause between words; when inserted in the middle of a blank line, refers to omitted material, e.g.,

Here go Spiderman.

   . . . [omitted material]

I'm not doing nothing
but scribble-scrabble.

3 Kindergarteners as Writers and Readers*

Elizabeth Sulzby
Northwestern University

INTRODUCTION

Little children show us delightful glimpses of the growth of thinking, feeling, and doing. Unfortunately, they typically give us these glimpses when our taperecorders are turned off, our pencils are neatly in their jars, and our bodies are ready for rest, recreation, or food. Researchers who wish to record the development of children are prodded by the nature of their young subjects to reconsider traditional methodology. This chapter contains one part of my wrestling with methodology with the goal of learning more about kindergarteners as writers and readers.

I will recount two studies, one an interview and one experimentally-structured, done in the fall of 1979 with a group of 24 kindergarteners and funded in 1980 by the Research Foundation of the National Council of Teachers of English (NCTE). These studies followed 2 years of piloting means of getting young children to reveal their growing knowledges[1] about written language and preceded a longitudinal study of writing and reading development funded by the National Institute of Education. This entire body of work has been done under the acronym BRDKAWL, or "Beginning Readers' Developing Knowledges About Written Language." In all of these studies, I have been "experimenting" with a methodology that would preserve some of the benefits of experimental design and incorporate some of the benefits of more naturalistic observations, using the different kinds of methodology to provide checks and challenges to my reasoning.[2]

---

*This chapter is a revision of *Kindergarteners begin to read their own compositions: Beginning readers' developing knowledges about written language,* a final report to the Research Foundation of the National Council of Teachers of English who funded the research reported herein. The author, however, is solely responsible for the statements and opinions expressed in both the report and this chapter.

[1]See page 128 for an explanation of the genesis of my use of the term *knowledges.*

[2]In this chapter I omit most details of scoring and statistical analysis. These are found in Sulzby (1981).

The first study is called "General Knowledges About Written Language." It is based on a structured interview in which the children were asked to write anything they could write and read anything they could read and to describe what they knew about writing and reading to the adult examiner. The second study used the structure of a repeated-measures factorial design; in this study children composed and re-read stories about the same basic topic, learning to ride a big wheel or bike, under two conditions. In one session the child composed the story as a real story about himself or herself and in another session, about a fictitious character, Little Prince or Princess Charming. I will explain each study's design and purpose in detail later.

Because these studies were done 4 years ago, I find that my thinking and the language that I now use about the research has changed somewhat. For example, in the final report I wrote for the NCTE (Sulzby, 1981, pp. 10–27), I described the overriding goal of the project as being a tracking of the "transition from pre-reading to reading" and treated children's compositions as one kind of written text that they experience while learning to read. I wrote that the focus of these studies was on how children became able to read from their own dictated and handwritten stories. Now I consider the goal of the overall project to be a description and, hopefully, explanation of the emergence of literacy, treating writing and reading as importantly-related aspects of literacy.

The original report has a long theoretical chapter. Because my thinking has developed since I wrote that chapter I will distill, briefly, a few important points and will move quickly into a description of the children's writing and reading and of the knowledges about oral and written language relationships that they revealed. I will also weave in other comments about theoretical considerations as the data are presented. (I expand these ideas in Sulzby [in press-c] in detail that space does not allow here.)

Points of Departure

First, the project was designed to describe how children become able to read from their own dictated and handwritten compositions. I hold that these and other kinds of texts (for example, commercial storybooks or basal readers) present a trade-off of supports and constraints for the young child learning to read conventionally. Children are acquiring knowledges about written language from the cradle. I use the term knowledges (plural) to emphasize that children's knowledge is not organized like that of the idealized adult but that individual children's knowledges are organized differently; furthermore, as children develop toward conventional reading and writing, there is a constraint from traditional orthography and the mature reading process that "presses" toward a more conventional organization of these knowledges. Experience with each text type appears to differentially present empirical and process information about reading, writing, and the reader-writer relationship to the young child. Dictation and handwritten compositions are both based in the child's experience and support the child's awareness that writers compose pieces of writing, yet these texts are constraining in that the child does not have to predict the composition of an external, absent author. In handwritten compositions, the child will be exploring writing systems, and eventually, in depth, an alphabetic system with its complex letter-sound relationships, whereas, in dictation, a scribe carries the burden of dealing with conventions of the writing system.

Second, dictated and handwritten compositions are of interest theoretically and not just practically. Children learn to read and write not as a transition from oral to written language, but from *within* oral and written language. From the cradle, children in literate cultures are developing written as well as oral language. Furthermore, oral and written language are related to each other in complex ways. The NCTE project, as well as my later research (Sulzby, 1982a, 1983a), assumed that children could reveal both what they knew about written language and how they conceived oral and written language to be organized in relation to each other. I used the structural paradigm of conversation, storytelling, dictation, and handwritten compositions, with re-reading and editing both of the written forms as an idealization of conventional ideas about oral-written language relationships. Eliciting samples of each of these kinds of language performance could reveal whether this idealization was appropriate for each child and children's adaptations of the tasks could further reveal the concepts they held.

Third, the project was designed in the belief that development needed to be studied "in the process of happening." Retrospective interviews with parents of precocious readers (Clark, 1976; Durkin, 1966) or writers (Read, 1970) had led us to ask questions about how all children develop. Goodman (1980, and various lectures) and Harste, Burke, and Woodward (1981) were pointing out that examining samples of children's scribblings and invented spelling after-the-fact could lead to mistaken conclusions about children's development. Additionally, research techniques from linguistics, anthropology, and the broad field of child development had led us toward more innovative designs, including both structured and unstructured observations.

Thus, I decided that I needed to look at children actually reading and writing. At that point in my own development, I knew that I, even using techniques such as ethnography, wouldn't understand unstructured observations without years of study; I needed the structure of interviews and experimental design in order to collect sufficient data to be able to see patterns, both those that replicate or fail to replicate findings of other researchers and those that indicate possible relationships between oral and written language that differ from our conventional cultural idealizations (see Olson, 1977; Tannen, 1982).

Fourth, this project looked at children before they were reading and writing conventionally and attempted to trace their development (briefly) toward conventional reading and writing. I thus found myself with the problem of defining what I meant by reading. However, as I thought through that problem I realized that the project really was designed to *discover* definitions and that the working definitions I began with had to be held tentatively (like exploratory hypotheses) and adjusted by what I found out from young readers and writers. For example, I used a working definition of "dictation," yet we found that children adapt the task of dictation in various ways. For some children, dictation is more like conversation and they scarcely seem to notice that a scribe is writing, or they ask incredulously what the adult is doing with the pencil. Still other children make exaggerated pauses for the scribe.

One set of definitions that is essential for the reader at this point, however, are those that center around what to call the young children. Are they "readers" and "writers"? In some sense they are, yet I think it is important to realize that there is a difference between the 3-year-old using a scribbling-type writing system, the 5-year-old using invented spelling, and the 7-year-old using or demanding the use of conventional orthography. Similarly, I think it is important to recognize differences in reading behaviors as children develop. I choose to use the terms *emergent literacy, emergent writing,* and *emergent reading* to distinguish them from conventional literacy, writing, and reading. I take the term *emergent* to indicate that the early behaviors are important and are real writing and reading behaviors that develop into conventional writing and reading. By conventional writing and reading, I simply mean that the "person on the street corner," witnessing a child writing or reading would assent that the child was "really" writing or reading (see Sulzby, in press-d; Teale & Sulzby, in press).

I think these definitions also do away with the notion that there are a set of pre-reading or pre-writing "readiness" skills that the child must be taught. The definitions do not address the issue of sequence of development; however, the research does. My research indicates that we can talk of *sequences* (plural) rather than sequence; we can also talk of individual variation but not of random patterns of literacy development. I will address this later.

Finally, I looked at current classes of theories of the reading process. Rumelhart (1977) and others (Anderson, 1977; Perfetti & Roth, 1981) have divided theories into categories using the computer processing metaphors of "top-down," "bottom-up," and "interactive." I held that neither a top-down nor a bottom-up theory had the power (a) to describe the development demonstrated by young children and (b) to include both writing and reading. Bottom-up theories, or theories that posit that "mechanics" such as letter recognition and decoding are prior to the higher-level processes of comprehension, are often defended on developmental grounds because young children appear to need to develop the mechanics prior to being able to comprehend written texts. Top-down theories hold that comprehension processes, such as predicting and inferencing, are prior to and guide selective use of lower-level processes. Such theories have been assumed to apply primarily to the "proficient" reader.

I contended that interactive theories, in which people are described as being capable of and actually performing parallel processing of information from sources at all levels from the "lowest" mechanics to the "highest" levels of comprehension, were potentially more compatible with the developmental patterns seen in young children (such as the kindergarteners in this study) and with the inclusion of both writing and reading. I further held that research in development would show us that comprehension of written language in literate societies begins prior to the time that the child is writing and reading conventionally; hence, all of the components of an interactive theory, in some rudimentary forms, are available to the young child in literate societies and not just to the fluent writer/reader. Additionally, the "world knowledge" of the reader or writer posited by formulations of the interactive theories can also include the young child's developing internalized model of the reader/writer relationship.

No specified theory that I am aware of currently includes both writing and reading and also allows for development. Such a theory would include emphasis both upon what Smith (1979) calls the inside-out or self-initiated and self-regulated sides of writing and reading development and also upon the outside-in or environmental (human and material) sides of writing and reading stressed in most traditional research and instructional models. I believe that the two together, inside-out and outside-in influences, are necessary parts of the teaching/learning process, whether that process is through indirect or direct means. The interface between early informal learning such as that which takes place in parent-child interaction and the formalized learning such as schools provide is a problem area—one which has been misunderstood because we haven't recognized the importance of the knowledges about literacy that children bring to school with them.

We do need to know how to look, though, in order to see these early knowledges. We can learn how to look partly from theory and partly from close observation of children. Such theoretical and empirical attention to the literacy development of young children is increasing with researchers in many countries (see Teale & Sulzby, in press). In the two studies that follow, I looked closely at 24 children as they wrote and read and talked about writing and reading.

Children, Setting, and General Techniques

A kindergarten classroom was selected in which the teacher did not teach writing or reading formally. All children enrolled in the half-day morning session were included. The teacher's goal for the kindergarten year included each child's becoming more mature socially and more confident as an effective individual. The curriculum included much creative artwork, fieldtrips, and play activities designed to give practice to large and small muscle control, singing, dancing, and storybook reading. I chose this kind of classroom, in which children received warm and valuable instruction, but did not receive direct instruction in writing and reading, because I wanted to study the knowledges about written language that the children brought to school with them at an age at which many schools now introduce direct instruction. The hypothesis was that children bring a great deal of knowledge and ability with them, but that it takes a form not recognized by most adults.

For the 2 previous years, I had observed and piloted techniques with children in this teacher's classroom. Subsequently, I conducted a 2-year study (Sulzby, 1983a) of children in this teacher's class that built upon findings of the studies reported in this chapter. I agree with Bronfenbrenner (1979) that we need to understand settings as thoroughly as possible; in that sense, this study was conducted at an early point of my understanding of the setting, but the teacher was well acquainted with me and my assistants and the children were quite accustomed to having us visit their classroom by the time we began the formal studies.

The children were the 24 kindergarteners enrolled in a morning session of one classroom in a school in a northern suburb of Chicago. Children in this suburb come from middle-class and, occasionally, upper middle-class homes in which the standard of living is relatively high and literacy is valued. Although ability and achievement levels are high on the average, each year there is a range of "readiness" characteristics associated with success in formal instruction in reading and writing. Evidence of this range was collected by our own observations, by teacher judgment, by reading readiness test scores, and by children's success in first grade. Part of the evidence in first grade came from groupings for reading, but there was little evidence of differentiated instruction in writing. Subsequent research (Sulzby, 1983a) documented the range of writing ability of the children in first grade as well.

In October the children's average age was 5 years and 4 months (range, 4:11 to 5:10). Thirteen of the children were girls and 11 were boys. Fortunately, all 24 children were present for every session. In addition to these boys and girls, a number of children in the same teacher's afternoon session allowed us to practice our interviewing techniques with them.

In addition to the parents giving their permission in response to a letter from the principal, each child also was asked and agreed to "help" us "learn more about what boys and girls know about reading and writing, even before the teacher teaches you." At one point in the first interview, the examiner expanded this idea: "You have already learned something about writing and reading, things at home and at school. I want you to show me what you can do and tell me about what you know."

In my final report to NCTE I stated: "For each session, an examiner took each child separately to a quiet spot. . . ." Actually, that meant that we were allocated desks and chairs in the hallway outside the kindergarten room. While a stranger to schools might not call the spots quiet, for an elementary school setting we were gloriously protected from the interruptions of announcements, children and adults coming up to ask questions, and from the bustle of 24 active children. Each adult took time to talk with each child, to help put the child at ease and to explain the purpose of the study, including our curiosity about reading and writing described above. We asked the children if they had taperecorders or had used them before (most had) and allowed them to try one out. We told the children that the taperecorder was there because we were interested in "everything we say" and that the taperecorder would help us remember.

The examiners worked together to devise a script to use that would be natural sounding and would elicit cooperation from the children. Each of us worked hard to memorize the wording and to devise alternate encouragements to use. Encouragements were designed to approximate Vygotsky's (1962, 1978) notion of the zone of proximal development in reverse—beginning with a request that the child perform independently, then moving through graduated levels of slightly increased support from the adult. Of particular importance is the encouragement following an increased urging to "try—do it your way." That encouragement was for the children to "pretend," a wording taken from children themselves as reported in Holdaway (1979), Sulzby (1981, 1983a) and others.

Every part of each session was taperecorded and subsequently transcribed and double-checked by the examiner. In addition, for the recordings of Study II, a trained assistant rechecked half of the tapes (containing 44% of the children), taken at random, against the typed protocols. The typed protocols also included the examiner's notes on the child's behavior during the sessions and copies of the children's writing and scribe's dictation, along with records of re-reading and editings. We attempted to keep a complete record of each session, including both child and adult statements and actions.

This section introduces the reasoning behind the two related studies and gives the general techniques we used. In the sections that follow, I will describe each study's rationale, method, and results separately, then I will conclude with ideas and questions of significance that I think these studies contribute to our understanding of emergent literacy.

GENERAL KNOWLEDGES ABOUT WRITTEN LANGUAGE: STUDY I

The first purpose of the structured interview was to find out what the child could already do in writing and reading—to gather actual samples of the child's unaided writing and reading performances. By the child, I actually mean the range of performances that could be found in a kindergarten classroom of this type in the United States. Hence, I include numbers when they are relevant.

The second purpose of the interview was to investigate what the child is beginning to learn about writing and reading. Samples were taken of the child's verbal explanations about things s/he could not yet do or explanations about the conditions under which s/he might be able to perform writing and reading tasks. Kindergarteners are interested in their own growing knowledges and, if approached in an encouraging, candid manner, will volunteer their own explanations. The adults were given scripts which included instructions to encourage the child to "pretend" or to tell what s/he thinks people need to be able to write or read. The adult was to follow the script for the basic interview, and then "to follow the child's lead," adding questions or tasks as needed. However, the adult was instructed not to introduce terms or ideas, but to explore the child's use of these.

The interview was designed to give information about these questions:

1. What can these 5-year-old children write?
2. What can these children read?
3. What do these children say about literacy tasks that they cannot yet perform?
4. How do these children characterize knowing and learning?
5. What do these children know about how to handle books and how one reads books?
6. What literacy-related language terms do these children use and how do they use them?
7. What do these children know about the variables of topic and audience?
8. How do these children perform as conversational partners?

Data collection. Each child was taken from the classroom by an examiner who said casually, while turning to go: "Oh, by the way, why don't you bring along one of your favorite storybooks?" Then the child was taken to a desk in a quiet spot on which the examiner had arranged the taperecorder, unlined ·8½ ″ x 11 ″ paper, fat and skinny pencils without erasers, and a package of crayons. Rapport was established and the taperecorder introduced. Then the examiner proceeded to conduct the "General Knowledges About Written Language" Interview.

The Interview Schedule consisted of six sections:

1. Writing Interview
2. Transition from Writing to Reading
3. Reading Interview (including Book Parts)

4.   Conversation Sample
5.   Prior Knowledge About Real and Make-Believe Stories
6.   Pilot Interview About Child and Adult Audiences

Writing interview.   The Writing Interview was designed to elicit an
actual sample of the writing performance, and metalinguistic and metacognitive explanations about how writing is identified and learned. The child was
also asked questions about how grown-ups write, including verbal descriptions, imitations, and again, metacognitive probing.

I am indebted in part to Clay (1975), Goodman (1980), and Harste,
Burke, and Woodward (1981) for ideas used in creating this section of the
script. One distinction added in this study, however, should be noted. That
distinction was made by asking questions that did not presume that the child
treated *knowledge* and *learning* as synonymous:

HOW DID YOU KNOW WHAT THAT WAS?
HOW DID YOU LEARN THAT?

The questions in the Writing Interview were sequenced so that the examiner could observe the order in which the child added items (see Goodman, 1980) and thus the child's orientation to space and directionality. This
spacing of elicitation also enabled the examiner to hear verbalizations during writing in order to make the use of invented spelling and writing analyses more valid.

Transition from writing to reading.   The purpose of this section of
the interview was to explore the child's metacognitive awareness of reading
and, briefly, the relationship between reading and writing. This transitional
section was used to avoid making the presumption that the child's labelling
of words and other written material during writing was considered by the
child to be instances of reading. The child was told that the examiner knew
s/he had told the examiner what things were during writing but now to re-
read what s/he had written. The examiner was able to observe the order as
well as accuracy and ease with which the child read, whether or not the child
omitted the "pretend grown-up" writing, the child's intonation, and whether
the child was looking at print.

At the end of reading the writing sample, the child was praised ("Hey,
you are getting so that you can read what you write!") then asked questions
about how s/he and other people learn to read, what they need to be able to
read, and why s/he thinks people need whatever s/he said.

Reading interview.   This section of the General Knowledges interview
was designed to tap the child's developing knowledges about reading and, in
particular, about books. It is an adaptation of Goodman and Altwerger's

(1981) Book Handling Task and Clay's (1972) *Concepts About Print* task (*Sand*). The version used in this study asked the child, first, to show the examiner the book and then to read the book to the examiner. (This task has been revised in Sulzby [1983a] to put emphasis on sharing the book as a literary event before encouraging or probing for "naming of parts.")

The purpose of encouraging the child to "show" the book first was to see how s/he interpreted that request. Some children take the request to mean tell about the book, others display the pictures, others begin to read or attempt to read. Some children volunteer names for book parts during their response to the "show" request.

Following the "show" requests, there were two additional script sections which were used if the child did not volunteer the relevant behaviors. First, the child was asked to identify and explain book parts (cover, pages, picture, print) and explain their functions. Second, the child was specifically asked to read the book.

The final three parts of the interview, a conversation sample, and interviews about real and make-believe topics and child and adult audiences, are not presented here. One important finding was that all 24 of the children could identify instances of real and make-believe story lines, could furnish instances, and had background knowledge about learning to ride a big wheel or bike, the topic for Study II's writing tasks.

KNOWLEDGES THE CHILD WRITERS AND READERS DEMONSTRATED

Writing Interview

The writing interview conducted in Study I had two purposes. The first purpose was to describe children's ability to produce and discuss writing. The second purpose was to compare children's writing performance in Study I with their writing performance when asked to write stories in Study II. The interview consisted of a writing sample and an interview about knowing and learning.

Writing sample.   Children were asked to produce and label anything they could write. Thus the child could control the task demands. There was one exception to this "basic competency level" and that was the request for a description and imitation of grown-up writing, but even in this task the expectation was established that the child was describing the behavior of someone else.

The writing sample data may be summarized around these questions:

1. What did the child write in response to the examiner's request?
2. What did the child call the writing or say about the writing and/or the task?
3. How did the child incorporate new resources?

4. How did the child respond to a task outside his/her current competency?
5. How did the child structure the writing on the paper?

Three scorers examined the protocols from Study I, and summarized answers to these five questions for each child. The results were then tallied.

What children wrote and said about writing. The most frequent response to the question, "What can you write?" is a prompt, energetic, and confident reply: "My name." Tallying across questions one and two, 22 of the 24 children wrote their names. Additionally, one other child added his name voluntarily at the end of the session. The final child was able to write his name and did so on direct request.

Children described this more frequent piece of writing by appropriate terminology. The most frequent description was to pronounce the name itself ("Jason" or "Irene Walsey") or to say "That's my name." Nineteen children used this form of description and three others were slightly more technical, including language about language (metalanguage): (a) "my name in *writing*," (b) "my name," then child said last four of six letters by letter name, spelling while writing, and (c) "the *letters* in my name."

The children wrote a number of other things besides their own names. These offerings could be described as discrete units rather than compositions intended as texts (in contrast to Study II). Children wrote the names of other people, other individual words, the alphabet (in whole or part), individual letters, or their telephone number. Two children drew pictures. Of the 24 children, 13 produced these additional responses. The following is a display of descriptions of the products and the children's verbal labels.

Child	Writing	Label
#4	An upper-case letter	"R"
#5	Alphabet, in sequence	"the whole alphabet in small letters," "T-V-V-W-X-Y-Z"
#7	A word list consisting of cat, sat, do, doe, dog, hat, mat, rap	Called words by names.
#8	Cat, hat	Called words by names.
#11	Telephone number in numerals	"My telephone number"
#12	Drew picture and wrote names	"Pictures and names"
#13	Drew a face	"a face"
#14	Numerous letters	Called by letter names
#15	Full alphabet in upper-case	Sang the alphabet song
#17	love	"I love you" "L, O, V, and E"
#20	R, F	"An R and a F"
#21	Telephone number in numerals, gun, exit	"My telephone number," "gun," "a gun," "exit" "E-X-I-T"
#23	Alphabet in upper case, dog, cat	"A-B-C...Z" "dog and cat" "D-O-G-C-A-T"

Incorporation of new resources.   For the request, "what can you write?" children produced items they could write in conventional English orthography. They used conventional and accurate verbal labels for these offerings. This is in contrast to the new resources they incorporate when the tasks they attempt become more demanding, as in Study II, and in the request to show the examiner how grown-ups write. For questions one and two, only one child produced what might have been an invented spelling. The child said he was writing God. The production could come from sound-letter matches or from attempting to remember a visual array.

   Tasks outside current competency.   As mentioned above, children did incorporate new resources when a more difficult task was set for them. Question three asked: "How do grown-ups write? Show me (pretend)." This task was treated as a reasonable question by the children, but it clearly required them to call upon new physical and verbal resources. Two children had improper elicitation probes for question three, and both children refused to try the task. Of the 22 with proper elicitations, only two (9%) refused the task.

   The responses show that children had abstracted features of adult writing and could imitate cursive writing, incorporating those features. (This ability to imitate script was then used as a resource by some children in Study II.)

   What was the nature of children's attempts to "write like grown-ups do"? Nine children produced scribble-like forms. (One child produced a scribble-like motion in the air but refused to do it on paper.) Four children (including two of the nine scribblers) produced letter-like joined forms. Three other children were able to produce elements of actual cursive writing. Five children produced variations, four of which were explained as reasonable by the child. For example, one child had written letters randomly spaced over the page as samples of his own writing. For grown-up writing, he wrote six uppercase letters in a line together like a word and said: "They write in a line." One other child gave a stylistic distinction; grown-ups write his formal first name whereas he writes his nickname. Two other children wrote lower case letters or smaller letters for grown-up writing as compared to their own larger writing. Only one production was not easily interpretable as showing features abstracted from adult writing. The product looked like a triangle. The child's label ("a triangle") did not aid the interpretation and she did not respond to other probes.

   What was the nature of children's attempts to describe grown-up writing? In addition to the brief examples given above, children used three major labels for adult writing: "scribble," "script," or "cursive." These responses were given by 10 children, and 9 children gave other responses all related to features of adult writing.

The "other" responses included saying grown-ups write like the examiner who actually was writing in cursive during the interview. Two children said grown-ups write "just like you" or "like you write." Two children commented on the continuity or linearity of adult writing: "when you do it all together" and "they write in a line." Two children commented on the size and/or form of letter differences: "they write with little letters," and "they write in little letters and big letters."

The ability to abstract features from writing that is in advance of the current competency level is thus seen in two areas. Children could physically form these features with their pencils and they are able to describe these features verbally.

Structuring of the page. Children had been given a sheet of 8½ " x 11 " unlined paper. The purpose of this kind of paper was to observe what knowledges children would display about the directionality and spacing of writing. Twenty-three of the 24 children were assessed in this way. One child was erroneously allowed two pieces of paper and wrote one entry on each page, thus directionality and spacing could not be described.

Only one child seemed to place items at random on the page. Most children (15) wrote items top to bottom; two additional children wrote primarily top to bottom. Three wrote bottom to top and two others added some items to the top.

In addition to the direction in which items were placed, children were able to display their knowledge about how items get joined and separated. In this interview, children did not produce sentences and larger texts. Children's structuring choices were either to display items in columns (16), lines (3), both columns and lines (3), or randomly (1 child).

In summary, children showed a level of basic, conventional competency both in performance and in verbal description. The emergence of any aspect of conventional performance is important. Hildreth (1936) has traced children's natural acquisition of name writing and has shown that they abstract features of their own name long before they master the conventional form. More recently, Simner (1981) has documented the pervasiveness of natural patterns in letter-printing acquisition even in the face of direct teaching of other systems. When natural acquisition from the literacy culture evolves toward the adult convention, an important new kind of baseline is established.

This new conventional baseline and the baselines of natural acquisitions are both important complementary parts of a description of acquisition. Thus we pushed the children above their conventional limits. When pressed above their current level of conventional performance, children call upon new resources that they have abstracted from the written language they see used around them. The contents of the new resources consist both of written performance itself and of verbal description of this performance. Part of the written performance extension of resources is evident in Study I. Study II presents more evidence. The next section will discuss aspects of children's verbal description.

Interview about knowing and learning. Two questions were designed to explore the child's understanding of his/her own knowledge and learning about writing.

HOW DID YOU KNOW WHAT THAT WAS?
HOW DID YOU LEARN THAT?

The questions were asked after each request for the child to write (questions 1 and 2). Later, in the optional parts of question 3, the child could have been asked how grown-ups learned to write. This third question was inserted to compare the child's understanding of his/her own learning with that of older members of the literate society.

Children attribute their learning both to other people, to their own efforts and knowledge states, and to things in the environment. The behavior of children agrees with the retrospective literature on early reading and writing (Clark, 1976; Durkin, 1966) in that they think they learned to write by being taught by relatives, particularly by their mother or both parents.

All 24 children answered these questions. Nineteen of these children (79%) mentioned other people as teachers or providers of help. Mother was mentioned alone by eight children; both parents by six; and mom in combination with other relatives, by 16 children. Friends were mentioned twice and a teacher only once. It is possible that two other children intended references to teachers, but they only mentioned "my other school" and "learned at school."

Of the five children who did not specifically mention people other than themselves, three mentioned specific cultural artifacts and agents associated with literacy: the ABC's, the alphabet, my other school, TV, knowing how to spell. Two children gave vague answers: "I just learned," "just did," and "fooling around." These latter answers were also used by other children and may refer to mental activities like thinking, puzzling, discovery, and so forth, about which children do not typically talk.

While the children did refer to other people as teaching them, particularly parents, they also attributed learning to their own efforts and knowledge states. Fourteen of the 24 mentioned their own efforts as contributing to their learning. They mentioned copying, learning the alphabet, "practice," wanting to know and asking someone, spelling, and "learning myself." Six children described their knowledge states as "just knowing" and two further specified that they knew because they could read what they wrote.

Some of the children distinguished between knowing and learning; others did not. Data mentioned above combines answers to both questions. Here is an example of how children treated the two questions as being different and requiring different answers.

One girl explained that her mother taught her and that her own maturation and effort were important as well:

Question 1—
  HOW DID YOU KNOW WHAT THAT WAS?
    My mom taught me.
    I wanted to know how my name was in writing.
  HOW DID YOU LEARN THAT?
    Well, I copied it sort of.

Question 2—
  HOW DID YOU KNOW WHAT THAT WAS?
    Cause I am a growing girl.
  HOW DID YOU LEARN THAT?
    It just takes practice.

Seventeen of the children were asked the optional question about how grown-ups learned to write. Nine children attributed the learning of grown-ups to parents as well. Only three children mentioned school as a source of grown-ups' knowledge. Four children said they did not know how grown-ups learned and one child gave an unprobed, irrelevant response. There was a tendency for children to attribute their own learning strategies to grown-ups. There was a real discrepancy in only two cases; children who said grown-ups learned in school, but they themselves learned from parents.

Transition From Writing to Reading

Each child was asked to re-read what s/he had written in entirety, as a separate act of reading. All of the children were able to perform this task with ease and were praised for learning to read what they could write.

The children were then quizzed about how they and other people learned to read and what people need so that they can read. Once again the children mentioned other people as sources of help. The response categories were similar to those for writing. When responses were classified by primary reason, 11 children gave other people as the source of learning to read. "School" was mentioned by only three children. Five children mentioned their own efforts alone. Two children said they did not know the answer and one simply said, "I don't know. With a pencil."

Many of the explanations contained combinations of sources. Here is a combination answer that stresses the child's own efforts:

Well, first you have to start to memorize, then you have to look real hard and then you know all those other things, and then pretty soon you'll start to read.

In this example, interaction between people over books involving parts of the effort is outlined lucidly by the child:

Sometimes they sound out the letters and sometimes people read them to them. They just read them and whoever is listening to the book can learn how to read by just the letters.

The results of the Transition from Writing to Reading Interview can be compared with the name writing results from the Writing Interview. Both present evidence that adult-like, conventional performance is already capable at some point for all of these 5-year-old children. They have both feature-like emerging abilities and a point of conventional performance as acquisitional baselines. Thus it can be argued that their concepts of reading and writing contain aspects of natural acquisition and also of the conventional model they are moving toward.

Reading Interview

In the Reading Interview children were asked to display their knowledge about book parts (cover, page, print, picture) and their purposes. They were also asked to read any part that they could of a favorite book. I am going to give only an overview of the results for two reasons. First, our work in 1979-80 was exploratory. The examiners were concerned with not frustrating the children and did not yet have good techniques to encourage children to press their limits. Second, our subsequent work has shown that children's performances were much richer if the storybook reading was first and if the examiner responded to it solely as a sharing of literature.

Book parts.   All children in this study picked up and oriented their chosen book correctly and distinguished most parts functionally. Overall, their labels and explanations for book parts were quite good. Children seem to prefer some labels over others. For example, book *covers* are more often called the *front* of the book; first *pages* are often called the *starting*. Often, labels were hard to elicit until after the child mentioned the function. A few children said *pages* were "for writing on," or "for the pictures to be written on." These responses might be early cues that children are aware that books have authors.

Storybook reading.   When we asked children to re-read their favorite books we found that the attempts seemed to fall into categories which I have developed more fully in subsequent studies (Sulzby, 1983a, 1983b, in press-b; see also Sulzby & Otto, 1982). The subsequent studies indicate that children's reading attempts can be ordered developmentally in ways that show their growing awareness of distinctions between oral and written language. The current study served as pilot data for the subsequent work.

Below I give three examples to illustrate these behaviors. First is a child who refused to read but explained his concept of reading. Second is an example of a reading in oral or *telling* language, and third is a version filled with book-like language.

The child who refused to read explained how he would be able to read when he got older and also that he could read *some* things now. He seemed to be focusing on what memory for text furnishes the beginner.

> If I were in first grade it would be a little cincher, like a friend of mine is. You already—I know how I learned to read. First I just have to listen to people read. Then [I] can remember it and then [I] can read it. That's how I learned to read—I can read lots of books of my own at home. (Later he mentioned *Curiour George*.)

The second example is from a child who was classified as using *telling* language. In this sample, she appears to be already at a point where her *telling* is the creation of a textual entity with clear awareness of the examiner as an audience. She began to "read" with very little urging:

> (Rapid speech) One day the mother told them to go out and teach them how to swim. The other ducks went in the water and took water—and the mother duck went in with the other ducks swimming—and the seven little ducks—and the other ducks went in the water and watched the other ducks—and the mother said, "You have to go out there and try to swim with the other little ducks."

> Well, he did one day with his mother and he did it, but when the mother took the other ducks to the shore and it dived for a fish, the mother dived in to help, and the six little ducks dived, but the seventh little duck didn't dive, and, um, and then they said, "It's time to go up from the river and go to sleep." So they went to sleep and the next morning they said to the seventh little duck, "Sorry, you'll have to leave because you're not ready." And they left. And an apple dropped right on him and he went under the water and the mother and father got him back and then they learned how to dive. Finished.

This *telling language* label may become clearer when compared with a child who uses *book language,* or phrases rarely heard in normal speech (see Cazden, 1983; Holdaway, 1979). Below I have underlined book-like phrases.

This girl also paused between "sentences" and turned the pages as if reading.

> Once there was a girl named Peggy and she found a penny. She put the penny in a gumball machine but she didn't get, get a penny, a gumball, she got a shiny ring. She wanted it, she wondered if the shiny would come off if she rubbed it. She rubbed it and the thunders came out as loud as she ever heard. Peggy—but soon appeared a little boy angel. "Who are you?" asked Peggy. "I am a little boy angel. I am here to grant you one wish." "I thought it was supposed to be sweet and everything," said Peggy. "Well, I can leave you one wish." (Then the child told the examiner she couldn't do any more.)

These results showed us that these 24 children were quite accustomed to handling, talking about, and "reading" the kinds of commercial storybooks available in their classroom. They were eager to attempt to deal with these storybooks and seemed to choose a "favorite" without trouble. They indicated to me at that time that storybook reading was a rich avenue to explore with kindergarten children. Since the time of the study, research in storybook reading has grown in richness and quantity (Cochran-Smith, 1984; Doake, 1981; Heath, 1982; Otto, 1984; Snow & Ninio, in press, Sulzby, 1983a, 1983b, in press-a, in press-b; also see Sulzby & Teale, 1983; Taylor, in press; Teale, 1982).

The overall results of Study I show clearly that many kindergarteners enter school with a wide and complex range of knowledges and abilities as writers and readers. What they know and how they use what they know do not appear to match expectations of typical school "readiness" tests and programs, however. In Study II, the evidence becomes clearer when we ask the children to perform more relevant writing and reading tasks.

REAL AND MAKE-BELIEVE STUDY PRODUCTIONS: STUDY II

The purpose of Study II was to examine children's story productions, explanations, and behaviors when asked to "write a story." A further purpose was to examine children's abilities to re-read and edit their own stories. Three basic modes of composition (telling, dictating, and writing) were used in order to examine oral and written language distinctions made by kindergarten children.

Two topic variations (real and make-believe) were used. The children had been interviewed in Study I about both the basic topic "learning to ride a big wheel," and the notions of real and make-believe contents in stories. Thus we were assured that the children had sufficient background knowledge for us to detect effects of the distinction between real and make-believe.

This study began my exploration of topic effects both upon writing and upon children's ability to re-read their own compositions. Topic effects upon writing should affect the comprehensibility of the text both in terms of information included in the text and in general decontextualization or provision of intra-text context. Topic effects upon re-reading should be evidenced in the degree of stability between the child's dictation and writing (or words said during writing) and the re-reading attempts.

This study was designed to explore the validity of the speculations about topic effects. It was also designed to yield data that could be analyzed in numerous ways. Some of the analyses that follow the children's distinctions between oral and written language, others focus upon the real and make-believe contrast, and others combine both sets of distinctions. All of the analyses are subsumed by the purpose of describing kindergarten children as writers and readers.

For the story collection sessions, three language productions were obtained from each child: a told story, a dictated story, and a handwritten story. Additionally, samples of re-reading and editing were gathered for each of the two written versions. The six possible orders of telling, dictating, and writing were counterbalanced and assigned to subjects at random, with re-reading and editing following dictating and writing whenever they appeared in the order. Real and make-believe story topics were assigned at random across the two sessions and coordinated with the mode orders as well. Thus there were 12 orders with two children assigned to each order; children had the same order across the two sessions.

The examiner asked the child in each session "to write a story for me." An abbreviated version of the directions are given below:

General directions	I WANT YOU TO WRITE A STORY FOR ME. WE WILL DO IT THREE WAYS. NOW I KNOW YOU DON'T REALLY KNOW HOW TO WRITE LIKE A GROWN-UP YET BUT YOU KNOW A LOT ABOUT WRITING. I'LL HELP YOU.
Telling	ONE OF THE THINGS PEOPLE DO TO WRITE A STORY IS TO TELL IT TO SOMEONE FROM THE BEGINNING TO THE END TO BE SURE THEY HAVE IT THE WAY THEY WANT IT TO BE. THAT'S WHAT I WANT YOU TO DO NOW. TELL ME YOUR STORY, YOUR WHOLE STORY FROM BEGINNING TO END...(Story directions)
Dictation	ONE OF THE THINGS PEOPLE CAN DO TO WRITE A STORY IS TO LET SOMEONE ELSE

WRITE IT DOWN FOR THEM. THAT'S LIKE
HAVING A SECRETARY. WE CALL IT *DIC-
TATING* WHEN YOU TELL YOUR STORY AND
SOMEONE ELSE WRITES IT DOWN FOR YOU. I
WANT YOU TO DICTATE YOUR STORY FOR ME
THIS TIME...(Story directions)

Writing   SOMETIMES WHEN PEOPLE WRITE A STORY
THEY DO THE WRITING ON PAPER ALL BY
THEMSELVES. EVEN LITTLE BOYS AND GIRLS
CAN WRITE THEIR OWN STORIES. YOU CAN
WRITE YOUR OWN STORY FOR ME YOUR
OWN WAY. IT DOESN'T HAVE TO BE JUST
LIKE GROWN-UP WRITING. YOU CAN JUST
DO IT YOUR OWN WAY. NOW I WANT YOU TO
WRITE YOUR STORY...(Story directions)

The story directions were inserted into each of the three mode directions. The directions to tell, dictate, or write were then reiterated. The story
directions asked alternatively for real and make-believe topics. The topic
variation is shown within parentheses.

Story directions   I WANT YOU TO TELL ME YOUR STORY (DIC-
TATE YOUR STORY TO ME, WRITE ME YOUR
STORY) AND IT'S A REAL (MAKE-BELIEVE)
STORY ABOUT YOU (LITTLE PRINCE/PRIN-
CESS CHARMING) AND HOW YOU (S/HE)
LEARNED HOW TO RIDE A BIG WHEEL:
   ABOUT HOW YOU (S/HE) LEARNED TO RIDE
   A BIG WHEEL.
   WHAT MADE YOU (HER/HIM) WANT TO DO
   IT,
   AND HOW YOU (S/HE) DID IT.

Directions for re-reading were simple:

Re-reading directions   GOOD JOB. NOW I WANT YOU TO READ BACK
YOUR STORY TO SEE IF IT IS JUST LIKE YOU
WANT IT TO BE.

If the child protested that s/he could not read, the examiner said she could
help the child and asked what help was wanted. If the child did not specify
the kind of help but still said s/he couldn't read, the examiner initiated
choral-reading and used fading techniques to deterine if the child could use
memory for text to continue without the examiner's help.

Editing could occur in a number of ways. The child could make voluntary changes during or following composition. All voluntary editing was

recorded. Additionally, two kinds of questions were used to encourage editing that the child wanted or could do. Editing in this sense was taken to indicate that the child treated the text as an entity and could be reflected upon and manipulated. The first probed editing asked the child to make judgments of desirability, and the second part probed for possible changes in these three aspects of reading: word stability, letter/sound relationships, and comprehension. Only the first editing directions are given here.

Editing directions   IS THE STORY JUST THE WAY YOU WANT IT? HOW ABOUT THIS PART? IS IT LIKE YOU WANT IT? WHY? HOW ELSE COULD YOU HAVE MADE IT?

Each examiner was instructed to observe the child's reactions to the directions and to note any deviations from the suggested procedures that were used, either at the child's or adult's instigation. The sections that follow examine children's writings and readings and what they said and did in writing and reading situations.

COMPARISONS OF REAL AND MAKE-BELIEVE STORIES WITHIN AND ACROSS MODES

Introduction

We can look for children's knowledges about written language in multitudes of ways long before they are writing and reading conventionally. I have divided my "looks" into five categories of inequal length and detail. In the first set of results, Children's Knowledges About Writing, I will focus on the children's handwritten stories, particularly upon the way orthographic forms, re-reading attempts, and comments during and about the storywriting task inform us about what the children know about writing and reading. In this section, I will also make comparisons with the children's writing in Study I.

The second section is an analysis of the children's emerging ability to read from their own compositions, comparing and combining their re-reading of dictation and written stories. The third and fourth sections emphasize distinctions and adaptations that children make between the modes of conversation, telling, dictating, and writing.

The fifth section is composed of three closely related analyses of the content and structure of the transcripts of told and dictated stories. This section includes the most direct contrasts between the real and make-believe topic variation included in this chapter. The first contrast involves adult readers' judgments about the overall comprehensibility of the children's stories as pieces of "autonomous" discourse. The second analysis concentrates on specific means by which children can re-create a context for the reader/listener. The final analysis is an examination of semantic/structural properties of the stories, using an adaptation of story grammar techniques. The section concludes with examples in which children's success or failure in distinguishing between real and make-believe appears quite evident on the surface of the typed transcripts.

Throughout the five sections, I have liberally used examples of the performances of the 24 kindergarteners. In this way, the "data base" of emergent literacy examples that I examined can be used by the reader to make judgments about the adequacy or inadequacy of the techniques I used. Researchers may use these examples to devise new research approaches and teachers may use them to devise better diagnostic techniques to use in teaching young writers and readers.

Children's Knowledges About Writing

Three questions about the children's handwritten compositions are addressed in this section: (a) What knowledges do these 5-year-old children have about how compositions get written? (b) How do children choose to write a composition, given the knowledges they have available to them? (c) What do children reveal in their writing about their concepts about authors, audiences, and reading? While the focus of this section is primarily upon the mechanics, broadly conceived, of composition, it will be clear that we cannot understand the form separated from the communicative intent of the composer.

While the primary data used here are the two handwritten story attempts from Study II, including things the children said during composition and re-reading attempts, the Writing Interview data from Study I are also used in order to make comparisons across tasks. To add to the broader descriptive analysis, the writing data from both studies were categorized by three independent judges, with final agreement reached through discussion. These categories were used: use of page space, word boundaries, directionality, graphic representation (scribble, joined letter-like forms, elements of actual cursive script, drawing, printed letters), composition representation (conventional, invented spelling, other), production style (speed, vocalization, pauses), editing (voluntary, general, elicited), and re-reading.

Knowledges about how compositions get written. Clay (1975) and others (Bissex, 1980; Ferreiro & Teberosky, 1982; Goodman, 1980; Graves, 1983; Gundlach, 1982; Read, 1975) have documented aspects of children's early writing attempts. Much of this evidence concerns the use of inventive writing systems. However, in Study I we noted that these children used both conventional spelling and letters as their overwhelming choice when asked,

"What can you write?" I consider these children to have at least some conventional writing in their repertoire; this took the form of names and isolated known words, numerals, letters, and letter sequences such as parts of the alphabet.

Furthermore, when the children were pressed to go beyond their conventional resources in Study I, they demonstrated that they could imitate grown-up writing in certain ways. In Study I, however, they showed no evidence of trying to compose a text.

In Study II, we asked the children to compose stories. The demand was increased from a request to write anything they wanted to a demand to create a whole text. Additionally, the children were given a specific topic, albeit a familiar one. For these children, this demand meant that they had to deal with a task outside their conventional resources. In Study II, we found the range of writing systems reported by other researchers such as Ferreiro and Teberosky (1982). I believe, however, that these writing systems are part of a many-featured repertoire, not a strictly developmental sequence. Indeed, children seemed to fall back on lower-level knowledges in order to accomplish a higher-level goal. I will discuss this further in the next section when I present examples from the children's stories.

Among the kinds of knowledges that children have is the knowledge that you can refuse to write. If you have a notion of what a task demands, you can assess whether or not you can do it. These children all knew conventional written graphics and spelling for at least one word, their own name (see also Ferreiro & Teberosky, 1982). They could compare their ability to write their name to the task of writing a story and could say: "I can't do that."

Even the child who refused, though, knew that s/he could imitate or pretend about writing beyond his or her conventional knowledge. The children had demonstrated that in imitating grown-up writing. An expectation might be that all of the children would simply use an imitation cursive.

The children, in fact, showed a far greater range of knowledges. They knew that writing is connected to other forms of representation. Some children choose to draw their story, or to talk about writing a story, explaining how they might do it. Other children used writing-like forms, such as scribbling or separated curved forms. Others used strings of letters or name elements to stand for their stories. Still others used invented spelling systems, varying from one letter to stand for one syllable, to non-exclusive spelling where one graph may exist simultaneously in two syllables, or exclusive, sequential spellings of the kind Read (1970) and Beers and Henderson (1977) have described. Some vocalized while writing and others did not. A few children used a number of conventional spellings and/or enlisted the examiner as an informant.

One important finding, no matter what knowledges the children used or in what task order the writing request occurred, was that children tended not to write long compositions. Most stopped before completing the composition as compared with their storytelling, dictation, or verbalized intention, including re-reading. Writing required effort and the 5-year-old children told adults about it: "Whew! That's all I can do!" So the knowledge they all implied was: compositions get written with effort.

How children chose to write compositions. The knowledges described above were used by the children in writing their stories. In the description that follows, I will give examples in an order that seems to start from the form most removed from conventional English alphabetic orthography and move to the most conventional writing. However, I must stress that these examples do not indicate a strict developmental sequence. In some instances, the child seems to be using what might be considered an underlying conceptualization (see Ferreiro & Teberosky, 1982), but in others the child appears to be using a lower-level resource in order to accomplish a more complex task. We must also remember that the children all had some conventional spelling and writing in their repertoire. Ferreiro and Teberosky (1982) note that holding such disparate knowledges may lead the child to conflicts which will force reorganization of the conceptual system concerning writing systems and literacy. Since our interviewing techniques are so different, I cannot address the issue of whether these children could be said to have one underlying conceptualization that could be placed sequentially. From the data (the patterns of which have since been replicated [Sulzby, 1983a], it appears that even the children who used lower-level writing forms were fairly certain that "real writing" was different. In particular, note the first two examples in which children drew for their story.

Figures 1–10 come from nine of the 24 children and other children are discussed in the text so that the variety of writing forms can be examined. The examples fall into these categories, again with the warning that the categories are not to be taken as a developmental ordering: writing via drawing; writing via "scribbling"; writing via letter-like forms; writing via well-learned units (such as name elements or alphabetic strings); writing via "invented spelling" (approximately one graph per syllable; non-discrete or overlapping letters; discrete and exclusive units, both with conventional or non-conventional use of word-boundaries); and writing as conventional English orthography. In order to give as many examples as possible, I have abbreviated the discussion whenever I felt it would not detract from understanding.

Of the 24 children, only one child, a boy, completely refused to attempt to write in both sessions of this study. He took part in all other parts of the study, including editing his dictation. He had written his own name and *mom* in Study I. He had described grown-up writing as *scribble* but refused to try it on paper. His only explanations for refusing in Study II were statements that he couldn't write and that he was tired. The examiner thought he might cry in the first session and that he was giving exaggerated almost-fake yawns in the second session. The possible significance of these yawns should not be overlooked, however. Writing was his last assigned task. We observed children yawning and giving other signs of fatigue and effort during writing attempts, even when they refused to stop when we suggested it. As mentioned earlier, writing requires effort and kindergarteners are well aware of that.

Writing via drawing. The first two examples (see Figures 1 and 2) come from children who offered drawings for writing. (Both children had the same examiner and same task order with writing first.) While children see books that contain both printed text and pictures and the two representations typically are combined to "tell a story," I believe that children's use of drawing for writing is not just a simple confusion of contiguous experiences. From evidence in both writing tasks and in reading tasks such as storybook reading attempts (Sulzby, in press-b), I have found evidence that the children take an approach which is Vygotskiian, treating both drawing and writing as related forms to represent intended meanings.

Figure 1.   Luanne

Figure 2.   Bethany (Retraced in crayon)

Children do not typically maintain that drawing *is* writing (Ferreiro & Teborosky, 1982; Harste, Burke, & Woodward, 1981) but they often reveal ambivalence or perhaps simply the inability to explain the relationship clearly. Vygotsky (1978) considered pretend-play with objects, gestures, drawing, and writing to be progressive abstractions away from real-life events. He described children's speech during drawing as often sounding as if the pictures were evolving. Thus Luanne's speech, the text following Figure 1, is a fairly mature example; she seems to have a theme of the picture pretty clearly in mind while she draws, even though her speech indicates an evolving story. (Other children use both "evolving picture" speech as well as evolving story speech.)

Luanne's language while composing:
I gotta make the person.
(Okay.)
He's low—that down there
    is nose.
(Okay.)
Now. (4 second pause) That's criss-cross. (2 second pause) That stuff comes
    out of—(3 seconds)—He's bleeding.
(Oh, he is?)
Here's the hot cap.
This one. (Pointing.)
That one's all the way back here.
(Uh-huh.)
Now here's (mumbled) and there's the (mumbled).
Okay, has to have square windows.
He's just leaving.
He's just leaving his home.
He's running away.
I should say driving away.
Now let's see, here's a good door.
It's a two-story house.
There's land (Repeated in response to adult's "what?")
Here's the grass.
This is a bumpy board.
Of course, he's riding on the grass!
There's a little weed growing there.
(A little weed?)
Yeah, I mean a little—yeah,
    it's a little weak—just a little weed
    growing down in the grass.
Oh the house we don't have to
    make a thing.
(No grass under the house?)

Mm-hm. Let's make the mud and the gook
  and the mud and the gook
  and the gook and the mud and the gook.
(Okay, that's a good job. Your story done now?)
Un-huh.

When Luanne was asked, she re-read without hesitation. During the
first two sentences (marked thus because of her sentence-final intonation),
she looked at the picture and spoke deliberately. Then she looked up in the
air and her intonation shifted into a more conversational tone. Notice how
her wording deteriorates, as if she's editing the verbal output in mid-sen-
tence. Nevertheless, the "read" story maintains past tense and recaptures
the ideas expressed actively during her composition.

Luanne's re-reading:
Once upon a time there was
  a little kid.
He was running away.
And he was—he wasn't very running away
because his mom wanted him to run away
and his dad wanted him to run away.
And he—boy—all the way out.
and they all went—his people. (Long pause.)
(Okay. All right.)
They have—they have kids too.
They have two other kids.

Bethany's story (Figure 2) isn't as poignant as Luanne's. Nor is her
speech during drawing as revealing about the story she eventually re-reads.
However, she is used as an illustration because she reveals the ambivalence
that I have found many children to seem to hold about whether drawing (a
picture) can be writing. Eventually, however, she states fairly clearly that
drawing is an alternative resource.

Bethany began by attempting a conversational response to the "write"
request. When pressed to write, she refused and negotiated a drawing.

Bethany's speech during drawing:
I can't write.
(Try.)
Well, I'll make a picture.
I can't draw very well
  but here's one wheel....
  (She continued labelling till the end.)
I can't make my body.

(How's that?
That's a nice drawing.
Have you written your story?)
This is a picture.
(Is it writing a story?)
Yeah.
(It is? How is it that
    it's writing a story?)
It's a picture.
(Is that the same thing
    as writing a story?)
Yeah.
(How come?)
Well, because, you know, sometimes
    you can't write things like grown-ups so
    you have to make a picture

Writing via scribbling. Paul wrote the lines of scribble in Figure 3 from top to bottom, left to right. He recited a story both while composing and re-reading.

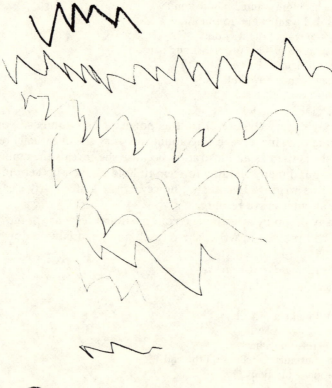

Figure 3.   Paul

Another child, Clifford (not shown), used a form similar to scribble that was somewhat unusual. The most impressive part of his system was that it *sounded* like adult, fluent writing to the examiner. He "wrote" left-to-right, top-to-bottom, making semi-circularish marks, rapidly. He used a slender pencil and made two distinctive sounds on paper. He struck the paper with a staccato-like impact, then made an emphatic writing-like sound while he formed the shapes. He filled three pages, then went back and struck the second paper with the pencil near the bottom between two of the marks. When asked what that was, he said it was "a dot," "to split the word," "when it comes to make a new word."

This was Clifford's second written story. In the first story he had refused to write anything except his conventional repertoire, similar to Study I: his name, his telephone number in numerals, and *no*. Both of his told and dictated stories were long, conversational, and complicated, yet he finally resolved one into a well-formed complex story. His concept for reading involved speed; he said that when he could read he would be able to go *vroom* over the lines. I speculate that Clifford was working on making the low-level processes work as fast as his ideas and that slowing-down would be an important step for him both in learning to write and read.

Writing via letter-like forms. Brant (Figure 4) refused to write, saying he could only write his name. He then asked to copy his dictated story. When urged, he sat quietly as if thinking, then picked up a red crayon and began to create these letter-like forms. He did not vocalize during writing, but recited a story for the re-reading attempt while looking at the examiner. When asked to name the letters later, he said he did not know what they were. (Typically, letter-like forms do not resemble conventional formations to the detail that Brant's letters do.)

Writing via well-learned elements. This is a pattern that I have subsequently found a number of times even with children who are reading from conventional print (Sulzby 1983a). The child may use some well-learned sequence, such as elements of his or her name and re-order them to create either "new words" or new undivided strings. Jessica (Figure 5)[3] used name elements and Eddy (Figure 6) used elements from the alphabet, along with some known or figured-out letters and some notion of matching "length" of sound to print. Eddy did a lot of voicing during composition, including evidence of keeping track of a gradually emerging sentence. He also elicited aid from the adult by asking for precise information: "I need—he made—he made—he made—umm-uh, need an "E.""

---

[3]To preserve anonymity and still use writing samples from real children, I have substituted a sample from a different child collected as part of a different study. Jessica's example differs from the child in this study in that she uses alphabetic strings as well as name elements.

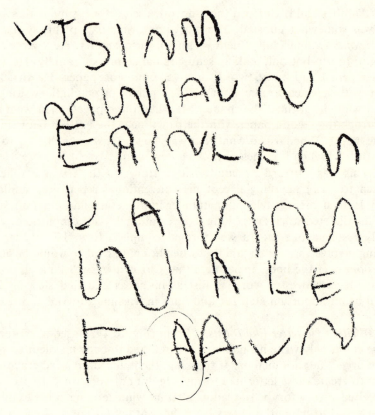

Figure 4.   Brant

Writing via "invented spelling."   Since Read's (1970) and Chomsky's (1970) research, many researchers have documented children's use of phonetically-based "invented" or "inventive" spelling. We have found that many kindergarten children can and do spell in this manner, far more than the early research would suggest and perhaps less than some more recent accounts would imply. Children do indeed use invented spelling when writing, but it appears in many forms and is augmented by other ways of writing as shown in the examples and figures.

In one of the least mature forms of invented spelling, children use approximately one letter per "syllable" (Ferreiro & Teberosky, 1982). In pilots and in subsequent work, we have found a few examples of children using one letter per "syllable." However, in this study I found only one example that could even vaguely be described as one letter per syllable. In rereading with pointing, Beegie seemed to stretch his finger pointing out to match each letter; however, the letters were not phonetically appropriate, except twice (*my* and *big*). His composition and voicing indicated that he

Figure 5. Jessica

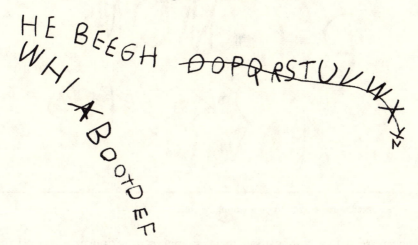

Figure 6. Eddy

157

was probably aware of the match between *my* and M. He wrote, right to left and backward:

His re-reading, with elongation on the initial *M*'s, sounded as if he were using letter-sound knowledge: "Mmmmy mmmom—bought mmme a big big wheel," even though most of the spoken units did not match phonetic, nor phonemic, features of the graphs. His second story led me to believe he was working on phonetically-based notions above, because he wrote

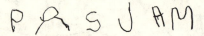

These letters were intended as the two words "Prince Charming," left to right, and are in quite full invented spelling. *PRS* captures the major consonantal sounds of *Prince*. *J* is closely related to *Ch* as shown by Read's (1975) experimental studies of speech sounds in English, while *JAM* as a unit is a full rendition of the first syllable of *Charming*.

A more mature form of one letter per syllable can be seen in the example below, but in this instance Arlene is indicating both knowledge of word boundaries and knowledge that the letters only "stand for" fuller spellings. This is Arlene's second story; in her first story she had used full invented spelling with no spaces between words.

[a] Retraced in red crayon to omit editing by child.

She re-read this composition in telegraphese, tracking print, as "Prince Charming. ($\mathcal{L}$ = J; compare with Beggie's JAM.) Mom helped. (Dictated as *owned*.) King owned castle. (KO) A nest laid." Her oral stories sounded like stories from a basal reading series or like abortive attempts to use literary language.

Arlene, Dictation:

> Prince Charming's dad helped to learn how to ride a big wheel. The owner of the palace was Prince Charming. A nest laid in a tree in the palace. The end.

In the examples shown in Figures 7–10, children who are using invented spellings show complex notions of how spacing and orthography relate. Only by watching and listening to the composing session would another person understand some of these examples. Alison (Figure 7) appears to have written nonsense; however, she reads it as:

Once	(YOWS in line 1; the W in 1a was crossed out for the /ʌ / in *upon*)
/ʌ / (of	(line 2 which was actually composed as /pɔ n/,
upon)	the second half of upon; evidently, she treated the crossed out syllable as if it still counted)
pon	(line 3, PWN)
a	(line 4, although both WT in 3a and WA in 4 were written as /ʌ /)
time	(line 4a, tiM)

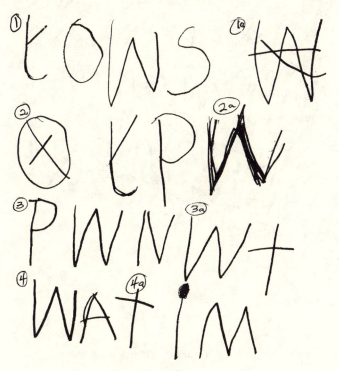

Figure 7.   Alison

Alison appears both to be figuring out how letters can represent the sounds she hears in the words she says to herself in writing and also to be working on how many times you write the letters for a given unit of speech. This same problem, of whether written units are composed of discrete, non-overlapping units, caused a great problem for a more mature speller, Linda, who wrote the long story in Figure 8.

Linda used very full and logical invented spelling. For instance, Line 1 includes the title: Little (LatLL) Princess (PRASAS) Charming (CRMAG). Like many inventive spellers, Linda used a linear line containing a number of words but no spaces to show word boundaries. In contrast, Alison had evidently been using a columnar display to deal with the issue of word or unit boundaries. Linda seemed partially to understand that words are discrete, non-overlapping units in English, but as her writing became longer and more crowded, she began to lose track and occasionally to compose nondiscretely. For instance, in Lines 5 and 6, she composed: "She started to grow and she wanted to have a big wheel." Note that in Line 6, she does not use one nonexclusive unit each for *have, a,* and *big*; instead HB appears to operate as *have,* A operates as the article *a* and also as part of BAG for *big* which includes the final consonant encoded for *have.*

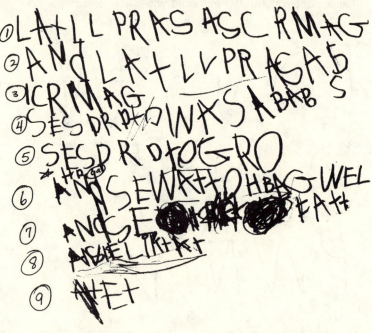

Figure 8.   Linda

Linda complained during re-reading that her writing in the middle sections was too hard to read. When the writing became difficult, she seemed to stop using her memory for the story she had composed both in writing and in dictation and to attempt to "sound out" the graphic record. Even with prompting from the examiner about remembering what she has written, she seemed to find the task confusing and complained that she couldn't remember.

The story can be read as:

Little Princess Charming
And Little Princess (was a baby)
Charming
She started to (was a baby)
She started to grow
And (her was inserted later) she wanted to have a big wheel
And she fitted
And she liked that
(Probably two attempts at the closing word *end*)

The final two examples come from Andy. In Figure 9, Andy used discrete units for each word and also a columnar display to set off what he seemed to treat as segmented units. That is, even though *torid* is written

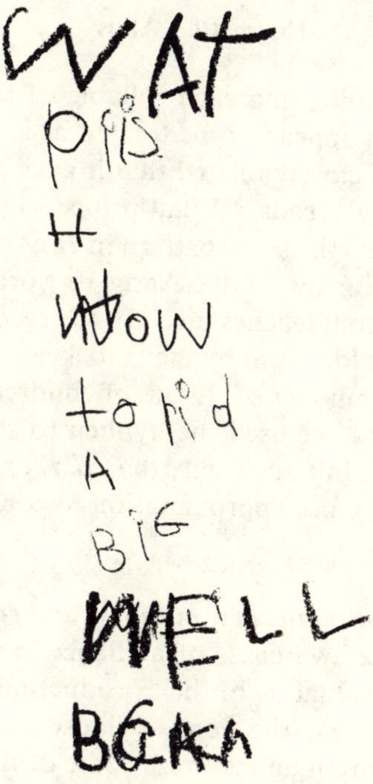

Figure 9. Andy

Figure 10.   Andy

together, the letters representing each syllable of *to ride* are separate and treated discretely. *Torid* appears to be treated as a "word" by Andy, or at least to be treated as so closely related that it goes on the same line. By the way, the abortive "story" reads, "What prince—how to ride a big wheel."

Figure 10 may show the same pattern in *ILrn* and *MYMOME,* but the second part is an editing by Andy. Andy re-worded, "I learn from my mom," to read, "My mom teaches me." In the second sentence, he may be using a graphic placeholder (the hyphen) to keep the word units apart, a technique reported in a number of studies of children's early writing. On the other hand, Andy may have used the hyphen to stand for the part of the phonetic unit that he didn't spell out, the /$\mathcal{I}$z/ on the end of *teaches.* At any rate, Andy shows a close approximation to conventional spelling in the second story.

Knowledges about audiences, authors, and readers.   The children in this study showed some awareness of audience in the sense that they used some monitoring and evaluating of their productions. I use the term editing, because the revisions were at the word or clause level and certainly were not extensive re-writings or reorganizations. Some of the children edited voluntarily, seemingly on the basis of some internal criterion of correctness of expression. Their efforts still seemed to be governed more by what they could do and the effort that it required than by a strong sense of adaptations that would help a reader. Of the elicited editings, only one child, Andy (Figure 10), edited at the clause level, rewording an entire sentence. Most editings were at the word level, like Arlene (above) who replaced MOM with ꊱꋒ and K⊕ (*castle*) with ꝗ for *palace*.

Children occasionally refused to re-read their nonconventional writing attempts, but these refusals did not directly reveal awareness of audience considerations. Rather, the refusals seemed to be based more upon the writing as production rather than upon the writer as producer: "It doesn't say anything." Nevertheless, the kindergarten children did have the beginnings of a set of standards concerning whether or not another person could read the composition.

Audience awareness seems far more evident in the less effort-requiring modes of telling and dictating, as would be expected. These modes both involve speaking and children are used to making self-corrections in speech; however, as we will see later, the children do not just treat their speech as oral language, particularly in the mode of dictation. This awareness does not, however, result in the kind of "decontextualization" that would help an absent audience understand all the aspects of the story, as we shall see later in the sections on context and structure.

During the writing task itself, the children participated in activities that illustrate things authors have to do. The children paused and planned, they encoded sound into print, they scratched out and edited, they re-read for accuracy and for sense, and they rejected the possibilities that they were able to do certain writing tasks in a way that a reader could read. The children in this study ranged widely in their ability to perform these activities. One indirect way to gauge their understandings of the writer-reader relationship is to look in more detail at children's emerging abilities to re-read their own dictated, as well as handwritten, compositions, particularly because this comparison includes both conventional orthography and the children's inventions.

Children's Emerging Reading Abilities With Dictated and Handwritten Stories

In the preceding section, we saw that the children used a wide variety of writing systems in order to compose stories. We had no theoretical suspicions about whether this variety could be related to children's reading attempts. In this section I will attempt, nonetheless, to pair the writing attempts and dictations with re-reading attempts. Such a pairing is evident in the data when one considers the child's behavior in attempting to write or dictate, the actual written text in whatever writing form the child uses, and the child's speech and behavior during re-reading. In other words, in the writing task, the child is not penalized for using an unconventional spelling system such as scribble or letter-strings as long as the composition intent can be inferred. This is particularly significant in light of Sulzby's longitudinal follow-up study (1983a). In that research, case study techniques were used and we found that some children who already were reading conventionally from print used lower-level writing systems in order to do a higher-order task, such as composing a story.

One explanation for this phenomenon may be increasing knowledge: invented spelling alone "won't do" because the child also knows that words have a conventional spelling, not just a phonetically-based one. Thus, the child may use letter-strings. Or the child may simply be impatient with a task that takes so much effort and hence revert to scribbling. Another intriguing idea is that these children, who are reading "before instruction," are used to figuring things out for themselves. Some of the children discuss writing as "This is the way I do it!" with a stress on I. One girl explained her own writing system and how it was different from her sister's; neither system was conventional and both girls were "precocious" readers. If indeed writing and reading are conceptually-based and children develop prior to instruction by figuring things out, then this attitude toward learning may be one that has worked and will continue to work well.

Analysis.   The protocols were content-analyzed to determine whether the re-reading attempts could reasonably be paired with dictations or the handwritten compositions. All of the children had given an initial response, either to refuse to try to read or to try using different strategies. The Emergent Reading Ability Judgments scale (Table 1) was constucted from the content-analysis based only on the child's initial attempt or attempt after a "try" prompt; in all cases, the re-reading attempt and composition were treated as a unit. Details of the scale and examples are provided in Sulzby (1981).

Two judges scored all the protocols independently, using the scale. One score was given for each reading/writing pair, handwritten or dictated, then these scores were averaged. Agreement was 96% between raters for each of the two sessions.

Results.   The ranking of the children's scores between the two sessions appeared to be significantly more similar than would be expected by chance ($rho = .77$, $p < .01$). As I reported in Sulzby (1982), there was also a significant correlation with the standard school-administered readiness test. However, it is not clear what this second correlation means, given the different theoretical bases of the two measures. I prefer to withhold judgment about the relationship with a more traditional measurement tool, particularly given the exploratory nature of the current research in emergent literacy.

TABLE 1
**Emergent Reading Ability Judgments
for Dictated and Handwritten Stories**

Score assigned	Behaviors Observed

(For 1–2, the productions are not considered to be stories or connected discourse; for 3–7, productions can be interpreted as being intended as connected discourse. Note that a child may stop with one clause but that there is evidence that the intended discourse was longer and that the child stopped in fatigue or for other reasons. This can be inferred from comparisons with told stories and from other comments by the child.)

1   The child did not dictate nor handwrite in response to the request. Thus there is also no attempt to re-read.

2   When asked to write a story, the child does not show evidence of attempting to write connected discourse in any recognized writing system. The child may produce random-looking marks but will refuse to re-read them. When asked to dictate, the child's speech does not seem to be dictation but has characteristics of conversational turn-taking. The child may refuse to re-read or re-read with need for conversational elicitations.

(For 3–7,   connected discourse is either produced or clearly intended.)

3   Child dictates and writes stories; however, s/he refuses to re-read. For handwritten story, child often says, "It doesn't say anything," and for dictation, "I can't read."

4   Child attempts to re-read dictation or handwritten story but does not keep eyes on the print. The story recited is similar to original production but is not stable with it. (Stable in reference to re-reading stories throughout this analysis means that no clause-level units have been added, omitted, or placed out of composed sequence.)

5   This appears to be a situation in which the child cannot simultaneously maintain eyes on print and recite a stable story. For this level, either (a) the child's eyes are on print but the story recited is similar to original but not stable with it, or (b) child's eyes are not on print but the story recited is stable with original.

6   Child's eyes are on print but the child is not tracking the print visually. The story recited is stable with the original composition. (The writing system used may not be conventional or phonetic but there must be clear evidence of the intended composition from voicing during composition or from the previously told story.)

7   Child's eyes are tracking print and child is matching voice to print, appearing to be reading conventionally from print. For purposes of this study, the story must consist of more than one complete clause; if only one clause or less, it was rated as a "6."

In particular, as I noted earlier, the Emergent Reading Ability Judgments for Dictated and Handwritten Stories is based upon very broad categories that may mask important developments. For instance, during later longitudinal research (Sulzby, 1983a), I have noted fluctuations and seeming regressions as new knowledges and abilities are added. The system described above is not yet sensitive to such fluctuations. Additionally, it does not distinguish between kinds of writing systems used which I suspect will become more important as we learn more. Finally, its tie to a theoretical base is not as strong as I would like it to be, and not as strong as is the system which I have been developing to describe the emergent reading of favorite storybooks (Sulzby, 1983b, in press-b).

In the two preceding sections, Children's Knowledges About Writing and Children's Emerging Reading Abilities with Dictated and Handwritten Stories, I looked at the children's productions in the context of describing emergent writing and reading abilities more-or-less directly. In the next section, I will look at the related modes that use speech: telling and dictation and their relationships to interactive conversation and the language typically conceived to be appropriate to writing. First I will look at the distinctions children make between telling and dictating; then at adaptations toward conversation and writing; and, finally, at the told and dictated stories using criteria typically applied to written-language-like texts.

Distinctions Between Telling and Dictating

The children had been asked to tell the same story in two modes that involved oral language: telling and dictating. For a child not yet reading or writing conventionally, these modes might appear to be exactly the same—you tell a story. However, for the child with increased awareness of written language, we would expect that the modes would differ. Indeed, we found that the modes did differ for children who seemed to have greater awareness of written language and that children with lesser awareness appeared to differ less vividly or almost not at all. These findings have been replicated in a follow-up study (Sulzby, in press-a), but for the current study I was interested in whether or not I could find relevant ways of detecting such distinctions. I chose three ways of going about the search: I asked raters to listen to tape-recordings of stories in the two modes and to describe what they heard in narrative form; then we analyzed the intonational contrasts; and, finally, we used pauses as a measure of fluency assuming that storytelling pauses would sound quite different from dictating pauses.

First, it was concluded that over half of the children distinguished clearly between storytelling and story dictation. An example of one of the narrative descriptions given by raters for a child who failed to distinguish the modes was the following: "The child dictated very fluently, running all ideas together with no regard for the examiner's writing. She used a conversational intonation."

Children's intonational patterns included using a word-by-word, staccato-like intonation, often associated with reading (Cook-Gumperz & Gumperz, 1981; Sulzby, in press-a); using falling intonation, rising intonation, or a continuant intonation at clause or phrase boundaries; or using high pitch with exaggerated "character" voices or exaggerated stress patterns. These patterns showed subtle differences between the two modes. Many children used the reading-like intonation for dictation or something that I now consider to be dictation intonation (see the discussion of pauses). Other children made distinctions as subtle as simply using voice falling intonation at the ends of the sentences in telling and voice continuant intonation in dictation (see Scollon & Scollon's [1981] discussion of the continuant voice means of signalling that a young child composer would continue creating a text rather than allow conversational interchanges).

Children used both filled and unfilled pauses. In filled pauses, they said um, uh, or partial words which were self-corrected. In unfilled pauses, there was silence. Raters could judge whether or not these unfilled pauses sounded like the brief-second-or-so endurance typical to conversation or face-to-face storytelling, or sounded as if they were timed for a scribe's writing. Children did use pauses to indicate distinctions between storytelling and dictation, but often with surprising effects as I will explain in the section on how children adapt the modes.

Adaptations Toward Conversation and Writing

In the section above, I described how children differentiated between storytelling and dictation, two modes that could be treated identically—as an oral monologue. Prior to researchers' turning their attention to early signs of knowledge of written language in oral delivery form, such distinctions were largely ignored. Now, however, we even look for other relationships across language modes. For instance, young children have been characterized as not being able to maintain an oral monologue or to narrate an account understandable to a nonpresent audience. One way of re-looking at this claim is to re-examine the data to describe the children who have this difficulty. I found that many children, particularly those who showed the least awareness of characteristics of written language, adapted their storytelling and, particularly, their dictation toward conversational exchanges. For example, they inserted comments in storytelling and dictation as if they were directed to the examiner for answers; or the child only responded if the adult continually asked questions.

On the other hand, this was not a case of either-or for these children. As we have seen, all of them had a fair amount of knowledge about written language. In the dictation mode this could be detected by the intonation and fluency patterns described above. However, some of the children "over-adapted" toward what they conceived to be the needs of the scribe: they used exaggerated pauses without actually watching the scribe to observe the speed of writing, or they used first long, conversational exchanges and then used exaggerated pauses sporadically. One over-adaptation came from two children who sounded as if they were dictating when they told their stories. These two children were very advanced in writing and were close to reading independently from print. At first, this adaptation seemed very bizarre until I recalled that the directions clearly said that the children were to tell and dictate as "things people do to write a story." Perhaps, for these advanced children, oral language used in the service of written composition should always sound like written language. On the other hand, given the variations which children use to signal distinctions between modes, the children could have been using a "reading intonation" for all of these tasks. (To my knowledge no one has yet differentiated technically between reading intonation, the intonation used in voicing during writing, and dictation intonation.)

A more technical analysis of pauses in telling and dictating and the features that judges treat as differentiation between the two modes can be found in Sulzby (in press-a). In that study, children high in emergent reading ability were found to distinguish between the prosodic features used in the two modes over four trials extending through kindergarten into the beginning of the first grade. During kindergarten, children moderate in emergent reading ability treated both modes as situations in which they should talk more slowly and pause more often than they did in normal conversational situations while the children low in emergent reading ability spoke rapidly and paused little in both modes. By the beginning of first grade, however, both of these groups began to distinguish between the two modes similar to the way in which the high group had distinguished all along. Naive linguistic judges used similar bases to those reported in this study for asserting that children distinguished between telling and dictating modes.

The analyses in the sections above have focused on content-free characteristics of the children's told and dictated stories. Those characteristics include how the child sounded while giving the oral version of both the told and dictated stories. In the extended section that follows, typed transcripts of the told and dictated stories will be examined in terms of how the child presents the content so that it can be comprehended as "written language" (language that an absent audience can comprehend), oriented toward the content needs of the audience, and structured the way a reader expects a story to be structured. In this final section, the real and make-believe distinction will also be explored.

Comparison of Told and Dictated Transcripts

In the previous two sections, we saw that the children differentiated between storytelling and dictation in the prosodic features of their speech and that some children showed features of oral language in the dictated mode by requiring conversational or interrogative exchanges and other children over-adapted to the needs of the scribe in dictating. However, children were asked to tell the story and to dictate the story as things that people do when they write a story, in order to get the story just the way they want it to be. In this section, we look at the stories to see how adequately the children created stories that can be judged as successful "written language stories."

For a story to be successful as written language, it needs to be understandable to an audience that cannot ask the composer questions directly. All answers need to come from the text, if not explicitly, then implicitly. A writer can provide a context from which a reader can generate inferences to complete the ideas in the text. According to Olson (1977), written text tends to be more explicit and decontextualized than oral utterances and thus is more understandable to an absent audience.

We must, however, take into account the development of the children in our analysis and not just apply adult criteria to the children's compositions if we are to understand their knowledges about oral and written language and writing and reading. For that reason, I looked at the told and dictated stories in three different ways. First, I asked naive judges to read matched pairs of the stories and make judgments of their relative "understandability," given that the judge was not allowed to ask the child composer any questions. The second analysis looked at the degrees of specification of context in the children's texts, using a "completeness of context" analysis adapted from that of Menig-Peterson and McCabe (1978). Finally a story grammar adapted first for production (rather than for recall), and second for this corpus of stories, was used in order to estimate the structural well-formedness of the stories. Story grammars thus far have not directly addressed issues concerning features of written language, so this section also discusses aspects of written language that were relevant in the adaptation of the grammar or that were overlooked by the analysis. The section concludes with examples of real and make-believe stories to illustrate the individual variation noted in the three sets of analyses.

Understandability Analysis. The purpose of this first analysis was to explore whether readers acquainted with the speech of 5-year-old children would be able, without an externally-imposed standard, to detect differences in the understandability of stories by these children when these stories were composed under different conditions related to written language. Thus, I asked two "naive" judges to make paired-comparisons of the transcipts of stories by the same child and to judge which of a pair was more understandable. Each judge was to ask herself: "Which of these two stories do I find more understandable, given that I cannot ask the author any questions directly?" After making each forced-choice comparison, each judge was to write an explanation of the basis for the judgment. The bases used by naive judges were then compared with other analyses to see in what ways naive judges used criteria similar to or different from more formal tools.

Full details of this analysis are available in my final report to NCTE (Sulzby, 1981). In summary, the judges first examined pairs of told stories and dictated stories (mode comparisons). Second, they compared pairs of real and make-believe stories (topic comparisons). Judges differed, first of all, in their ability to reach the same judgment: 95% for told stories, but only 74% for dictated stories; 76% for real stories and 89% for make-believe stories. The difference between these percentages treated as the difference between two independent proportions was not significant in either case. In addition, the total number of preferences for each type of story in the paired comparisons occurred almost exactly at a chance level.

These results indicate that if there was a difference between the stories in terms of understandability, it was not evident to untrained adult readers, even those acquainted with the ways young children talk and think. However, the criteria that the judges reported using were highly informative.

The following description can be considered to be criteria used intuitively by adults when asked to judge young children's typed stories for how understandable they are. Content analysis revealed that, although the judges were not highly compatible in their better/worse comparisons, they were nevertheless using an overall criterion that could be called understandability which consisted of three component clusters: topic, wording, and completeness. (Many of their justifications contained multiple criteria.)

Explanations that centered around topic focused on the main idea of the story. Judges used the phrases "the subject" or "what is being talked about" in these explanations.

Example 1:   Told [story] has more detail and it stays primarily on the topic of the bike.
Example 2:   Dictated story mentions the object *big wheel*. Told story gives no specific reference to what is being talked about.
Example 3:   Stuck more to the topic. R[eal] started out okay, but then wandered.

In other explanations, the judges focused on aspects of the wording, or how the child phrased the ideas in the story. One judge used the words "smooth" or "smoother" quite often. When she was asked to explain this response, she indicated she meant that the actual wording sounded more fluent. Other wording explanations mentioned word choices that differed across the pairs of stories or flow from sentence to sentence due to wording.

Example 1:   Used "guy" instead of "somebody."
Example 2:   The sentence structures are much poorer in the MB story. The way it is told makes it difficult to follow. I got very confused. Except for too many "*and*'s" joining the sentences in the R story it was easy to follow.
Example 3:   Almost exact same story. Told was worded better.

The explanations that emphasized completeness often referred to aspects of topic and wording; however, the main thrust of these explanations was upon whether or not the story was either a whole unit or a better unit than the other story. Judges seemed to have an intuitive sense that the author should create a whole. These explanations often referred to genre expectations.

Example 1:   Neither story is complete and neither makes mention of the object being talked about but the dictated story has a little more detail.

Example 2:   The R story was only a single statement. The MB story sounded like a complete story and it was logical and easy to follow.

Example 3:   MB is more complete and is more of a story with some action taking place. R seems like it needs more follow-up—what happened then?

Completeness of Context Analysis

When authors write stories, they need to provide readers with enough information to understand what they are writing about. Authors must give information specifically or explicitly enough for readers to re-create the message from the text. Unlike the face-to-face interaction of conversation, the author and reader are separated in time and place from one another.

Even in oral interchanges it is often necessary to give a conversational partner some contextual orientation. One such oral interchange occurs when one narrates a past event to a person who did not witness the event. We made use of one tool for analyzing personal narratives developed by Menig-Peterson and McCabe (1978) to study children's developing awareness of the needs of a conversational partner.

Menig-Peterson and McCabe (1978) were concerned with how young children would orient a listener to the content of narratives they told about their own lives. One of their analyses, which they referred to as "completeness of context," will be described below, following a discussion of how their narratives differ from the narratives in this study.

Menig-Peterson and McCabe used more naturalistic procedures than were used in this study. Also the listeners who elicited narratives interacted conversationally with the child. The interactions were well-defined so as not to introduce new material, but they were more interactive than our procedures in which the listener did not interact except to say, "anything else," and so forth (as detailed in the procedure section above).

The Menig-Peterson and McCabe study reported analyses for only the three longest narratives for each child. In addition to these narratives, there were also instances in which children did not produce a narrative in response to a prompt, but rather let the topic "die," and instances in which children produced much shorter narratives. Since Menig-Peterson and McCabe (1978) wanted to elicit optimum narratives, and since those narratiaves were structured as face-to-face interactions, the narratives analyzed by their system differed from our narratives. In our study, children were repeatedly told that their goal was to *write* a story and that all the modes were things that people sometimes did while trying to write a story. While there is no way of knowing precisely in what ways that goal remained in children's memory while doing the task, there is evidence that it was a goal for many of the children, perhaps in terms of how much knowledge they had about written language and how varied that knowledge was.

Furthermore, our topic was given to the children as a direction and it had some specification to it. Children were given the topic (or the "what"): *big wheel* (or *bicycle*). They were given the protagonist (or "who"): *you yourself* or *Little Prince/Princess Charming*. Accompanying the protagonist specification was the further stipulation that the *you* story had to be *real* and the *LPC* story had to be *make-believe*. Additionally, they were given directions about the content of the "how": tell *how* you/LPC learned to ride a big wheel. Finally, they were instructed to discuss the "why": *what made you/LPC want to do it.*

Since Menig-Peterson and McCabe were concerned with children's natural use of specification, they analyzed their narratives in terms of how well children specified information for their listeners that would answer the traditional questions: *who, what, when, where, how,* and *why.* For each question, they used a scoring range for the specifications that were present in the children's narratives. This range was appropriate to apply to our stories for some, but not all of the questions, thus the analysis was adapted to fit these stories when it was appropriate (see Sulzby [1981] for complete details.)

One adaptation was particularly important. The interpretation of the relative importance of the six questions was, of necessity, different for our study. Menig-Peterson and McCabe were interested in answers to all six questions, but did not direct children to address any of them (although they did model similar narratives as elicitation probes). While a child could include information addressed to all six questions in the current study, the directions focused children's attention directly on four of the six questions. Those four questions were *who, what, how,* and *why.* The *where* and *when* questions were not alluded to by the examiner although a child could choose to include material giving the location and time context to the audience.

It should be noticed that this scoring penalizes the child who redefines the task (for example, saying "I just learned," then going on to detail other actions very clearly). There were, however, few children who redefined the task in this way. The clearest case was one girl whose narratives otherwise were also confusing to an absent audience. Her redefined story action, going off and getting married, contained some confusing elements for the new context.

Scoring.   Scoring was done by two raters. One person scored all the children's stories for the six categories. That scorer trained a second rater on the first 12 children's stories in each category, then the second scorer completed the scoring independently. The percentages of agreement ranged from 88% for "why" to 96% for both "where" and "how." Disagreements were due to errors in not following the criteria, except for "why" in which some disagreements arose over implied causal relationships.

Results.   The completeness-of-analysis scoring system was used to compare overall differences and differences in each of the six scoring categories (measures) due to topic (real and make-believe) and/or mode (told or dictated), using analysis of variance for repeated-measures (details in Sulzby [1981]).

There were significant individual differences in the specificity of context by these 5-year-old children. This finding was not surprising and confirmed other reports in the literature about the variation found among children at this age level. These differences must be held in mind as we analyze the differences within individuals.

In the analysis of completeness of context, the mode distinctions of telling versus dictating did not result in a significant factor. Children did not differ significantly in how specific they were in providing essential information for their audience in told mode as opposed to dictated mode. The topic was held constant in this comparison, so it would appear that children held their basic information similarly across the two modes.

A further question was whether children always provided basic context-setting information in the same degree of specificity if other factors, such as topic, varied. The topic variation, real versus make-believe, did produce significant differences, both overall and in interaction with the six measures of context specification. (The overall significance of differences among measures was not tested due to the fact that the same metric was not used across the six measures.) The mean scores for the interaction of measures by topic (real and make-believe) are shown in Table 1 converted into percentages of the total possible score in each category.

TABLE 1
Scores for Context Specification in Informational Categories Using a Real and Make-Believe Topic Variation

	Real	**Make-Believe**
WHO	58[a]	69
WHERE	24	29
WHAT	77	68
WHEN	28	22
WHY	55	71
HOW	38	61

[a] All figures are percentages of possible score for that category.

The real and make-believe stories generated by these 5-year-old children differed overall in how completely the child specified information to answer the basic *who, where, when, what, why,* and *how* questions. By examining each category, one can see that the make-believe stories tended to provide more specific information about the *who, why,* and *how* in the story. Make-believe stories were also slightly more specific about location, *where,* but so few children specified location at all that these differences should be disregarded. The real stories, on the other hand, were more specific in explaining *what* the object was and *when* the event took place.

The *who, why,* and *how* specification advantage of make-believe stories partially presents some support for the speculations in the literature (Peterson & McCabe, 1983; Sulzby, 1980) that fantasy frees the composer to add features resulting in a better-formed story. The *who, why,* and *how* scoring includes an introduction of the protagonist (*who*) as well as the specific goal, attempt, and outcome (*how*). *Why* scoring is simply an indication that the story contains some signalled causal relations. These elements certainly form the heart of a complete narrative.

The support is only partial, however, because the real stories show an advantage over the make-believe in specifying *when* the event took place and in specifying objects in the story (*what*). *What* is particularly keyed to the main object of the story, the big wheel or bicycle. The age you are when you learn to ride a big wheel or bicycle seems to be very important to people who have only lived a few years. Age and kind of vehicle are very specific memories so it is possible that these elements are easily retrieved whereas *how,* for example, may be quite fuzzy. I will return to these speculations after considering the specific overall and category means for this study (Table 1) as compared with those reported by Menig-Peterson and McCabe (1978).

Menig-Peterson and McCabe presented data from 96 children, broken into groups of 16 children at each of six age groups from 3½–4½ up to 8½–9½. The mean age of our children was 5:4 (range 4:11 to 5:10) in October with the final data collected mid-December. Our overall mean score using the system we adapted from theirs was 6.72 of a possible 12. The mean for their youngest group was 7.52 (range, 7.52 to 9.81) of a possible 13. These means, converted into proportions, indicated that our sample earned approximately 56% of the possible score and their 3½ to 4½-year-old children earned approximately 58%. See Table 2 for these comparisons.

In five categories our children scored as low or lower than Menig-Peterson and McCabe's youngest sample. One category, *when,* exceeded the score of their oldest sample. *When* was also one of the two categories in which our real stories exceeded the make-believe in specifying the contxt. As mentioned previously, the age at which children learned to ride a big wheel or a bicycle seemed to be extremely significant in their real-life memories

TABLE 2
Comparison of Children's Specification of Context
in Two Story Elicitation Situations

| | Telling Stories Under Writing Directions (Sulzby data) | | Telling Stores With Conversational Elicitation (Menig-Peterson & McCabe data) | |
	Percentages	Ages	Percentages	Ages
WHO	64	5½	63	3½–4½
WHERE	26	5½	54	3½–4½
WHAT	73	5½	83	3½–4½
WHEN	75	5½	60	8½–9½
WHY	63	5½	71	4½–5½
HOW	49	5½	86	3½–4½

and showed up frequently, particularly in their real stories. The mean for make-believe stories, while lower than for real, was also higher than Menig-Peterson and McCabe's 8½- to 9½-year-old's.

If we take specification of context as an indication of language appropriate for written communication, then it would appear that Menig-Peterson and McCabe's rural children used more written language-like detail in a face-to-face conversation than these suburban children did in a "writing" situation. We also see a similar depression in story structure when these stories are compared indirectly to storytelling data. However, since all these data were gathered in different studies, direct comparisons cannot be made.

In a follow-up study (Tinzmann, Cox, & Sulzby, 1983) we found no effect of specific categories being requested in our directions except when the information was actually given rather than requested. For example, giving the content of *what* as a "big wheel" increased the likelihood that the object would be named in specific terms. However, just referring to a content-free category, "what we did," did not increase the specification of related categories.

In general, children did not provide sufficient specification for stories to be understood by a nonpresent audience. This finding has also been replicated and documented using cohesion analysis (Cox, 1983; Cox & Sulzby, 1984). In these analyses, stories were found to be contextualized to the situation via the examiner's directions (see King & Rentel, 1981).

Structural analysis. In the previous analyses, we examined the transcripts of children's told and dictated stories, first, by having adult readers judge how understandable the stories were as written texts, and, second, by examining the children's provision of specific pieces of information needed by a nonpresent audience.

Another way of analyzing children's stories is to look at their structure. In this section I will use a story grammar adapted for story production or composition (Glenn & Stein, 1978; Stein & Glenn, 1981) and further adapt it for the conditions used in this study. Story grammars (Mandler & Johnson, 1977; Stein & Glenn, 1979) were developed to describe the structure of folk-tales that had endured within cultures. In research the grammars are typically used to generate "well-formed" stories and then to measure recall of those stories by listeners, on the assumption that, within a culture, people develop a schema that reflects the grammatical properties of well-formed stories. The better-formed the story, the more likely that people will recall a veridical version of the story and deviations of different kinds should predict certain effects upon people's memory for the stories. Indeed, research with story recall has documented these kinds of effects.

If children's memory for text is an important factor in learning to read, we need to explore the issue of memorability of texts. Sulzby (1983b, in press-b) examined the nature of children's use of memory in reading favorite storybooks. In this study, I explore the children's use of memory for text in two ways. The first and primary question is whether or not children's text differs in well-formedness, using an adapted story grammar analysis, either across modes of telling or dictating or across the real and make-believe condition. Second, can we detect any difference in the children's re-reading attempts related to structural differences.

Instructional research in the language-experience approach (see Stauffer, 1970) has claimed that children will learn to read more easily from materials in the child's own language about the child's own experiences. Holdaway (1979), in contrast, speculated that these "stories" or accounts are composed of less memorable language than is used in other text-types, particularly children's storybooks. In a follow-up study (Sulzby, 1983a), I compared children's readings of these different text-types, but it is clear that the stories differ in far more ways than simply the real and make-believe distinction. None of the previous instructional research dealt with issues of memorability due to structural well-formedness.

Story production research (Glenn & Stein, 1978; Stein & Glenn, 1981) has addressed the issue of well-formedness without addressing reading. One study (Peterson & McCabe, 1983) found that samples of real-life narratives of young children were more well-formed and more complex structurally than were Glenn & Stein's (1978) fictional stories elicited from children of similar ages and descriptions. No published story of which I am aware has yet tested real versus make-believe effects upon the structures of stories produced by the same children, nor have any other studies of reading development examined this factor within the same text-type.

Research in story production conducted in conditions in which children are asked or encouraged to tell stories (Applebee, 1978; Glenn & Stein, 1978; Peterson & McCabe, 1983; Sutton-Smith, 1981) has found that children's stories often differ from the idealized structure proposed by story grammars. Additionally, different kinds of analyses yield different results because they address different questions (Peterson & McCabe, 1983).

While none of the existing techniques captured all of the features of written language with which this study was concerned, the story grammar techniques illuminated structure in a particularly helpful fashion since they also addressed memorability. The existing story grammar techniques had to be adapted, but were useful as discovery tools (as was the case in the analysis of completeness of context in the previous section). For instance, in the discussion of the use of story grammar analysis, I report that the children often omit information about the story setting; this finding is understandable, when we consider that kindergarteners do not produce fully "decontextualized" stories, but often use features of oral interactive speech in their story productions (under "write a story" conditions), whether those stories are told, dictated, or written (Cox, 1983; Cox & Sulzby, in press; King & Rentel, 1981).

Nevertheless, the adapted story grammar can be used to address the primary question dealt with in this section—whether or not children's stories differ in well-formedness. That question can be re-stated to indicate our concern with the stories as written compositions: In what ways can children be said to compose structurally well-formed stories that would be understandable to an absent audience when obvious signs of composition mode (telling or dictation) are removed, that is, when the children's stories are transcribed, typed, and read? Will signs of mode still be present in the written transcript and will there be effects of the real versus make-believe topic variation? Our judgments of emergent reading ability can then be used to explore effects of structure upon re-reading attempts.

In the section that follows I will describe the general outline of the story grammar used for analysis, discuss considerations related to this particular corpus of stories and, finally, give details about the adapted scoring system. These details will furnish examples from the children's stories. The results of applying the story grammar are then reported in terms of frequency of structures and relation to emerging reading ability. At the end of the section, I will give examples of real and make-believe story differences that are not captured by any of the three analyses thus far, but which are nonetheless clearly observable to a reader.

General outline of the grammar. A story grammar as described by Stein and Glenn (1981) depicts the "ideal" (or idealized) structure for an orally-told story. The Stein and Glenn (1979, 1981) grammar does not include all cultural differences in story composition and memory (for example, Scollon & Scollon's [1981] work with the interactive, four-part structure of Athabaskan stories), but it does fit cultures like that of the children in this study. The ideal structure is composed of two primary divisions, a setting and an episode structure. The episode is the major unit of analysis and is composed, again "ideally," of five parts: the initiating event, an internal response, an attempt, a consequence, and a reaction. The grammar contains rules which define when parts can be deleted and enables predictions to be made about the results of such deletions upon the memorability of the story produced. Most of the research in story grammars has used the method of recall to test the psychological validity of the grammatical definitions.

Glenn and Stein (1978; Stein & Glenn, 1981) have described the use of their grammar with story productions rather than with recall. They elicited make-believe stories from kindergarteners, third-graders, and fifth-graders by providing them with "story stems" that provided the protagonist and setting. (For example, "Once there was a big grey fox who lived in a cave near a forest.") This tool has also been used by Peterson and McCabe (1983) to analyze more naturally-occurring narratives told about real events in a child's past; their children, were as young as 3½-years-old. Both sets of researchers conclude that the story grammar successfully measures structural aspects of story productions as predefined by the episode and event structure, although they differ about the relative importance to assign to subcategories and elaborations within and concerning the structures.

Few children in our corpus produced "ideal" stories, consisting simply of a setting and a single episode. However, I have chosen this example to illustrate the "ideal" episode for the reader; other examples will be given to illustrate other points. It should be noted that in this example the active nature of the attempt must be inferred (and was substantiated by other versions by the child).

Examples of a One-Episode Story (Sulzby corpus)

SETTING: (elaborated with literary conventions)	Once upon a time... there was a girl named Prince Charming
INTERNAL RESPONSE: (elaborated)	And she didn't know how to ride a big wheel And once she wanted to ride her big wheel But she didn't know how to
INITIATING EVENT:	One day her brother came out and said: Want—do you want some tactics how to ride your big wheel?
ATTEMPT: (abbreviated and inferential)	And her brother taught her how to

CONSEQUENCE:	And she finally knew how to ride her big wheel
REACTION: (with literary convention)	And she kept on riding it round the block. The end.

Compare this example with the perfect balance of a story formed by the idealized grammar, as illustrated by Stein and Glenn (1979, and elsewhere):

Example of a One-Episode Story (Stein and Glenn grammar)

SETTING:	1. Once there was a big grey fish named Albert.
	2. He lived in a big icy pond near the edge of a forest.
INITIATING EVENT:	3. One day, Albert was swimming around the pond.
	4. Then he spotted a big juicy worm on the top of the water.
INTERNAL RESPONSE:	5. Albert knew how delicious worms tasted.
	6. He wanted to eat that one for his dinner.
ATTEMPT:	7. So he swam very close to the worm.
	8. Then he bit into him.
CONSEQUENCE:	9. Suddenly, Albert was pulled through the water into a boat.
	10. He had been caught by a fisherman.
REACTION:	11. Albert felt sad.
	12. He wished he had been more careful.

While the grammar example or ideal is perfectly balanced and meets definitional requirements, Glenn and Stein (1978) and others admit that children's actual productions vary from the ideal. The claim is, however, that the variation is understandable and not random and that the grammar provides a standard from which a more adequate description of the production structure may be derived. The grammar can thus be used to make comparisons, whether or not it captures all the relevant aspects of children's productions. The nature of this corpus and the conditions under which it was obtained must be held in mind, particularly how they differ from oral recall or production studies not concerned with written language.

The current study.   The corpus of "stories" being compared in this analysis consists of 83 productions taken from the children's transcripts. To review, each child in this study had been asked to produce stories under both told and dictated conditions, with both real and make-believe topic directions. Thus each child could have produced four stories for a total of 96 stories from the 24 subjects. In fact, there were 13 instances in which stories were not produced, but only one child refused to produce a story at least once under these four sets of conditions. That child's performance was believed to be a valid indicator of her ability. (She produced a handwritten story for the second session, discussed the composition, and attempted to re-read it. Subsequent informal evaluation confirmed that she was at a very early stage of literacy acquisition.)

Three aspects of this study's design bear upon the issue of the appropriateness of the analyses. First, this study was concerned with finding evidence of "written language" knowledges and the story grammar was designed primarily to apply to orally-told stories or re-told oral stories. Second, our directions specified an event in children's memory that was potentially spread out over time, rather than occurring at one memorable occasion. Third, our directions specified some parts of a "story grammar" for a child, but did not provide a model for the child to repeat or paraphrase, as story grammar researchers have done.

Knowledges about written language can be shown by children in numerous ways in writing and reading tasks. In the corpus of told and dictated stories being compared here, however, that knowledge is particularly evident in three ways. First, children begin to insert literary language—conventional phrases coming from book-like stories. "Once upon a time there was a girl named Prince Charming" is one example already presented. "Once upon a time *there lived* a princess" (underlining mine) is even more formal. One child's somewhat abortive attempt to sound like a book is given below. She was starting to read preprimers at the time and dictated with reading intonation.

> Prince Charming's dad helped to learn how to ride
>   a big wheel.
> The owner of the palace was Prince Charming.
> A nest laid in a tree in the palace.
> That's all.

Another way in which children show knowledge about written language is in their intonation. (This is discussed at more length in the section on adaptations of modes.) Children would dictate using word-by-word phrasing, staccato-fashion, or even "list-reading" intonation.[4] Others use pauses between units closely tied to the scribe's speed of writing. These intonation patterns indicate knowledge about how reading sounds to a beginner and about what the demands of handwriting are.

A third sign of knowledge about written language is found in asides children would make during composition. These asides indicate that the child is treating the composition as an entity with special status. Such asides often are evident by change in intonation as well as content. Below is an example composition with 1-second pauses indicated by each diagonal mark, examiner's comments in brackets, and examiner's words in parentheses.

> I want a bicycle. I'll tell you the same way I
>   told you the first time for a bicycle. [This
>   is clearly preface addressed to the examiner.]
> My//sister/Mazie
> [(Mazie?)]
> Yeah, taught///me///
> how///to///ride///a///big///wheel
> No, a bicycle. Erase that.
> [Normal conversational prosody on: "No, a bicycle.
> Erase that." (///OK.)]
> Then///I///learned///
> how///to///ride///a///big///wheel.
> That's the whole story. [Conversational prosody.]
> [Notice he tried to change to *bicycle* but ended up
> with *big wheel*. He recited it as *bicycle* later.]

These kinds of knowledges about written language are not directly measured by the story grammar. The semantic content and grammatical structure of the literary language would be scored, but the knowledge about reading and writing implied by intonation must be dealt with in adaptations of mode. The third kind of knowledge, that the composition is a special entity that can be commented upon, has been used prior to the application of the grammar *when the child is skillful enough* to make the distinction clear to the examiner and transcribers. By keeping notes on observations during the sessions as well as making full transcripts we have tried to detect these distinctions between text and comments. Below is an example in which examiner first thought the child was telling a story, then realized the child might be explaining a problem about the story content.

---

[4]In contrast with adults who often read lists with a rising intonation at the end of each word or phrase, children often use an abrupt falling intonation.

I saw everybody
riding a big wheel
[Long Pause.] Can't think. I don't know anything
more. [Pause]
I was born
and I couldn't hear when I was born. [Then she told the
examiner couldn't hear when she was born, not until
age 3.[5] Examiner asked if she could remember about
big wheels and she said no. Then examiner asked
about bike: (Do you remember how to ride a bike?)]
Yes.
Well, my babysitter taught me
and he lef go of me
and I kept going
I tried
and tried
and tried
and I learned.
Then I went out
and rode my bike
all the way to their house
and it took a long time.

Fortunately, after adjusting the topic, the child was able to complete her story. If the examiner had misinterpreted the statement, "and I couldn't hear when I was born," the resulting "story" would have been scored as poorly structured and hard to comprehend. (Also, the examiner would have failed to comfort the child over her past problem and would have missed important diagnostic information about this girl, who had some difficulty abandoning the conversational mode.)

A second consideration regarding the use of the story grammar with this corpus is the nature of the event we asked children to relate, learning to ride a big wheel (bicycle). While there is controversy over exactly what a story is or minimally consists of, there is some evidence that the episodic structure is well within the core of the concept, and may well be prototypical for middle-class American children (Policastro, 1981). McCabe (personal communication, 1981) has pointed out that the event structure is an important factor, often reflected in the past tense verb, which serves as a clue to whether or not a discourse can be considered a story, or narrative. There is a change of state at one point in time that marks the beginning of a discrete set of occurrences. Glenn and Stein's fish Albert exists in a pond (his state), when there is a change (a juicy worm wriggles by). Albert begins an attempt

---

[5]According to the teacher this was an exaggeration, but the child had had recurring problems with ear aches.

that results in a dire outcome. Peterson and McCabe's children tell events that happened to them personally at discrete points in time. Their children help butcher hogs, have car accidents, or drench fathers with water.

The incident, learning to ride a big wheel, or some variant such as a bicycle or "green machine," was remembered by all of the children. Some of the children remembered the occurrence of learning as a discrete event in time (the day the brother offered some tactics, or the day a cousin came to visit). For other children, however, the event was spread out over time. What had to be decided was whether or not our stimulus precluded the use of more advanced structures by some of the children. From content analysis and application of the grammar to the corpus, I decided that the event was appropriate to episodic narration even when spread over time.

The narratives that did not have the expected past-tense verb structure fell into two categories: those that legitimately fit into nonepisodic categories of the story grammar and those in which the child was *planning* a possible narrative, using procedural language, rather than actually narrating. Both of these categories could be classified by the grammar since the procedurally-stated narratives nevertheless reflected one of the primary structures. There were only three compositions that were primarily stated in procedural language. Two of these had an underlying action sequence structure and, for the third, the underlying structure was an incomplete episode. All of the passages our children produced could be legitimately placed into the Glenn and Stein categories, by making this adaptation of observing the relations of verb structure, event structure, and function (narrative or procedural) of the passage.

The final design consideration is the content of the directions given to the children. These directions differ from the elicitation procedures used by Glenn and Stein (1978) and by Menig-Peterson and McCabe (1978, Peterson & McCabe, 1983). Glenn and Stein gave children story starters or stems and asked them to complete the story. Menig-Peterson and McCabe elicited narratives by having the examiner give a brief account, ostensibly about her own experience, asking the child if anything similar had ever happened to him or her. The Glenn and Stein stems were designed to be considered as a part of the total production, whereas, Menig-Peterson and McCabe's procedures were designed to elicit a free-standing narrative.

In the current study, the directions specify four potential categories: (a) setting information (the protagonist is specified); (b) consequence/goal information ("how you learned to ride a big wheel"); (c) internal response information ("what made you want to do it"); and (d) action information ("how you did it"). A child could respond to these directions as if they were part of the narrative, contingently, or re-state them to create a free-standing narrative. One of the primary purposes of this study was to determine the conditions under which children would create a decontextualized, written language-like composition as compared with a contingent composition showing signs of an oral language-like interactive mode. That question was addressed by the completeness of context analysis in the previous section, but was also analyzable through the categories of the story grammar. For instance, the setting was often omitted in stories from this corpus. Children often did not introduce the protagonist seemingly because the directions specified the protagonist. Yet other children with advanced knowledge introduced themselves by what Scollon and Scollon (1981) call "fictionalization of self."

> Once upon a time, once upon a time there was a little girl named Kimberly, K-I-M-B-E-R-L-Y.

In all cases, when the child's composition was scored credit was not given for information in the directions unless the child re-stated the information in some way, with the exception of the presupposed setting.

Description of story grammar classification. Stein and Glenn (1981) divide children's orally-told narratives into three types. They call them all *stories* since they arise as children's responses to the directive, "tell a story," although it is not clear that these variants necessarily are limited to the story genre (see Peterson & McCabe's [1983] discussion of the reactive sequence, but also see Policastro [1981]). The three types are as follows:

1. Stories which are not organized around a motive resolution sequence;
2. Stories which contain a single motive resolution sequence; and
3. Stories which contain more than one motive resolution sequence.

Each type then has sub-categories. For convenience, I have divided the structures into only two parts, pre-episodic and episodic. The examples given come from this corpus.

The pre-episodic structures consist of four categories:

1. No structure.
2. Descriptive sequence.
3. Action sequence.
4. Reactive sequence.

The episodic structures also consist of four categories:

5. Incomplete episode.
6. Simple episode.

7. Complete episode.
8. Multiple episode.

No structure. Stein and Glenn (1981) use the category "no structure" both for children who do not produce any statements and for those who produce only one or two statements (the second being just a paraphrase of the first). In the scoring used for this study, a distinction is made between (1a) "No Story" and (1b) "No Structure," but Stein and Glenn's definition is used for "No Structure."

Subject 2, Dictation, Real:
I just pedal and steer.

Descriptive sequence. The descriptive sequence is merely a description of habitual states, acts, and surroundings of a protagonist.

Subject 1, Dictation, Real:
I ride on my big wheel so fast.
I ride it slow and fast.
My mommy rides my bike with me
and I color
and I walk outside
and open the garage
and ride my bike.
That's all.

Action sequence. The example given for a description sequence includes actions of the protagonist, but they are not goal-directed. Rather, they are habitual. In contrast, the action sequence may have occasional goals, but they are locally attached to actions and are not goals for larger structures. Stein and Glenn compare the action sequence to a "script."

Subject 2, Telling, Make-Believe:
Well, one day he just learned
and somebody taught him how to pedal and steer
and that's all.

Reactive sequence. The reactive sequence, according to Stein and Glenn (1981), is more advanced but still a developmental precursor to the motive sequence.

[T]here is no planful behavior on the part of the protagonist which would result in the attainment or non-attainment of a goal. Rather, the events related

have a beginning and an end and are causally related, but are out of control of
the protagonist. (p. 15)

The events seem to happen to the protagonist rather than being actions
planned by the protagonist. There is a change of state and a causal relationship between events and results, but there is no evidence that the protagonist
plans the results.

> Subject 16, Dictation, Real:
>> My mom and dad bought a big wheel for me
>> and they pushed me on it with my feet on
>>> the pedals
>> And then I learned how to ride it.
>> That's all.

Incomplete episode. The incomplete episode contains a goal and implies, but does not describe, planful behavior. Also the consequence may be
sketchy and there is no reaction. Basically, it may have a setting, it must
have either an initiating event or an internal response, but it lacks an attempt
and reaction.

> Subject 12, Dictation, Make-Believe:
>> Once upon a time
>> there was a girl
>> named Prince Charming
>> And she didn't know how to ride a big wheel
>> And one day her mom came outside
>> to teach her how to ride a big wheel.
>> And finally she knew how to ride a big wheel.
>> The end.

Simple episode. The simple episode adds one component, the Attempt,
to the incomplete episode. All other options remain the same as for the incomplete episode. The Reaction category is still missing, hindering the simple episode from being complete. Also, the consequence seems to have a
more legitimate status.

> Subject 5: Telling, Make-Believe:
>> Well, one time, see, she tried to ride one
>> and, and, see, and pushed one
>> tried she [sic].
>> One time she tried to ride a big wheel
>> and they pushed
>> and soon she was riding a little bit

and she pushed
and soon she was riding a little bit
and she pushed
and pushed
and soon she was riding it.
And that's the end.

Complete episode. The complete episode is described as the ideal structure, containing the five parts of the episode, along with a setting. In other words, it consists of setting, initiating event, internal response, attempt, consequence, and reaction. From examination of the examples Glenn and Stein (1978; Stein & Glenn, 1981) provided and from my own corpus, however, it appears that the setting may still be omitted, except for "contextualized" references to the protagonist ("I," "he," or "she"), and either the initiating event or the internal response may be omitted as long as the goal is clear.

Subject 17, Dictation, Real:
Well, my daddy tried to teach me
and—well, well, you see,
and I learned
and learned
and learned
until I could ride it myself.
So then I started riding it at Grammy's
    more and more and more.

Multi-episode. All the episodic structures can be linked and embedded to form larger multi-episode units. Additionally, nonepisodic structures may function as elaborations with a descriptive sequence, for instance, to form an elaborated setting. While this classification is too broad for larger passages, the one category of multi-episode is sufficient for this corpus.

Subject 14, Dictation, Real:
I learn, I learn
when I was four years old
and how I learned
The first thing I learned was how to pedal
And then I practiced
and I practiced
and suddenly I just did it
and I got too big for that
so my friend has a two-wheeler
So I always practiced on it

and I was still four years old.
And I didn't have a two-wheeler just like his
or I didn't even have a bike
And then one day my mom was looking in the paper
and then there was a place
where they wanted to sell a bike
Because they didn't want it anymore
And then we went to go get it
and I'm still four years old
And then when I start
my dad put on the training wheels
and then I practiced
and rided my bike
and I learned to keep the training wheels off
   the sidewalk
and then my dad took off the training wheels
and then I learned how to ride a two-wheeler.
That's the end.

Scoring. All stories were classified by an examiner with extensive experience with story grammar scoring. As a check on the scoring, 20% of the stories were used to train a second scorer who then independently scored an additional 25% of the stories. The two examiners agreed about the overall structure of all but one of the stories. That disagreement appeared to be due to whether or not one could infer a consequence from the child's wording. In subsequent use of the story grammar analysis techniques, we found it easier to begin by deciding whether or not there was a goal or motive and then making a tentative decision about overall structure before looking for internal categories.

Frequency of structures. All 96 instances were categorized from "no story," and "no structure," through "multi-episodic structure." Scores of 0 through 8 were assigned in order to use statistical techniques; these scores should be considered an ordinal scale although there is some question about whether or not the reactive sequence is a category that is ordered developmentally as Stein and Glenn indicate it is, or is found at all levels of development as Peterson and McCabe (1983) suggest. In these stories, and in the follow-up study (Sulzby, 1983a), the reactive sequence appears to be ordered as Stein and Glenn (1981) report. A frequency distribution of the stories from this study is shown in Table 3.

The distribution of story structures indicates that these stories tend to be less complex than those elicited using the story starter method of Glenn and Stein (1978) and much less complex than the narratives elicited by Peterson and McCabe (1983). However, it should be noted that, in a longitudinal replication (Sulzby, 1983a), the percentages of structures of a smaller group of children paralleled the Glenn and Stein percentages.

TABLE 3
Frequency of Story Structures

Structure	Session 1		Session 2		
	Told	Dictated	Told	Dictated	Total
No Story	4	5	2	2	13
No Structure	3	2	1	1	7
Descriptive Structure	0	1	1	2a	4
Action Sequence	4a	3a	11	7	25
Reactive Sequence	4	6	4	8	22
Incomplete Episode	2a	1	1	2	6
Simple Episode	1	1	1	0	3
Complete Episode	4	4	1	0	9
Multi-episode	2	1	2	2	7
Totals	24	24	24	24	96

[a]Contains one "procedural" narrative.

A subjects-by-measures analysis of variance indicated that there were no significant effects of mode (telling or dictating) nor of topic (real versus make-believe). The only significant effect was a mode-by-individuals interaction.

In other words, at the level of overall structure the children's stories did not differ when they were supposed to be real or make-believe stories, although it was expected that the make-believe stories might be more complex. The children's stories did not differ consistently in structural complexity in mode; we would have expected that these stories would be essentially the same when told or dictated. Instead, individual differences in structural complexity were evident in whether the story was told or dictated.

The individual scores making up the mode by subjects interactions were examined. There were two clusters of children, one group in which the told stories were superior and one in which the dictated stories were superior. There was a mix of children in each group who were high and low in emergent reading abilities as determined by the scale described in the previous section. An analysis of covariance calculated using these scores[6] as a covariate confirmed the findings of the examination of the individual scores.

My interpretation of these findings comes from a close look at the children and the stories they produced. It appears that when children are attempting to write and to read, the stories they produce are affected by numerous factors beyond those that would be present in oral storytelling sessions. Remember that a few children had sounded as if they were dictat-

---

[6]Although there is a slight use of "structure" in the Emergent Reading Ability Judgments, it is not the kind of structural analysis used in the story grammar scoring.

ing when they were telling stories; internal pausing and planning for a written story seemed to result in sparse productions. On the other hand, some "low" children produced better-formed dictated stories than some of the "high" children, yet showed less awareness of the relevant conditions for dictating.

Additionally, almost all of the children showed knowledges about written language that were not indicated directly in the structural scoring. If story grammar techniques are used in future research in emergent literacy, I would suggest gathering children's stories generated as true storytelling to compare with those generated as part of a writing task. I can also add that our subsequent research has continued to document the task and setting differences partially reported in these studies. For example, in Sulzby (1983a), I found children's stories to differ in complexity when they were collected in a group setting in the classroom in contrast with individual sessions. Often, however, the type of writing system used by the child also changed.

The story grammar was designed to examine structure and also the gross semantic notions of the grammatical categories. In order to apply it, we also had to take specific semantic content of the stimulus, learning to ride a big wheel, into account. Even with this adaptation, the story grammar was not sensitive to the specific details of the real/make-believe manipulation used in this study. In previous sections, we saw that the stories were not judged by adult readers to differ in overall "understandability," but that specific items were differently specified in real and make-believe stories.

The real and make-believe distinction could, nevertheless, be judged for some children by direct examination of their stories. I will present examples of children who did and who did not vary their story according to the real and make-believe distinction.

Real and make-believe distinguished. Kimberly showed a great deal of knowledge about written language as noted in previous examples taken from her dictation (page 184). Her first session was make-believe. She introduced a fictional protagonist using literary language and then put her in a problematic situation with the big wheel that only another suitable literary device, the prince, marriage, and "happily ever after" could solve. In contrast, her real story appeared to be tied to actual events she could remember in the telling condition. (In the dictating condition, she tried to tell what happened to herself when she grew up but then quit saying that she couldn't remember.)

Kimberly, make-believe, telling:
> Once upon a time there lived a princess
> that learned how to ride a big wheel.
> But by the time she grew up

she didn't know how to ride it
and a prince came along and taught her how to ride it
and married her
and lived happily ever after.

Kimberly, real, telling:

Well, I learned, well, I actually knew how
to ride a bike when I first got it.
I got it for my birthday.
I actually like to ride my bicycle.
A couple of times I tipped over sometimes
but I don't do it anymore.
And (3 second pause) I can't think of anything more—
And I liked it a lot.
And I shared it with a friend.
And that's all.

Real and make-believe not distinguished. A number of children simply took the same basic composition and changed the pronouns. Matt's two told stories are examples of this strategy. The only difference that appears to be a distinction is the introduction of another (unspecified) person to teach the make-believe character how to ride.

Matt, make-believe, telling:

Well, one day he just learned
and somebody taught him how to pedal and steer
and that's all.

Matt, real, telling:

I learned to ride something around.
I just steered and pedalled.
I just did it.

In subsequent work I have found children to be far more willing to use elements of fantasy in situations that are more free than the type of interview sessions used here. This finding has been reported by other researchers as well (for example, Sutton-Smith, 1981). The current study did not indicate that make-believe conditions of the constrained sort used here resulted in more complex stories, nor that emergent reading ability was directly enhanced by whether or not the child had composed a real or make-believe story. I believe that the relationship is far more complex and, for now, consider the real and make-believe condition to be more helpful as one means of getting fairly comparable stimulus items. A more appropriate comparison of writing about real topics and fantasy topics would involve more naturalistic research with composition and revision over time.

SUMMARY OF RESULTS

These two studies reveal many insights into what 5-year-olds know about writing and reading before they are introduced to formal instruction in schools. In the summary that follows, I will focus first upon the children's knowledges about writing and then about reading. Then I review observations about the children's "knowledges about knowing and learning," which includes metalinguistic and metacognitive awarenesses. Finally, I will comment upon the patterns of development and of individual differences seen in the performances of the 24 children in this study.

Writing

These 5-year-old children from literate backgrounds came to kindergarten knowing a tremendous amount about writing. Graphically, all of the children knew how to form some letters and many knew how to form all of the alphabet letters. Since I avoided the typical testing/inventory procedures, these findings probably underestimate the number of letters known conventionally, but they also pick up partial knowledge or approximations that conventional testing would have missed.

There is evidence that children acquire the ability to use handwriting as a result of abstraction, rather than direct imitation. This evidence is quite striking when the children's attempts to produce "grown-up writing" are examined.

These children were also aware of how writing is displayed graphically on pages. They showed this awareness both in their inventories of what they could write, which usually were list-like, and in writing stories. Additionally, they used this awareness to indicate what should get read in storybooks, although when they tried to read those books themselves, most of the children did not keep their eyes on print.

The children also showed a great deal of knowledge about the communicative function of writing. They all encoded meanings. All of the children wrote their own names and most of the children wrote additional items. Most of the isolated items were rendered in conventional orthography.

Generally, the children were aware of what they could do both by conventional standards and when they were using idiosyncratic means, "doing it my way," or "pretending." They vocalized, made comments, and asked questions while writing so that adults could observe the composition process and make inferences about the children's knowledges.

Most of the children attempted to write the longer, more complex messages requested for Study II, called "stories" by the examiners. The children typically used resources other than conventional orthography to make these attempts. Their writing attempts illustrate relationships between representational systems that have been found in other studies (Clay, 1975; Ferreiro & Teberosky, 1982; Harste, Burke, & Woodward, 1981; also Vygotsky, 1978). They write via drawing, scribbling, letter-like forms, strings of well-learned elements, and various forms of invented spelling, as well as via conventional orthography.

The young writers were also aware of and sensitive to the effort that writing required of a beginner. They accommodated for the effort required in various ways, such as reverting to a rapid, pretend-writing to encode a complex story or laboriously sounding-out a few words, then stopping in fatigue.

While I set out to compare the children's handwritten stories with their dictated and told stories, I could not make direct comparisons because the effort and fatigue required hindered most of the children from completing the handwritten composition. Thus the closest parallel comparison of the oral and written modes came through the told and dictated stories. Nevertheless, the partial handwritten compositions can be described meaningfully and interpreted along with the children's re-reading attempts.

As dictators, children made use of a more literate member of their society to write for them, just as novices have done historically and still do in less literate cultures (see Scribner & Cole, 1981). The children varied in their awareness of the needs of the scribe as they dictated their stories. This variation seemed to be related to how close the child was to being able to read independently. Children's dictated stories showed some features of oral language, but they also showed awareness of characteristics of written language. Child dictators signalled awareness of the scribe's needs by pausing to allow the scribe to write; they varied in whether or not they paused voluntarily, in how realistic their pauses were, and in whether or not they responded to prompts by the scribe. Additionally, the children varied in whether or not they turned dictation into an interrogation session, maintained an oral monologue without aid, or clearly signalled when their speech was to be taken as dictation or as an aside (see Sulzby & Otto, 1982).

In general, these children can be described as having knowledges that are correct by conventional standards and knowledges that are emerging toward the conventional along logical paths based upon features of written language, both in its graphic form and in its functions.

Reading

The children in these studies were emerging in reading ability as well. Their reading abilities were displayed in four different tasks: re-reading their own conventional writing (which was usually a list); reading a favorite storybook; re-reading their own handwritten and dictated stories; and re-reading all or parts of those stories in order to edit them.

Reading from their own conventional writing provides some evidence that children can perform in conventional ways with reading tasks, that is, in ways that the "adult on the street" might consider to be "reading." However, these performances varied from reading with eyes on print to reading with eyes gazing into space or at the examiner. The children typically used a list-like intonation for this task, but they varied in whether they simply said or described the words written: Emily vs. "my name." Even when the child's eyes were on print, however, it was not possible to be certain that s/he was reading independently since the items could be recognized from various clues, including memory for the composition itself. While it sounds reasonable that children should be able to read what they write, particularly when they write conventionally, I have come to question whether or not children automatically make that connection.

In this study, many of the children attempted to read from favorite storybooks. There was some evidence that the attempts could be ordered developmentally and follow-up research has confirmed this (Sulzby, 1983b, in press-b). Children's reading attempts included refusals along with statements about what they would need in order to be able to read the book. Other reading attempts included speech that could be considered more appropriate to storytelling than to storyreading while some children used book-like language even when they were re-creating the story.

Children's reading attempts with their own stories, both handwritten and dictated, could also be ordered developmentally. This ordering required a suspension of the requirement that the writing be conventional and involved a comparison of the "re-reading" with the composed version, even when that version was only inferrable from the child's speech while composing. The scale developed to make these judgments has been used successfully in follow-up research; however, I think that its success may be due to its broad character which may mask important regressions and fluctuations in the children's performances. Nevertheless, watching where the children's eyes are looking, listening to the wording and intonation of the child's speech while re-reading, and comparing the composed and re-read versions for semantic similarity furnishes enlightening evidence of children's concepts about reading. One of the most intriguing pieces of evidence comes when a child learns that s/he can track and re-track the printed version to get memory, voice, eyes, and even fingers aligned; Clay's (1979) research revealed that children gradually learn such aligning, rather than automatically making the connections in one step. Some of the children in this study explored this type of learning during re-reading tasks and others only through the examiner-prompted editing tasks. In all cases, the child appears to be constructing an internal representation of the composed unit to compare with the printed unit, be that unit written in conventional orthography or the child's developing orthography.

In the various reading attempts and in children's explanations about how one learns to read, children gave evidence of the numerous knowledges that eventually become coordinated into independent reading. These knowledges include how the prosody of reading sounds, what the wording of written language is like, how words get sounded-out, how memory for words and for entire texts is used, how finger, voice, and print can be coordinated, who writes texts, what the reader-audience can expect from a writer-author, what goes into texts, and even why one cannot yet read a given piece of writing to one's satisfaction.

Knowledges About Knowing and Learning

The children in the current study responded to a number of interview questions about how they know and learned certain things about writing and reading. Additionally, they volunteered explanations and labels having to do with literacy activities and items. They offered explanations about what they could or might do under certain circumstances and what they have yet to learn. These responses, taken collectively, indicate that children's metalinguistic and metacognitive verbalizations are a rich source of information that we can explore further, keeping an open mind to try to understand the world of literacy from the child's view.

One finding that was particularly intriguing was the emphasis by the children upon learning in the home in contrast with their few mentions of learning in school. At first I thought this might be an artifact of the sample, but this finding has been replicated in a subsequent stury (Sulzby, 1983a). Additionally, it confirms evidence from retrospective studies of early reading (Clark, 1976; Durkin, 1966).

Individual Differences and Patterns of Development

Both the descriptive and quantitative analyses indicated individual variation in both writing and reading tasks. There was also evidence of patterns of development emerging toward conventional performance. My interpretation is that we can expect children to differ in how they develop, but to differ in logical and not random ways. Writing and reading are not mirror images, as pointed out by other researchers (Bissex, 1980; Read, 1979). Also, writing and reading are done by real people, real children, with notions about how the task is done conventionally and how it might be done more easily or interestingly. In subsequent research using case study techniques, we have found some behaviors that appeared bizarre, at first, but always turned out to be a logical way of dealing with a literacy task. Literacy is developing in a whole child; we must not forget that. On the other hand, we can look for patterns of development that can be seen even with all of the individual variation.

IMPLICATIONS

One clear implication of all of the research in emergent literacy is that children know far more than we have acknowledged in our schools and instructional programs at the point when children begin formal schooling. But they know it differently than we would have expected. Most programs are based on a conventional model of writing and reading which most children entering formal instruction do not yet share (see Teale & Sulzby, in press). While many middle-class children appear to be successful even with programs that are not developmentally appropriate, many less-advantaged children are not so successful. For those children, we may need programs that are more like the kind of instruction and discovery that these middle-class children are getting at home and from other sources prior to kindergarten. Or, we may discover through more in-depth research with non middle-class children that more precise descriptions of the knowledges that they bring to school with them may lead to a greater variety of programs. One of the strongest implications I would draw is that teachers of young children face a complex intellectual task and need the strongest support of the public and research communities.

REFERENCES

Anderson, R. C. (1977). The notion of schemata and the educational enterprise. In R. C. Anderson, R. J. Spiro, & W. Montague (Eds.), *Schooling and the acquisition of knowledge*. Hillsdale, NJ: Lawrence Erlbaum Associates.

Applebee, A. N. (1978). *The child's concept of story: Ages two to seventeen*. Chicago, IL: University of Chicago Press.

Beers, J. W., & Henderson, E. H. (1977). A study of developing orthographic concepts among first graders. *Research in the Teaching of English, 11,* 133–148.

Bissex, G. L. (1980). *GNYS AT WRK: A child learns to write and read*. Cambridge, MA: Harvard University Press.

Bronfenbrenner, U. (1979). *The ecology of human development*. Cambridge, MA: Harvard University Press.

Cazden, C. B. (1983). Peekaboo as an instructional model: Discourse development at home and at school. In B. Bain (Ed.), *The sociogenesis of language and human conduct: A multi-disciplinary book of readings*. New York: Plenum.

Chomsky, C. (1970). Reading, writing, and phonology. *Harvard Educational Review, 40,* 287–309.

Clark, M. M. (1976). *Young fluent readers*. London: Heinemann Educational Books.

Clay, M. M. (1975). *What did I write?* Auckland, New Zealand: Heinemann Educational Books.

Clay, M. M. (1979). *Reading: The patterning of complex behavior.* Auckland, New Zealand: Heinemann Educational Books.

Cochran-Smith, M. (1984). *The making of a reader.* Norwood, NJ: Ablex Publishing Corporation.

Cook-Gumperz, J., & Gumperz, J. J. (1981). From oral to written culture: The transition to literacy. In M. F. Whiteman (Ed.), *Variation in writing: Functional and linguistic-cultural differences. (Vol. 1).* Hillsdale, NJ: Lawrence Erlbaum Associates.

Cox, B. J. (1983). Tracking "it" through woods and down the trail from emergent to independent reading. *32nd NRC Yearbook,* 243–250.

Cox, B. J., & Sulzby, E. (1984). Children's use of reference in told, dictated, and handwritten stories. *Research in the Teaching of English 18,* 345–356.

Doake, D. (1981). *Book experience and emergent reading behavior.* Unpublished doctoral dissertation, University of Alberta.

Durkin, D. (1966). *Children who read early.* New York: Teachers College Press.

Ferreiro, E., & Teberosky, A. (1982). *Literacy before schooling.* Exeter, NH: Heinemann Educational Books.

Glenn, C. G., & Stein, N. L. (1978). *Syntactic structures and real-world themes in stories generated by children.* Mimeographed paper. Urbana, IL: The University of Illinois.

Goodman, Y. M. (1980). *The roots of literacy.* In M. Douglass (Ed.), *Claremont Reading Conference Forty-Fourth Yearbook.* Claremont, CA: The Claremont Reading Conference.

Goodman, Y. M., & Altwerger, B. (1981). *Print awareness in preschool children: A study of the development of literacy in preschool children.* (Occasional Paper No. 4). Tucson, AZ: Program in Language and Literacy, College of Education, University of Arizona.

Graves, D. H. (1983). *Writing: Teachers & children at work.* Exeter, NH: Heinemann Educational Books.

Gundlach, R. A. (1982). Children as writers: The beginnings of learning to write. In M. Nystrand (Ed.), *What writers know: The language and structure of written discourse.* New York: Academic Press.

Harste, J. E., Burke, C. L., & Woodward, V. A. (1981). *Children, their language and world: Initial encounters with print.* (Final report to the National Institute of Education, NIE-G-79-0132). Bloomington, IN: Indiana University.

Heath, S. B. (1982). What no bedtime story means: Narrative skills at home and school. *Language in Society, 11,* 49–76.

Hildreth, G. (1936). Developmental sequences in name writing. *Child Development, 7,* 291–303.

Holdaway, D. (1979). *The foundations of literacy.* Sydney, Australia: Ashton Scholastic.

King, M. L., & Rentel, V. M. (1981). *How children learn to write* (Final report to the National Institute of Education). Columbus, OH: Ohio State University.

Mandler, J. M., & Johnson, N. S. (1977). Remembrance of things parsed: Story structure and recall. *Cognitive Psychology, 9,* 111–151.

Menig-Peterson, C. L., & McCabe, A. (1978). Children's orientation of a listener to the context of their narratives. *Developmental Psychology, 13,* 582–592.

Olson, D. R. (1977). From utterance to text: The bias of language in speech and writing. *Harvard Educational Review, 47,* 257–281.

Otto, B. (1984). *Evidence of emergent reading behaviors in young children's interactions with favorite storybooks.* Unpublished doctoral dissertation, Northwestern University.

Perfetti, C. A., & Roth, S. (1981). Some of the interactive processes in reading and their role in reading skill. In A. M. Lesgold & C. A. Perfetti (Eds.), *Interactive processes in reading.* Hillsdale, NJ: Lawrence Erlbaum Associates.

Peterson, C. L., & McCabe, A. (1983). *Three ways of looking at a child's narratives: A psycholinguistic analysis.* New York: Plenum.

Policastro, M. (1981). *The concept of a story: A comparison between children and teachers.* Unpublished doctoral dissertation, Northwestern University.

Read, C. (1970). *Children's perceptions of the sounds of English.* Unpublished doctoral dissertation, Harvard University.

Read, C. (1975). *Children's categorizations of speech sounds in English* (NCTE Research Report 17). Urbana, IL: National Council of Teachers of English.

Read, C. (1979). Writing is not the inverse of reading for young children. In C. H. Frederiksen & J. F. Dominic (Eds.), *Writing: Process, development, and communication.* Hillsdale, NJ: Lawrence Erlbaum Associates.

Rumelhart, D. E. (1977). Toward an interactive model of reading. In S. Dornic (Ed.), *Attention and performance VI.* London: Academic Press.

Scollon, R. & Scollon, S. B. K. (1981). *Narrative, literacy, and face in interethnic communication.* Norwood, NJ: Ablex Publishing Corporation.

Scribner, S., & Cole, M. (1981). *The psychology of literacy.* Cambridge, MA: Harvard University Press.

Simner, M. L. (1981). *Printing errors in kindergarten and the prediction of academic performance.* Paper presented at the Biennial Meeting of the Society for Research in Child Development, Boston.

Smith, F. (1979). Conflicting approaches to reading research and instruction. In L. B. Resnick & P. A. Weaver (Eds.), *Theory and practice of early reading* (Vol. 2). Hillsdale, NJ: Lawrence Erlbaum Associates.

Snow, C., & Ninio, A. (in press). The contracts of literacy: What children learn from learning to read books. In W. H. Teale & E. Sulzby (Eds.), *Emergent literacy: Writing and reading.* Norwood, NJ: Ablex Publishing Corporation.

Stauffer, R. G. (1970). *The language-experience approach to the teaching of reading.* New York: Harper & Row.

Stein, N. L., & Glenn, C. G. (1979). An analysis of story comprehension in elementary school children. In R. O. Freedle (Ed.), *New directions in discourse comprehension* (Vol. 2). Norwood, NJ: Ablex Publishing Corporation.

Stein, N. L., & Glenn, C. G. (1981). *The concept of a story: A study of story telling.* Mimeographed paper. Chicago, IL: University of Chicago.

Sulzby, E. (1980). Using children's dictated stories to aid comprehension. *The Reading Teacher, 33,* 772–778.

Sulzby, E. (1981). *Kindergarteners begin to read their own compositions: Beginning readers' developing knowledges about written language project* (Final report to the Research Foundation of the National Council of Teachers of English). Evanston, IL: Northwestern University.

Sulzby, E. (1982). Oral and written mode adaptations in stories by kindergarten children. *Journal of Reading Behavior, 14,* 51–59.

Sulzby, E. (1983a). *Beginning readers' developing knowledges about written language.* Final report to the National Institute of Education (NIE-G-80-0176). Evanston, IL: Northwestern University.

Sulzby, E. (1983b). *Children's emergent abilities to read favorite storybooks.* Final report to the Spencer Foundation. Evanston, IL: Northwestern University.

Sulzby, E. (in press-a). Children's development of prosodic distinctions in telling and dictating modes. To appear in A. Matsuhashi (Ed.), *Writing in real time: Modelling production processes.* New York: Longman.

Sulzby, E. (in press-b). Children's emergent reading of favorite storybooks: A developmental study. *Reading Research Quarterly.*

Sulzby, E. (in press-c). *Emergent writing and reading in 5–6 year olds: A longitudinal study.* Norwood, NJ: Ablex Publishing Corporation.

Sulzby, E. (in press-d). Writing and reading: Signs of oral and written language organization in the young child. In W. H. Teale & E. Sulzby (Eds.), *Emergent literacy: Writing and reading.* Norwood, NJ: Ablex Publishing Corporation.

Sulzby, E., & Otto, B. (1982). "Text" as an object of metalinguistic knowledge: A study in literacy development. *First Language, 3,* 181–199.

Sulzby, E., & Teale, W. H. (1983). *Young children's storybook reading: Longitudinal study of parent-child interaction and children's independent functioning.* Proposal to the Spencer Foundation. Evanston, IL: Northwestern University.

Sutton-Smith, B. (1981). *The folkstories of children.* Philadelphia, PA: University of Pennsylvania Press.

Tannen, D. (1982). *Spoken and written language: Exploring orality and literacy.* Norwood, NJ: Ablex Publishing Corporation.

Taylor, D. (in press). Creating family story. In W. H. Teale & E. Sulzby (Eds.), *Emergent literacy: Writing and reading.* Norwood, NJ: Ablex Publishing Corporation.

Teale, W. H. (1982). Toward a theory of how children learn to read and write naturally. *Language Arts, 59,* 555–570.

Teale, W. H., & Sulzby, E. (in press). Emergent literacy as a perspective for looking at how children become writers and readers. In W. H. Teale and E. Sulzby (Eds.), *Emergent literacy: Writing and reading.* Norwood, NJ: Ablex Publishing Corporation.

Teale, W. H., & Sulzby, E. (in press). *Emergent literacy: Writing and reading.* Norwood, NJ: Ablex Publishing Corporation.

Tinzmann, M., Cox, B., & Sulzby, E. (1983). Children's specification of context in told and dictated story productions. *32nd National Reading Conference Yearbook, 32,* 267–274.

Vygotsky, L. S. (1962). *Thought and language.* Cambridge, MA: MIT Press.

Vygotsky, L. S. (1978). *Mind in society: The development of higher psychological processes.* Cambridge, MA: Harvard University Press.

4 Children's Writing in an Elementary School Postal System

Jennifer E. Greene
The Literacy Workshop
Santa Monica, California

BACKGROUND FOR THE PROJECT

Jennifer: Of the different kinds of writing you do in your classroom, which do you like to do best?
Miguel: Colmar Mail.
Jennifer: What is special to you about doing Colmar Mail?
Miguel: You can talk to a person like that, in a silent way.

Introduction

Miguel has learned that writing can communicate his intentions to someone effectively, just as talking can. What Miguel knows about writing, as a fourth grader, is something too many children do not have the chance to learn before they decide that school writing is difficult, unpleasant, and not really good for anything personally meaningful anyway. Miguel is one of 32 second, third, and fourth graders who participated in a year long study of their use of a school-based postal system at Colmar Elementary School in Bell Gardens, California. He may be more articulate than some, but I do not think it is unreasonable to consider his point of view typical of the others'.

The purpose of this background part of the chapter is to establish two separate but closely related contexts which are necessary for an understanding of the project. The first pertains to the theory and research which guided me, and the second, to the nature of the operation of the postal system at Colmar. The following sections discuss the theoretical rationale which motivated the study; describe the design, development, and implementation of the postal system at Colmar, as well as its daily operation; discuss my aims in selecting classrooms and students to participate in the project and describe different styles of managing the postal system on the classroom level; discuss data collection, both linguistic and ethnographic methods; and describe my basic approach to this research project and my aims in presenting the findings. It is clear throughout that the phenomenon I was investigating had a great deal of impact on the method of approaching it and the shape the study would take.

Theoretical Rationale

By the time children first enter school, they have accomplished the extremely complex task of acquiring proficiency in one, and often two or more, languages. Their linguistic knowledge encompasses not only structural rules of how to create grammatical utterances, but also social rules of language use, the understanding of what is appropriate to say to whom on what occasions. Recent research on literacy development (e.g., Cook-Gumperz & Gumperz, 1981) points to the importance of allowing children to draw on their rich oral language tradition as they make the transition to written literacy. Too often instructional methods do not make use of what children already know in the effort to move them into new areas of literacy development. In writing instruction, the focus is often on mechanical matters such as handwriting or spelling and rhetorical matters relating to formal content, with the result that children rarely have the opportunity to just "talk on paper" to grow comfortable with the medium. As Miguel described above, the postal system at Colmar provides students with precisely that opportunity.

From the point of view of an observant outsider looking in, it seemed that there were several important ways in which use of the postal system would allow children to draw on their oral language as they made the transition to literacy. First, in writing letters they could draw on the full range of language functions that is part of their oral language competence. When children talk, they invite, insult, apologize, brag, compliment, complain, ask, inform, and so forth. Typically, when they write in school, they are only asked to inform, one small piece of their oral language competence.

Second, it seemed that, like oral communication, communication in letters would be functional. Children would write letters in order to say real things to real people. What they wrote would be self-generated, rather than teacher-generated. It would be intended to accomplish communicative goals truly felt by children rather than external goals imposed by a teacher.

And, third, it seemed that communication in letters, like oral communication, would be interactive. Unlike most school writing tasks, which are designed for an unknown audience, children would write letters to a known recipient, and they would write with the expectation of a response.

The value of functional, interactive writing in writing development had been documented by Shuy (1981) and Staton (1982) in the context of dialogue journals, where a teacher and a student wrote to one another on a daily basis. The postal system at Colmar provided another context, with somewhat different operational rules, in which to observe the effects of such writing. Some pilot work that I had done at Colmar during the 1980–1981 school year, (Greene, 1981) indicated that functional, interactive writing, which employed a range of language functions, was indeed being done. And it revealed some of the formal aspects involved as children learned to use the postal system.

The purpose of this study was to use linguistic and ethnographic methods to investigate two questions. First, I wanted to find out what children used the postal system for, what they wrote about, and what language functions they employed. I wanted to know how the postal system entered into their personal, social, and academic lives. Second, I wanted to find out what was involved in learning to correspond, to interact with someone through the medium of writing. This seemed to me to be the essence of being able to use the postal system. I viewed learning to use the postal system as the acquisition of a cultural tool, in Vygotsky's (1978) sense. With the few changes involved in the transition from the Colmar postal system to the United States postal system, children were acquiring use of a tool that would be of value to them for the rest of their lives.

The Colmar Postal System

Understanding precisely what this tool was that Colmar students were learning to use requires some explanation. As anyone who has been involved with successful educational innovation knows, implementation of the postal system at Colmar did not happen overnight. It started in a 2-3-4 bilingual classroom in another school where an observant and clever teacher noticed that her students were writing a lot of notes to one another. She decided to try to channel some of that energy into her classroom writing program by establishing a postal center. As she watched her students writing letters, she noticed such things as an increase in the amount of time her students spent writing, a desire on their part to send and receive letters, and the ease with which they learned correct letter writing form. By answering all the letters she received, she found that she could model adult writing for them and facilitate their writing development.

Then, she was promoted out of the classroom, to the position of reading specialist at Colmar. During her first year there she worked with many teachers, helping them set up language arts centers. In many classrooms they started postal centers, with good results. It was at this point that she started thinking about the prospect of a school-wide postal system. She presented the idea to the Colmar staff, and the staff approved. She formed a committee consisting of a cross-section of teachers, and together they developed the groundwork for the Colmar Postal System. The committee presented its plan to the staff, and the plan was enthusiastically received. Using compensatory education funds, they printed stationery, stamps designed by the students, direction cards, and directories. Aides made mailboxes for each class and a big one for the library. Finally, the teachers set up their individual classroom centers, a central post office was established in the library, and the postal system was ready to go. Everyday a mail person from each class delivered mail to the central post office. Two fourth grade clerks went to the library at 10:00 a.m. to cancel (they had their own cancellation stamp made) and sort the mail. Then at 10:30, two deliverers went to the library, put on mail helmets, filled their mail bags, and delivered the mail.

Thus, this was the school-level context in which letter writing happened at Colmar. At the time my study began, the postal system had been in operation successfully for 2 years. The reading specialist's leadership in the design, development, and implementation of the postal system, actively involving teachers every step of the way, was no doubt a large part of her success with the project. Winning a California School Boards award for innovative curriculum projects in 1982 helped to confirm the role of the postal system as an important institution at Colmar, and set an example for other schools to follow.

Choice of Classrooms and Students for Participation

After becoming familiar with the operation of the postal system during my pilot work, I developed a plan for this project which involved working in four classrooms with a total of 32 students. I wanted four classrooms in order to be sure of having some variation in teacher management of the postal system. Explaining my method for selecting classrooms requires some information about how Colmar operates. Because of overcrowding, Colmar is on a year-round schedule. The school is divided into four "tracks" (the groupings have no relation to student ability), each of which is in session for 9 weeks and then on vacation for 3. It is a neighborhood school, with each "track" consisting of one quadrant of the neighborhood. Thus, the children who are in school together are also on vacation together, and it is among children on each "track" that most friendships tend to be. Because I knew from my pilot work that most letters were written between friends, I wanted the four classrooms I chose to be on a single "track." The "track" I chose had the most equal representation of second, third, and fourth graders. There were two 2-3 classrooms, one 3, and one 4.

In Mrs. F's classroom, one of the 2-3's, letter writing was a free time activity. She taught a lesson on letter form early in the year, but from then on (with the exception of class time taken to write to the Great Pumpkin and the Easter Bunny) students were on their own. Numerous times during my observations, I heard children requested to put their stationery away and to return to the task at hand. Letter writing was a popular activity there.

In Ms. G's room, the other 2-3, the children were divided into four groups, and each group went to a post office center one, and sometimes two, times a week. There, children were required to write one letter and allowed to write more if time permitted. Letter writing was also a free time activity.

In Ms. R's classroom, the fourth grade, the postal system functioned much as it did in Ms. G's room, as a weekly, or more frequent, center, and as a free time activity. A great deal of letter writing was done in Ms. R's classroom.

In Mr. D's classroom, the third grade class, management of the postal system was more carefully monitored. Letter writing was taught as a whole class activity on a weekly basis. Mr. D was insistent upon correct spelling and form.

Other aspects of the teachers' behavior with respect to the postal system will emerge in this chapter, but it is worth mentioning at the outset that individual teacher's management style did not affect the nature of children's use of the postal system to any noticeable extent. Certain letter writing habits emerged in certain classrooms, but the variation seemed to be more a matter of peer than of teacher influence.

In choosing students to participate in the project, I made certain at the outset to have a reasonable balance according to grade level, English language fluency, academic ability (as determined by teacher judgment), and sex. The community of Bell Gardens is one of the poorer East Los Angeles suburbs. The population of the school is roughly 70% Hispanic, and of the 32 children chosen, 27 had Spanish surnames. Of these 27, 23 spoke Spanish as their first language and had learned English more or less recently, with somewhat varying degrees of fluency. All were, at the time of the selection, considered bilingual, although in some cases, the degree to which they were bilingual seemed questionable. Four of the students with non-Hispanic surnames were Anglo, and one was Samoan, although his first language was English. Of the 32 students, 8 were in the second grade, 14 in the third, and 10 in the fourth. All of the students whom I invited to participate in the project agreed to do so, and received parental permission.

Data Collection

Data collection involved collecting written samples for linguistic analysis, and ethnographic methods of observing and interviewing. I gave all the students in each of the four classrooms a manila envelope in which to store the letters they received. On the front of the envelope was taped a form on which to record the date, recipient, and school address of all the letters they wrote. On a monthly basis I collected the envelopes and copied the letters written by the students in the project which had been received since the previous collection. On a weekly basis, and sometimes more often because of a special event, I observed in the classrooms when letters were being written and when they were being distributed.

When I was in the classrooms I played the role of a helper, happy to assist with spelling (the usual "problem") or other matters pertaining to writing. My specific behavior was partially a product of the particular classroom I was in and that teacher's style of managing the postal system. I also observed the children when they were on the playground at recess, noting who played with whom and the kinds of talk I heard.

In June I interviewed the 32 students in order to better understand their feelings about the postal system and its usefulness for them. At that time I also interviewed the four teachers, to hear from them how they felt the postal system fit into their overall writing curriculum, and to discuss the students.

Data Reduction and Analysis

The essence of my purpose in presenting the results of this study is to document what children who are in the process of learning to write do when a school-wide postal system is part of their educational environment. I wanted the children to be real and to be allowed to reveal themselves through what they wrote, what they said to me, and what I observed about them. I view the complete set of written data I collected as a whole, representing the full range of ways second, third, and fourth graders are likely to use the postal system. The children had the right of censorship, and for this and other reasons having to do with unavoidable slack in the collecting of letters, I am certain there are letters I did not see. But if the body of data I have is viewed as a whole, then each child represents some part of that whole. Of the complete range of concerns and language functions that appear in the letters, each child contributed one subset of them. Each child's subset may be slightly, or perhaps, markedly different from the others. I have noted the unusual, and focused my reporting on the more general.

I have not tried to fully portray each child. Rather, I have selected an illustrative set of letter writing strategies which, in my opinion, satisfactorily represents the whole. I have selected letters which illustrate clearly and interestingly the range of letter writing strategies I found. In this respect my methodology is more like the artist than the scientist doing qualitative educational research (Eizner, 1981). Rather than fully accounting for the whole by quantitative methods, I am allowing a part to represent the whole, knowing that the vitality that is so much a part of the children's use of the postal system will better shine through this way.

A story could have been told about each child, without question. But doing that was simply beyond the realm of possibility. There were a few cases, however, where it was impossible not to focus on one child at length, and in these instances a complete section is focused on a single child. The second section, How Children Use the Postal System, draws from the complete set of data to demonstrate how children across the grade levels use the postal system. The third section, Corresponding, draws from a much smaller set of data to illustrate what is involved as children learn to correspond. The final section suggests implications for education. The kinds of contributions a school-based postal system can make to children's writing development are discussed.

HOW CHILDREN USE THE POSTAL SYSTEM

Introduction

Any examination of how children use the postal system must, at least implicitly, also be concerned with their purposes in using it. Children's purposes for writing motivate and guide what they write. Purposes, however, are internal and, therefore, nonobservable. Children's concerns, on the other hand, the things which they consider important and interesting, are apparent in what they write. It is the purpose of this section to investigate the concerns that are manifest in the children's letters through an examination of the language functions in which these concerns occur.

Use of the term "concern" is intended to reflect the fact that much of the letter writing that children do does not have a topic in any usual rhetorical or linguistic sense. This writing might be called pre-topical in that it involves a somewhat amorphous, yet pervasive concern with interpersonal relationships. Certainly there are occasions when a specific topic, like a sport or a particular academic subject, is apparent, but generally even these are woven into the larger concern of interpersonal relations. The term "language function" is used here to refer to the surface level manifestation of the writer's intention, the goal to be achieved by a written sentence part, whole sentence, or series of sentences. The language functions, for example, complimenting or inviting, convey the writer's aims in communicating, and they also reflect his or her attitude with respect to the larger concern with interpersonal relations.

This section begins with a discussion of the most frequently occurring language function in the data. It is perhaps most accurately described as an affirmation of friendship. The child's concern in these instances is unquestionably with the interpersonal, "you and me." The second part investigates other language functions that occur in letters among peers, while the third examines what children write to adults. Finally there are case studies of two children, James and Caridad, who use the postal system extensively and yet in rather dissimilar ways.

Affirmations of Friendship

This function is treated first and in a section of its own because of its pervasiveness in the data. It seems to be the function that appears first in children's letters, the one from which others evolve. However, the reasons for
its pervasiveness are apparently as much socially based as they are developmentally based. Affirmations of friendship are a matter of convention in
children's letter writing. For reasons that will be suggested below, they become the standard of appropriateness. The letter in (1) illustrates one basic
form of the function.

(1)   Sept 21, 1981
            Dear Caridad
            you are my best
            frend
            (pic)
            Love
            Zoraya (Mr. D, 3)

(After each letter the author's classroom and grade level are identified. The
children's spelling, punctuation, spacing, line breaks, and placement of letter
parts have not been altered. Misspelled words of questionable decipherability
are corrected in parentheses. "(Pic)" appears between the body of the letter
and the closing, where the picture box is placed on the stationery, if the
writer draws a picture. A letter may be assumed to have been addressed to a
classmate, unless it is otherwise identified. When a writer does not sign a
letter, his or her name appears in parentheses at the end of the letter. A letter
written in Spanish is followed immediately by the English translation.)

There is another basic form which the affirmation of friendship takes,
illustrated in (2). Here there is an expression of feeling rather than a claim
of status.

(2)   9/2/81
            Dear
            Gina I love
            you very
            much
            (pic)
            Becky (Mrs. F, 2)

Typically a child who uses one of these basic forms does not use the other.
Children seem to settle on a particular strategy that feels right and to use it
as a foundation on which to build.

There may be a tendency for less-experienced writers to write more
simple, pared down affirmations of friendship than those for whom writing

comes more easily. For example, Julio, who as a fourth grader still had considerable difficulty with writing, wrote the undated (3) sometime in November. (Julio was retained in the fourth grade the following year.)

(3)   John you
        are my friend
        (Julio) (Ms. R, 4)

However, the trend toward simplicity cannot be attributed to ability or experience only. Students have other reasons for writing what they do. Five days after Becky wrote the letter in (2), she wrote to Gina again, as shown in (4).

(4)   Dear   9/7/81
        Gina I love
        you very much
        you are nice
        I miss you
        when I am at
        home
        (pic)
        Becky

(Becky's pictures are nearly always hearts, with or without arrows through them.) Here, in addition to her "I love you," Becky provides a reason for her affirmation of friendship, or an explanation for the basis for her feelings, "You are nice," and a statement about the effect of having these feelings, "I miss you when I am at home." Her letter is tight and coherent. Clearly, Becky makes choices when she writes as to how simple and short she wants her letter to be, or how elaborate. Most frequently during the year, she chose to write short, unadorned affirmations of friendship.

Similarly Zoraya is not limited to writing letters as streamlined in their affirmations of friendship as (1). She did (1) in cursive handwriting, a skill which was quite new to her as a third grader, and one which may have been distracting her from focusing on other aspects of her writing. Four days previous to writing (1), she had sent (5) to Caridad, this one printed rather than in cursive writing.

(5)   Dear Caridad   9/17
        I like you because you are
        nice to me. Cari you are my
        best friend
        (pic)
        Love Zoraya

Here she gives a reason for her feelings and uses an affirmation of friendship to create a powerful punch line. Zoraya's second letter to Caridad, in (1), may be simpler because of the strain of doing cursive writing, or because it was her second letter and she had already outdone herself in the first. (Caridad had written to her on September 17, too, so the brevity of Zoraya's second letter was probably not due to frustration at failure to get a response from Caridad.) Since native English speakers, as well as children whose first language is Spanish, write identical affirmations of friendship in English, it is also unlikely that a lack of fluency in English is the cause of the brevity of these letters. Whatever other factors may be involved, it seems clear that children write affirmations of friendship, at least in part, because that is the socially appropriate thing to do.

The remainder of this section examines an illustrative selection of letters in which an affirmation of friendship is the only or primary language function in an effort to describe and to explain, where possible, the variation that occurs. One of the more common means by which a letter containing an affirmation of friendship is enlarged is by reference to an activity in which the writer and the addressee participate together, In (6), for example, Becky names the general category of play.

(6)   Dear Julia
        I love you very
        much and I like to
        play with you.
        (pic)
        Love Becky (Mrs. F, 2)

In (7), Alex names a specific shared play activity in his letter to a friend in another classroom.

                Sept 24
(7)   Dear Mario
        I like to play
        kickball with you
        and I like you
        Mario
        (pic)
        by Alex (Mrs. F, 3)

(Alex addresses Mario directly in his letter, a common occurrence among some children. Also, he closes his letter with "by," an action which suggests that his letter writing is influenced by other school writing tasks.) In (8), Carlos names a specific activity, as well as his other friends who participate in it.

(8)   12-3-81
             Dear Guillermo
             You are my Best
             friend and we
             play monsters with
             jose and alejandro
             and alvaro
             your friend
             Carlos (Mr. D, 3)

Andy mentions another best friend, as well as a shared activity, in (9).

(9)   3-25-82
             Dear Eliseo
             your my best
             friend and Carlos
             and we play
             kickball
             (pic)
             friend
             Andy (Mr. D, 3)

The naming of a shared activity seems to provide a context for the affirmation of friendship. This in effect reflects a real world truth, that the shared
activity is, in a sense, the context in which the friendship is embedded. Contextualization has long been recognized as a feature of children's developing
language. It is not surprising, therefore, that as these children struggle to
connect with one another through the strange medium of writing, they draw
from the salient features of the contexts in which their friendships take
place.

    In (10), Alma not only names an activity which she and her friend
share, but also makes a boast (or at least states what she perceives to be a
fact), which makes the contextual background of the shared activity come
alive for her.

(10)   October 8 1981
             Dear Zoraya
             you are my best friend
             and sometimes you play
             with me tetherball and I
             win you all the time
             (pic)
             your best friend
             Alma (Mr. D, 3)

In (11), Julia's reference to shared activities occurs in an offer or bargain she is making.

(11)   Dec 7
            Dear Delfina
            I like you very
            much you are my Best
            Freind Delfina
            I am your Best Frend
            I will be in your club
            if you play house with
            me today
                    love   Julia (Mrs. F, 2)

There is the sense here that Julia is indirectly asking for friendship, perhaps that she is attempting to arrange for activities that will give the association a chance to grow. The concept of being best friends, as it appears in children's letters, does not seem to involve mutuality. "You are my best friend" is a statement about my feelings for you. "I am your best friend" is a statement about my behavior toward you; I am nice to you. Being a best friend does not involve exclusivity, either. As Andy's letter in (9) shows, it is possible to have more than one best friend. Furthermore, just as it is possible to have a best friend, one can also have a best cousin, as Carlos' letter in (12) to Philip, who is in another classroom, illustrates.

(12)   Sept 17 1981
            Dear Phillip
            Yuo are my Best
            cousin and we go to
            your house and we Play
            soccer and marbles and
            baseball and catch
            love Carlos (Mr. D, 3)

Naming a shared activity is a method several children use to elaborate an affirmation of friendship. They ground it, or lend it credence, by making reference to a familiar activity. There are other methods used to lend credence to an affirmation of friendship. What Caridad does is to tell her friends why she likes them, as in (13). A detailed examination of Caridad's use of the postal system is presented in a later section.

(13)   10/8
            Dear Margaret
            I like you because you are nice

to me and you are nice to
Norma to good by
Margaret
Your friend Caridad (Mr. D, 3)

Patricia's strategy for elaborating her affirmations of friendship is to promise a gift, as in (14).

(14)   4/21
          Dear Isela
          I like you and
          I will boing
          gum for you?
          Love Patricia (Ms. G, 3)

(Patricia has begun to take note of the question mark. Perhaps her use of it here reflects a question in her mind as to whether or not she will be able to bring gum for Isela.) Patricia's strategy is actually more general than (14) demonstrates. She follows her affirmations of friendship with a kind thought of some sort, which provides evidence of her good intention. (15) illustrates another example of this strategy.

(15)   Dear Elizabeth
          your my best
          friend and I hope
          you in my next
          class in 4
          (pic)
          Love Patricia (Ms. G, 3)

Toward the end of the year Patricia wrote a letter in which her concern with interpresonal relations seems to have grown into a real topic. The letter is clearly an affirmation of friendship, but here she is focusing directly on the topic of being friends. The letter, in (16), is written to a friend in another classroom.

(16)   5/17
          Dear Melissa
          How are you? I am fine thank you.
          I hope we all could be friend
          for every and every every me and
          Liz has so lets be friend like
          me and Liz
          (pic)
          Love Patricia (Ms. G, 3)

(This is Patricia's first use of what becomes a commonly used strategy among the more mature letter writers: asking a question of her addressee and then answering it for herself. "How are you? I am fine," actually becomes a standard, ritualistic greeting in many children's letters. Patricia is one of the few students who uses a question mark in the question answer sequence. Once children start using it as a standard greeting, they no longer perceive it as containing a real question. For Patricia "How are you?" still is a real question, and she even goes so far as to thank her addressee for hypothetically having asked it. This sort of play with language, pretending someone has asked a question and answering, demonstrates a growing control of the rules of language use.)

Even among some of the most mature fourth graders, affirmations of friendship are sometimes the sole concern of a letter. Cindy's letter in (17) demonstrates quite a sophisticated concept of what friendship is.

(17)   1/24/82
             Dear Yvonne. Hi I like you and your a
             special friend to me and nobody else is. And
             I like you very very much and I Love
             you as a friend. I will like you always
             even if we fight even if you mad at
             me I will always like you and love
             you. Love you Yvonne and I don't care if
             you lagh either
                      Love you always Cindy (Ms. R, 4)

Such demonstrativeness is by no means characteristic only of the older girls, as Nieves' letter in (18) shows.

(18)   October 1981
             I love you Lorena
             and you love mi to
             and I sent you This Letter
             because I love you
             so mutch
             (Nieves) (Ms. G, 2)

(Note the Spanish influence in Nieves' spelling of "me": *mi*.)

It is interesting to note that affirmations of friendship did not occur in the oral language of these children during observations of their face-to-face interaction. Friendships are negotiated, maintained, broken, and renegotiated in a myriad of ways in the course of the day's activities, but strong affirmations of friendship, as illustrated here, seem to be limited to letter writing. The question arises as to why they are so pervasive in children's letters. While there are no conclusive answers, several possibilities are available. The first, and perhaps the most obvious, takes this line of thinking: children write letters in order to get letters in return; saying something nice is likely to inspire a recipient to write back; an affirmation of friendship is something nice. There is no doubt some truth to this line of thinking, but it does not go deep enough.

Often in children's behavior there are evidences of precursors of adult behavior. Child forms evolve into adult forms as they make generalizations, and test and refine them. Since such direct affirmations of friendship do not occur as the sole language function in adult letters, it is reasonable to ask what adult behavior children might be approximating with their affirmations of friendship. Typically, adults write letters about mutual interests, topics that grow out of a shared framework of experience. Might it not be true that children, too, are searching for topics of mutual interest, and that affirmations of friendship focus on the most accessible candidate: you and me? That is, you and me in our entirety, the whole being easier than the parts, the whole person being easier to focus on than his or her attributes. It seems that affirmations of friendship might be the most available way to connect with a person through writing for writers who have not yet gained a sure sense of control over the medium. For these writers, too, a letter is a gift with a message. The message is important, but the giving of the gift, with the hope of receiving one in return, is more so. An affirmation of friendship in a letter, then, is a gesture which allows children to connect in writing from the start. It provides a way of taking a turn, giving the recipient something tangible to indicate that the turn is now his. Later it will be refined and broken down into a variety of less global, more adult-like functions.

Other Uses of the Postal System among Peers

In this section the concerns or topics children write about to their peers form the organizational basis for an examination of the language functions they employ. Interpersonal relations is the overriding concern among peers and is considered first, followed by school and free time activities.

Much of the strictly interpersonal writing takes place between girls. Compliments abound as children focus on writing something that will inspire a response. Zoraya's letter in (1) starts off with two compliments.

(1)   10-10-81
         Querida Lili
         tu eres bonita y tienes bonito
         pelo. y me gusta jugar contigo a
         tetherball. mira la estampilla
         si te gusta me dices y man

        dame una carta
        (pic)
        Love
        Zoraya P (Mr. D, 3)

        (Dear Lili
        you are pretty and you have pretty
        hair. and I like to play
        tetherball with you. look at the stamp
        if you like it tell me and send
        me a letter
        Love
        Zoraya)

As Zoraya gravitates toward a request for a letter from Lili by giving her a specific task ("look at the stamp tell me if you like it"), it becomes reasonable to infer that her intent in paying Lili the compliments is, at least in part, to contribute to the effort to get Lili to write back. "Say something nice, if you want a response."

The intent of Alma's compliment in (2) is more difficult to infer. Perhaps her entire letter is really an affirmation of friendship clad in a compliment. Certainly Alma's inexperience at paying compliments shows.

(2)   1-13-82
        Dear Zoraya P.
        I like your dress
        because it's like my dress
        and my dress is red
        and your dress
        is yellow
        (pic)
        Your friend
        Alma D (Mr. D, 3)

In Julia's letter in (3), there is a cumulative effect in her three compliments at the end, as she progresses from the merely descriptive to the superlative.

(3)   September 10 1981
        I like you
        missy y you are
        good to me
        I like to play with
        you on the swings
        with you

> Missy you are cute
> Missy how did you get
> so prite
> your the cuteest girl
> (Julia) (Mrs. F, 2)

In (4), Julia first uses an affirmation of friendship, then a simple yes/no question as to whether or not her addressee is her friend, then an invitation and another affirmation of friendship, all in aid of cementing the friendship. She follows these language functions with some information about herself, the intent of which is not absolutely clear.

(4)   9/29
> Dear Susy
> I like you very
> much. are you
> my friend Susy
> I what you to
> come to my House
> Susy V
> I like you very much
> I am seven years old
> my favrite animal
> is a tertle
> Love Julia (Mrs. F, 2)

Perhaps Julia's teacher or someone of influence in her life has told her that writing about herself is an appropriate thing to do in a letter, and she is giving it a try. She also wrote part of this same information, that the turtle is her favorite animal, to her teacher.

Just as they write about being friends in their letters, girls also write about not being friends. (5) is again from Julia. Here she is seeking friendship, as she has before, but in this instance she is considering why she might not be her addressee's friend.

(5)   12/4
> Dear Delfina
> I like you very much
> will you be my freind.
> I like to play with you.
> I am seven years
> old. I know why your
> not my Freind becuse I am
> littleer than you

I know that I'm only
                    seven
        Love
        Julia (Mrs. F, 2)

Julia's addressee in (5), Delfina, is older than Julia and a grade ahead. Here it seems that Julia's purpose in telling Delfina that she is 7-years-old is not so much to inform as to explain why Delfina doesn't like her better, and perhaps to imply that size and age are not justifiable reasons for a lack of friendliness.

Some girls write not only about their own friendships, but also about the friendships of others. In (6), Judith wants to control her addressee's choice of friends.

(6)   3-30
        Dear Shirley
        tu estas Bonita
        y Shirley no
        seas a miga
        de otras ninas
        solo de Beatriz
        y yo
            Love
            Judith (Ms. R, 4)

        (Dear Shirley
        you are pretty
        and Shirley don't
        be friends
        with other girls
        only with Beatriz
        and me
            Love
            Judith)

(Notice that Judith's opening and closing are in English. Sometimes bilingual or Spanish speaking students who are learning English do just the reverse, opening and closing in Spanish and writing the body of the letter in English. Clearly, these children perceive a letter as having distinct parts.) The friendship Judith wants to organize is a triumvirate made up of Shirley, Beatriz, and herself. Others are to be excluded.

Occasionally girls are more explicit about with whom an addressee is to not be friends. Such is the case in Yvonne's letter in (7).

(7)   March 3
        Dear Lizzy
        I think that you are a very good

friend and I have Notice that you
are not Melissa friend and eather
is Patricia or me and I think
that is the best thing
    Love
    Yvonne (Ms. R, 4)

Such writing demonstrates a type of behavior educators do not want to nurture. Certainly the ground rules that each teacher lays for letter writing would advise against such unkindness. However, it seems important to acknowledge that this sort of writing does sometimes occur, and that it expresses feelings that will be manifest in other forms if they are not written. An occasional unkind letter does not constitute a reason to stifle the privacy or freedom of choice children have in their letter writing.

It may even be true that if children feel free to express the worst of what they feel, they can then explore the full range of their feelings in the letters they write. In (8), for example, Patricia makes a complaint and then goes on to affirm her friendship with her addressee.

(8)   3-3
    Dear Lizzy
    I not like you when you
    seit (cheat) in thrreball and I like
    you when you play with me
    and I hope you will be in
    my calss in my nast calss
    and now good-by Take
    care writh back
        Love
        Patricia (Ms. G, 3)

Similarly, it is possible to express regret in order to keep a friendship going, as in (9) and (10).

(9)   Dear Sonia
    I am sorry what
    I did that day
    I like you for a
    Best frend. I hope
    you like me for
    a Best frend
    I like you o.k.
        Missy (Mrs. F, 3)

(10)   1/21/82
    (Pat)
    I'm sorry for what I said and

thanks for the candy. It is good
and I really am sorry and I
hope you will forgive me for what
I said and I like you a lot
    by your
    freind
    Liz (Ms. R, 4)

The purpose of writing letters is not only to say what is easy, but also, perhaps, what is hard.

It is not to be suggested that only girls engage in writing that is solely concerned with interpersonal relationships. Boys do it too, but not as much. In (11) and (12), respectively, Jose and Julio seem to be selecting characteristics of their friends that stand out to them. Both letters are descriptive and, in a sense, nonengaged.

(11)   1/18
      Dear Glen
      Glen you are a bad boy you are
      a good friend and you are a good
      dodgeball player and good-by glen
         Jose A (Ms. R, 4)

(12)   1/21
      John
      you are funny
      and you are my freind
      and you like Spainish dogeball
         (Julio) (Ms. R, 4)

Most of the writing that is really about interpersonal relationships is either between girls and about girls, or between boys and about boys. In two of the classrooms where the research project was conducted, it was fashionable to be interested in the opposite sex, and in two it was not. And in the two classrooms in the first category, the interest in the opposite sex was apparent in some children's letters. In Mrs. F's room, for example, (13) was written.

(13)   12-9-81
      Dear Wendy
      Do you like
      Rodney I like
      him I hope
      you Do like
      him all the

girls do But sonia
likes Gabriel
from
No   Yes   Missy (Mrs. F, 3)
☐   ☒

Missy asks her question of Wendy at the outset and later repeats it. (Asking if the addressee likes a particular person and supplying boxes to be checked in the affirmative or negative is a popular custom in Mrs. F and Ms. R's rooms. This is a method of treating the postal system as if it is informal note passing, in which the same note gets passed back and forth.) Missy's letter provides some information as to Rodney's standing with the girls in Room F. Then Rodney's letter in (14) provides some information as to where he stands amidst all his popularity.

(14)   12/1/81
            To kose from Rodney
            Dear Kose how are you
            Tell sonia Dus she Love
            Gadriel I She dus Tell
            her why dusent she Love
            me better then Gabriel
            If she Love Gabriel better tell
            her thet Im going to get Gabriel
            I Love Sonia
                To Kose
                (Rodney) (Mrs. F, 3)

(Note Rodney's two uses of "tell" rather than "ask." He provides evidence for Chomsky's (1969) finding that children over-generalize their use of the verb "tell" before they acquire mature awareness of the distinction between the two verbs.) After Rodney's formulaic greeting, he makes a request of Kose to get some information for him. Contingent upon the answer to this first question, he requests that Kose get some more information for him. And contingent upon the answer to this question, he asks Kose to convey a threat for him. Then he tells how he feels about Sonia, which, in effect, is an explanation for everything that preceded. As well as writing about Sonia, Rodney also writes to her a few times during the year. (15) provides an example before they became, in their teacher's words, "an item" in Room F.

(15)   10/13/81
            sonia
            Dear sonia I like you
            if Roul hits you tell

me and if any body
hits you I will get them
(pic)
        (Rodney) (Mrs. F, 3)

Later, Rodney wrote Sonia one or two short love letters.

In Room A-3, Karla and Joseph are interested in one another. Karla is the pursuer, and Joseph the sometimes reluctant pursuee. Joseph's interest in girls is apparent in a letter written early in the year to Danny, shown in (16).

(16)   October 8 1981
        Dear Danny
        did you like when
        the girls were
        chasing us. x
                from
                Joseph (Ms. G, A-3)

Karla's letter in (17) is undated, but the issue of chasing is still certainly pertinent.

(17)   Joseph

        Joseph I am
        going to
        shaes (chase) you
        if you do
        what we said
        to do we will
        not shaes you
                (Karla) (Ms. G, A-3)

Here she threatens Joseph with pursuit. (Note Karla's spelling of "chase." Because the variety of Spanish she speaks does not have the *sh* sound, but has the very similar *ch,* she is having difficulty determining just where each sound belongs in English. As for the vowels, she knows which ones belong in "chase," but she hasn't mastered the final *e* generalization that would tell her where they go.)

During the last month of school, Karla and Joseph actually correspond with each other (see (24) for the letters). Karla complains that Joseph doesn't write to her just because she is a girl, and he acknowledges that she is essentially correct, he does not want to be the target of embarassing remarks. The postal system provides an additional arena in which boys and girls can explore their relationships with one another.

Among academic or other school-related concerns, writing letters gets written about quite a bit. Sometimes the concern is with getting a letter in return, as Octavio's letter in (17) demonstrates.

(17)   Sept 17
             Estimado
             Alejandro
             te traigo esta
             carta porke
             eres mi mejor
             primo
             te mando esta
             carta paraque
             me mandes tu
             una carta
             (Octavio) Ms. G, 2)

             (Dear
             Alejandro
             I am bringing you this
             letter because
             you are my best
             cousin
             I am sending you this
             letter so that
             you will send me
             a letter)

Among the youngest writers, such as Octavio, it is likely that writing letters about writing letters is a kind of contextualization of the activity. It is the natural thing to write about because that is what is happening. Octavio is absolutely open and direct about his reason for writing to Alejandro.

   In (18), Caridad's talk about writing letters seems to be used as evidence for the existence of her friendship with Ruth.

(18)   10-81
             Dear Ruth
             I like you because you are
             nice to me and I wrote
             you back and I know you
             wrote me. the End and good by
             (pic)
                  Love
                  Caridad M (Mr. D, 3)

(It is Caridad's custom to tell her addressee why she likes her. Again, a fuller discussion of Caridad's use of the postal system is given in a later section.)

Alma focuses on the appearance of a letter she received from her fourth grade friend Debbie in (19), and gets swept into the spirit of complimenting her.

(19)   9-16-81
              Dear Debby tank you
              for your cart I lik it
              it was beatiful an you
              ar beatiful to becouse you
              always Play with me.
              (pic)
                 You friend
                    (Alma) (Mr. D, 3)

(Alma's spelling of "thank" is influenced by the variety of Spanish she speaks, which does not have the *th* sound that English does. She may well have Spanish "carta" in mind in her spelling of "card." For other instances of her nonstandard spelling, it is difficult to be sure whether the influence of Spanish or difficulty with the intricacies of English spelling is the cause. In some cases both are, no doubt, operating.)

Debbie's return letter, in (20), expresses thanks for Alma's letter and corrects her on a matter of spelling.

(20)   Sept 24
              Dear Alma
              Alma tank you for the cartd you gave
              me and you don't spell my name like
              this Debby you spell my name like
              this Debbie I will give your teatherball
              back Sunday
                 good by
                    you Friend
                       Debbie (Ms. R, 4)

In (21), Judith thanks Shirley for her letter, tells her she likes it, says it is pretty, refers to what Shirley said in it about how she is, tells Shirley again that she likes the letter, and asks for another card, please. The whole letter can be regarded as an extended affirmation of friendship.

(21)   3/11
              Shirley
              querida Shirley yo quiero
              a ser tu me Jor amiga
              grasias por tu carta a mi
              me gusto tu carta
              esta ba muy Bonita

como estas tu yo
esto muy bien
y tu en tu carta me
dises que estas bien
Shirley me gusto tu
carta mucho sheirley
me escribes otra
carta por favor
    By
    (Judith V (Ms. R, 4)

(Shirley
dear Shirley I want
to be your best friend
thank you for your letter
I liked your letter
it was very Pretty
how are you
I am just fine
and you in your letter
tell me that you are fine
Shirley I liked your
letter a lot shierley
write me another
letter please
    By
    Judith)

Alex received a long letter that he liked from James (see the section entitled James for a discussion of the nature of his use of the postal system) and wrote (22) a month or so later, perhaps in response.

(22)   9/17
    Dear
    James I hope
    you send me
    more and
    more letters
    I like you
    (Alex) (Mrs. F, 3)

In (23), Joseph registers a complaint, in a somewhat indirect manner.

(23)   October 8

    Dear Manuel
    I don't Now why

you dont write
back to me
I wrote 2
letters.
(pic)
      from
            Joseph (Ms. G, 3)

Clearly, getting letters is a major concern among users of the postal system, and that goal in itself is reason enough to write a letter.

While the postal system is part of the academic program at Colmar, the manner in which children write about it, compared to the manner in which they write about other academic subjects, sets it apart from the rest of the curriculum. There is a sense of urgency in the sending and receiving of letters. Furthermore, in contrast to the many letters about writing letters, there are very few, among peers, about specific academic subjects. In (24), Cindy is writing about a writing test the fourth grade class took. The fact that she found the event worthy of a letter suggests the significance it has for her.

(24)   Dec 14, 1981
            Dear Yvonne
            When I took the heart test I wrote
            about when I had to go to the hopsital
            because the wood in my foot. What
            did you write about?
            Love always
                  Your friend Cindy (Ms. R, 4)

In (24) Liz complains, and perhaps commiserates with her addressee.

(25)   (Susan)
        I hate math quizes dayda?
        I mean I relly hate math quizes
        We are going to work in your
        commeits
              by
                  Liz (Ms. R, 4)

Among the fourth graders, James, too, writes about academic subjects. (Again, the section entitled James is focused exclusively on his use of the postal system.) Among the younger children, Maria's letter in (26) provides a rare example of focus on an academic subject among peers.

(26)   June 18, 1982
            Dear Yesenia

> how were you i'm
> good at spelling you
> are to very good at
> spelling by yesenia
>> your frind
>> Maria A

It may be that Maria is bragging about her spelling ability, but it seems more likely that she is identifying something that she and her addressee share, the fact that they are both good at spelling. Thus what looks like a compliment may actually be the other half of this identification process.

Just as there is a limited amount of writing about academic subjects among peers, so is there a limited amount of writing about other school-related concerns. When fourth graders are "off track" at Colmar, that is, on their 3 week vacation following 9 weeks of school, they have the opportunity to work at school as tutors, helping younger children. This is what Liz writes about in one letter to Pat, in (27).

(27)   Pat   1/21
>   do you what to be a tutier
>   and I what to be one—
>   and Melissa whats to be
>   a tutier.
>>   Liz (Ms. R, 4)

It is also possible to work in the cafeteria, as Yvonne writes about in (28).

(28)   9/22/81
>   Dear Beatriz
>   thank you for sighning up to work
>   in the cafeteria I hope you like
>   working in there. on Friday lets
>   sighn up
>>   Love
>>   Yvonne (Ms. R, 4)

In (29), Sandra expresses great pleasure at having secret knowledge of the date of her teacher's birthday.

(29)   3-15-82
>   Dear Regina
>   Only me and you now
>   when is Mrs. F's
>   birthday. Don't tell
>   nobody ok. You are
>   my best friend

          (pic)
          Don't tell
          nobody o.k.
                  Love,
                  Sandra (Mrs. F, 3)

Sandra's concern with keeping the matter secret is clear with her two directives. Her affirmation of friendship is designed to secure the secret. A best friend does not reveal such important matters.

In a previous section, it was demonstrated that the first elaborations of affirmations of friendship were often statements that the writer and addressee played a particular sport or game together. Whether school related or not, sports and games are written about frequently, when an affirmation of friendship is not the main focus of the letter. The boys play and write about kickball and dodgeball, while the girls are most interested in tetherball. Nieves' letter in (30), which focuses on kickball, illustrates his characteristic effusiveness.

    (30)   October 1981
                  Dear Soseph Im
                  so Happy if you Play
                  wath my on
                  Recess ckikball
                  and Im going to di
                  on your tiem Thanks
                  for the leter
                          (Nieves) (Ms. G, 2)

(A number of interesting points could be made about Nieves' spelling. It has some strikingly nonstandard features, some of which reflect his native Spanish and others which bespeak his conscious efforts to master some of the quirks of English. Particularly noteworthy is "ckikball;" he knows about the *ck* combination, but he hasn't yet mastered where it occurs.)

Also on the subject of kickball is Joseph's letter to Raul in (31). Here Joseph compliments his addressee and issues what is probably intended as an invitation in the form of a yes/no question. He also requests a letter in return, suggesting that getting a reply is an integral part of his purpose in writing.

    (31)   October 1981
                  Dear Raul
                  you are a good kicker.
                  Do you want to play kickball.
                  Please writ back
                          From
                          Joseph (Ms. G, 4)

In (32), Andy seems to be waxing philosophical about the outcomes of both soccer and kickball games.

(32)   11-30-81
       Dear Ruben
       yo y tu jugamos
       soccer y tambien
       jugamos kickball
       y algunas yo gano
       y algunas tu ganas
       y tambien hay empate
       tu amigo
           Andy H (Mr. D, 3)

       (Dear Ruben
       I and you play
       soccer and also
       we play kickball
       and sometimes I win
       and sometimes you win
       and also there are ties
       your friend
           Andy H)

And in (33), Bobby gives Jose a suggestion about how to play dodgeball.

(33)   Jose
      Why in Dogball you allwes
      Duck Just let them get
      you out ok
         By
         Bobby (Ms. R, 4)
         yes

It is not clear why Bobby is telling Jose how to lose the game.

In (34), Liz combines a concern with tetherball with some other school-related matters. Her compliment on Melissa's ability at tetherball is followed by a statement about her own ability, which establishes a rather competitive tone.

(34)   9/22/81
       Dear melisa,
       you can play
       tetherball reall
       good. and I can
       allmost win you
       out! and melissa

what level are
you on. I'm on
leve 4 melissa!
I like work
in the Learning
Center I wish
you could work
wiht me please
write   Love
back   Liz (Ms. R, 4)
Melissa!

Liz carries the competitive spirit over into the subject of spelling, where she asks Melissa how she is doing. The repeated exclamation point indicates Liz's confidence in her own standing. Her final statement softens the competitive edge and serves to affirm the friendship.

Miguel's letter in (35) is another that combines focus on a sport with other interpersonal concerns.

(35)   April 14, 1981
Dear John
We are going to play Hockey
today. But that still does'nt
mean Im not going to get back
at Micheal. Micheal shouldnt
do bad thing. ooh ooh
by I have to leave
          (Miguel) (Ms. R, 4)

Implicitly on the subject of sports and games, but explicitly focusing on interpersonal relationships, are Rodney's letters in (36) and (37).

(36)   1-18-82
Dear Alex
you pass our gang
your a leader
you and Gabriel
and me and Kose
I will tell you
hus in are gang
me Kose you Luis
Gabriel christ
Butch Phillip and

          YOU PASS
          #1
          (Rodney) (Mrs. F, 3)

(37)   1-19-82
Dear Alex
will you take over
leader for me if I'm
not her
(pic)
      (Rodney)

In (36), Rodney is welcoming Alex into the gang and informing him about it, and in (37), he makes a request. The dates on the letters indicate that focus on a particular concern can carry over from day to day. Rodney has a customary face that he draws, rather than signing his name to his letters.

    In (38), Jose asks to borrow one or another of Roberta's games.

(38)   January
           12-1982
Dear Roberta
Roberta iF you
could bring the
Football game
or the hocky
game could
you lend me
your Foot ball
score game
you are a
nice girl.
let me and
Robert and Glenn
     your Firend
     ~~Jose~~
Munch (Ms. R, 4)

It is natural to wonder if Jose's compliment is not a fairly obvious effort to get Roberta to comply with his request. Munch or Munchy is Jose's nickname, and he wanted to be associated with it here.

    Sports and games blend into other free time activities. In (39), Jose is writing about a boxing match coming up on television that evening.

(39)   September 1981
Dear Miguel
Miguel Who do you
go for in the fit
today in the nigth
I go for Herns I
bet you go for Sugre

Lonr We do not no
Who is ging to
win iym going
to see it
in my houes
    Good By.
    your friend
    Jose (Ms. R, 4)

Among free time activities, plans for play activities are important to write about. In Missy's letter (40), concern with interpersonal relations is closely interwoven with ideas for how she and Sonia might get together.

(40) Dear sonia
      are you my friend I
      want to be your
      friend. If you want
      me to go to your
      house I will. can you
      to to my house when
      it stops raining. I will
      pick you up if your
      mom lets you go
      bo you like Wendy
      yes or no. I like
      □   □ you
      much
          Love
          Missy (Mrs. F, 3)

Delfina's letter in (41) is quite similar to Missy's in that the suggestion for how they might get together to play is prefaced with a question as to whether her addressee is her friend.

(41) Dear
      Wendy are you my friend
      yes or no can you go
      □   □ to my house
      I cod go down your house
      I'm staying over your house
      o.k. I like you wendy
      last nith my rother het me
      and I codden't Brether
      it was sade I was cring
          Love
             Delfina

After her offer to visit Wendy and spend the night, Delfina affirms her friendship with Wendy, and then confides in her about being hit by her brother and having the wind knocked out of her.

Going to the library is another free time activity, which Yvonne writes about in (42).

(42)   3/11
           Dear Cindy
           how have you
           been ask your
           mom again if
           you can go to
           the libery on
           Wednesday but
           please don't
           ask your father
                Love
                Yvonne

Major holidays, especially Christmas, receive a lot of attention in letters as they approach, as Kose's letter in (42) illustrates.

(42)   12-10-81
           Dear Rodney
           how are you what are you
           going to get for Christmas
           I'm getting a racing track
           good By
                SOS #1
                   (Kose) (Mrs. F, 3)

As well as curiosity about family Christmases, children are also concerned with giving gifts to one another, as shown in Rodney's letter in (43).

(43)   12/16/81
           Dear Delphina
           thaks for the rubecub
           I like for a friend
           I will get you somthing
           for Christmas goodby
                (Rodney) (Mrs. F, 3)

Other special events are occasions for letters, and going to Disneyland is certainly one of these, as Miguel's letter in (44) illustrates.

(44)   May 27, 1982
            Dear John
            I cant wait for June 8, 82
            that is the day we go
            to Disneyland it is
            going to be fun and
            if we get lost that
            would be real fun
                Your friend
                    Miguel (Ms. R, 4)

When a child must move, the separation is an ordeal both for the child moving and the friends left behind. Liz's letter in (45) deals with Patricia's impending move. She both focuses directly on her feelings and talks about free time activities that are of mutual interest to the two girls.

45)   (Nov 23, 1981
            Dear Patricia,
            I'm glad you are still
            hear. Because I like you
            alot. And I don't whant
            you to go because you
            are my Freind. and I
            like you very much and
            I don't whant you
            to go. did you
            see Mary Poppins on Sunday
            night because it came
            on at 8:00. and it was
            Funny. I made some
            dogs and the two
            pretty whants are you
            and me.
                Love
                Lizzy

In writing letters to their peers, children use the postal system as an added dimension in carrying on their social lives. Among the less experienced writers, the strain of writing limits what gets put down on paper. As children's experience with writing increases, their letters become more and more reflective of the full range of their concerns in their relationships with their peers.

Letters to Adults

This section approaches children's letters to adults in the same manner that their letters to peers were previously considered. The topics or concerns written about form the organizational basis for an examination of the language functions employed. The majority of letters to adults are concerned with interpersonal relationships and/or academic matters. And it is perhaps not surprising that the most common language function is the compliment. There are good reasons for demonstrating deference to those in power.

Among less-experienced writers writing about interpersonal relations, the expression of one simple compliment can be difficult. In (1), the part of Octavio's letter beginning with the unstruck out "because" is written in the classroom aide's hand.

(1)   Dear Mrs G
        you are the best
        Teacher ~~becuase~~
        because you are nice
              (Octavio) (Ms. G, 2)

It may well be that Octavio spent his entire post office center time getting up to the "because" part and asked for help in completing his thought before cleanup time. Since he had addressed the letter first, he was able to finish, although he did not get a chance to sign it.

Karla, in (2), had an easier time.

(2)   Sept 21 1981.
        Ms. G
        Ms. G
        .I like you I tinke
        yuo are the
        best ticher
        (pic)
        Ms. G
              Karla (Ms. G, 2)

In an important sense, children's expressions of liking or loving their teachers are no different from the affirmations of friendship discussed at length in a previous section. Yet it is clear, from the implied expressions of reverence that are present in their explanations of why they have strong feelings about their teachers, that these children sense the social distance between their teachers and themselves. As expressed in (2), Karla assigns Ms. G's excellence in the superlative. In (3), Patricia focuses on her teacher's relationship with, or attention to, her personally.

(3)   Dear Mis G
            I like you so
        much because
        you are a good
        teacher with me

        (pic)
        Love
            Patricia (Ms. G, 3)

In (4), Zoraya identifies a particular thing that her teacher does that
has special meaning for her.

(4)   Sept. 21, 1981
            Dear Mr. D,
            you ar my best teacher,
            because you play with me.
            (pic)
            love
                Zoraya P. (Mr. D, 3)

While it is possible that Zoraya is demonstrating particular precocity by observing her teacher's ability to get down on his students' level, it is more likely
that her letter does not reflect that level of thinking. There are a number of
similar letters to teachers in which students do not demonstrate awareness
of the distinction between student and teacher roles. This is not to suggest
that these students do not have this awareness, but rather that their writing,
in these cases, does not reflect it.
    While the letters in (1)–(4) are all written by children who wrote to
their teacher only occasionally throughout the school year, there are a few
children who either made it a regular habit to write or went through a short
period of writing frequently to their teacher. Becky is a student in the former
category. Frequently during the year she wrote letters that varied very little
from (5).

(5)   Dear Mrs F
        I love you
        you are nice
        Love Becky (Mrs. F, 2)

Most of these letters are undated, leaving little possibility of determining
when they were written in relation to some much longer and more complex
letters that Becky also wrote to her teacher. In (6), there is evidence of the
very important role Mrs. F may play in Becky's life, and of the fact that the
postal system may provide Becky with a means of expressing this importance.

(6)   9/29/81
            Dear
            Miss F
            I Love you very

much and I ~~whoud~~
woud Like to
have you as
my mom Becuse
you are Nice
and you Can come
To my Birthy
Party
(pic)
      Becky (Mrs. F, 2)

The date on (6) places it early in the year, indicating that it is not a matter of ability, but rather of choice, which induces Becky to write sometimes short and sometimes long letters. Becky is not the only child who mentions the desirability of having her teacher as a parent. It is impossible to know either the seriousness or the actual nature of her intent, but there is no doubt as to the strength of the compliment. Her invitation to her birthday party, "You can come. . ." presupposed that her teacher wants to go. This is not an unusual feature of children's invitations.

In a sense, Becky's invitation to Mrs. F in (6) can be viewed as a compliment, that she likes her teacher enough to issue the invitation. However, Becky's writing about interpersonal concerns does go beyond complimenting. In (7) she gives a directive.

(7)   March 17 1982
      Dear Miss F
      I love you very much.
      how are you doing I'm Doing
      fine. tell angel to cwit
      shooting and Alex and Jon
      and Plhimp and Rotney
      and Kose O.K.
          (Becky) (Mrs. F, 2)

And in (8) she seems to be doing some perspective-taking, asking questions of her principal as she thinks about what his life might be like.

(8)   March 11, 1982
      Dear Mr K
      How are you Doing?
      and how is it Being
      a Pricble is it Horbell
        Becky R (Mrs. F, 2)

Kose is a student in the second category mentioned above (he went through a short period of writing frequently to his teacher). Between September 18 and September 30, he wrote six letters to her, all of which are very similar to the one in (9).

(9)   Sept 25
             Dear Mrs. F
             How are you
             and I like you and
             I love you
             and goodby
                  Kose (Mrs. F, 3)

Again with Kose, however, it is evident that writing a short, sweet letter is a matter of choice, rather than of ability. During vacations, it is Mrs. F's custom to give her students stationery and a stamped envelope and to invite them to send her a letter through the United States mail. For many students the change of context prompts a distinctly different type of letter, as Kose's letter in (10) illustrates.

(10)   April 23, 1982
             Dear Mrs. F
             I I'm playing baketball and
             my Dad is vs his friend
             jon he woork xxxx withe
             him and the scra (score) was
             81 to 20 my Dad hit
             30 more and all
             I I'm Doing is playing
             and hleping my Dad
             and how are you
             and your fambley
             in Lahabra and
             when we go in 4 grad
             and we xxxx tell
             you that we want
             to stay in room
             F Do we still
             go to the Bell high
             school to swim But
             if you won't put a
             Black dit in Box yes no
                       □ □
             and if we Do I'm happy
             xxxx then.
                  your friend Kose
             (pic)
                       please writhe
                       Back to me

While Kose's message is not always easy to decipher in this letter, the range of concerns he writes about and the range of language functions he employs are quite remarkable in comparison to his other letters to Mrs. F. He not only describes in a general way what he is doing over vacation, but provides specific details about a basketball game that obviously impressed him. He asks about his teacher and her family, and expresses the wish to stay with her when he moves on to grade 4. He asks about swimming at Bell High School and gives Mrs. F "yes" and "no" boxes to check appropriately. Then he expresses his hope for an affirmative answer, signs off, draws a picture of an eagle (which may or may not represent some connection with the United States mail), and requests a response. Such letters as this hint at some of the constraints which are present when children are writing to people whom they see every day, a point which will be taken up in a later section. It seems likely that for students like both Becky and Kose, the short, frequent expressions of affection are intended to align their relationship with their teacher in a manner that satisfies some of their personal needs. And for Becky, who wrote many such letters to her peers as well, they seem to be her definition of the norm for letter writing, from which she deviates when there is good reason.

Frequently in letters to their teachers, children blend interpersonal with academic concerns. For example, in (11), Julia compliments Mrs. F, expresses affection for her, tells her how she feels about one school-related subject, and how she feels about her performance in two others.

(11)   March 10, 1982
          Dear
          Mrs F.
          You are a Good teacher
          I Like you
          I Love math and you are
          very Good to me
          But I am not Good at
          writing I Do art
          Better
          (pic)
                    Love
                    Julia (Mrs. F, 2)

(For the "I's" of "I Like you" and "I Love math," Julia drew rebus eyes. her letter was also punctuated with two hearts and a smiling face.)

In (12), Andy expresses gratitude to Ms. R, whose classroom he goes to for reading, for her help in that subject.

(12)   Dear Miss R
        y wich that y was in your

clas your the one that make
me ride nise you help Eliseo
me, caridad, carlos D,.
   Whit love
   Andy (Mr. D, 3)

(The influence of Spanish is evident in several aspects of Andy's spelling. His use of "y" for "I" probably has two sources. The first is the similarity of "y" to Spanish "yo," which means "I." The second is that "y" is itself a meaningful "little" word in Spanish, meaning "and." The substitution of one "little word for another is not unusual. Next is his spelling of "wish" with *ch*; since Spanish does not have the English *sh* sound, *ch* is the closest approximation. And last, of the most noteworthy Spanish influences, is the spelling of "reading" with an *i*. Using Spanish *i* gives "reading" the correct pronunciation.)

In (13), Maria wishes her teacher's aide well for the following year, since she has been sick this year, and acknowledges her help on particular projects the class undertook. Maria is a Spanish speaker who is learning English, and she is making a big effort to write in English because the aide does not know Spanish.

(13)   Dear
       Miss B
       I hope
       you are
       next year
       to be all riht you
       sick on this year
       you help us in
       bird, Mexico, Hawaii.
          your friend
          Maria (Ms. G, 2)

While some of the more experienced fourth grade writers are more at ease with the medium, their concerns are still a blend of the interpersonal with the academic. For example, in (14), Cindy opens with an expression of pleasure at being in Ms. R's class, then focuses on spelling, her skill and progress, and ends with acknowledgement of her teacher's kindness toward her and an expression of affection.

(14)   Nov 23, 1982
          Dear Miss R
          I like being in your class
          and I like spelling because
          I do it fast and I'm going

       to be in level 15 pretty soon
       You are nice to me and I like
       you alot.
           by now.
              your student
   (pic)   Cindy (Ms. R, 4)

Clearly Cindy feels good about her performance in spelling and wants her teacher to be aware of it.

    In (15), Jose opens with a question to his teacher which he answers with respect to himself, no doubt with pleasure at his academic sense of appropriateness. Then he thanks Ms. R for her assistance in math, and closes with two compliments.

  (15)   Jan 18, 1982
       Dear R
       Miss R What are
       you doing I am
       gest writing and
       riding Ms R
       thank you for
       shoing me how
       to do math.
       You are a good
       teacher and a nice
       lady.
       good-by
          Love
          Jose (Ms. R, 4)

(Interpret "riding" as "reading," as in Andy's letter in (12).) It is interesting that Jose divides Ms. R into a teacher and a lady, describing the former in terms of skill and the latter in terms of kindness. Perhaps he is working on developing literary style, or perhaps he has other reasons for separating two of Ms. R's roles and ascribing to them different kinds of attributes.

    In (16), Yvonne focuses on math and the significance of knowing one's multiplication tables.

  (16)   Nov 24, 1981
       Dear Miss R
       My math is very
       easy now that
       I know my time
       table's. Cindy told
       me that her

sister missy knows
all her time table's
by hart and
she is only in
third grade.
        Love
        Yvonne (Ms. R, 4)

It is significant to her that a mere third grader could achieve this difficult task.

The topics and language functions discussed to this point present a picture of children's writing to adults that captures its general nature. There is a small set of letters, each of which stands out because of something it reveals about the nature of letter writing, that has not yet been described.

Ms. M is the very popular reading specialist who left Colmar in the middle of the year as the result of a promotion. It was she who implemented the postal system, and she who received and wrote more letters than any other single adult in the school. Her basic activities as reading specialist involved having students who were experiencing difficulty in their classroom come to her for help with reading and writing, and visiting classrooms for special discussion occasions. While she was still at Colmar, she received many letters complimenting her and expressing appreciation for her efforts. She also, occasionally, received letters such as (17), in which Zoraya, not understanding why her classmates had the privilege of visiting Ms. M, expresses envy and the desire to be selected too.

(17)   1-13-82
        Dear Ms M
             I wish you
        take me to why do you
        take George and Maria
        Lupe? Take me to and I love
        you.
        (pic)
        Love
             Zoraya (Mr. D, 3)

When Ms. M left Colmar, she invited students to write to her in her new office, and she was deluged with mail. There were many requests for her to return to Colmar, as well as wishes for happiness in her new position. Several letters from one child reacting to Ms. M's departure appear in the section entitled Caridad. On one letter writing day when I was observing in Mr. D's classroom, he suggested that students write to an adult who was not in the classroom. Ms. M's name came up, and many children decided to write to her. Andy's letter in (18) was not at all like the other letters written that day.

(18)   2-17-82
        Dear Ms M,
        I wich I know
        who you are. Ms M
        Write me back
        (pic)
        Love
              Andy (Mr. D, 3)

There are several possible interpretations of Andy's letter. Perhaps he simply meant that he wished he knew her. Certainly the social pressure was on to write to Ms. M. Andy's willingness to write to someone whom he does not know, and to acknowledge that he does not know her, is somehow suggestive of his lack of experience at letter writing. His tolerance for participating in an activity, the customs surrounding which he is still a little uncertain, is admirable.

    When I observed in classrooms at letter writing time, children sometimes decided to write to me. Since my official role was to help with any writing problems, usually spelling, I received many compliments on my ability as a writer/speller. One letter in which the writer did not employ the usual compliments was (19).

(19)   september 15, 1981
        Dear Jennifer greene,
        I like lerning how
        to write so far I have writtin
        one letter and I wrote to
        John i wrote to him
        about the Phite.
              Miguel (Ms. R, 4)

In the picture box Miguel wrote the alphabet cursively from *a* through *m* and signed his name. The rest of the letter was printed. It was not clear whether his first sentence was about writing cursively or about writing letters, but his letter was clearly very carefully designed for its recipient.

    Kose wrote (20) to me after he had written four letters telling me that he liked me, to which I had tried to tactfully respond that I was happy to receive his letters but he was not giving me very much to write back about.

(20)   Dear Mis Green
        I like you and

                    if you have a
                    son wirte to me
                    and tell me how
                    old is he and if
                    he go to school
                    and if he does't
                    go to tell that
                    to
                    (pic)
                            (Kose) (Mrs. F, 3)

Unquestionably, Kose got my message, and a good long letter from me in response. He was ready to be inspired to something new. Vygotsky's notion of the zone of proximal development can explain this kind of readiness. With adult encouragement (it could have been some other impetus of a social nature), Kose used abilities that he possessed that would have gone untapped, at least temporarily, if he had been left to his customary ways. He needed a reason to stretch to something new.

Among the four classroom teachers involved in the research project, Mrs. F was the most enthusiastic letter writer. Her responses to children often involved elaborate pictures, or jokes or riddles. Perhaps related to this, or perhaps because of a host of factors related to Mrs. F personally and to the nature of the operation of the postal system in her classroom, she was the recipient of two letters which stand out from other letters to adults for their openness and complexity. The first, in (21), was written at the start of the year from a former student.

(21)   August 24, 1981
            Dear Miss F How are
            you. I am fine. how is your
            class. I bet Thay are doing
            good. My work is hard in This class
            and Sandra and Shirley sit next
            to me but we sit by boys
            do you know why? Miss R Thinks
            we wont but we talk alot
            more but we don't talk all The
            time. will I have To go
            now. by
            your freaind
                    Elizabeth (Ms. R, 4)

As children grow older, former teachers become more like friends than current teachers, yet there remain some important distinctions. Liz finds herself in an interesting bind, that of wanting to confide and possibly brag about getting away with "misbehavior," while simultaneously wanting to be a good girl in her former teacher's eyes.

In (22), Sandra confides some of her feelings about a very big issue in her life, that of moving.

(22)   6-1-82
        Dear Mrs. F
        We are going to move
        next week but my mom sed
        that we will finish this year
        in this school so that's wy
        I am happy, but I am
        not going to be here next
        year now that's bad news. I
        am going to mis you
        and all my friends.
        But I will be back to
        this school because I am
        a girl scout so I am not
        too sad but Regina F
        is sad becaus I am movein
        too another house but Regina
        gave me her adress for
        I can send her a letter
        I mitht send you a letter too
           Allwise your
           friend Sandra
        YOU ARE VERY PRETTY

Sandra has learned that when distance separates friends, they can stay in touch through writing letters. The postal system has become truly functional for her.

Not all children write to adults in the school, but many do occasionally, and a few do so frequently. Many stay with the usual interpersonal concern of liking and being liked by the adult in question, and in letters to their teacher many combine interpersonal and academic concerns. There are a few instances in which some feature of the writing context encouraged a child to stretch beyond his or her usual letter writing customs.

James

James is a bilingual fourth grader who writes, at least at school, exclusively in English. He is described by his teacher as a good writer, and he, himself, acknowledged his proficiency in writing during the interview, citing as evidence 10 good-writer-of-the-year awards he received when he was in the third grade. As a letter writer, James is outstanding for the variety of apparent purposes for which he writes. He writes about the same concerns that his peers do, but he writes about other things as well. In his lack of inhibition, he calls to mind Art Linkletter's well worn observation, "Kids say the darndest things." He is an observer and monitor of his classmates' behavior, and seems to have strong feelings about what they do. Yet in many cases he is supportive at the same time that he is critical.

James is creative in his use of the postal system. He makes his own lined stationery on sheets of colored construction paper cut to various shapes and sizes. He adds lines in the picture box of the standard stationery when he finds he needs more writing space. For a short while he experimented with using three colors of ink in a single letter, changing colors cyclically every two, three, or four words. This creativity is a reflection of James' confidence as a writer. His control of the medium affords him considerable flexibility in using it.

There are 60 letters from James in the data pool, written to 24 people. In addition, James' list of addresses indicates that he wrote 30 letters which were not made available to the project. Why this is so is not clear. While it is the case that some of James' letters were not entirely complimentary, it is also true that other such letters from him were contributed to the project. Another consideration of relevance here is that James did not receive nearly as many letters as he wrote, in spite of the fact that he has good friends. There are 17 letters to James on record. Perhaps a boy who is such a prolific writer is bound to be disappointed with the number of responses he gets because many of his peers are less inclined to use the postal system as extensively as he does. Or perhaps James has not learned how to inspire people to write back on a regular basis.

Although James' use of the postal system is not entirely representative of his peers, it is interesting because writing letters is, apparently, such a useful communicative tool for him. Examination of a representative sample of James' letters permits a look not only at manifest topics and functions, but also beyond, to some of his assumptions about what letter writing is for, and how it is to be done.

In July or August, at the beginning of the school year before the NIE project began, James wrote the letter in (1) to Alex, who had been a classmate in their second-third grade class the previous year and was now a third grader in Mrs. F's room. From this early point in the year, James seems to be comfortable as a writer and confident of his ability to make the medium work for him. He responds directly to a topic raised in a letter Alex sends (which, unfortunately, is not in the data pool) and goes on to reminisce about events that took place the previous year.

(1)   Dear Alex. I got your letter
        you sent me. You where write

I am on M-10. But you got it
wrong I had to moved to B-2.
Do you whant to now why I
moved. It because the main
billden is being carpet because
the old carpet is riped so
we have to move to B-2.
So thats the story Alex
we had to move. Do you remember
when we usto go to B-2.
Do you remember Miss R and
Miss G. Remember we played
kickball and we made Homeruns
over the head. Remember we
played a game we (with) E-1
we won them. Remember we had
Cristmas party's in the class
room we had a Cristmas
tree and we had a (all) the
girls dacneing. Miss R was
dacneing we the boys. You
and Rodert were untieing the
striig of the Cristmas
tree and it fell on my head.
Write dack Love James

The occasion of being in B-2 while his classroom is being recarpeted prompts James to think about his past experiences there with Alex. His use of "Do you remember" and "Remember" may perform a significant function in the writing process itself by helping him stay on target, calling up the memories. It seems to be a technique for moving the text along, for getting from one idea to the next. It also functions to actively engage the recipient. After two uses of the full phrase, just the single word is enough. And after three uses of the single word reminder, James' memory of the Christmas party, with all the details, comes flooding in so surely that there is no need to call attention to the recall process.

Like most boys his age, James writes about sports in his letters. But unlike many others, James' concerns go beyond the mere fact of playing, or even winning. In (2), he is concerned with the position he is going to play in hockey, and the need for practice if the team he and John are on is going to win.

(2)   March 27, 1982
         Dear John
         arent you happy we
         are going to play
         hocking. But there is

still one problem we
do not kown yet who
is going to play
senter foword. I never
play senter foword but
I still want to win the
hockey trofee and we
butter pratus hard.
I think we are going to
lose the trofee. We better
pratus. Your friend
    James G.

It is not clear whether or not James thinks he can help his team if he plays center forward, but he is definitely focusing on what the team must do in order to win, a certain lack of precision notwithstanding. A letter can function to inspire team spirit. (Notice James' spelling of *know* in the seventh line: "kown." Previously he has written "now." Now, although he has lost the appropriate vowel sound, he has supplied the "silent" *k,* a significant step toward the standard spelling.)

In another letter written on March 27, 1982, James chastises Manuel F. for not showing up at hockey practice to help the team out as its goalie. His concern with winning is still evident, and it is apparent that James thinks it is acceptable to express his anger in a letter. But if he can express anger, he can also demonstrate his understanding of fair play. In another letter to John, also about sports, he tries to arrange an exchange which will draw on both his and John's strengths. This letter appears as (3).

(3)   Jan 11 1982
        Dear John
will you so (show)
me how to
be a good
dodgeball
player. If you
show me I
will show
you how to
kick hard
and be a
good player
in kickball.
Your my friend.
    Your friend
    James

With diplomacy, a letter can be used to persuade someone to act in one's own interest.

While many children make requests of the people they write to, James is more precise and provides more details about the context of the event than most. In one instance (see the section entitled Corresponding with Continuous Discourse, (4)), he tells of his plan to give a ball to a friend, describing a mark on the ball and how the mark is different from the one on his own ball. In (4), he is precise in proposing a small business deal.

(4)   March 16 1982
             Dear Julio
             are you going to sell
             the rubeck cubs. I will
             buy you it for
             a dollar.
                  Your friend James

In addition to sports and games, the academic performance and class-room behavior of his friends are recurrent topics in James' letters. (5) is illustrative of his concern with classroom behavior.

(5)   september 22 1981
             Dear Keith
             why are you so lasy
             in the class when the teacher
             tell you don't lessen to the
             teacher Heres a picture of you lasy
             (pic)
             why do you take oof your shoe at home
                  white back love James

While it is possible to interpret this letter as being quite critical, it is not clear at all how James intended it. He might be asking honest questions, or perhaps offering friendly advice. When he spoke in the interview about how writing letters differed from other school writing, he said at one point, "...you make new friends, sometimes you break up with other friends..." Typically, when a child "breaks up" with another in a letter, he or she is very direct: "You are not my friend." There are not letters of that sort from James in the data. James closes his letter to Keith by asking him to write back, and signs it "Love." Those are not the gestures of someone who is ending a friendship. It seems reasonable to conclude that James' intent is not to offend, but rather to be of help. A similar conclusion is appropriate for the letter to Manuel R. in (6), where academic performance is the focus.

(6)   Jan 14, 1982
            Dear
            Manual R. how
            are you going to finish
            your Rreading. I hope
            you finish your Reading
            because your in big
            trouble because if you
            don't finish your
            your things at the
            right time you will
            get in trouble.
            You are my best
            friend I ever
            had in my
            classroom. You never
            call me names ore
            you never teas me
            You are my best friend
                    friend
                    James

The juxtaposition of this strong affirmation of friendship to the discussion of Manuel's completion of his reading serves to eliminate the likelihood of ill intent in what might otherwise seem offensive.

The letter to Manuel in (6) introduces another topic that is of concern to James, that of name calling. In three letters on the same day, James writes about name calling, in each case asking one of his classmates why he is called a particular name and offering some kind of help or consolation. The letter to Benjie in (7) illustrates.

(7)   Jan 14 1982
            Dear Benjie
            way do they
            call you dog.
            If they call
            you call you
            benjie the dog
            just tell the
            teacher they were
            calling you
            names. Well
            John got the
            pretty flower
            so what John
            can keep that

old flower.
So what you
look better than
John you look
like Shierlook
homes. In way
you are my best
friend Benjie
    friend
    James

Here James' offer of help is the suggestion that Benjie tell the teacher if "they" call him names. He also seems to be consoling Benjie about not getting the pretty flower that John got by telling him that he looks better than John, in fact like "Shierlook homes". Although the punctuation indicates that Benjie is James' best friend "in way", it also seems possible that the period was misplaced and that James thinks Benjie looks like Sherlock Holmes in a way instead. However, it is certainly possible that James has in mind a way of qualifying his best friendship with Benjie. While James unquestionably does say things that other children do not, he also quite clearly demonstrates sensitivity to their feelings.

James had 5 or 6 days during the school year when he was very prolific, and January 14, 1982, when he wrote the letters in (6) and (7), was one of them. On that day he wrote nine letters to as many people. As mentioned above, three of them involved the issue of name calling. Two others, including to one to Manuel R. in (6), focused on classroom performance. Yet across these topics, each of the letters was so carefully designed for the recipient that there was no hint of repetition. Often when less proficient writers write more than one letter in a sitting, the second is very nearly a duplicate of the first. James' skill allowed him more versatility. Another concern of James' on January 14, 1982, a recurrent one throughout the year, was getting a letter in return. He wrote a number of follow-up letters during the year, as (8) illustrates.

(8)   Jan 14, 1982
      Dear George
      You got my letter
      I send you. I hope
      you did. George I
      think when we to to
      cottarsam (?) I can't
      jump over the fence
      because when we
      did jump over the
      fence my pants

got a little
bit wrip. So what.
Did you got my
letter. I think
I can't jump
over the fence
because my
pants wer a little
bit wrip. Your
a good dogeball
player your my friend
    friend
    James

Twice James asks whether George has received a previous letter. It is difficult to determine his purpose in referring to his ripped pants and the problem of not going over the fence. If his primary intent is to motivate George to write to him, his method is indirect. He neither requests a letter, nor pointedly asks George something he can write back about.

It would be interesting to know the sequence in which James wrote his letters of January 14, 1982. While some of them are quite pointed in purpose (whether or not the intent is unambiguously inferrable), others are less clear. In (9) he seems to let his thoughts flow in stream of consciousness fashion.

(9)   Jan 14, 1982
    Dear Glen
    this is the first time I
    ever wrote to you. I ever
    never had wrote to you
    most of the time because
    the teacher doesn't give
    us a little bit of time.
    The teacher is a little
    bit of mean but I think
    she not so mean because
    she lits us have P.E.
    Teachers are fun
    to be around with
    us. The teacher makes
    lots of good
    things to do in
    school. Some people
    have lots of fun
        your friend
        James

While it is possible to trace how each thought in this letter led to the next, doing so is beyond the present purpose. The point is to demonstrate that here, unlike many children, James is not hindered by perfectionism. He thinks as he goes and feels free to change his mind along the way.

On another day when he wrote several letters, he wrote one to Julio in which he told him he had played all the video games (in a particular arcade) and that he had also drawn them. Then he wrote the letter in (10) to Manuel F., who is generally recognized as the class artist.

(10)   March 17, 1982
          Dear Manuel F
          I wrote a letter to
          Julio and I told
          him that I did all
          off the video and
          I draw them and
          color the(m) all
          can you draw video games.
               your friend James

The question arises as to why James wanted to inform Manuel of his letter to Julio, and the answer is not readily apparent. Sometimes he seems to write without any identifiable purpose, almost as though the content of his message is rather beside the point. His purpose, perhaps, is to write a lot of letters. On the other hand, the question to Manuel about whether or not he is able to draw video games is highly appropriate, because of the class-wide recognition of Manuel's artistic talent.

In the interview James said that one of the reasons he likes to write letters is to make friends. Writing letters, he also said, makes him feel happy and attached to friends. In (11) he offers help and information to a boy who comes to his class for reading in a direct effort to make friends.

(11)   Dear Gillarmo
       do you
       no wher
       I sit down
       for late reading
       why don't
       you sit
       in the
       sit in the
       emty desk.
       You now
       wher I sit
       next to

me ther
is a emty
desk so
you can
put in your
things.
Will you
be my
friend

James is concerned with maintaining his sense of connection to adults through the postal system, as well as to his peers. Early in the year he comes to the defense of his principal with the letter in (12).

(12)   september 22 1981
Dear Mr. K,
you are the tallest
principul in colmar school
some people say you have
sticks. I said he a tall man
(pic)
love James
wite back

"Sticks" is in all probability to be translated as "stilts." Since Mr. K is the only principal at Colmar, he is without a doubt the tallest, but it is also true that he is tall, a fact not missed by the students who are under his authority.

Another adult with whom James made an effort to maintain contact was Ms. M, the reading specialist. In February Ms. M was promoted to a district level position, and James, as well as many of the other fourth graders, wrote to ask her to come back to do Junior Great Books discussions with them. A rather lengthy correspondence developed between James and Ms. M (a total of 11 letters, 7 of which were from James), marked by delays in delivery because two postal systems (Colmar mail and the district's inter-office mail) were being used, rather than just one. The letter in (13) is James' first letter to Ms. M after her departure from Colmar.

(13)   March 5, 1982
Dear Ms M
thank you for the
2 years we had
with you. How
are you in
youre new school
do you have

your own office.
Ms M when
are you comeing
back for Juinor
Great Books
Descusin. You
saw me in
the treller (trailer) wher
all of those boxes
wher all your
what were in
all off those boxes.
I hope you
come back to
colmr school
and stay with us.
We all love you
        (James)

By March 16 James had not heard from Ms. M so he wrote to her again (14). His concern for her welfare had intensified, and his request for her to return for a Junior Great Books discussion went from a direct question as to when she was coming, to an indirect statement about waiting for her.

(14)   Mar 16, 1982
        Dear Ms M
        how are you I hope
        you fine in the
        office I hope
        you all right.
        Some of us
        are waiting for
        you so we
        can have Junior
        Great Books
        Will you right
        back so we
        now your
        all right.
                Love
                James

Unbeknownst to James, Ms. M was writing to him on the very day that he wrote the letter in (14) to her. Soon he had two letters from her, and this was occasion to write to his friend Benjie about hearing from her. The letter is in (15).

(15)   March 27, 1982
              Dear Benjie
              I rote to Ms
              M. Benjie I got
              allready got two
              letters from Ms M.
              I got two letters
              from Ms M
              how many
              letters have
              you get from
              Ms M
              On my letter she
              said if Ms R
              calls her for Juinor
              Great Book she will come
                   Your friend
                   James

James' pride and happiness make him sound a bit boastful. Certainly two letters from an important grown up is delicious abundance, and James is fairly sure that he is one-up on Benjie. It is important to note that it is not just the fact of hearing from Ms. M that pleases him, but also the fact that he can report what she said, namely, that she will come for a Junior Great Books discussion if their teacher asks her. One of James' purposes in writing letters is to get action. After a lot of inaction during the year, he is probably proud of what he perceives to be his role in getting Ms. M back.

Any sample of James' letters is bound to miss interesting and informative things that he said, and this one is no exception. However, it is at least illustrative of the range of topics and functions he employed as a fourth grader. In the interview he seemed to be aware of a functional difference between the United States mail and Colmar mail. The former, he thought, allowed people to report urgent personal news to friends and relatives who lived some distance away, whereas Colmar mail did not have such an important built-in function. More than most children, James was exploring the potential uses of a school-based postal system. While his writing was in decided need of the development and application of editing skills, James' willingness to use letter writing to explore and test his relationships with people was unusual. Writing, for him, had become a useful and valuable tool.

Caridad

Caridad is a bilingual third grader in Mr. D's classroom. Although Spanish is her first language, she does not, she says in the interview, know how to write in Spanish. Most of her literacy instruction has been in English. Her teacher thinks that she was pushed a little too hard too early to move into English reading, and that this has caused her unnecessary difficulty with phonics activities in reading, and with spelling in general. While it is certainly true that Caridad is not an accomplished speller, her difficulty does not diminish the pleasure she finds in using the postal system. She invents her spellings as she needs them, and while she willingly accepts correction when it is given, the need for perfection does not prevent her from getting things written. She loves to write letters, and, even more, she loves to receive them. Caridad is of particular interest, however, not only for what she writes, but also for her ability to use the postal system to fulfill her social and personal needs. In the interview she reveals a conscious awareness of social aspects of language use that most children possess but do not articulate. The following brief description of her letters is designed to provide the contextual background for a discussion of the postal system as a cultural tool in Caridad's life, the major focus of this section.

In contrast to James, whose letters are quite varied in topic and function, Caridad's letters are noticeably repetitive. Of the 20 letters in the data pool she wrote to peers, 11 begin with the statement "I like you because," followed by a reason. The letter to Marisela in (1) is Caridad's prototype, the original, stripped-down form.

(1)   3-82
         Dear Marisela,
         I like you because
         you are nice to me,
         write me back good
         bye (pic)
              love
                   Caridad

Caridad does vary her prototype, however, and her thoughts often go far beyond simple affirmations of friendship. The letter in (2), for example, written to her closest friend, reflects a somewhat sophisticated view of friendship.

(2)   4-19-82
         Dear Norma
         I like you because
         you are nice to
         me and when
         you get mad at
         me we get back
         to geter and

```
          this is me
          (pic)
                Love
                Caridad
```

Caridad acknowledges that deciding what to say in a letter is difficult. At one point in the interview she says, "Sometimes, um, when they write to me, I hardly know what to say, so sometimes I write the same thing." It is not clear whether she means that she writes the same thing that was written to her, or the same thing that she usually writes. Whatever the case, she is aware of the difficulty of deciding what to say, and of her customary way of coping with it. When asked what kinds of things she says in a letter, she replies, "I say, like for example, 'Dear Norma, I like you because you are nice to me and, um, here is a picture for you.' And I do the picture for her and then I go, 'Your best friend, Cari.' And then I fold it, and then I do a picture on the back."

In one of the rare letters in which Caridad does not speak directly of liking her addressee, the feeling is strongly implied.

```
(3)        8, 1981
          Dear ALma
          I hope you bring your homework
          so you won't get a check
          and write me back.
          good by ALma
          (pic)
          your friend
                Caridad M.
```

In another letter Caridad registers a complaint and makes a request, all in aid of setting a friendship right.

```
(4)   1-4-82
          Dear Zoraya,
          I like you but you always
          play with Norma and you don't play
          with me and please play
          with me now and I will
          like you and write me
          bake good by Zoraya
                Love
                     Caridad
```

(Notice the alignment of the date and greeting in (4). Caridad had drawn her own lines for indicating the placement of the letter parts on an unlined Christmas card that was part of Colmar's holiday stationery.)

Pictures are an important part of Caridad's letters. She draws them on all of her letters, even if there is no picture box on the stationery and she has to draw over the lines meant for writing. If the primary purpose of writing is to affirm friendships, the offering of a picture is an important part of the entire gesture.

It should not be assumed that because Caridad is exclusively concerned with friendship in her letters to her friends that she writes all of her letters about friendship. She has a keen sense of audience, of what it is appropriate to say to whom. One of the most noteworthy instances in which this is revealed is her letter to the Great Pumpkin.

It is the custom at Colmar to write to the various traditional holiday characters. While Santa Claus and the Easter Bunny have been the subject of centuries of lore and their identities are well established, the Great Pumpkin is a newcomer on the scene. No one is quite sure just who he or she is. There are those students who stay with the familiar "You are my best friend" in their letters. For those who are curious about the identity of the Great Pumpkin, the most obvious conclusion to draw is that he or she is the bearer of candy, since the quest for candy is the focus of Hallowe'en for most children. A handful of children go beyond the obvious in an effort to uncover significant information about just who this character might really be, and Caridad is one of this small group. She gets right to the heart of the matter with the letter in (5).

(5)   10-15
        Dear Great Pumpkin
        I have a question
        and here it
        comes do you
        have powers! please
        answer me back
            (pic)
        Caridad M.

Caridad calls attention to her question, first, by announcing it and, second, by punctuating it with an exclamation point. She has identified a key issue and does not want it to slip by unnoticed.

To her teacher Caridad writes to ask "If I'm gonna pass grade and if I do good work." In letters to her principal and the former reading specialist, who had moved to another school, she is concerned with making her identity known to her addressees. In a sense she is testing to find out if she is recognized. These letters, in (6) and (7), also reflect her awareness of her audience.

(6)   11-19
        Dear Mr. K
        remember when you saw

me at the monkey bars
my name is Cari good
by Mr. K
write me back.
    (pic)
    Caridad M

(7)   2-7-82
Dear Ms. M
I like you. Maybe You don't know me
but I know you. My name is Carry
write me back. the End
    (pic)
    love
        Carry

(Caridad seems to be exploring her sense of self in another way in these two letters. She is experimenting with the spelling of her nickname. As well as "Caridad," she is "Cari," and "Carry" here. Another variation she uses during the year is "Carriy.")

In addition to possessing audience awareness, Caridad has a strong sense of linguistic appropriateness, of the interpersonal aspects of language use. In the interview, when asked if she has ever expressed anger to anyone in a letter, she tells of being angry with Lupe for calling her names.

> ...so the next day we had letters and I wrote her a letter. (I said) "To Lupe." I didn't write "Dear Lupe." Instead I wrote "To Lupe," because I was mad at her. I wrote "To Lupe: Lupe, don't call me names no more. Or else." And then I put my name.

She does not open a letter to someone she is mad at with "Dear." Similarly, she reports not signing a letter to her mother's male friend with "Love." That will happen when she knows him better.

Caridad is sensitive to nuances of language use and able to use the postal system to meet her personal and social needs. While the range of things she says to her friends is narrow, the basic function of letter writing in her life is similar to the function of the friendly letter for adults, except that adults are generally concerned with relationships with friends or relatives some distance away.

Caridad is outstanding among her peers for the extent to which she has integrated writing letters into her daily life. In the interview she tells of taking school stationery home and writing letters there, because she does not have time to write all she wants to at school. She describes putting real street addresses on her letters, giving them a touch more validity than the classroom addresses used at Colmar. Then she runs to her friends' houses to deliver the letters, being careful to avoid being seen. Writing and delivering letters is part of Caridad's free time fun. She demonstrates her control over using the postal system by changing the rules to suit her purposes.

Receiving letters is very important to Caridad, too. It is a measure of her popularity. When asked in the interview what her favorite kind of writing to do in school was, she responded by saying "Letters." When asked what she liked about writing letters, she immediately focused on the receiving end of the process: "I like it when they write me back, and then, the pictures that they draw." The letters she receives become fond mementos. During a lull in school work, she takes her letters out of her desk and rereads her favorites. She says she likes to get long letters better than short ones because there is more to read at such times. She describes taking 38 of them home and putting some up on the refrigerator. Others she put in her dresser, up very high where her two little sisters could not get to them. Her mother wishes she would throw them away because there are so many, but she wants to save them so that "When I grow up I could see the letters that they sen' me." Clearly, Caridad's letters are valued possessions.

One letter she received was from a boy, and this was a very big event as it was the first time it had ever happened. When asked what the letter said, she replied, "He told me that I play a lot with Norma and things like that." And, indeed, he did. The letter, which she carefully saved, is in (8).

(8)   9-28
          Dear Caridad
          tu juegas
          con norma
          y con Alma
          tambien y
          ustedes juegan
          a tedrball and
          camprop and
          yu play alot
          with Zoraya tu
          yuo ar norma
          best frend
               love
               Eliseo

          (Dear Caridad
          you play
          with Norma
          and with Alma
          too and
          you play
          tetherball and

    jumprope and
    you play a lot
    with Zoraya too
    you are Norma's
    best friend.
        love
        Eliseo)

What Eliseo wrote is wholly appropriate in Caridad's eyes. This is the letter she identifies as her favorite among all that she has received, because "It was the first time that a boy wrote to me," and "It's so important to me, and like, it seems as if that boy cares about me, and things like that."

Caridad is a child who has tried on the postal system and found a good fit. Writing and receiving letters enables her to use and develop her sensitivity to language use. It also fulfills important social and personal needs for her, and enhances her self image. It seems certain that as Caridad's writing abilities develop, her use of the postal system will grow in depth and variety. The postal system truly is a functional cultural tool for her, which at once helps her grow and reflects her growth.

CORRESPONDING

Introduction

The notion that writing can be interactive is not necessarily obvious to children being taught to write in school. That is an idea which, for some students, evolves in time, as they gain experience using the postal system. As it turns out, however, it is quite possible for children to correspond, in the sense that they exchange letters, without writing interactively at all. This is not to suggest that it is possible to correspond without interacting in some way. The key to the matter is the level at which the interaction takes place, whether face to face in the classroom, embedded in the content of the letters, or somewhere in between.

Increasingly, researchers (e.g., Harste, Burke, & Woodward, 1981) are noticing that young children who are acquiring oral and written language competence are not using subcategories of adult models. Rather, they engage in the same language processes, for example, listening, speaking, reading, writing, that adults do, but they feed different data into the processes (Farr, 1983). In the case of corresponding, it can be said that, from their first efforts, children are engaged in an interactive process, just as are adults who correspond with friends. The difference, again, is the level at which the interaction takes place.

In order to understand what is involved as children feed increasingly sophisticated data into their corresponding, it helps to have in mind a picture of the interactive process adults engage in when they correspond with friends. At its most basic, adult corresponding requires that some person, A, write a letter to another person, B, and that B respond by writing a letter to A. A's letter prompts B's response. This structural framework is supported by several important underpinnings. Presumably A writes to B for a reason, and the reason influences what A writes about and the style and tone s/he employs. The reason for the friendly letter is typically to maintain contact over a distance, and the method involves informal talk about topics assumed to be of mutual interest. Finding topics of mutual interest involves self-reflection and perspective taking. At a minimum, B's letter to A "connects" to A's by acknowledging it (e.g., "Thanks for your letter."). This is a surface level connection to be distinguished from a deeper level of connecting which involves incorporation of or collaboration on a topic which A introduces (Ochs & Schieffelin, 1976). Incorporation of or collaboration on a topic between writers results in continuous, or interactive, discourse. The terms "continuous" and "interactive" are essentially interchangeable.

Adult corresponding does involve taking turns. And it is possible for the locus of the interaction to be more in the turn-taking than in the discourse itself. A writes to B about his concerns, and B writes to A about his, with a minimum of overlap. Many correspondences between friends are ongoing, however, with each correspondent's turn consisting of some new topics and some continuation of old ones. The turn-taking is similar to spoken conversation in its informal, interactive nature, yet different in that each turn is typically longer and covers a wider range of topics. Experience is required in order for writers to learn to control these longer, more complicated turns.

Of course, the rules for corresponding are slightly different at Colmar, because children are writing to people they see every day. It is natural that face-to-face interaction would play a part in their corresponding. The fact that interaction takes place on other levels than in the discourse itself makes the process of identifying the instances of corresponding somewhat difficult. A certain amount of detective work is required, and, because of the difficulty involved, there is a good chance that the detective work is incomplete. However, four general categories of corresponding became apparent when all the identifiable instances were sorted.

The four categories may be roughly described as follows. In the first, children agree orally to write a letter to one another on the same day. While the writing grows out of the interaction, the interaction is primarily oral rather than written. In the second category, the letters are written on different days, but the proximity of their dates (or another clue, such as holiday or special occasion stationery) provides an indication that A's letter probably motivated B's "response." As in the first category, there is no written interaction. In the third category, interaction appears in the letters, but it is located at the turn-taking level rather than at the actual letter content level.

B may thank A for his or her letter, or otherwise acknowledge receipt of it, but makes no reference to anything A says. Finally in the fourth category, there is interaction in the content of the letter, that is, interactive discourse, typically about a single topic which A initiates.

I have used the word *category* consciously in order to avoid the implication of stages which children must go through sequentially from first to last. And yet clearly in the ordering of the categories, there is evidence of growth from more concrete to more abstract, from contextualization of the interaction to decontextualization. The locus of the interaction is increasingly remote from the child and embedded in the writing itself. Among the Colmar students who participated in the research project, none went through each of the four categories sequentially, as if they were developmental stages. However, each child who reached the final category and did not start out there at the beginning of the year, passed through at least one of the first three in preparation for the last.

Simultaneous Corresponding

When two children agree to write to one another at the same time, they gain assurance that their efforts, at the moment of writing, are yielding a return effort. Being able to eliminate any question as to whether or not a letter will get a response is a definite strong point, perhaps particularly in a world where the teacher may not allow time for letter writing when a person needs it.

Often simultaneous correspondences are about the same topic, probably growing out of a recent or even current conversation. Missy and Wendy's letter in (1) illustrate.

(1a)   Dec 9
       Dear Missy
       are you Rodney's
       friend I am
       are you how are
       you doing in math
       I'm doing fine
         No   yes
         ☐   ☐
         (Wendy) (Mrs. F, 3)

(1b)   12/9/81
       Dear Wendy
       Do you like
       Rodney I like
       him I hope
       you do like him

> all the girls do but
> Sonia likes gabriel
> from
>   No   Yes
>   ☐   ☐
>   Missy (Mrs. F, 3)

Wendy and Missy's letters share not only a common topic, but also a common form, the yes/no question with the yes/no answer boxes for the response.

Seven of the eleven instances of simultaneous corresponding occurred in Mr. D's class. While it might be possible to hypothesize a reason for this based on the nature of the classroom context in which the postal system operates, it is probably more to the point that five of these correspondences involve a single student, Caridad. In (2), Caridad and Margaret write to one another, with Caridad, as usual, telling why she likes her addressee.

(2a)   8, 1981
> Dear Margaret
> I like you because you are
> nice to me and you are nice
> to Norma to good by margart
> (pic)
> Your friend,
>   Caridad (Mr. D, 3)

(2b)   10-8 1981
> Caridad
> Dear Caridad,
> I like to watch
> you play tetherball
> (pic)
>   Your friend
>   Margaret (Mr. D, 3)

Margaret's letter focuses on observation rather than participation, perhaps reflecting a feeling of distance from, or admiration of, Caridad.

In (3), it may be that Caridad has influenced the content of Zoraya's letter, since Zoraya does not usually tell her addressee why she likes her.

(3a)   Sept 17, 1981
> Dear Zoraya
> I like you because you are
> funny but I still like you
> because you are fun to play
> with and I like you. the End

(pic)
    love Caridad (Mr. D, 3)

(3b)   Sept. 17. 1981.
Dear Caridad
I like you because you are
nice to me. Cari you are my
best friend
(pic)
    Love
    Zoraya (Mr. D, 3)

Caridad and Norma are good friends who write to one another many
times during the school year. Two of these occasions for writing appear to
be instances of simultaneous corresponding, in which holiday giving is the
concern.

(4a)   12-3
Dear Norma
I like you because
you are nice to me
and I already have your
present Merry " Merry
Christmas
    THE END
(pic)
    Love Caridad (Mr. D, 3)

(4b)   12-3
Dear Caridad
I like you very
much and are
you going to get
presents. I might
give you one. and
have a merry christmas
(pic)
    love Norma
    your friend

(5a)   12-16-82
Dera Norma
I got you a valentine card
did you get one for me? I hope
you did write me backe.
(pic)
    Love
      Cari (Mr. D, 3)

(5b)   2-16-82
          Dear Caridad
          You are nice to me and I
          like you and are
          you going to Bring Valentine cards.
          (pic)
                    Your friend
                    Norma (Mr. D, 3)

Later in the year Caridad and Norma write to each other on the same day, but this time the correspondence is markedly different from the earlier letters. The interactive nature of the writing, as well as the absence of an address on the second letter, provide evidence that the postal system is being used for passing notes in class.

(6a)   6-3-82
          Dear Norma
          I wont to be
          your friend but I
          can't and don't tock to
          me evr agen write
          me back
          (pic)
                    Love
                    Carry (Mr. D, 3)

6b)   6-3-82
          Dear cari
          why can't I talk
          to you could I
          talk to you in
          class
          (pic)
                    your friend
                    Norma

(Caridad's letter in (6a) provides interesting data for the ongoing effort to understand what writing is for children. For her, writing and talking seem to have different functions; during a fight talking is not acceptable, whereas writing is. Perhaps it is the appeal of the privateness of writing, in contrast to the publicness of speaking, that enables her to continue communicating with her friend via writing during their fight [Farr, personal communication].)

Corresponding on the same day is not characteristic only for the younger writers. Fourth graders Judith and Beatriz engage in it early in the year, and here the writing does not even seem to grow out of verbal interaction in the classroom.

(7a)   9-15-81
              Para Beatriz
              tu eres mi amiga y yo
              soy tu amiga y tu eres mi
              mejor amiga y tu eres
              buena con migo y yo quiero
              que seas mi mejor amiga
              (pic)
              yo te quiero porque tu eres buena
                    (Judith) (Ms. R, 4)

              For Beatriz
              you are my friend and I
              am your friend and you are my
              best friend and you are
              good with me and I would love
              for you to be my best friend
              (pic)
              I love you because you are nice
                    (Judith)

(7b)   Sept 15 1981
              Dear Judith
              I like To
              play Tetherball plus
              you het har and I
              like you for a friend
              (pic)
                    Beatriz (Ms. R, 4)

It is possible, of course, that Judith and Beatriz' writing to one another is
due purely to coincidence. (Beatriz did, in fact, write another letter to Judith
2 days later in which she seems to respond to Judith's affirmation of friendship, as well as reiterating her enjoyment of tetherball.)

Two other fourth graders, Liz and her friend Patricia, each wrote four
letters to one another on January 21, during their postal center time. For
Liz and other students participating in the research project, both sending
and receiving large quantities of letters took on importance at this mid-point
in the year. There was a competitive surge of letter writing. Although it is
impossible to be certain of the order of Liz and Patricia's letters on January
21st, one pair, in (8), does apparently contain interactive discourse.

(8a)   1/21
              Dear Liz
              To Liz I like you
              for a friend and how
              do you like the candy

that I got you. You are
a special girl to me
and I will be glad
to get you a (illegible)
That's all I have to
say to you
       (Pat) (Ms. R, 4)

(8b)   Jan 21, 1982
(Pat)
I'm sorry for what
I said and thanks
for the candy It
is good and I really
am sorry and I hope
you will forgive me
for what I said and
I like you a lot.
(pic)
     by your
     Freind Liz (Ms. R, 4)

Patricia's other letters on January 21st are all affirmations of friendship. Liz' letters contain questions about school-related matters (e.g., "Do you like this school?" and "Do you want to be a tutor?"), which Patricia does not answer in writing. There is the sense that most of the interaction between Liz and Patricia takes place face to face, in the classroom, and that just a small portion of it is contained in their writing.

It appears that simultaneous writing by agreement, without interactive discourse, is an access to corresponding which some children choose to use. At the outset it grows out of oral interaction, enabling the writer to feel a sense of working in the here and now, and it assures each writer of a "response." Simultaneous corresponding may grow into traditional note passing or more mature kinds of corresponding, yet it always remains an option, and may be returned to when new goals, such as generating a quantity of letters, become important.

Sequential Corresponding Without Continuous Discourse

The second category of corresponding involves instances where the proximity of dates indicates that the receipt of the earlier letter may have in some sense caused the writing of the next letter. Because children often omit dates, it is difficult to distinguish correspondences which fall into this category from instances of simultaneous corresponding. But, fuzzy as the demarcation lines may be, this category is real and interesting because the recipient of the first letter responds without giving any indication of having received the letter. There is neither acknowledgement of the letter, nor interactive discourse. The letters in (1) illustrate this category of corresponding.

(1a)   septiembre-22 1981
Querido Andy
Andy tu eres mi mejor
amigo tu juegas con
migo y con Orlando
y con Carlos D
(pic)
con amor
    Eliseo (Mr. D, 3)

     (September-22 1981)
Dear Andy
Andy you are my best
friend you play with
me and with Orlando
and with Carlos D
(pic)
with love
    Eliseo)

(1b)   9-23
Eliso
Dear Eliseo
I like When
We play KicKball)
(pic)
mi amigo
Andy (Mr. D, 3)

While it may not be mere coincidence that Andy's letter, like Eliseo's, is concerned with play, there is no indication of interactive writing.

    The correspondence in (2) takes place between students in different classrooms.

(2a)   Oct 8 1981.
Dear Susi
Susi yo soy tu amiga
I Veronica esta in mi
clase yo te mado esta
cart para que me
quontestes
(pic)
quirira susi
    Karla (Ms G, 2)

(Oct 8 1981.
Dear Susi
Susi I am your friend
And Veronica is in my
class I am sending you this
letter so that you will
answer me
(pic)
dear susi
          Karla)

(2b)   October 13 1981
Karle yo
te quiero mucho
puedes ir a mi casa
a ora
di le a tu mama
i a tu papa
que si puedes
ir a mi casa
          Susy (Mrs. F, 2)
          tu amiga

          (October 13 1981
Karle I
love you a lot
can you go to my house
now
tell your mother
and your father
if you can
go to my house
          Susy
          your friend)

Karla says that she is writing so that Susy will answer her, yet she does not ask any questions or make any statements that directly require a response. Apparently to her, a letter itself, apart from its content, is sufficient to warrant a response. Susy (note her use of "tell" rather than "ask," as observed in the writing of other Spanish and English speaking students) responds to the spirit of Karla's letter without any linking of discourse.

It does not seem justified to conclude that all respondents whose letters fall into this category are unable to write interactively. For some children, sending a letter is much like giving a gift, and while the giver may hope for something in return, he or she does not expect the two gifts to connect in any way. Fourth graders, as well as younger students, do this type of corresponding, as shown in (3).

(3a)   JaNuary 11, 1982
               Querido Jaems
               Jaems tu eres mi mejor
               amigo y poresa te mado
               esta cart y Juegas muy bien
               querido amigo
               (pic)
                    Manual R
                    tu amigo (Ms. R, 4)

                    (JaNuary 11, 1982
               Dear Jaems
               James you are my best
               friend and so I am sending you
               this letter and you play very well
               dear friend
               (pic)
                    Manual R
                    your friend

(3b)   Jan 14, 1982
               Dear
               Manual R how
               are you going to finish
               your Rreading. I hope
               you finish your Reading
               because your in big
               trouble because if you
               don't finish your
               things at the
               right time you will
               get in trouble.
               You are my best
               friend I ever
               had in my
               classroom. You never
               call me names ore
               you never teas me
               You are my best friend
                    friend
                    James (Ms. R, 4)

After his warning to Manual, James does pick up the friendship theme that is the main thrust of Manual's letter. Because affirmations of friendship are so frequent in the data, it is virtually impossible to say whether this is in response to Manual's letter, or, for example, an effort by James to explain why he felt free to issue the warning. (See the previous discussion of James' use of the postal system.) Similarly, Jose's motivation for issuing the affirmation of friendship in (4b) is unclear.

(4a)   October 12 1981
Dear Munchy (Jose)
You are my best
friend so you can
youes my makers (markers?)
so you can
Here is a picture of
you in the store
(pic) cute
Whrite back
          love James (Ms. R, 4)

(4b)   October 14, 1981
Dera James
James you are my
best best firend. you did
not pick me on
today. Lets play tag
(pic)
          Your friend Jose (Ms. R, 4)

In Jose's letter the affirmation of friendship seems so automatic that it might be a response to a greeting, as when two acquaintances in a work situation pass one another and one says "Hello" and the other replies "Hello." It is possible to infer a complex relationship between the affirmation of friendship and the complaint which follows it, such that the affirmation provides a reason why the thing complained about should not have occurred, but it is impossible to know if setting up that inference is Jose's intent, or whether, in making the affirmation of friendship, he is simply responding in kind to the spirit of James' letter.

Acknowledging Receipt of a Letter

In the two kinds of correspondence that have been discussed up to this point, there is no direct indication that the second letter is a response to the first. The third category marks a distinct break from the first two in that the respondent makes direct reference to receipt of a letter. And typically, this is the only way in which the two letters connect. (1) and (2) are classic examples of third and fourth graders, respectively.

(1a)   Oct.1
Dear Eliseo
Dear Eliseo your
My best friend. When ever
we're going to
play kickball

I wish if you our
on my team
Andy (Mr. D, 3)

(1b)   10-3
Dear Andy
ya agarre tu
carta que me mendates
y yo quiero que
le mandes una
carta a Carlos D
y a Orlando tamdien
y vamos juara
cickball y tamdien
en lonche tamdien
vamo a jugar
en lonche comemos la comida
con amor
Eliseo (Mr. D, 3)

(10-3
Dear Andy
I already got your
letter that you sent me
and I want
you to send a
letter to Carlos D
and to Orlando too
and we are going to play
cickball and also
at lunch also
we are going to play
at lunch we eat together
con amor
Eliseo)

(2a)   9/18
(Judith)
How are you? I am find
do you like the day today?
I like the day today
hos your best friend? My best
frend is Sandra
Good luck
by   from
Veronica (Ms. R, 4)

(2b)   9/23/1981
Veronica
gracias porque me

mandes te una carta
Veronica yo soi
Judith y qui si era
a ser tu amiga si
tu quieres a ser mi
amiga te tienes
que juntar con miga
yo quiero a ser tu
amiga Veronica
manda me una carta
porque sino me mandas
yo no te mando manda
me una carta
    Judith (Ms. R, 4)

    9/23/1981
(Veronica)
thank you for
sending me a letter
Veronica I am
Judith and I would like
to be your friend if
you want to be my
friend you have
to get together with me
I want to be your
friend Veronica
send me a letter
because if you don't send me one
I won't send you one send
me a letter
    Judith)

Judith's letter may also actually respond, somewhat indirectly, to the content of Veronica's letter. If Judith feels left out of Veronica's friendship with Sandra, she could be understood as making a rather strong plea for friendship with Veronica herself.

Luz' response to James in (3) is outstanding for its absence of both a response to his offer and an answer to his question. However, the intervention of 5 days, with all the potential for face-to-face interaction, may have made direct responses irrelevant.

(3a)   March 26, 1982
Dear Luz
do you want I
ball. I will give you
one. I will give you

a ball with a
red line on it.
Luz are you going to see the
Wisserd of Oz. It is a 8:00
on challen 2.
     Your friend James (Ms. R, 4)

(3b)   3/31
Dear James
Hi I got the letter you
gave me and I want to
be in the classroom at Suva
because you are a good friend
to me and I get to go now good by
James
     Love Luz (Ms. R, 4)

Telling James she wants to be in his classroom next year because he is a good friend may be Luz' indirect means of expressing gratitude for his generosity.

    (4) and (5) offer the opportunity to compare correspondences between the same children early and late in the year. Manual R was trying to learn to speak and write English at the beginning of the year and the strain took its toll on his writing as shown in (4a). When he started writing in Spanish, his writing improved markedly, in (5a).

(4a)   9-22-81

ay jaem
me en Jens
we play
spanes hash
bool your
fren Manual R (Ms. R, 4)

(Dear James
me and James
we play
Spanish dodge'
ball your
friend Manual R)

4b)   October 12, 1981
Dear Manual R
I got your letter and
I got it and I read it.
You are my best friend
and I like you very much

    Here is a picture of you and me
    playing a game
          White Back?
          love your friend James (Ms. R, 4)

(5a)   June 23, 1982
    querido james
    te mando esta carta
    porque tu eres mi me
    jor amigo dime
    si siempre vas a
    jugar socer en la
    carta que me mandes
          tu querido
          amigo Manual R (Ms. R, 4)

          (June 23, 1982
    Dear James
    I am sending you this letter
    because you are my
    best friend tell me
    if you are always going to
    play socer in the
    letter you send me
          your dear
          friend Manual R)

(5b)   June 25, 1982
    Dear Manual R
    I did get your
    letter I know your
    my best friend what
    class room are you going to
    I am going to room 403
          good By
          James (Ms. R, 4)

Manual's letter in (5a) is significantly more mature than the one in (4a), and more elaborate than the one in the section entitled Sequential Corresponding Without Continuous Discourse, (3a). It is difficult to know whether his direct request for information, "Tell me if you are always going to play soccer in the letter you send me," is also intended as an indirect request for a letter, or whether he simply assumes that James will write back. Whatever the case, he has certainly learned to make writing work for him. James, in both of his letters in (4b) and (5b), acknowledges receipt of Manual's letters and affirms their friendship, but he does not seem to pay attention to any of Manual's mentions of sports. His statement in (4b), that he read Manual

R's letter, may be intended as reassurance to Manual that his letter was indeed decipherable. Such sensitivity on James' part is in contrast to his rather critical letter to Manual, also in the Section entitled Sequential Corresponding Without Continuous Discourse, (3b).

By acknowledging receipt of a letter, a respondent is, in a sense, putting out a sign that "This is a correspondence." It is a key step in mastering the last of the formal rules of corresponding: A writes to B; then B writes back to A *because of* A's letter. The next step is to bring the interaction into the writing itself.

Corresponding with Continuous Discourse

In theory every respondent has a choice as to whether to continue a topic introduced by the initiator of the correspondence or to introduce one or more new topics himself. And yet, in reality, continuation of at least one topic from the initiating letter seems to be a feature that characterizes correspondences where there is a sense that the writer is comfortable using the postal system. Perhaps the best evidence for the case that continuation of one of the initiator's topics reflects growth comes from cases in which the respondent seems to be learning how, or exploring ways, to continue a topic. The first part of this section focuses on such instances.

The strategy which Carlos uses in (1) appears to be to copy what Phillip wrote, while adding more information.

(1a)   9/81
          Dear Carlos D
   I am your Best
      cosend
   and we Play soccer
   and Basbal
   by soccer
   (pic)
   Phillip D (Mrs. F, 3)

(1b)   Sept 17, 1981
   Dear Phillip D
   Yuo are my Best
   cousin and we go to
   yuor house and we Play
   soccer and marbles and
   baseball and catch
   (pic)
     love
       Carlos D

Clearly this is not corresponding in any sophisticated sense, and yet Carlos' effort to stay on the topic Phillip introduced is unmistakable.

Julio's strategy for continuing the discourse in (2) is to draw a conclusion, or state an assumption about why Manual F wrote what he did.

(2a)   March 16, 1982
       Dear Julio do you know that the Dodgers
       played the Heaston astros and the dodgers
       and they won 7-4
          Manual F (Ms. R, 4)

(2b)   Manual you like the Dodgers because
       the won the scrt 7-4
          (Julio) (Ms. R, 4)

In Ochs and Schieffelin's terms (1976), Julio incorporates Manual F's discourse topic into a new proposition. If he had answered Manual F's question, he would have collaborated on the topic. Julio's writing conveys his discomfort with the medium; what has been written to him very rigidly defines what he can write back.

Manual F's letter in (3) illustrates topic collaboration in a respondent's letter, this time with some elaboration.

(3a)   September 17, 1981
       Dear Manual
       as you know sugar-
       ray won the fight sugar-
       ray nocked him out 2 times
       in the 13th and in the 14th
       please write back. By
       (pic)
          your friend Miguel (Ms. R, 4)

(3b)   Sept 24,
       Dear Migel
       I no that sugar Ray
       won the fit sugar Ray nock
       down hearns 7th rown
       sugar ray mest up hears
       (pic)
          Manual F (Ms. R, 4)

The extent of Manual F's interaction with Miguel is actually considerable. First is his response to Miguel's "as you know" to open his letter. Miguel's use of the expression is quite unusual for a child of his age. Manual F reacts to it quite literally, responding to it much as if it were a question in need of an answer. Second, Manual F contributes the name of Sugar Ray's opponent in the fight, thus adding information that Miguel had omitted. And third, Manual F goes on to provide further details, designed either to correct Miguel, or to fill in more of the complete story.

Manual F's use of "I know" to respond to Miguel's "As you know" is illustrative of a successful, if somewhat awkward effort of a writer to refer to something the initiator of the correspondence said. A slightly different sort of awkwardness appears in Jose's response to James in (4).

(4a)   March 26, 1982
            Dear Jose A
            I am going to give
            Luz a ball. I am
            going to give her
            a ball with a
            red mark. You now
            how I have my ball with a
            blue mark. I am going
            to put a red mark on her ball
                Your friend
                James (Ms. R, 4)

(4b)   3/30/82
            Dear James
            Hi How are you
            to day I am fine.
            I herd you are
            going to give Luz
            a ball. try to give
            me a ball to. or let
            me baro one
                Goo-by
                your firend
                Jose A (Ms. R, 4)

Now it may, of course, be true that, in addition to reading it in James' letter, Jose did actually hear in conversation with friends that James was going to give Luz a ball. There is no way of knowing. But since Jose is writing in response to James' letter, it is reasonable to assume that his choice of the verb "hear" in "I herd you are going to give Luz a ball" is his method of acknowledging what James had written to him. Possibly this is a case of misplaced indirectness; Jose wants to make his request for a ball for himself as polite (indirect) as he can, but instead of attaching the indirectness to his request, he attaches it to the method by which he received the message about James' gift to Luz. In any case, Jose's responding to James' very direct message with "I herd," as if it had come from some unidentified or anonymous source, comes across as an inexperienced correspondent's practice at learning how to make reference to something written to him in a letter.

Because it is impossible to know how classroom interaction may have influenced each instance of written correspondence, as well as to understand how certain things that get written are actually intended, there is no clear line between what appear to be initial, slightly strained efforts to continue discourse, and more successful, mature ones. In the following examples, the manner in which something is said does not distract attention from or interfere with understanding of what is said, and this, at least from an adult point of view, is one of the best barometers of developing maturity and naturalness in using the postal system.

In (5), Yvonne responds very positively to the closing of the letter she received from Lily.

(5a)   Monday, September, 14, 1981
            To Yvonne
            Yvonne you are pretty and
            I wish you wer my best
            frend and I like
            How you right on spelling
                    Love is alwis
                    From Lily M (Ms. R, 4)

(5b)   Sept. 15, 1981
            Dear Lily
            Thank you very much
            for your letter.
            I liked when you
            said love is always with
            Lilly. I will be your
            best friend now and
            I will play teatherball
            with you and Cindy.
            One of these days I
            will ask my mother
            if you could come
            over my house
            Your new best friend
                    Love
                    Yvonne (Ms. R, 4)

(Note how Yvonne uses the standard spelling of 'always,'' rather than Lily's spelling. She is making the standard spelling available to Lily, and perhaps Lily will notice and learn it in this very personal context.) Yvonne also responds directly and affirmatively to Lily's wish (request) for best friendship, and makes promises in order to confirm the seriousness of her intent.

(6) is a correspondence between third and fourth graders Alma and Debby, respectively, in different classrooms. Alma has some difficulty with her letter, and there is the sense that Debby is trying to ease Alma's discomfort, to assure her that it doesn't matter.

(6a)   November 18 1981
       Dear Debbie
       You are my best frind
       and I play
       tetherball white me
       and I like to
       play tetherball god
       by Debbie
           Your frend
             Alma (Mr. D, 3)

(6b)   November 25, 1981
       Dear Alma D
       how come you do not come to my house
       to play tetherball with me ane we can
       play a lot of games and we can play
       with my friend Cindy at school and I
       like to play with you because you are
       very pretty and you are very nice
       to me. and your mom is very nice
       to me and you.
          your friend
            Debby G (Ms. F, 4)

Debby's method of responding is to pick up Alma's tetherball theme by inviting her to her house to play (the invitational intent of "how come you do not come to my house..." is made clear by the following "...and we can play..."). While the fit of the two letters is not tight with respect to interaction, the thematic linking is unmistakable, as is Debby's interactional intent.

Some of the complexities of male-female relationships are the issue in (7). Karla has apparently written to Joseph before, without getting a response. In (7), after remarking on Joseph's progress with respect to kindness toward two members of the opposite sex, she lodges a complaint.

(7a)   6-19-82
       Joseph
       Joseph you are geting
       to be nice to me

and yesenia
When I rite to you
you don't answer me
just because I am
a Girl
(pic)
      Love
      Karla (Ms. G, 2)

(7b)   Dear Karla
      I didn't wrate
      back because Jesus
      will say something
      to me.
      O.K. By
      (pic)
         from
         Joseph (Ms. G, 3)

Joseph acknowledges that Karla is essentially correct; he doesn't want his friend Jesus to know that he wrote to a girl because of the teasing it will cause. But while Joseph is explaining why he didn't write to Karla, there he is writing to her after all. Her second letter cannot go ignored.

(8) contains three letters exchanged between two fourth grade girls who demonstrate the desire and ability to write interactively early in the year.

(8a)   Sept, 15 1981
      Dear Yvonne
      Hi how are you well
      for me fine I like
      you and I want you
      to go to my house
      for Missy's birthday
      and you'll be with me
      and missy's firends will
      be with her including
      my cousins one is 11 and
      7 I think your my best
      friend and Lilly
      is but your my 1st
      best friend I would
      write more but I'm
      running out of lines
         Your friend
         Always Cindy (Ms. R, 4)
         P.S. Write back

(8b)   Sept. 17, 1981
              Dear Cindy
              Hi thank you very much for
              your letter. I'm fine to
              just like you. I will ask
              my mother if I could go
              to Missy's birthday party and
              if I don't go I will try
              and get her a presand and
              if I don't get her a
              presand or go to her
              birthday party then I don't know
              what I will do but
              I will try very hard
              to go. Wall it is time
              for sighlent reading so
              I have to go now
                    And love is always
                          with Yvonne (Ms. R, 4)

(8c)   Sept 18 1981,
              Dear Yvonne
              thanks for the letter. well I
              hope you could to to missy's birthday
              party. and I promise you you
              don't have to be with Missy because
              your going to be with me. I hope.
              well I have to go now because
              were going to have to go to lunch
                    love always your
                    best friend Cindy (Ms. R, 4)

The correspondence continues with Yvonne writing on September 22nd to express regret at not having been able to attend Missy's (Cindy's younger sister's) birthday party. Although Cindy and Yvonne's concerns about the birthday party seem to be somewhat different, their ability to sustain a topic over turns is apparent. Each is comfortable using the postal system, and has acquired the ability to write interactively with fluency.

Both (5) and (8) demonstrate Yvonne's ability to write interactively in her corresponding. Another correspondence into which she entered has implications for the effect of the social context in which letter writing takes place upon what children write. Toward the end of the school year, after I interviewed each of the students who had participated in the research project, I wrote and thanked each one for his or her participation. My letter started a correspondence with Yvonne, which is shown in (9).

(9a)   June 17, 1982
        Dear Yvonne
             Thanks for coming to talk with
        me today. It was a big help
        and fun too.
             What are you going to miss most
        about Colmar next year? And what
        are you going to like best about Suva?
                  Write back!
                       Love,
                       Jennifer

(9b)   6/21/82
        Dear Jennifer
        thaks alot for
        your letter
        remember the
        one you rought
        me about innerviewing
        on me. Well I like
        it. To bad we
        woun't be able
        to do that again
                  Love
                  Yvonne (Ms. R, 4)

(9c)   June 23, 1982
        Dear Yvonne,
             Thanks for the letter.
        Yes I do remember the one
        I wrote you about our interview.
        I'm glad you had a good time.
             How do you feel about the
        school year ending? I feel
        a little bit sad because I
        won't be seeing the friends
        I made here this year.
             Please write if you have
        time.
                  Love,
                  Jennifer

(9d)   6/24/82
        Dear Jennifer
        I did like the
        inner viewing
        it was fun
        to bad we

can't do it
again but
I wish I could
Write back soon!
   Love
   Always
   Yvonne (Ms. R, 4)

In both of my letters, through my questions, I made an effort to write to Yvonne about what struck me as important personal issues. And in my second letter, I answered my question to her with respect to myself, hoping that by sharing my feelings I could encourage her to share hers. Yvonne steadfastly resists my efforts, choosing instead to focus on the "inner view." (Her spelling reflects a refreshingly different and appealing notion of what interviewing is, and she is clear enough about her perception of the event that she does not notice the standard spelling in my second letter and correct to it in hers.) Clearly the interview had a big impact on her, and she wants to hold on to it. But her letters do not demonstrate the facility at interactive writing seen in her letters to her peers. There is the sense that she is being very careful in a relationship where she is a little awed. For example, in (9b), when she thanks me for my first letter, she reminds me of what it was about, with the implication that I won't remember without her assistance. While there is no way to be absolutely certain, it seems likely that the stress of interacting with an adult of some importance to her about a momentous event inhibited the rather sophisticated writing facility which Yvonne has demonstrated in more relaxed settings. Unfortunately, there are no other instances of Yvonne responding to an adult to use for comparison. In typical child–adult correspondences, the child initiates, the adult responds, and the interaction stops.

There is another instance of child–adult corresponding worthy of mention here because of its contrast to the situation in (9). In this instance, nothing in the social context interferes, and the adult is able to motivate the child to write interactively. Judith (see the section entitled Simultaneous Corresponding, (7)) is one of the less mature fourth grade letter writers, and with her peers she does not do any writing that is clearly interactive. However, her teacher is able to help her to move beyond what she typically does with peers. Judith wrote three letters in rapid succession to Ms. R which were repetitive expressions of affection. In an effort to give Judith something else to write about, to share more of herself, Ms. R wrote to Judith and asked if she had any brothers and sisters, and if so, their names and ages. Judith's response, three weeks later, appears in (10).

(10)   11-13
      Miss Rose
      You are nice

with me Miss
Rose a like one
of your letters and
that was very nice
and in that letter you
tol me wat was the
name of my sisters
and Broders one of
the name of my
broder is Eddiee
and the another Hes
name is jorge
and the big siste
is Rose Mari have
a happy day Miss
Rose
     form
     Judith

(Again, notice the use of "tell" instead of "ask." Also there are interesting evidences of the influence of Spanish in Judith's spelling. "I" becomes "a;" in Spanish /a/ is the closest approximation to the English dipthong /ay/. Similarly, "brothers" becomes "broders" because /d/ closely approximates the English voiced interdental fricative *th* sound which does not occur in Spanish.)

The careful, labored way in which Judith refers to Ms. R's letter and what she feels is the main question in it, and then goes on to answer the question, reflects the effort she must exert to respond to the content of Ms R's letter, that is, to respond interactively. There is the impression that she is stretching here, both in her use of English and in her skill at writing letters, making the most of her teacher's assistance to achieve more than she could have without the incentive. (It is interesting that Judith does not answer Ms. R's first question about whether or not she has any brothers or sisters. This may reflect a lack of perspective taking on Judith's part, in that her brothers and sisters are such an integral part of her life that a question about whether or not she has any simply slips by unnoticed.) Again, Vygotsky's notion of the zone of proximal development helps to explain Judith's ability to exceed her usual ability in this case. What she can do with her teacher's encouragement now, she will be able to do more readily in written interactions later.

The notion that writing can be interactive seems to be one which evolves as children gain experience using the postal system. Because corresponding by its very definition is an interactive process, the act of doing it helps children to move the locus of the interaction from the here and now of the classroom to the more remote content of the writing itself. When correspondents emerge who make demands on their correspondees, the process is hurried along. The facilitator may be an adult, but, as will be seen in the next section, it need not be.

Karla

Karla is an academically successful second grader in Ms. G's class. While her first language is Spanish, she is bilingual, and she writes letters in English unless her recipient is more comfortable with Spanish. Two of Karla's 23 letters are in Spanish, and in both of these the greetings and dates are in English. Perhaps Karla writes these before she really begins to think about to whom she is writing. Or, since the closing of one of these letters is in English too, perhaps Karla is simply accustomed to doing these formulaic parts of the letter in English and tailor-makes only the body of her letters for the recipient.

Karla is popular and social, and not just among girls in Ms. G's classroom. One day Patricia, a good third grade friend of hers, announced to me in Karla's presence, "She writes to boys." And indeed she does, at least to one. She seems to consider boys to be regular people, which is not entirely usual for girls her age. Karla also writes to older children (two fourth grade girls in Ms. R's class) and it is the development of a correspondence with one of these students, Shirley, that is of particular interest here.

It was seen previously that a teacher can help a student to write at a level she has not reached on her own. It appears also that an older child can facilitate the progress of a younger one by modeling more mature writing. It is not that Shirley intentionally plays the role of model, but rather that Karla makes use of what she sees Shirley do for her own advancement.

In the first pair of letters, written in March, Shirley initiates the correspondence, and Karla responds with a letter of the type discussed in the section entitled Sequential Corresponding Without Continuous Discourse except for one interesting exception. While the words of Karla's letter do not give any hint that she is responding to Shirley's letter, the thematic relation of the art work in the two letters is unmistakable. To Shirley's picture of two straight-haired girls labeled "you" and "me" playing tetherball, Karla responds with two curly-haired girls labeled "you" and "me" also playing tetherball. In Shirley's picture the ball is on "me's" side; in Karla's it is on "you's" side. The written messages in this first pair of letters appear in (1).

(1a)   March 5-82
              Hi Krala
              How are you? I am Fine
              How are you going in School
              are you good? I am. I

thing so. are you geting
better in tethir-ball. I
am. will I have to go
     by you'r Frined Shirley (pic)

(1b)   3-15-82
Dear Shirly
shirly I like you
because you play whith
me   love (Karla) (pic)

It may be that Karla assumes Shirley knows she is talking about tether-ball, and that Karla is correct in her assumption. Perhaps only an adult researcher looks for such literalness. In the second pair of letters, again initiated by Shirley 2 months later, there are no pictures, and Karla's verbal message is more specific because it has to carry more of the meaning. The second sequence appears in (2).

(2a)   5/18 1982
Dear Karla
How are you. I am Fine. How are you
geting in teathball Hope better. are
you Fine is school work. what Book
you in math and in reading well
I have to go by you'r Friend

    Shirley
oh say Hi to Elizabeth and Sonia

    by agin!

(2b) Dear shirly I like
you because you
play with me and
we play tether
ball.
    love
    Karla

Karla's first two letters to Shirley are done in cursive writing, and it may be that her concentration on handwriting interferes with the composing process. She gives the impression of not having noticed most of what Shirley writes to her, picking up on only the tetherball topic. Or it may simply be that for an inexperienced letter writer the many questions in Shirley's letter are simply overwhelming.

Karla's third letter is in marked contrast to the first two. Here she initiates the correspondence and gives Shirley something to write back about.

She is learning about the usefulness of asking questions in her letters, because they require answers, they motivate the recipient to respond. This third sequence of letters, of which the first was written in early to mid-June, appears in (3).

(3a)   Dear Shirly I
       Like you because
       you play Chinice
       Jump Roap with me
       how are you
       doing with your
       Riding.
              Love
              Karla

(3b)   Date
              June 15-1982
       Hi Karla
       How are you.
       I am Fine.
       and I like
       to play chinice
       Jump rope with
       you too. and I
       am Fine in reading
       too. Krala How
       old are you. I am
       10 year's old, and
       I am a 4th grader
              by your
          Friend
              Shirley B.

Once again Karla tells Shirley why she likes her, although this time she focuses on a different activity in which she and Shirley participate together. She asks Shirley how she is doing in a particular school subject, reading. It seems quite likely that Karla has learned from Shirley's letters that such questions are appropriate.

Shirley writes back a model response, in (3b). She performs the ritualistic greeting, asking her addressee how she is, and then answering with respect to herself. She comprehends the intent of Karla's "I like you because you play Chinice Jump Roap with me," and responds appropriately that she likes to play the game with her, too. Shirley knows how to spell "rope" and does so correctly; she apparently does not know how to spell "Chinese" and therefore stays with Karla's spelling. She answers Karla's question about how she is doing in reading, again changing to the standard spelling. Shirley then goes on to ask a new question, to answer it with respect to herself, and then to give some additional information (which Karla presumably already knows). Shirley's letter is definitely not a model of creativity, but a model of how to respond appropriately and sensitively.

Shirley does not hear from Karla within a week, so she writes her to find out why. Karla writes back to apologize for not responding sooner, writing interactively for the first time. This represents a major step in the development of her ability to correspond. This final sequence between Karla and Shirley appears in (4).

(4a)   June-22-1982
          Hi Karla
                    How are you.
          I am Fine. How come
          you don't wirte back
          or the letter that
          I sent you has
          not got to you.
          and How are you
          in math. I'm just
          Fine. what book are
          you in Math. what
          Book are you in
          reading. well I have
          to go by your Friend
                    Shirley
                    P.S. Wirte Back!

(4b)   6-28-82
          Dear Shirly
          I am sorry because I dindt
          answer you. I didn't have any
          time so if you could send
          me another letter by now
          Frind (pic)
          Love Karla

Karla's apology and explanation that she didn't have time constitute an appropriate and sensitive response to Shirley's question (or complaint) about not hearing from her. Karla does not respond to any of Shirley's other questions. She responds directly to the part that may have important social implications for her relationship with Shirley, but she disregards the rest of the letter and asks for another one.

Karla's request for *another* letter from Shirley reveals an interesting assumption about the rules for corresponding with which Karla is operating. The particular rule at issue pertains to the question of what constitutes a letter in need of a response. Is it simply a matter of turn-taking, or might there be something actually written in the letter itself that could motivate a response? Her request in (4b) suggests a feeling on her part that the communicative intent of Shirley's earlier letter is somehow cancelled by Karla's failure to respond to it before another one arrived. Both the turn-taking sequence and the content of the letters have significance. A letter that she wrote early in the year suggests that her answer at that time focused almost exclusively on the turn-taking aspect of corresponding. This letter, written to the principal, appears in (5).

(5)   Oct 8, 1981
        Mr K
        Mr K
        You are a very nice man.
        Please answer me. My
        name is Karla (pic)
        Love Karla

Here it is the act of writing a letter, that is, taking a turn, that is supposed to elicit a response. If Karla has any notion that the message in a letter might be deliberately designed so as to require an answer, she demonstrates no awareness of it. At the same time of year she writes to Susy, a second grade friend in Mrs. F's class, "Yo te mado esta cart para que me quontestes" (I am sending you this letter so that you will answer me.). Again, the message in her letter does not give its recipient anything concrete to answer. What Karla is after early in the year is a return letter. It is the physical presence of the letter, more than its symbolic content, that constitues its significance. The letter is the concrete manifestation of a turn taken, the signal for the recipient to do his or her part.

By the end of the year, the message in a letter has taken on more importance to Karla. Its physical being is still a major concern, but she has discovered, with Shirley's help, that she can interact with a friend through what they write to each other. This is no small revelation, for it makes the writing of friendly letters a useful communicative tool, rather than a largely ceremonious gesture. Certainly Karla has more to learn about corresponding with a friend, but through her experience with models of writing more mature than her own she has made important progress.

IMPLICATIONS FOR EDUCATION

Introduction

It is obvious that the postal system at Colmar is not instantly producing great writers. Much of the writing is labored and very limited. And yet, children who would not otherwise be writing are choosing to write letters of their own accord. Clearly something important is going on. Furthermore, these children are getting the idea that something they might actually want to write is important enough to be a school activity. Certainly this paves the way for positive attitudes toward writing. And children who find pleasure in writing early on are more likely to be willing to work to make their writing improve as they go further on in school than children for whom writing has been drudgery from the start. In the final part of this chapter, I would like to look at what using the postal system may be contributing to children's writing development.

The Notion of Text Ownership

When I set out to study interactive writing, I had no idea how little of it I would find. And yet when I reflect on my own experience corresponding with friends, I notice that not a great deal of that writing is interactive either. Certainly part of it is, but the turn-taking aspect of corresponding is important with adults, too. The major difference I notice between my experience with corresponding and what I found in children's letters at Colmar has to do with what I have best heard referred to as text ownership (Farr, 1983). Experienced writers have a certain sense of command over their writing which is very clearly missing with inexperienced writers. I once watched Lawrence, a second grader in Ms. G's classroom, laboriously write to his sister, April: "I see you play with Laura at my house." After finishing that letter he still had a little time, so he decided to write a letter to Laura, his sister's friend. This is the content of his letter to Laura: "I see you play with April at my house." The messages are identical, except for the change of names. This to me represents the epitome of a lack of text ownership; reusing the same message because of the supreme effort involved in thinking of it and getting it down on paper. What is perhaps most remarkable about the use of the postal system among some of the children at Colmar is their willingness to struggle to get something written to send to a friend or an important adult. They want to send and receive letters.

There are several instances in which children play, either with language or with the rules of letter writing form, and these instances seem to convey a growing sense of text ownership. For instance, Becky (Mrs. F, 2), who wrote so many affirmations of friendship during the year, on one occasion wrote to Wendy (Mrs. F, 3), "I love you You are nice and I like you. You yourself and you." The "you yourself and you" inserted in the picture box conveyed to me the message that Becky was feeling a sense of power over the medium. Similarly, in a letter which Miguel (Ms. R, 4) wrote to John (Ms. R, 4) about the Tommy Hearns-Sugar Ray Leonard boxing match, the address on the front was "From: Miguel going for Tommy Hearns," and "To: John going for tommy." Miguel, too, seemed to be feeling powerful, in charge of his medium. In contrast to inexperienced writers such as Lawrence, when more experienced writers write several letters at one sitting, each one is different, tailor-made for the recipient. These writers make the medium work for them, rather than feeling controlled by it.

Notes on Development

The design of the project, without a control group, makes it impossible to attribute the cause of development in children's writing to use of the postal system. However, examples such as (10) in the section entitled Correspond-ing With Continuous Discourse in which Ms. R encourages Judith to strug-gle with interactive writing, and the story of Karla and Shirley in the section entitled Karla certainly point to a particular kind of growth directly attri-butable to use of the postal system. Since there are no other occasions for interactive writing in the writing curriculum, it is only logical to assume that the development is taking place within the context of the postal system.

There is another type of situation in which use of the postal system may not be the cause of development, but it may be a vehicle for revealing development. One particular child comes to mind. Susy began the school year fluent only in Spanish. She was a newcomer to the school and, quick to make friends, she soon found writing letters a good facilitator of the process. Early in the year she wrote several letters such as (1).

(1)   10-81
           estimada Roselia yo to quiero
           mucho vas a mi casa aora cuando
           igamos de la escuela aora
           tu amiga susy

           (dear Roselia I love you
           very much go to my house now when
           we leave school now
           your friend susy (Mrs. F, 2)

Since making friends was on her mind, it comes as no surprise that her letter would contain an affirmation of friendship and an invitation. During the first half of the year, Susy's letters, all in Spanish, grew from just a few lines to double or triple that length. Then, on her own initiative, she started writ-ing in English, and her letters became short again temporarily. By the end of the year she was inspired to write the letter in (2). The occasion was the death of her friend's brother in an automobile accident.

(2)   6-82
           Dear Delfina
           I like you If I cut (could)
           go to your hous

Il gook (cook?) Delfina.
To see your mam
I Love your mam.
she is prette.
You ar cut (cute) to Delfina
ar you Wendy's Frend
yes-or-no ansser
me Ples I houp
you fill bette and
your mam to
I love you Delfina
Love Sus
Your fend Susy (Mrs. F, 2)

Certainly there is much that could be said about Susy's spelling, and in one place it is not precisely clear what she means, but it appears that she has written a letter of condolence, the basic content of which many adults would have difficulty improving. To console Delfina and her mother, Susy offers to help them (to cook), tells them she loves them, compliments them, and tells them she hopes they feel better. She also takes care of a little business ("are you Wendy's frend yes-or-no"), as if to remind Delfina that life is still going on, waiting for her to return.

While using the postal system cannot be said to have caused the development of either Susy's English language proficiency or her writing, the fact that she enjoyed writing letters and did it frequently could only be to her advantage. The postal system provided a supportive environment in which her writing development could flourish.

Conclusion

It has been my intention throughout to let the Colmar students themselves reveal how use of the postal system enters into their lives. They are not learning editing skills in this process, but they are learning that writing is fun and rewarding. They are developing fluency and developing skill at a particular kind of writing that will be useful for the rest of their lives.

There is another advantage to the postal system at Colmar that is extremely significant, given the state of American education today. Many teachers feel unsure of their own writing abilities, and shy away from putting themselves in the position of evaluating their students' writing. Many other teachers simply feel overwhelmed at the amount of paper work they have to do. A postal system such as this one creates a situation in which the students do a lot of writing with a minimum of responsibility on their teacher's parts. Teachers need to create a context in which the writing can happen, and then, simply let it happen. It is reassuring to know that something that is fun is also good for the people involved.

REFERENCES

Cholewinski, M. & Greene, J.E. (1982). Colmar postal system. *California School Boards, 41* (8), 10–13.

Chomsky, C. (1969). *The acquisition of syntax in children from 5 to 10.* Cambridge, MA: MIT Press.

Clark, C. & Florio, S. (1982). Understanding writing in school: A descriptive study of writing and its instruction in two classrooms (Research Series No. 104). East Lansing, MI: Institute for Research on Teaching.

Cook-Gumperz, J. & Gumperz, J. (1981). From oral to written culture: The transition to literacy. In M. F. Whiteman (Ed.), *Writing: The nature, development, and teaching of written communication* (Vol. 1). Hillsdale, NJ: Lawrence Erlbaum Associates.

Eizner, E. (1981). On the differences between scientific and artistic approaches to qualitative research. *Educational Researcher, 10* (4), 10–12.

Farr, M. (1983). *Written language growth in young children: What we are learning from research.* Washington, DC: Dingle Associates.

Graves, D. (1981). *A case study of observing the development of primary children's composing, spelling, and motor behavior during the writing process.* (NIE Final Report NIE-G-78-0714). Washington, DC: National Institute of Education.

Green, J. L. & Wallat, C. (Eds.) (1981). *Ethnography and language in educational settings.* Norwood, NJ: Ablex Publishing Corporation.

Greene, J. E. (1981). *A study of functional interactive writing in a school-based post office system.* Paper presented at the annual meeting of the American Educational Research Association, Los Angeles.

Gundlach, R. A. (1982). Children as writers: The beginnings of learning to write. In M. Nystrand (Ed.), *What writers know: The language, process, and structure of written discourse.* New York: Academic Press.

Harste, J., Burke, C., & Woodward, V. (1981). *Children, their language, and world: Initial encounters with print.* (NIE Final Report NIE-G-79-0132). Washington, DC: National Institute of Education.

King, M. & Rentel, V. (1981). *How children learn to write: A longitudinal study.* (NIE Final Report, Vol. 1, NIE-G-79-0137 and NIE-G-79-0039). Washington, DC: National Institute of Education.

Ochs, E. & Schieffelin, B. (1976). Topic as a discourse notion: A study of topic in the conversations of children and adults. In C. N. Li (Ed.), *Subject and topic.* New York: Academic Press.

Shuy, R. (1982). A comparison of oral and written language functions. Paper presented at the annual meeting of the American Educational Research Association, New York.

Staton, J. (1982). *Analysis of dialogue journal writing as a communicative event.* (NIE Final Report, Vols. 1 and 2, NIE-G-80-0122). Washington, DC: National Institute of Education.

Vygotsky, L. (1978). *Mind in society: The development of higher psychological processes.* Translation edited by M. Cole, V. John-Steiner, S. Scribner, & E. Souberman. Cambridge, MA: Harvard University Press.

5 Learning to Write in a Workshop: A Study in Grades One Through Four

Susan Sowers
Harvard University

INTRODUCTION

A study of development in context, Graves's 2-year case study describes children's early growth in the writing process. With adult assistance in classroom workshops, the children acted upon, and thus partially constructed, their own context for learning to write. The children's learning became visible in a series of scenes or episodes in particular settings among other children and adults whose histories as learners were described. As McDermott said of context, "Behavior does not occur *in* contexts the way alphabet soup shows up in a bowl...[O]ur language fools us by including the preposition where it does not belong" (1980, pp. 14). In describing the context of learning to write, I will attempt to document several workshop settings and to report on some episodes of learning. I will present some features of workshops as instances of cognitive learning in social situations and will describe the sequences in which children learned to write in these workshops.

As part of a naturalistic, longitudinal case study of children's development as writers funded by the National Institute of Education, Donald Graves, Lucy Calkins, and I observed and interviewed children as they wrote in their public school classrooms. Although not intended to be instructional in nature, the study might also be taken as a model of collaborative instructional innovation. At the start, the research team selected 16 children, half in first grade and half in third grade, to observe for 2 years. The 16 children represented a range of developmental differences and high, average, and low academic achievement in grades one through four. As the study progressed, the research team observed and interviewed many other children as well. The researchers directed focal attention to the case study children, and the context of the writing received peripheral attention until later analyses of the data.

The research procedures, particularly the interviews with children about their writing, seemed to generate the kind of talk about writing which the children later internalized to regulate their writing processes. Although designed to be unobtrusive, the researchers' interventions unintentionally became a model for instruction. Thus, an apparent methodological short-coming produced one of the significant outcomes of the study.

The research team recorded children writing and discussing their writing. They took protocols of children composing by making detailed notes or videotaping everything the writers did related to the act of composing: writing, talking, drawing, reading and rereading, and interrupting their own writing. Several kinds of talk predominated. Children composed aloud, usually in a word-by-word rhythm, each word unnaturally distinct as they segmented the sentence into words. They seemed to be dictating to themselves in a special register similar to the beginning reading register. Children orally segmented words into syllables and sounds while they wrote. They elaborated on the stories their drawings and written texts represented; what they wrote was only the gist of a story. They made procedural comments and spontaneously evaluated their own and each others' productions.

Researchers manually recorded children's composing behavior, sitting among the children on child-sized chairs. Although some data was lost through the limitations of writing speed, the interaction among the children about writing informed the researchers about some of the social dimensions in learning to write. When videotaped, children wrote in relative isolation without talking to other children. Unlike the manual recordings, videotapes recorded all visible writing behavior. The researchers interrupted children to question them informally about their decisions in their text and their plans. At intervals during the year, they interviewed the children more formally. In addition to protocols of the children's composing behavior, the researchers collected photocopies of all the case study children's writing products over 2 years.

The researchers entered the school with prepared questions but did not restrict themselves to those questions. Intrigued by the children's answers to the research questions, the teachers also began to ask children questions similar to the researchers'. As a result, the questions became part of writing instruction and the basis for writing conferences. The children, in turn, asked each other similar questions about each others' writing. One category of questions tapped the writer's concept of good writing: What does a good writer do? What do you have to do to be a good writer? If the question seemed incomprehensible because it was too abstract, the researcher made it concrete by taking a piece of the child's writing and saying, "You're a good writer. Tell me—how did you write this?" or "What did you have to know to be able to write this?" Researchers hoped the children would make their criteria for good and skillful writing explicit. If the criteria remained implicit, they attempted to discover them by asking writers to evaluate their work. Researchers asked: Which of these pieces of writing is your best?

Why is this a good piece of writing? What did you do to make it good? What do you think is the best part? The worst part? Why? What does your teacher think is your best piece of writing?

With a second category of questions, the researchers attempted to discover how far in advance the writer planned: What will happen next? What will you do next? Anticipating the next step or several steps ahead was considered a mark of maturity.

In a third category of questions, the researchers asked the writer to give an account of his or her writing process. Although the researchers could not always accept this introspective data at face value, the writers' accounts provided evidence that was useful and interesting in combination with their writing products, observations, and earlier accounts. The adult might ask the child: How did you write this piece? How did you get the idea to begin it? Why did you change that part? What was the most difficult problem to solve?

The questions and the study assumed that the writing process could be separated into phases or temporal stages: rehearsal or prewriting, drafting, revising, and editing. However, as many have pointed out, the act of writing is recursive. For example, the writer engaged in rehearsal or prewriting might generate ideas, revise recent plans, and draft lists and outlines. In an attempt to clarify terms, I will identify the cycle of craft, conveniently if artificially divided into temporal stages, as "the writing cycle." The underlying processes which characterize the thinking that may occur in all the stages of the cycle will remain "the writing process."

Reporting the context in which the children wrote originally was intended to be a task secondary to the study of the children's development as writers. The natural setting—the classrooms—was expected to remain in the background, static. However, the workshop or process-conference approach to instruction was a product of collaboration between teachers and researchers over the course of the study and influenced to an unanticipated extent the findings of the study. Young writers altered the instructional climate for each other as they grew more knowledgeable about writing. An interaction between writers could be viewed simultaneously as evidence of one writer's individual growth in articulating a concept and the context for another writer's application of that concept in a shifting figure-ground relationship. Each child who learned about writing became a repository of information for others. Instruction became diffuse, embodied in routines of listening to and commenting on drafts and the exercise of informed judgments about writing. The boundaries blurred. The competence of an individual writer could not be isolated with certainty. The effectiveness of an instance of instruction could not be measured with any validity by the number of words changed in a resulting draft, nor could the effectiveness of an instructional technique be relied upon under all circumstances.

Birdwhistell compared context to a rope: "The fibers that make up the rope are discontinuous; when you twist them together, you don't make *them* continuous, you make the *thread* continuous" (McDermott, 1980, pp. 14–15). In the sections of the report that follow, I will attempt to examine several strands of the study: First, the organization of writing in the classrooms, a theme and its variations over time and among several rooms; second, a series of writing conferences and an exploration of reasons for their effectiveness; and third, a description of children's growth in writing.

CLASSROOM ORGANIZATION FOR WRITING

Graves and his associates observed children in their natural settings, the classrooms at Atkinson Academy, the public elementary school for Atkinson, New Hampshire. A small town which grew to accommodate commuters to jobs around Boston, Atkinson is predominantly white and middle class. Although it is only 30 miles from the University of New Hampshire, the two communities had little contact before the study. The Academy is a four-room schoolhouse nearly 200 years old with a series of more recent additions attached to it. It includes a second building with three classrooms about a quarter of a mile away, The Rockwell School.

According to the Statistical Update from the Center for Field Services (1980), during the years of the study, New Hampshire ranked last among the 50 states in the percentage of financial aid provided to school districts by the state, so school budgets depended on local property taxes. Of New Hampshire's 168 school districts, 135 were more fortunate than Atkinson in the value of the property they taxed. Atkinson residents' tax rates were four times higher than those in the wealthiest district, an industrial town, yet Atkinson's taxes generated only half the school revenue per pupil. Two results of Atkinson's budgetary limitations influenced the study indirectly. First, there was no public kindergarten in Atkinson. Second, most of the faculty left and new teachers were hired in a bitter strike only 5 years before the study.

The research team imposed no writing curriculum. Instead, they became a catalyst for change in writing instruction at Atkinson. The programs or techniques attributed to the study evolved from collaboration between teachers and researchers. Graves contributed his knowledge of children's development in the writing process (1973, 1975). A pioneer in research in children's writing processes, Graves had observed the behavior of 7-year-old children while they composed instead of simply analyzing their written products. Graves was also director of the University of New Hampshire's Writing Process Laboratory, an interdepartmental group of writers and teachers of writing who constituted a supportive and challenging community behind the research team. They advocated self-chosen topics, conferences between teacher and writer about work in progress, writing for real audiences, and revising only promising pieces of writing in successive drafts. Murray's *Learning by Teaching: Selected Articles on Writing and Teaching* (1982) exemplifies the contributions of the members of the Writing Process Laboratory to the body of practice and theory made available to Atkinson.

When the research team arrived in September 1978, the Atkinson teachers continued to assign writing and return corrected papers to students as they had always done. Some allowed children to write in ungraded journals. The teachers' first departure from their customary writing instruction was to schedule time for writing more regularly to accommodate the researchers' schedules. Soon, however, teachers and researchers were exchanging anecdotes about the children's writing during free time at recess and lunch periods. As trust grew, a spirit of inquiry and experimentation took hold. The interaction between teachers and researchers resulted in an unforeseen collaborative effort.

The teachers accommodated the intrusive videotape equipment and increasing numbers of visitors, and Graves lent support to the teachers' explorations in the teaching of writing. He encouraged their development as active professionals who addressed their colleagues at conferences and in print.

The teachers formulated new theories and tested them in action. They learned to look at writing as adults listen to children's early attempts to talk and asked themselves what the child knows rather than what the child doesn't know. They looked first *through* language to the meaning before they looked at the language itself, again following a principle to which adults instinctively adhere when they talk to young children. They modeled the separation of meaning from form and dealt with meaning first. Perhaps paradoxically, by looking at meaning first, children learned to treat language and the properties of stories as objects sooner than anyone expected.

Writing without assigned topics began in first grade with Atkinson teacher Mary Ellen Giacobbe's visit to the classroom of a first grade teacher in another school—a teacher who did not make assignments and allowed her children to write through invented spelling. She returned to Atkinson with several "books" written in the other class, edited for correct spelling. She read these to her children and asked if they thought they could write books, too. "That's cinchy," replied a few of the bold ones. She equipped a writing table with a variety of paper—lined and unlined, stapled into big and small books, or left in loose sheets—as well as pencils, felt tip markers, and crayons. Each day a few children experimented with writing. They brought their products to the teacher, read them to her, and then read them to the whole class at the regular meeting time before lunch. Soon all the children were writing. Other first grade teachers in the school experimented with invented spelling and unassigned writing, and they adapted what they found useful and consistent with their philosophies of teaching.

The third grade teachers began by bringing personal items from home. Janet Dresser brought her ice fishing gear and Pat Howard an x-ray of her dog's broken leg. Their students interviewed them and learned which questions elicited a simple "yes" or "no" and which a wealth of information. The interviews anticipated the questions children were to ask each other in conference. Before, during, and after writing, children interviewed each other. They quickly learned to focus on information. They rehearsed, developed, and revised their writing by asking questions. These questions, internalized, became guides to more independent writing and to critical evaluation of their own and other writers' work.

After the children interviewed their teachers, the teachers modeled writing on the blackboard for the children. Each began with three leads, or beginnings, and chose the most satisfactory with which to begin a draft. The children observed that (a) writing was not a simple process for adults, for they reread, rephrased their sentences, and evaluated their writing according to criteria they struggled to make explicit, and (b) writing was prompted by a desire to convey a message about a subject the author knew and cared about.

In the second year of the study, the researchers continued to observe the same case study children in the next grade. The children who had been in the "readiness" class—6-year-olds judged too immature for first grade—went to first grade, the first grade children to second, and the third grade children to fourth grade. Many Atkinson teachers experimented with writing regardless of the presence of case study children in their classes. To begin writing in the second year, the teachers simply asked the children to write. No models were necessary for teachers or children. When Atkinson teachers and the research team demonstrated the teaching of writing in other schools, they simply requested the students to write about something they knew about or had done. They helped older students brainstorm topics or subjects. Nonfiction was encouraged at first, but first and second grade children were not usually subject to that rule. Students wrote willingly, often to their teachers' surprise. The request to write seemed to be taken as a sign of confidence in the writer.

A visitor at Atkinson saw two teaching styles, one that was open and non-traditional and a second that was more traditional in which students worked on the same subjects at the same time. The activity-centered classrooms were divided into areas where children pursued projects in science, math, art, blocks, reading, and writing. Classrooms of this type were found in "readiness" (the class for children not mature enough for first grade work), first grade, and second grade. One room had a "pretend" area with old clothing and costumes for play or improvised drama. Another had a well-stocked art area; paints, easels, and clay were available throughout the morning. The rooms had inviting libraries with rugs and shelves of fiction and nonfiction books. Children contributed to the library final published versions of their own books, which were edited, typed, and bound into attractive wallpapered covers stitched with dental floss.

All but one teacher used basal readers for reading instruction at the beginning of the study, although two teachers of 6-year-olds abandoned the basals when they saw that their children had learned reading skills of phonics, comprehension, and critical thinking through writing. Standardized testing at the end of the year confirmed their informal observations that writing as they taught it was as effective as basal reader programs. These teachers did not exclude basal readers from their children's choices of books or workbooks when they had a choice of activities. They were simply one type of reading material offered along with trade books and books the children wrote.

A second, more traditionally-structured style of teaching prevailed in grades three and four. Unlike the lower grades, writing did not occur throughout the morning or the day, but at regularly scheduled periods. Some of the teachers dropped formal spelling programs or grammar and usage programs and taught those subjects through editing, and some teachers maintained their language arts programs unchanged by the innovations in writing instruction.

The teachers' expectations of writing genre varied. In readiness, first, and second grades, the teachers accepted both fiction and nonfiction. The third and fourth grade teachers expected the children to begin by writing personal experience narratives, but by the end of the year the children also wrote reports based on research in books and interviews. Some wrote fiction as well. The teachers believed the high standards for clarity, use of information, and interest to the audience established for personal narrative could be transferred to report writing and fiction. With some instruction, children transferred their ability to revise, read critically, and select and focus on a subject in personal narratives to the writing of reports and fiction.

In Judith Egan's second grade classroom, children reinvented many modes of writing within the rich instructional setting. They wrote fiction, personal experience narratives, "all about" collections of facts, reports based on reading and observation in the science and social studies areas, journals of plant growth, scripts for plays, letters to classroom visitors, lists of interview questions to ask a visiting speaker, and notes on the speech. One pair of girls wrote critiques of each others' published books, reinventing the book review. When introduced to children's literature, they wrote letters to favorite living authors and biographies of authors and compared the authors' styles to their own. They did not, however, imitate their styles.

Teachers arranged for time and materials to match their students' levels of maturity and their own styles of teaching. The first and second grade teachers made writing an activity available anytime in the morning, and the teachers devoted much of their morning time to writing conferences where writing, reading, and the other language arts were taught. One teacher expected her students to write daily. Another expected hers to write when they felt ready since she believed she wrote best when she felt the need to commit something to paper. She monitored their work and encouraged frequent writing. The third and fourth grade teachers, whose classes were more traditionally structured in blocks of time for subjects of study, scheduled writing at regular times. Three, four, or five times a week their classes wrote and conferred together for three-quarters of an hour to an hour.

Teachers accommodated individual differences in their students' needs for attention. They realized that a child experimenting with a difficult subject—one that required library research, for example—or with a new genre, needed steady encouragement. Children in unsettled periods or writing slumps also had quicker access to the teacher's attention. The immature child who wanted attention might come to the head of a short line of children waiting to confer, while more mature writers were asked to read their drafts to each other. A teacher might invite a restless child to break with custom and interrupt the teacher's conference with another child for a word of encouragement. In general, however, children were expected to observe established customs for conferences in their classes.

The children wrote at their own pace, and quantity varied accordingly. The most prolific first grader produced 117 pieces of writing, yet a few third and fourth grade students finished only about a dozen pieces in a year. They were encouraged to abandon unpromising drafts as unworthy of revision. The older children wrote two or more drafts and in rare instances, more than five. For first graders, a piece of writing might range from a sentence or two as a caption for a drawing early in the year, to a 350-word composition on lined paper stapled at the left margin as a book much later in the year.

Teachers did not assign dealines for each paper. Except for the beginning of the year and the return from vacations, children rarely began new pieces as a whole class. Children in readiness, first, and second grades anticipated class publication of one in every four or five books they wrote. Published books were made part of the class library with library cards and pockets. Children checked books out overnight to read to family and neighbors. In third and fourth grades, children made collections of their writing, but no publication comparable to that of the younger children took place. They edited next-to-final drafts for correctness once all revisions were made and copied them neatly as a final draft.

Children heard teachers identify qualities of good writing in their own and their classmates' work, and they adopted the terminology and the standards as their own: an abundance of information; a beginning, middle, and end or other means of giving order; an appropriately narrowed focus; an exciting lead or beginning; vivid language; and concrete, specific details. Also, the children prized a long piece of writing or complicated series of revisions for the process behind the product. Similar standards applied in the upper grades. The greatest difference was the third and fourth graders' preference for a middle-beginning-end pattern in chronological development. They began in the midst of the action and filled in the details the reader could not infer once the action was launched, just as adult writers of nonfiction might.

The selection of drafts for publication conveyed sane and wholesome messages about the writing process. First, conferences in which authors selected and evaluated writing became the occasions to discuss qualities of good writing. Second, children and teachers were not subject to the unrealistic expectation that each piece be a masterpiece at the child's level of performance nor a major leap forward in maturity. Children's writing development exhibited its share of crests, troughs, and plateaus. Teachers and researchers who might have become anxious about a child's lack of progress restrained the desire to intervene prematurely. They learned to wait and observe. They asked themselves what kind of nonpunitive intervention was likely to be effective, how long a slump was likely to last, what its course was likely to be, and what produced the peaks of performance the other children had achieved.

Conferences

Writing instruction took place in conferences. No drafts were submitted for written critiques and no writing lessons were taught without illustrations from the children's drafts or accounts from the writers themselves about their processes. Teachers provided a number of formats for conferences: two individuals, small groups, whole class group; with the teacher, with peers, with both; teacher-initiated and writer-initiated. Teachers new to conferences began by conferring individually with children and by inviting those who had finished a draft to read it to the entire group for a response. By mid-year, the patterns of writing conferences had proliferated. The conferences became more differentiated as reasons for writing conferences multiplied. Children anticipated writing and wanted to discuss possible topics. They wanted quick checks for reassurance while drafting. Conferences guided revision. A writer might need to elaborate, focus, or reorder; check for clarity; apply criteria for good writing to the draft; identify the most and least successful parts of a draft; give an account of the process behind the draft; and finally, edit and learn skills of spelling, punctuation, and usage. A child, the teacher, or the class routine itself might suggest the form and content of a conference. Typically, children had vague expectations and objectives for a conference early in the year, but with experience children learned to request specific help.

In an individual conference, teachers responded to a child's writing according to its stage of completion—rehearsal, drafting, revision, or editing. The teacher might paraphrase the content, ask the writer to think aloud about the direction of the draft, or tell the story one more time. Children were requested to evaluate their work throughout the writing process—to tell what they liked and disliked in their drafts and to compare their earlier drafts. Children were questioned not only by researchers but also by their teachers about their decision-making in writing, no doubt enhancing their awareness of the writing process.

The original model for the individual conference at Atkinson may have been the research interview. Researchers elicited children's criteria for good writing at intervals during the study. At first, most said good writing had to be neat, correct, and long. When asked about the best parts of a piece they had written, most replied, "It's *all* good" or "I like the whole thing." When asked what made it good, they usually said it was good because it was about a particular subject, and they liked that subject. The teachers did not contradict such immature or incorrect answers given in conference. Instead they listened with the attitude of researchers, noting which children adopted and applied new criteria for good writing. Many other qualities of good writing were identified at other times.

In a conference with the whole class, the children usually assembled on a rug in a circle and the author held the floor—reading, telling what kind of help was wanted, and calling on other children. The teacher was always present and the author called on her if she wished to comment. Usually, she left the routine bulk of the comments to the children and added only what they could not be expected to know. In this way, the teacher introduced new procedures and criteria for good writing to the class as a whole. Teachers rarely taught a principle of writing until a child first demonstrated it. Ready to achieve something new, a child might have been coached to a point where s/he could demonstrate the lesson to the class. The whole class meeting was a forum for sharing work in progress and admiring finished pieces.

Peer conferences occurred when children had permission to talk to each other while writing. In some classes, formal peer conferences could be arranged by a pair, who moved to a corner or a table at the periphery of the room to talk and read. They might be requested to sign up for the opportunity or to report in a brief memo on the main topic or suggestion made in the conference. First graders, however, often talked aloud to themselves and freely made unsolicited suggestions to each other. In most classrooms, quiet talk with a conference partner was encouraged for the benefit of the writer and the listener.

In most classrooms, teachers enjoyed the small group conference for its intensity and the care with which children listened to each other's work in progress. The four to six children focused on how the draft succeeded in representing the author's intentions and how to improve it. The small group conference in first and second grade was the occasion for the author to judge his or her best piece of writing, worthy of publication, and to hear responses from peers. In third and fourth grades, the teacher-led small group conference provided a more focused response to a draft than was likely in an informal conference with a peer.

Few teachers used all the conference formats, and all adapted them to their styles. For example, the first grade teacher found her first class succeeded in small group publishing conferences, selecting their best book, defending their choice for publication, and finally hearing suggestions for improvements. However, her class the next year was not sufficiently mature for such discussions so the children made their selections and final revisions with her alone. She had borrowed the small group conference from the third grade. The second grade teacher increased the number of whole group conferences at the children's request. They wanted still more ideas for improving their drafts just before publication. The second graders after mid-year relished their new fluency and the ease with which they could alter and clarify their drafts.

One of the greatest benefits to the children from conferences may have been their acquisition of the language of writers. Stereotypical judgments about schoolwork—right, wrong, neat, messy—had to be overcome. An early draft was usually both wrong and messy, yet it could be promising. The children used verbal tools to isolate parts of a draft from the flow of words and to identify qualities of writing. Planning for writing was fostered in conference. Even first graders could be overheard planning—what to play outside or make in blocks, for example—yet they were rarely asked to plan their school work. Listening to instructions was usually considered more important.

Materials

Writing folders were essential to teaching, evaluation, recordkeeping, and research. All teachers used them, and some had two sets of folders. All work in progress and previous drafts remained at school, available to parents in conference with the teacher. The children reviewed the collections of writing with their teachers and the researchers. The researchers photocopied hundreds of pieces of children's work. In classrooms where two sets of folders were in use, current work was kept in one and old work as it accumulated was transferred to a second, less accessible, set of folders. The year-long collection of work was a visible reminder to researchers, teachers, parents, visitors, and children of the children's progress. A period of slow growth in March fell into perspective beside work from September. When children reviewed their old work, they spontaneously commented on their own development as they might while looking at their baby pictures in the family album. Some children denied that they had done the writing or drawing from early in the year because it was so different from their recent work.

In the second year of the study, the teachers began to use the surfaces of the folders as a site for lists which extended their own and the writer's memory. On the outside cover, children were asked to list the titles of the pieces they had finished. The previous year, one teacher had listed titles on a long sheet of shelf paper across the bulletin board, adding new titles in the column below the author's name when the writing was completed and highlighting in color published titles. On an inside cover of the folder, children kept a second list—"Things that I can write about." Exciting ideas for future topics were generated at the moment an event was spontaneously recalled. Now the ideas could be recorded before they were forgotten, but without the requirement that they become a piece of writing. Perhaps this idea was most effective at the level where it originated, second grade. Interviews with children at grade levels from one to five at the end of at least 1 year of writing instruction revealed that in fourth and fifth grades, and to some extent in third grade, children knew many more potential topics, as well as procedures for generating topics, than the younger children. Another procedure developed in second grade was a box of file cards listing special knowledge and experience each child had. The teacher called the class together and asked them to tell her about each member's area of expertise. The children often learned their classmates perceived them as knowledgeable in subjects they had previously taken for granted.

A third use of the writing folder was as a record of proofreading responsibilities, "Things — — — can do." Teachers approached the addition of a new item ("I think you're ready to spell these words correctly every time, *too, two,* and *to*") as an achievement, rather than as a failure, to comply with the conventions of written English. Again, this was an adaptation of a proofreading list kept in a conference journal, a record keeping form developed in first grade.

A booklet called a conference journal or writing diary was a brief record of each conference between child and teacher, and it was sometimes kept in the folder. Dated entries provided brief notes summarizing conferences and documented growth in writing concepts and mechanics. For example, if an important issue in a conference was the child's follow-up revision after the conference and the child was expected to work without the direct aid of the teacher, the note in the conference journal was a sufficient reminder to both. The child checked the journal after the conference ended and the teacher a day or so later at the next conference. Skills not sufficiently automatic to list as proofreading responsibilities might be noted in the conference journal. Teachers who used the children's writing in the first two grades as a major part of the reading and language arts program found conference journals useful record keeping tools. Along with collected work, these records replaced cycles of pretesting, seatwork, and post-testing of specific skills in basal reader programs.

Environmental assistance to writing abounded. Instruction was diffuse because not only the conference, but also the tools became messages about writing—folders, special places for writing and conferring; staples and staple removers, tape, and scissors for revision; and materials for publication.

CONFERENCES: INTERNALIZING THE DIALOGUE ABOUT WRITING

One item on the list of proofreading expectations appeared in the writing folders of many children: "Go back over my writing." Children in the writing and conference areas of the room could be seen reading aloud to a partner, reading in a low voice alone, or reading silently. Graves asked Hilary, a second grader, what she was doing when she was reading her draft. "I have an individual conference—with myself," she replied. Asked what she did in her solitary conference, she said she read her book again and again and thought of questions the other children would ask about it. She gave an example of a question she anticipated about one page in her current book, "On the Farm:" " 'Your horse's name is Misty. Well, do you ride it or feed it or what?' So I'm going to put, 'I ride her every day unless it is raining.' "

Hilary's response showed she internalized conference dialogue to help her regulate her revision process. First, she formulated an audience's response. She summarized a sufficiently detailed section of her draft: " 'Your horse's name is Misty' " from an audience's point of view. Second, she probably empathized with classmates confronted with a skimpy draft when she asked herself: " 'Well, do you ride it or feed it or what?' " Then she committed herself to revise: "So I'm going to put. . . ." Finally, she decided how to satisfy the implicit criterion of sufficient detail: " 'I ride her every day unless it is raining.' "

Hilary imagined her peers' response to the bald fact that her family owned a horse named Misty, and that process was fostered in conferences. At Atkinson, conferences were the heart of writing instruction. Conferences were usually brief oral readings and discussions of writing or plans for writing. The teacher's tone was respectful yet not overly solicitous, an expression of confidence that inadequate writing could be made adequate and good writing could be made even better. The conference was an occasion to listen to the writing. The tone of conferences, in fact, was more readily replicated than the patterning of the content, and the tone may have conveyed as much to beginners about what it meant to write for an audience than any direct statement. No doubt the affective tone of conferences was internalized along with the pattern of dialogue.

Just as children learned to anticipate the cycle of writing—rehearsal, drafting, revising, editing, and publishing—they anticipated a sequence of questions and a predictable range of issues in the writing conference. The dialogue between teacher and writer and between reader and draft in conference can be described in terms of *scaffolding*. According to Cazden (1982, p. 6):

> A scaffold is, literally, a temporary framework for construction in progress. Metaphorically, the term 'scaffold' was first used by Jerome Bruner to refer to adult assistance to children's language development.

The metaphor of scaffolding may be applied to two kinds of construction in writing. First, conference dialogue may serve as a framework for the writer's construction of a reflective stance toward any piece of writing but especially toward his or her own drafts. Second, conference dialogue may serve as scaffolding for the construction of a piece of writing. In this sense, writers do not outgrow the need for dialogue about writing. Scaffolding may change as a writer matures—just as conferences among fourth graders will be shown to differ from those among first graders—and temporary, external support in the form of dialogue may sustain writing in progress over a long career in writing, not just in childhood writing.

In the remainder of this section, the metaphor of scaffolding informs the commentary on a series of conferences among children. Conferences among first and second grade children serve as a framework to help them achieve fidelity to good sense, order, and completeness. Among the third and fourth grade children, the earlier framework seems to have been dismantled as the writers work from a secure new platform of coherence. They use the conference as a scaffold to support the achievement of voice in writing, and they frequently specify the support they must have.

Finally, at the end of this section, implications for a theory of instruction based on dialogue will be drawn largely from the work of Bruner, Piaget, and Vygotsky.

First Grade

Even the 6-year-olds knew how conferences were to be conducted. In the following interview, visiting researcher Barbara Kamler asked first grader Donna how a teacher should conduct a conference. Donna had just completed a conference with her teacher and drew her examples from it.

Donna: Well, what you have to do is you have to have a piece of writing— well, you have to have words written on them, and then you have to take it to the teacher and show it to her, and you have to read it to the teacher. And when you read it to the teacher, also, when you do that, she has to write something when she can't read it. She has to write something when she can't read it. She has to write what you read to her. (Donna's invented spelling was often difficult to decode, and she is correct in this detail.) And if she can read it, she doesn't write anything. And so you have to talk about it and make a little change sometimes. And sometimes you don't need to make changes and sometimes you do.

Kamler: How do you know when you need to make changes?

Donna: Well, the teacher points out—either you decide it doesn't make any sense or the teacher points out to you—it's wrong, this thing.

Kamler: Did this just happen in your conference with Mrs. Giacobbe?

Donna: She pointed out that the 'g' was wrong, she pointed, that a couple of my 'g's were wrong. She had a little talk with me when I had my conference with her.

Kamler: About what? Just about 'g's?

Donna: About my story. That's how we have conferences. So we have a little talk to see if it makes sense or not.

Donna discussed a familiar pattern: take the finished writing to the teacher, read and decode it, have "a little talk," and sometimes make changes (revise). With probing, she told about two conditions under which revision was undertaken: (a) either something is wrong and doesn't make sense and "the teacher points it out to you," or (b) "you decide it doesn't make any sense." Donna revealed her role as an active evaluator of her own writing. The teacher was not the sole arbiter of the text's meaning. Donna defended her writing from misinterpretation and willingly took steps to revise it. Until her writing always "makes sense," she can expect "making sense" to be a predictable issue in conference. In the conference she referred to before the interview, Donna had initiated the discussion of making sense by asking her teacher whether she, too, thought this book made better sense than an earlier book, "The Fantastic Whale." They agreed that it did.

In peer conferences, teachers encouraged children to appreciate, diagnose, and offer remedies to their peers. In the first grade group conference that follows, the children told Allen, the author, that his piece confused them. Their teacher allowed them to discuss the draft until they reached an impasse. Something was wrong, but no one offered a solution. At that point, the teacher took a more active role.

Allen read his practice book, "My Trip to the Football Game," which he judged the best of his previous five pieces and good enough for publication. The other three children were prepared to listen carefully, suggest improvements, and identify the parts they liked. Allen's writing typified the apparent regression in skills associated with an ambitious attempt to write about a new topic. Organization had never been a problem until he stretched his capacity to organize in this piece.

Allen: My Trip to the Football Game
                    We had to drive to my dad's work. We got on a big bus. It
                    took us to the game.
                    We had a picnic when we got there.
                    The Patriots and the Jets played. The score was 55 to 21.
                    The Patriots won.
                    We saw two men in long underwear and funny glasses and
                    noses.
                    There was over fifty buses.
                    There was a bathroom on the bus.
                    And we saw a man and he had a pumpkin on his head.
                    The policeman made us throw our Coke in the garbage.
Shannon: It wasn't about one thing. It went hippety-hop from one
                    thing to the next.

Chris agreed with the hippety-hopping.

John: Why would a guy have a pumpkin on his head?
Shannon: Yeah, but it didn't have anything to do with the book.
Chris: Yeah.
Shannon: It's like Allen went to sleep and had a crazy dream.
Allen: That's how I saw the stuff. And I didn't see the whole game.
Mrs. Giacobbe: When you went to the game, Allen, what happened?

Allen retold the things he saw and did, and she wrote them in a list.

Chris: (interrupting) You should put the Coke thing between the
                    picnic and the stadium.

Allen reread his book, ending with "The policeman made us throw our
Coke in the garbage."

Mrs. Giacobbe: What could Allen do to put this page in the beginning?

    The children volunteered ideas: erase and rewrite the book, cross out
the words, scribble over, write the whole thing again, and draw arrows from
page to page to show where each part belongs. The children had many ideas
about sequence and coherence, yet they knew very little about manipulating
print on the page.

Mrs. Giacobbe: You could number the pages so when I type it I'll know
                    where to type them. Now, the last page.
Allen: "The policeman made us throw our Coke in the garbage."
                    Oh, boy. (He knew it was out of place and required work to
                    fix it.)

Chris:	I'm glad he told the score. It tells how the game ended. Maybe he could tell who got a touchdown. It's easier to see what's in his head.
Allen:	Well, it was in October, and I don't remember. Besides, I couldn't see it.
Chris:	*Now* he tells us it was in October. That explains why he had a pumpkin on his head.

After further conferring with his teacher, Allen removed the staples from his book and rearranged the pages. In addition, with Mrs. Giacobbe's probing, he expanded his narrative to include the fact that he was unable to see much of the football game since taller adults blocked his view of the field. He made explicit the connection between the time of the year and the Halloween pumpkin on the man's head.

Allen's alert classmates were not tactful about telling him his "hippety-hopping" did not meet their standards for logical order, although Chris later told him he appreciated being told the score and learning why the man wore a pumpkin on his head. The children's complaints were delivered in a business-like tone. A confusing draft, though, was not a cause for shame, nor was revision a punishment.

Second Grade

Second grade students (Hilary, for example, whose conversation with Graves, reported earlier, showed her to have internalized some of the questions her classmates were likely to have asked) were probably more sensitive partners in conference than Chris, Shannon, and John were for Allen. Kamler (1980) reported that second grader Jill, Hilary's classmate, was asked by her teacher to read her draft to a classmate before a one-to-one conference with her teacher. Although Jill did not copy a second draft, she made six changes in her original 54 word piece, deleting 12 words and adding 25. Jill did not need as much explicit instruction as Allen nor was she, on that day, ready for an individual conference with herself. Kamler (1980, p. 684) explained that for Jill, her partner's "presence was crucial to the content revisions of the draft. . . . [She] seemed to make the concept of audience visible for Jill."

The following conference between second grader Katy and her teacher, Judith Egan, reveals that she had recently solved the problem that troubled first grader Allen—orchestrating a mass of chronological details—and that this is a new accomplishment for her. Mrs. Egan did not push for further refinements or interrogate her to draw out even more details. Instead she and Katy together evaluated Katy's growth, comparing her current piece to an earlier one which required considerable social support for revision. Here, Katy was able to formulate the kind of knowledge she brought to bear upon the task of writing, and her teacher acknowledged this accomplishment with the statement, "You remember what you now know how to do? That's good, Katy."

Katy:
(reading)   The first thing we done in Boston, we went to The Children's Museum in Boston. This museum is really big. We got to go in it.
(to Mrs. Egan) Happy, I was happy.
(Katy anticipated a question about how she felt and answered it unprompted.)
(reading):   They had a McDonald's next to The Children's Museum.
(to Mrs. Egan) Hitched on to it.
Mrs. Egan: Really? Hmm.
Katy:
(reading)   We saw a lot of things like how the Indians lived, how the handicapped people lived, and all different things in life.
Mrs. Egan: What a good word—handicapped. What does that mean?
Katy: When people are crippled or they ride in wheel carriages or they have a broken leg.
Mrs. Egan: Is that the display where you can ride in a wheel chair and see what it's like to be handicapped? I think there were games that let you know what it would be like if you didn't see or hear correctly. I heard that's a really good exhibit, Katy.
(Mrs. Egan responded to Katy's writing by looking through the language to the content. Katy's comments, "Happy, I was happy," and "Hitched on to it" show Katy anticipated this line of the discussion.)
Katy: I like the next one.
(reading)   I came to the doll houses, and I saw one of the houses. And I said, "That looks like Beatrix Potter's doll house," and it was. I was so happy I hollered, "Mom! Mom! Look at that! This is Beatrix Potter's doll house!"
                 She said, "It must be because it has a story about the two bad mice."
                 I said, "That is the house that was in the story."
                 And then she read the story to me. When she got to the part when she said the doll house, they were both the same color and they looked the same.
Mrs. Egan: Which looked the same, Katy?
Katy: The book and...they both looked the same.
Mrs. Egan: The picture and the doll house itself?
(Mrs. Egan has now made some metalinguistic comments about Katy's language, the word "handicapped" and her question about the ambiguous reference, "they looked the same." Katy, too, has now commented on her story, "I like the next one.")
Katy:
(reading)   Then we got to the computers and we played hangman, tic tac toe, and inchworm. I had a lot of problems.
Mrs. Egan   Using the computer?

Katy: I pushed the wrong button.

Mrs. Egan: I remember when we had the computers at the children's museum in Nashua. I had a hard time with them, too.

(Again, Mrs. Egan made a conversational response about a shared experience and carried it beyond the subject of the writing, inviting Katy to do the same.)

Katy: My father works with them some days at his work.

(reading)   And we got to play in a Volkswagon. We saw how the gears work.

(pointing to her illustration)

                 That's the stick thing, the shift. That's the emergency brake. The gas, the brake, the wheel, and the clutch.

(reading)   I got to go down a manhole. All it was was wire and pipes. And then we went to the little store in The Children's Museum. And I got a little car and a book by Beatrix Potter.

Mrs. Egan: What was the book that you got?

Katy: *Squirrel Nutkin*. Says in the back.

(reading)   Then we left the museum. We went to the No Name Diner, and I had chowder.

Mrs. Egan: Had you ever been to the No Name Diner before?

Katy: My first time.

Mrs. Egan: I've been there before. They have super chowder.

Katy: I had fish chowder. It had mostly meat.

Mrs. Egan: Did it? Do you know that their chowder is famous and that the people from the No Name Diner have actually served it at the White House? To the president?

Katy: My grandfather told me that. 'Cause he goes in there all the time. In Boston. I went on some other trips. I half forgot about them.

(The conference shifts from the content to an evaluation of Katy's progress.)

Mrs. Egan: You know what I notice in this book? Your book about your trip to Pennsylvania with your family—remember how you really had to work on the order and getting the order of everything? (Katy laughs.)
                 Something I notice in this book you *have* done...

Katy: ...put it all in order!

Mrs. Egan: I see everything in the beginning of the book is about the trip to The Children's Museum,...

Katy: ...then McDonald's, then handicapped and all about Beatrix Potter's doll house, the computer, the Volkswagon, the manhole, then at the No Name Diner.

Mrs. Egan: You have everything about the museum together, everything about eating together. I also like the way you wrote this at home over vacation, Katy. It's kind of nice to have a book right there when everything's fresh in your mind.

(Mrs. Egan recognized Katy's growth, and Katy was justifiably proud.)

Mrs. Egan: I also notice, Katy, that you remembered to use periods throughout the book, and it's nice to see that.

Katy: I didn't even look in my folder. 'Cause I looked in it, and I done
               it all.
(Katy's personal list of proofreading responsibilities was inside the folder
where she kept drafts before choosing one to publish.)
Mrs. Egan: You remember what you now know how to do? That's good,
               Katy.

Katy makes the steps beyond first grade writing visible. She has solved
the problems of chronological order in her first draft. She has a fullness of
detail that is absent from Allen's book and that her classmate Hilary was
striving for in her book "On the Farm." She added further comments in conference with her teacher—"Happy, I was happy" and about the McDonald's
at the museum, "Hitched on to it." Implicit in her favorite part of the story,
the Beatrix Potter doll house ("I like the next one"), is her excitement and
energy, a step beyond the often wooden accounts of children new to writing.
Mrs. Egan responded as any helpful adult might to the news in Katy's piece
and followed the principle of semantic contingency which caretakers are
observed to follow in talking with young children. The caretakers take their
cue from the child's utterance, just as Mrs. Egan did. She expanded the discussion by including her own feelings about computers, displays in another
children's museum, shared knowledge about a famous Boston restaurant, a
previous book Katy had written, the pleasures of writing about an event
outside school, and the principles of chronological ordering which Katy had
begun to observe with new ease.

Third Grade

In third grade, students provided a more sophisticated kind of help for each
other. As soon as children were able to generate a convincing fullness of
detail, their teachers asked them to select the most telling details. From that
point on, writing became a process of alternating cycles of elaboration and
selection guided by the questions: What kind of piece of writing do I want
this to be? What do I want to say? What do I mean?

   Here, Terry has just completed what he hoped was the last draft before
his final copy, and he asked Brian to be his reader. Brian agreed on the condition that Terry would read his draft as well. Brian laughed when he finished
his first reading of Terry's account of a bicycling accident he'd had to avoid
colliding with his younger sister. Brian asked Terry a few questions to confirm what he had read, then began rereading silently and paraphrasing with
great animation as he read.

Brian: I'd just say, "My sister was coming up the driveway with her bike."
         You're almost colliding...She cuts you off...You took a left. You
         hit the brakes. The brakes squealed (here Brian added squealing sound
         effects). "I hit a rock!"...You're going down the hill. Your sister's

in the way...you took a deep left. You were on dirt. You knew the
brakes wouldn't work. You hit them anyway. You hit a rock. You
crashed into the creek. You looked up. The bike! Oh, no, it landed on
you!

Terry thoroughly enjoyed Brian's dramatization of his piece. Brian
chided him, "You made a mistake when you turned the corner," and the
boys discussed alternative strategies that might not have resulted in the accident Terry described. This discussion and Brian's performance were vivid
proof to Terry that his piece had come alive for Brian. But he wanted an explicit evaluation.

"Did you like it?" Terry asked.

"Yeah, except 'My sister was walking up the driveway with her bike,'"
Brian said, quoting the sentence from the draft. It's not exciting. 'My sister
cut me off' is better."

Now Brian read Terry's piece for a third time submitting each sentence
to a test. After each, he asked, "Is it exciting?" All the sentences met his
criterion for excitement except the objectionable first sentence, "My sister
was walking up the driveway with her bike" and the last sentence, which
was funny instead of exciting.

Independent of their teacher, Janet Dresser, and her direct supervision
and immediate follow-up, Brian and Terry focused on the qualities of good
writing beyond sufficient information, order, and clarity. Excitement, interest, and humor were the hallmarks of successful writing in their third
grade class, qualities their teacher first identified in their writing and the
8-year-olds adopted as goals.

Fourth Grade

In the next example, a fourth grade student, Mark, who had been writing
regularly for a year and a half, had internalized many of the questions and
suggestions that might arise in conference with his teacher and classmates.
However, his conference partners offered him little help on this piece. As he
wrote, he talked aloud to himself and to the researcher seated beside him.
His talk was probably the outcome of the difficult task he set for himself—
to follow one of the oldest rules in journalism, "Show, don't tell."

In five sentences, Mark attempted to render his perceptions so scrupu-
lously that the audience would vicariously experience what happened to him
and feel his confusion and surprise. Yet the audience also needed a guiding
concept of the action in order to fill in the less-interesting details for themselves. Like a film editor examining the footage of his fall down the stairs,
Mark reviewed his accident from his perspective and the perspective of an
observer, cutting and juxtaposing segments, allowing the reader to be both
Mark (the participant) and a spectator at the scene of the accident.

Here is his first draft.

Milk Flying

I had a glass of milk in one hand, and in the other hand I had a chocolate chip square and a piece of blueberry cake.

I walked half way down the stairs. Then I slipped and yelled help. I saw milk flying all over the place.

My mother said, "Oh, Mark," she said, not in a happy voice.

Mark went to a classmate, Barb, for a conference and warned her about his working title, "This is a weird title, but I won't keep it." Then he read his piece aloud to her.

Barb said she liked it but pointed out his two "said"s in the last sentence. She explained she liked the second "said" better because it told *how* his mother said it. Here, Barb departed from the rule for discussing content first in conferences. Then she asked Mark if he liked it. He said he did, and Barb asked what he needed help on. With this question, she began to help Mark. Mark said he didn't know what to add, so Barb suggested he tell the story "in your own words."

"Well," Mark told her, "I kinda ran down the stairs and my slippers aren't the best in the world—they are slippery—and I stepped on the edge of the carpet and held to the glass, but the milk went flying."

Barb suggested he add something about his slippers and slipping on the carpet.

In the next week, Mark wrote two more drafts. He conferred with another classmate, Dana, after his second draft. Mark either disregarded or forgot Barb's suggestion to describe his slippers and slipping on the carpet. In his second draft, Mark reconsidered telling about the food. Then he rehearsed aloud versions of his walk down the stairs:

1. I ran down the stairs
2. I took two slow steps and then I walked fast halfway down the steps
3. I walked slowly and then I walked fast
4. I ran down the stairs halfway and then I slipped
5. I ran down the stairs so I would not miss the beginning of the show

Mark generated six more ways of explaining how he went down the stairs, only one with a reference to his slippers. After his eleventh attempt, Mark wrote:

I walked down the stairs halfway when all of a sudden it seemed like my legs were being pulled out. I fell flat on my back. I saw milk. My arm was flying around when I saw milk flying all over the place.

Then Mark read his second draft to the researcher. In her presence he took the role of naive reader of his own draft, reconstructing the event he literally described. He began to laugh at the incongruous picture of detached arms and legs his words might specify. "I just thought of something," he said. "Where it says 'pulled out,' it's like pulled out of my body!" He read on. A moment later he said, "I figured out another one. 'My arm was flying around'—in a circle! It's so crazy to think of my arm flying around...but how can I fix it?"

Mark's attempts to remedy the distortion his words might create were no more facile than the 12 attempts, in his second draft, to tell how he descended the stairs. Mark still juggled issues of whether to describe the carpet and the worn tread on his slippers, how he carried the food, and how to end the piece. It was an unusually brief piece. Did a short piece work, he wondered. With the additional question of his teacher who asked again how he slipped on the rug, and the researcher who asked how he could carry so much food, Mark came to a final draft, only three sentences longer than the first, but thoroughly examined in light of what good writing ought to be.

Oh! Mark

I was getting a snack to bring downstairs. I had a chocolate chip square and a piece of blueberry cake stacked up in one hand. And in the other hand I had a glass of milk.

I walked down the stairs halfway. When all of a sudden it seemed like my legs were being pulled out from under me. I fell flat on my back. I whacked my arm against the wall and saw milk all over the place.

"Oh! Mark," my mother said, not in a happy voice.

To achieve this degree of success, Mark had to know when to disregard others' suggestions as well as when to apply them. The children and adults who offered him advice may have, in Kamler's phrase, "made the concept of audience visible," but Mark remained the author. Barb's suggestion to retell the story "in your own words" and her request to know what Mark needed help on were valuable if they only sustained Mark's internal dialogue. Conferences in which Mark had taken part during the previous year and a half served as scaffolding for his construction of rules and judgments about writing. He did not approach suggestions made in conference as a list of instructions for revision. Instead, they stimulated his own sense of rules and procedures for writing. His most recent round of conferences seemed almost a ritual, perhaps necessary, but not sufficient for writing the work in progress.

To summarize the development in writing projects children took upon themselves, we began with Allen who attempted a chronological, list-like account of an important new experience, going to a football game with his father. In comparison with Terry's account of a bicycle accident, Allen's

piece was rather flat, wooden and without affect. Allen's classmates identified his problems quickly but had no remedy short of rewriting the whole
piece. Telling the score, one suggestion for improvement, would have brought
the piece into conformity with a script for attending a sports event. The children simply complained about disorganization ("hippety-hopping") and
perceptions unrelated to the event. The "man with a pumpkin on his head"
made it like "a crazy dream." The first graders had more experience judging
than revising stories. They had internalized criteria for good stories but not
techniques for revision.

Katy's piece reflects her automatic control over organization, the very
problem Allen faced. Her teacher identified this achievement, comparing it
to an earlier struggle she'd had to reorganize an out-of-sequence piece, and
Katy joined in the assessment. Another accomplishment her teacher identified and in which Katy shared the evaluation was a small victory in the use
of periods and proofreading. Using periods had become automatic. Part of
Katy's piece matched the excitement of Terry's—her excitement about seeing Beatrix Potter's doll house. She introduced that section of her draft by
saying, "I like this part," perhaps the beginnings of an awareness that the
two boys in third grade maintained throughout a piece.

By third grade, Terry controlled all the components of an accident
script—the cause, the characters and their motives, the sequence of events,
and the final injuries to his pride, his bike, and his body. Terry went beyond
Allen's neutral, factual account. He wanted to make his audience laugh and
wince, so he engaged Brian to help him judge how well he had achieved the
quality of excitement. Conferences on earlier drafts devoted to clarity allowed
Terry to be playful in this later draft. His partner, Brian, adopted their
teacher's technique of reading and paraphrasing. Again, thoroughness and
patience were the hallmark of the conference.

Mark's piece, like Terry's, was a version of an accident script. There
was surprise but no injury. The story would have been trivial without Mark's
exercise of craftsmanship. Mark's perceptions in the instant he lost his footing are the real subjects of the piece.

Theoretical Perspectives on Writing Conferences

In the section that follows, the ideas of Bruner, Piaget, and Vygotsky on the
role of social discourse as a medium for learning will furnish additional perspectives on learning to write in a workshop. Learning to talk often serves
as a metaphor for learning to write, and the preceding series of writing conferences illustrates the parallels between the two processes. Both learning to
talk and learning to write require social assistance. In talking, people not
only deliver the linguistic raw materials—phonological, syntactic, and lex-
ical—but also engage the child in social routines where the linguistic data

that constitute social discourse is cast in conversational turns. Scaffolding, mentioned earlier, is a metaphor for this type of social assistance to language learning.

Bruner (1981) has likened the social assistance to learning that adults provide to Vygotsky's (1978, pp. 84–91) notion of a zone of proximal development. With assistance, a child can perform at the next (proximal) higher level of learning or development, the level adjacent to the one at which s/he now performs alone. In the zone of proximal development, Vygotsky (1978, p. 57) states, "an interpersonal process is transformed into an intrapersonal one."

Bruner and his colleagues have investigated scaffolding in two studies and characterized adult assistance to learning in two situations, first, in a study of tutoring and problem solving (Wood, Bruner, & Ross, 1976) and second, of mother-infant interactions in which teaching the child to play social games mimics the social interactions in which the infants had learned to talk (Ratner & Bruner, 1978). From the first study, six characteristics of social assistance to learning have been identified and from the second, five. Together, these 11 characteristics illustrate the assistance that mediation in the form of social interaction can offer to the solitary and cognitive activity of writing.

1. "Focus the child on the task." Children watched others listen closely to their words. Jill, for instance, could not reread her piece effectively without her partner "to make the concept of audience visible," although their classmate Hilary reread her piece independently. Brian read Terry's piece sentence by sentence to help him locate the exact place where he had not met his criteria for good writing.

2. "Reduce degrees of freedom." Teachers limited their attention in conference to (a) reflecting and paraphrasing a draft, (b) discussing possible additions, deletions and substitutions, and (c) asking for an evaluation. Also, teachers limited the length of a piece to encourage revision. Conferences were orderly and predictable as Donna's account of guidelines for conferences makes clear. Teachers limited the legitimate business of a conference to content first with evaluation an optional part of the discussion which could occur at any point. In first and second grade, a few errors were corrected each time. After that, all errors were corrected in a final editing conference.

3. "Maintain the direction of the task." The rhythm of talk-write-talk-write was institutionalized in the workshop approach to writing instruction. Questions of where in the cycle or the draft a writer was working became routine, an orientation at the begin-

ning of a conference. Materials and record keeping systems such as folders and writing journals allowed children to progress to the next step once the teacher's directions were not necessary.

4. "Mark critical features." Teachers did not attempt to remedy every flaw in a draft. They focused on one or a few features. They identified new ways of meeting standards for information, order, vivid language, and the emergence of the writer's voice. Allen's teacher did not attempt to remedy his problems with both chronological order and extraneous detail (the man with the pumpkin on his head) at the same time. She helped him make the sequence on paper match the sequence in his memory. Then he attended to his other problems when his classmates drew his attention to them.

5. "Control frustration." Limited length, limited feedback, accessibility of others for help, and rewarding good work without punishing unsuccessful work limited the child's frustration. Unsuccessful work was acknowledged—Donna readily admitted "The Fantastic Whale" did not make sense—but such drafts were not a cause for shame. They were simply unsuccessful approximations, a fixed point of error from which to learn.

6. "Demonstrate solutions." Children read aloud successful pieces and discussed problems in drafting and their solutions. Barb suggested Mark tell his story in his own words to recover his voice. Chris told Allen he should include the score of the game, and Brian composed a sample "exciting" lead for Terry's last draft.

7. "Limit and make familiar the semantic domain." Children wrote about familiar experiences or chose the topic about which they wished to write. The language of discussing writing was also limited, specialized, and familiar. Donna used the terms conference, have a little talk, make sense, points out something right or wrong, and make a change. Hilary used the term individual conference for a one-to-one conference and by analogy applied it to reading her own draft. Terry and Brian applied judgments of exciting, funny, and boring to parts of a draft. Barb had a repertoire of responses to Mark's draft, even though she had no strong opinion about what he should do with it.

8. "Offer a structure in which utterances can be inserted." Children followed a process in writing and conferences in which they could make appropriate comments. The conference format of the reader asking questions whose answers s/he did not know allowed for maximum writer control. The fact that children to some degree replaced the teacher as a conference partner as early as first grade shows they were not merely spectators at someone else's lesson.

Allen's classmates were participants—listeners, teachers, and learners—at his conference.

9. "Reversible roles." Children took the role of conference partner with each other and then alone with themselves and their own drafts. A conference partner inexperienced in writing could not help by simply running through a list of questions. But a child experienced in writing and conferring about writing selects appropriate questions to ask another writer. For example, Hilary reconstructed an imaginary conference to help her elaborate her draft. Mark internalized a naive reader, easily confused by unclear descriptions. He imagined the ways in which his words might be misconstrued.

10. Tasks are "amenable to having their constituents varied." Writing and conferring demand quick changes in roles, the writer imagining a reader (for example, Mark and his imagined reader) and a character written about (Mark as a character slipping and spilling milk). The reader must reconstitute a character and infer a writer with a communicative intent. Allen's classmates attempted to picture his experience at the football game with some difficulty.

11. "The playful atmosphere doubtless permits the child to 'distance' himself from the task sufficiently to sustain a readiness to innovate. . . ." Writing was treated as play—as block construction or improvised drama. Children were not punished for unsuccessful attempts, nor even for a series of failures. Nor was ranking an issue since the qualities of children's writing emerged and became more important than any single dimension against which they might have been measured. They enjoyed and shared in each other's successes. This, of course, was a reflection of the teachers' attitudes.

Shannon playfully characterized as "hippety-hopping" Allen's trouble with chronological order. Brian dramatized his friend's piece, and Mark laughed as though he were an outsider reading that his arm flew through the air as though detached from his body. These children chose to represent as humorous the events from their life although writing about death, loss, and pain occurred along with the happier pieces.

Children incorporated the social and material assistance available to them as writers, and they, in turn, enriched the instructional context as they learned to write, read, and discuss writing skillfully. Thus, instruction was diffuse, and the boundaries between the competence of individuals and the class as a whole blurred. The class as a whole was a repository of perspectives from which to view a writing problem. The perspectives gave rise to multiple applications of a few guiding principles in any draft. For teachers, the tacit metaphor was a developmental one. In the garden they cultivated, growing organisms would develop—organize themselves—if the gardener tended chiefly to the conditions under which they grew. A watering one day would not produce fruit the next even in a thriving plant. The harvest was a distant objective with signs of maturation along the way sufficient reward for the present.

Just as organisms assimilate nourishment from the environment, children internalize elements in the activity around them to help them write. Internalization, in fact, has a long history of explaining thinking and conduct. Socrates believed critical thinking came about through internalizing a dialogue in three stages: exposure to critical standards, adopting the standards, and using them to monitor one's behavior. The Freudian view of the development of conscience is that the child internalizes the father's voice and then voluntarily follows its dictates. According to Mead (1934), the mind develops from social processes it internalizes. He emphasized the importance of vocal speech, which enables the child to hear himself or herself as others do. "It is in social behavior that the process of reflection itself arises," Mead (1934, p. 354) wrote. Paradoxically, he pointed out, the self comes into being when the capacity to get outside the self and see the self from another's point of view develops (pp. 365–366): "Out of addressing one's self and responding with the appropriate responses with another, 'self-consciousness' arises. The child through this period of infancy creates a forum within which he assumes various roles." Imitative and dramatic play and the identification with a role make possible later conversations with others and oneself about writing.

Piaget identifies social interaction, although he did not investigate it systematically, as a catalyst for cognitive growth. According to Flavell (1963), Piaget finds the child "frees himself from the grip of egocentrism" in social interaction with peers. Flavell (1963, p. 179) states,

> In the course of his contacts (and especially, his conflicts and arguments) with other children, the child increasingly finds himself forced to reexamine his own percepts in the light of those of others, and by so doing, gradually rids himself of cognitive egocentrism.

The child with a draft has fixed his or her position in relation to the subject of the writing. Not only may others take issue with the draft, but the author, too, may take a different position toward the subject from the one s/he took while writing. Flavell cites Piaget's belief in social interaction as motivation for the child to reexamine physical experience. Yet the impulse to defend a position surely arises in other aspects of the child's construction of a meaningful world. *In Judgment and Reasoning in the Child,* Piaget asks,

What then gives rise to the need for verification? Surely it must be the shock of our thought coming into contact with that of others, which produces doubt and the desire to prove.... The social need to share the thought of others and to communicate our own with success is at the root of our need for verification. Proof is the outcome of argument.... Logical reasoning is an argument which we have with ourselves, and which reproduces internally the features of a real argument. (Piaget, 1928, p. 204 in Flavell 1963, p. 279)

For Vygotsky (1978), internalization is the key to cognitive development. The child transforms *inter*personal processes into *intra*personal ones by working with a partner in his or her zone of proximal development. In this socially-mediated form of learning, the tutor maintains the zone of proximal development for the learner as "a vicarious form of consciousness," in Bruner's (1981) phrase. Vygotsky (1978, pp. 56–57) states,

the process of internalization consists of a series of transformations:

(a) An operation that initially represents an external activity is reconstructed and begins to occur internally...

(b) An interpersonal process is transformed into an intrapersonal one. Every function in the child's cultural development appears twice: first on the social level, and later, on the individual level.... All higher functions originate as actual relations between human individuals...

(c) The transformation of an interpersonal process into an intrapersonal one is the result of a long series of developmental events.

The preceding discussion may be summarized in Cook-Gumperz's (1975, p. 139) characterization of social science research: "When the guiding model has not been behaviorism, the internalization model has been taken to account for all the seemingly generative aspects of the child's actions." However, problems remain in explaining "[h]ow the social gets 'inside' and how the development of an individualized social being can be examined other than through exteriorized displays" (p. 140) as well as issues of competence and performance.

The conferences in the preceding pages demonstrate some of the forms of consciousness shared in the evolving context of writing process workshops. The dialogues show the penetration of the social context into the child's reflections and the child's heightened competence into the social context.

Allen, the first grader whose description of a football game seemed like a crazy dream, relied on his classmates and teacher. Second grader Jill needed a partner's presence to bring alive the concept of audience, although her classmate Hilary articulated the function of an internalized reader when she said, "I have an individual conference with myself." Brian helped Terry evaluate the effect of his piece on a reader as he laughed, dramatized the action, and solemnly evaluated each sentence as meeting the standards of exciting writing. At this level in writing and conferring, the writer constructs and reconstructs by "retrospective structuring" (Perl, 1979, p. 334) knowledge and experience in an attempt to represent them for himself or herself and to make them accessible to others. Finally, Mark's help from others was spotty in his current cycle of writing, but having internalized rules from previous conferences, the interaction in conference and talking aloud to the researcher sustained him and triggered the working out of his own intentions for the piece of writing.

It may be premature to speculate on the routes by which the information in the child and the context traveled. Nevertheless, I will set out two models for consideration.

First, information was created—articulated—in the interview-like transactions occurring at all points of exchange in the classroom. Chronologically, interviews began when the researchers asked children questions about their writing. Next, teachers asked many of the same questions in conference, having heard about the research interviews from the research team. The questions were often those to which the adults did not know the answer since they tapped the perceptions of the student. Teachers did, however, ask questions whose answers they knew when they acted in the role of a generalized reader. Thus,

1. teacher interviews child
2. child interviews child
3. child interviews self
4. child interviews draft

The interview assumes the questioner begins with some information, at least a general framework within which the writing or the experience that sparked the writing fits. The questioner often attempts to resolve and identify, define, or restate:

1 and 2. What have you written?
3. What did I write?
4. What did I do or feel when my words say...?

The second point of interaction, child interviewing child, is significant here for its implication that asking others may facilitate asking oneself similar questions at a later date. Also, the teachers' efforts are multiplied by students who willingly and capably do their job for them while they themselves profit from asking questions. The level of child-interviewing-child may be seen as a mediating level between teacher output and child intake of interviewing routines. This discussion of probes assumes that the value of the interviews lies in the answers the children attempt to articulate and the questions they articulate to maintain these routines with each other and finally with themselves.

Piaget's discussion of the child's internalization of moral standards lends some support to the value of the mediating level of child judgment of a peer's conduct.

> But between the spontaneous moral realism of the early years and the theoretical moral realism...there is an intermediate link that must not be disregarded —we mean the judgment made by the child, not about his own actions, but about the conduct of his equals. As far as he himself is concerned he succeeds fairly soon...in differentiating intentional faults from involuntary breaches of the moral code....But when it comes to the deeds of those around him, things appear in a very different light. Generally speaking, it is not going too far to say that the child—like ourselves—is more severe with others than with himself. (1965, p. 183)

Like the judgment of a piece of writing, moral judgment is a form of social cognition, a matter of understanding negotiated standards, not the physical properties of objects or time, space, and causality. Young children judge their own actions by their intentions, not outcomes. They are also likely to judge their writing by their communicative intent, not the outcome, before they can take into consideration another writer's intentions. Just as they judge the conduct of others by the outcome, they judge the writing of others as an outcome. Children apply stringent standards to others' writing before they apply it to their own, just as they do in their judgments of conduct.

To apply this account of children's ability to empathize with another's intentions and to judge their work by stringent standards, the writing conferences conducted as peer interviews offer children a forum in which they can take on new roles toward drafts. First, they can extend empathy for the author's communicative intent to drafts other than their own. Second, they can learn to apply critical standards to their own work. The range of the internal dialogue about writing may be extended in the application of judgments about writing which must be made in conferences.

A second model comes from a contrasting assumption: that a child cannot speak about an operation in writing meaningfully—although he or she may parrot someone else's words—until that operation is under his or her firm control. That is, children perform implicitly before they can speak explicitly about their tacit knowledge. The child's talk about a writing operation serves as evidence of a kind of competence. The pattern by which information travels from child to child as each articulates it appears in the following outline:

(1)   child performs an operation in writing (from tacit knowledge)
(2)   child articulates an operation in writing (explicit statement)
      under either of these circumstances:
      (a)   in response to a(n adult) question
      (b)   unprompted initiation of a comment or question

There is no conflict between the two models. The first suggests social routes by which the child may acquire probes that may provoke him or her to articulate, as sketched in the second model, what s/he implicitly knows to be true. If a child performs an operation spontaneously, without reflection, deliberation, or intervention, then the classroom talk can help the writer bring the operation under conscious control. The social interactions of writing conferences help a child gain conscious control of what s/he knows implicitly. The process of social mediation offers the child many occasions to articulate and affirm what s/he knows.

Many questions remain. Is talk important in initial learning, fine-tuning, or both? Do different kinds of questions follow different routes to internalization? How does the child search the environment for probes, questions, or answers? The issues of intake, input, and output in writing instruction can be added to quandaries about performance and competence. How does input become intake? What is the relationship between what is taught and what is learned? What is the nature of the hypothetical boundary at the site of intake—a gatekeeper, a monitor, or, to use a biological metaphor, a semipermeable membrane? Assimilation is the "filtering or modification of input," according to Piaget and Inhelder (1969, p. 6). To say a child's internal schemata determine what will pass through still does not explain how or why a child takes up information and rules for judgment from the context.

Perhaps the biggest question is that of the nature of the experience of writing for the children. Unlike most school subjects, the activity of writing for most children is easy and pleasant initially and later becomes challenging, frustrating, and occasionally exhilarating. A process-conference approach to writing requires sensitivity to the claims of traditional dichotomies: oral and written language, affect and cognition, the authority of the adult and authority of the child as author, and the pressures of group opinion and the autonomy of the individual. A fourth grade writer, Barb, explained why writing, despite the demands, was important to her:

You learn about yourself. You can learn that—maybe you've had a really tough day and everything—and nothing seems to be going right. And you think, "I can't do *anything*," you know. "Nothing's *mine*." Well, your writing *is*, you know. It's up to you whether you want to do it or not, really...

It helps you with your anger and frustrations and like that. And it is...fun. You can write on whatever you want. It's not like you write about "The Day I

Came to School,'' you have to write about that. Like, whatever you want to write you can write about. It's up to you if you want to change it or not. If you like it the way it is, you can leave it. Like, your mother can go, "Go up to bed right now!" You don't have to change the story, right this minute, like. And if you don't want to change it you don't have to. It's like you're the mother of the story type thing, and if you want to do it, you can.

If you're going to let somebody else take over your story, it won't be yours. It will be somebody else's in somebody else's own words and everything. And if they want to write about it, they can go and write about it in their own words. I'm not going to put it into *my* story. And it's up to me whether I'm going to let it be their story or if it's going to be mine. So I want it to be my story, not the class's story.

CHILDREN'S GROWTH IN WRITING

The study was designed to document writing as *development,* that is, the unfolding of the individual according to nature's plan, only incidentally related to instruction and social mediation. Instead, *learning,* or what was provided by the environment, proved to be closely intertwined with developmental data about what and how the child took from the environment for self-generated purposes. Writing instruction enhanced the children's performance. Boundaries blurred between a writer's competence and the environmental assistance the writer recruited in order to produce a piece of writing. Indeed, one measure of a writer's success might be the ability to extend the writing beyond what s/he could produce alone. In Barb's phrase, the writer was the mother of the story. Other influences played their roles. Still, the resources a writer sought depended on a vision of the final product and the writer's willingness to alter it.

If levels, stages, or phases were present in writers, then décalage, or uneven progress between stages, was not the exception, but the rule. Children with the most complex, differentiated processes were flexible. They were least reluctant to degrade their performances to a lower level or stage in order to achieve a desired end. They seemed to be guided by a very clear, separate, and distinct set of concepts about the ends and the means to their ends. For instance, the mechanics of handwriting, punctuation, and spelling and the adequacy of detail suffered while the writer sketched in first draft from the intended scope of the piece. Children who might have been expected to dictate in other classrooms because they forgot to leave spaces between words or spelled with very few vowels wrote unexpectedly complex pieces. Other children, recognized as talented editors by their classmates who competed for their help in conferences, wrote abbreviated pieces.

In the discussion that follows, four areas of growth in writing will be examined, beginning with the mechanics of writing.

Skills

According to Graves's (1979a) report on handwriting, several principles govern the child's growth in motor control and knowledge of conventions. First, written language for the child has its roots in drawing and speech. Children may not know that, unlike spoken language, written language must conform to spatial constraints. Children may write words without the boundaries of a space between them because oral language is fluid, without breaks between words. They may write from right to left, bottom to top, or in columns. Drawing "serves as a rehearsal for the text as well as an important bridge from speech to print" (1979a, p. 19). Child control of writing accounts for improvements in handwriting. The role of authorship entails responsibility for choice of subject for writing and the choice of means to express the subject's voice and the author's voice. Children may obscure their messages with illegible handwriting until they learn to control the content. Finally, children learn to differentiate between the need to record their message regardless of its appearance in quick early drafts and the need to observe the etiquette of neat handwriting on final copies of their drafts.

In the proposal for the study (Graves, 1977), six motor control variables in handwriting were listed as potentially important for the child's willingness to compose. Unexpectedly, observations in the initial weeks of the study made it clear to the researchers that lack of speed or fine control of a writing implement did not prevent any child from writing. Thus, progress in handwriting was not observed with close attention.

Calkins (1980b) investigated punctuation by comparing two third grade classes. In one classroom, the teacher taught punctuation within the context of writing, without drill; in another, children learned punctuation through patterned practice drills, but did little writing. Calkins examined the drafts written in both classes. She found a trend among children taught punctuation in the context of writing to experiment with an increasing variety of punctuation throughout the school year. Their writing required more *kinds* of punctuation since they wrote more. Although they never used as many kinds of punctuation as they needed, by the middle of the year they began to close the gap between what they needed and what they used. Calkins asked the children in both the writing and the drill classrooms to identify or define as many kinds of punctuation as they could from a list of 16 items. The children in the writing classroom identified, on the average, about half the items of punctuation while the children in the drill classroom averaged about a quarter of the list. Calkins hypothesized that the children who wrote found more uses for punctuation and therefore learned more about it. They wanted to give voices to their characters with quotation marks, express surprise with exclamation points, and show suspense with an ellipsis. Since writing was read aloud whenever it was shared, the need to express the characters' and the author's voices and to engage the audience was met through the reader's voice with the aid of punctuation.

Teachers followed no special order in their instruction in punctuation. Puncutation was usually taught individually through conferences. Children frequently borrowed punctuation from texts read before they were instructed in its use. The marks were attractive to the children, and they displayed their new acquisitions to each other. Overgeneralization was common. Apostrophes, for example, appeared before all final -s suffixes and quotation marks around indirect speech until they learned to differentiate among the situations that invited punctuation.

Spelling was another area of mechanics in which progress was highly visible. Spelling was directly taught in conference in first and second grade, and no special spelling curriculum was used beyond correcting writing. Invented spelling was permitted, and one or a few features were identified for the child in conference as examples of principles of spelling s/he was ready to learn next. A few of the incorrect features were also selected for correction and instruction.

Invented spelling refers to the systematic patterns of encoding words which children produce before they learn the conventions of sound-letter relationships. Their errors differ from other kinds of misspellings (Read, 1975). For example, if a child does not represent a sound with a letter, perhaps spelling "went" as WT, the teacher might ask the child to say the word and to listen for the missing sound. A 6-year-old spelling only the initial and final sounds when asked to listen for another sound would be likely to make either of two choices, WNT or WAT. WET, WANT, and WENT are possible spellings, but not as likely. The typical choice of the letter A or N to represent the medial sounds of "went" indicates the tacit knowledge of English phonology the child brings to writing. Inventive spellers do not rely on a faulty visual memory or incorrect sound-letter correspondences. Instead, they often rely on a correspondence between the name of a letter and the sound they wish to represent to make a spelling decision. The place of articulation in the mouth—not the sound-letter correspondences of phonics which readers know—determines inventive spellers' decisions. The choice of N to represent the medial sounds (WNT) indicates the child is using a letter name strategy to represent both middle sounds as an undifferentiated whole, both the short vowel "e" and the consonant "n." A subtle clue, the use of A (WAT) represents a similar approach to encoding. The child must first isolate the short "e" vowel sound and represent it, as is common among inventive spellers, as A. The name for A is articulated in the mouth closer to the position for the short "e" sound than to the name for the letter E. The omission of the nasal "m" or "n" before a consonant (WAT for went) is also typical of inventive spellers, since they use their mouths to spell and do not represent what they do not articulate. Nasals before consonants often are not articulated, and inventive spellers faithfully record this feature of English. A more correct spelling, WET or WENT, indicates knowledge of letter-sound relationships as a result of instruction or observation.

In making decisions about which spelling errors to correct, teachers attended to the pattern of errors in the current piece, recalled earlier conferences, and consulted earlier patterns of spelling errors in the child's writing folder. Their intention was not to teach children to be inventive spellers, but to allow children to use spelling to write and read more independently.

Children's spelling test scores did not suffer without a traditional spelling curriculum. At the end of first grade, the children earned scores on the district spelling test comparable to scores in previous years when they had studied weekly spelling lists. In second grade, the inventive spellers, many of whom had not written in their first grade classrooms, showed gains greater than expected on the district spelling test after the first half of the year. By the end of second grade, however, the inventive spellers scored some gains, but the size of the gains had decreased.

On a phonics subtest of a standardized reading test, first grade children scored on the average 1½–2 years above grade level, perhaps as a result of encoding English daily. Reading scores on the basal reader series tests indicated that the children achieved comparable comprehension levels without basal readers in first and second grade. An exception was one usually capable Readiness class in which the children gained far more in reading scores through their own writing without the basal reader instruction than previous Readiness classes had. No formal evaluation of the effect of writing on the children's academic growth has been undertaken by the school district.

Spelling instruction through writing in third and fourth grades consisted of the teachers requiring children to circle words they thought they had misspelled before consulting a dictionary. Incorrect words they failed to circle provided diagnostic information about their spelling, and the teachers helped children recognize errors they missed. The third and fourth grade children received traditional spelling instruction in addition to their writing.

Development in Space

As soon as children learned to use the space on the page in conventional ways—directionality from left to right and from top to bottom and spaces between words—they wanted to cover the entire page with words. Children often pointed with pride to a sheet of paper they had filled which required them to use the space on the back of the page. The least mature first graders usually preferred experience paper, large (18″ x 12″), lined sheets of paper with a space for drawing. Later, children wrote on paper stapled between construction paper covers. Many first graders attempted to use loose sheets of lined paper without space for drawing instead of the prepared booklets, and all but a few returned to books with pages after their experiment. Book forms were still popular in second grade, and they made possible easy addition of information on the facing page. Thus, revision was possible without laborious recopying. By third grade, children did not require space to draw and wrote on sheets of lined paper.

In third and fourth grades, children showed that they could anticipate revision by their use of space on the page. They wrote on alternate lines leaving space to substitute and add phrases. Some used markers such as asterisks to remind themselves that they were dissatisfied with a section of their text. Then they could easily return to that part of the draft and revise it. Willingness to write in the margins and cross out large sections of a draft was neither automatic nor easy. Even without adult emphasis, children wanted to write neatly, sometimes at the expense of content. When a child expressed a preference for a particular piece of writing because the printing was good or because there were no crossouts, teachers and researchers were surprised since they had not fostered those attitudes in school, and parents saw only the final edited products. The preoccupation with neatness seemed to arise naturally and early. Perhaps neat papers represented control over the medium to the children. Children resisted the adult notion that messiness on initial drafts was to be expected until they came to understand content or information as the most important criterion for good writing. For some, the acquired tolerance for early messy drafts did not come until the second half of the year.

Teachers were sensitive to the influence of their physical presence on a child's willingness to revise. Beginning revisers remained close to their teachers when they made their first attempts at revision, usually in a conference or after a conference. In first grade, some children revised spontaneously and independently before a conference, but the revisions had not been the result of deliberation or application of an articulated criterion to a text. To foster revision, teachers kept the children nearby to inspect their progress. As the children grew more mature and self-directed, they revised alone after a conference, across the room, or wherever they wished. A teacher might initially seat three novice revisers at a table after a conference in order to question, ask for retellings once more, make sure essential changes were made, and acknowledge the revisions as soon as they were made. Again, the child read the draft with its revisions and heard a response to the changes he or she labored over. In this way, teachers used the physical space in the classroom to help the children learn to write.

In interviews, the children described how they carried out thinking and rehearsal for a piece of writing outside the classroom. Although rehearsal began in first grade with a drawing on the page immediately preceding writing, older children sometimes cited a time for reflection away from the classroom. By February, for example, first grader Chris developed a dislike of revision, so he began to plan his books the night before writing. Bedtime was his favorite planning time. Before he fell asleep, he rehearsed what he would write the next day so he would have very few changes to make after his first draft.

Chris was not alone in reporting bedtime as the time for anticipating writing. In fourth grade, Marcy wrote three leads for her report on foxes, describing the fox hidden in its den. One day she wrote a fourth lead after she had completed the body of the report. The new lead was a dramatic improvement over the three previous attempts. At bedtime the night before, she told the researcher, she noticed her cat squinting at a shaft of light as her sister opened the door to her darkened bedroom. Marcy realized then that she had the image she needed to draw her readers into the piece in the first paragraph. The next day she revised the lead to include the fox squinting as a beam of sunlight entered its darkened den.

The children extended their thinking about writing over several different settings. They wrote about events in other places recalled in school, then reconsidered the event or their writing about it in still a third place. Like Marcy, some observed their environment with unusual care, storing impressions for future use.

Development in Time

As children extended their thinking about a piece of writing to other places, they also extended the amount of time in which they could maintain their attention on a piece of writing and the flexibility, stability, and change of focus necessary for maintaining an interest over time.

Related to the area of development in space is children's territoriality in writing. Graves found in his earlier study of 7-year-old writers (1973, 1975) that girls usually wrote in primary territory, that is, about home and school; boys, about secondary territory or the neighborhood; and only the most mature children of either gender in extended territory, the area beyond direct personal experience. In the third and fourth grades, the teachers enthusiastically supported personal narratives. In fourth grade, the children were taught to write reports using sources of information beyond their direct experience. The first and second grade teachers permitted the children to write about any topic they chose as fiction or non-fiction. Most teachers came to prefer personal narrative because of the richness of detail a young writer could command when writing about a known subject, and undoubtedly their unstated preferences were felt and reflected in teacher-child and peer conferences, perhaps resulting in fewer pieces in extended territory.

Boys wrote more often in primary territory than predictable from Graves's earlier study and unexpectedly included female characters. Girls, too, wrote in secondary territory. The only apparent difference in the subject or territory of writing as the children matured was the increasing preference for writing about social situations, particularly after school play with peers and favorite family stories, often about themselves as preschool children.

In general, the teachers adjusted their conferring and sharing sessions to children's lengthening attention spans in a piece of writing over time. In first grade, children needed more frequent but briefer meetings with the teacher, a quicker response to their writing. Not only their interest in content, but beginners' ability to read invented spellings seemed to suffer when longer periods of time elapsed between writing and reading to an audience. Children in first and second grades received instruction in almost every conference on some point of spelling or punctuation. Third and fourth grade students received more thorough corrections of errors less frequently, just before the final draft was to be written. Thus, teachers stretched the pattern of a response to content preceding a response to mechanics to cover a longer period of time and in more differentiated conferences.

Along with the ability to maintain an interest in a piece over a longer period of time came the responsibility to choose the subject of writing more thoughtfully. First and second grade children usually finished whatever book they started, few books requiring more than 2 or 3 days on a first draft, and many completed in one sitting. But children in third and fourth grades had the option of stopping after one draft if the subject did not seem to them—perhaps after a conference—as promising as it did before writing. So the older children maintained a more differentiated pattern in their drafting and revision. One third grade girl wrote 14 drafts of a short piece in an attempt to perfect an anecdote. The subject was her confusion seeing a squirrel and hearing a cat's meow. She wished to dramatize her perceptions in order to recreate her confusion for the reader and then reveal her discovery that a cat hidden from view was responsible for the meows. Fourteen was an exceptional number of drafts, but it demonstrated the kind of persistence a child might bring to unassigned writing.

The Writing Cycle

The writing cycle, divided into prewriting, writing, and revision, took on different patterns as children learned to write. In the area of prewriting, or rehearsal, the youngest children were encouraged to draw before they wrote. As they grew older, they drew after writing. Finally, they did not draw at all in relation to writing. Accounts of the relationship between drawing and writing are rare. Marshall (1963, p. 143) described a similar sequence among her students in a one-room school in a rural English village.

They, too, wrote books before they learned to read:

> These books are always profusely illustrated, the picture always being drawn
> *before the appropriate text is written.* Thought must precede written work,
> and the picture first serves to inspire and then order thought, so that the words
> flow with confidence and clarity afterwards....If the picture is always done
> first, one finds that the illustrations get fewer and fewer as the children gain
> more and more confidence in the use of words, finally disappearing except for
> those put in for sheer pleasure and the delight of making a good thing even
> better. (italics in the original)

Thus, children of another generation on another continent displayed similar
developmental patterns in their growth as writers.

In their practice books, the Atkinson children drew smaller and less-
detailed drawings as words carried more of the meaning of the story. By mid-
second grade, some drawings became quite abstract as in Katy's book about
her family's trip to Pennsylvania in which she illustrated one page about the
dress of the Amish girls with a simple outline of a sun bonnet. Jill, perfunc-
torily illustrating a page in a practice book about her favorite authors, included the sentence, "Beatrix Potter and Shel Silverstein are nothing alike."
She drew a square and a circle apparently cancelled with a diagonal line to
diagram how different the two authors were from each other.

Two of the younger case study children accompanied a change in their
composing with the appearance of figures in profile in their drawings,
which were part of their prewriting activities. Sarah, a first grader, made a
transition from writing predominantly non-narrative books to predominantly narratives, and during that period of time she also began to draw
figures in profile. This new form of representing her characters seemed to
give them more scope for action, suitable for narratives, in contrast to the
relatively static books listing attributes she wrote earlier (Sowers, 1979a).
Another child in second grade accompanied a new peak in the liveliness of
her writing, although she had been writing narratives for almost a year, with
figures drawn in profile, rehearsing the actions about which she wrote. It
was not possible to establish a causal relationship between the drawings and
writing, yet the changes in rehearsal and composing seemed to be coordinated.

The children in third and fourth grades were taught as a form of rehearsal to write several leads and choose the best. Other prewriting activities, such as listing possible topics and discussing them with a friend, were
based on the representation of the original experience in language, not in
pictures. Calkins (1980a) has shown how Andrea, whom she observed in
third and fourth grades, began, with the process of prewriting, a parallel
process of revising by narrowing and focusing her topic. In writing narratives, children often began writing leads at some distance from the center of

interest in their memories. A typical series of leads in such a situation is chronological, the writer inching closer to the most important part of the piece with each lead. As many have pointed out, the writing process is recursive, not a linear march through prewriting, writing, and revision. Writers do not leave prewriting behind when they begin to draft, and, as Calkins has shown, revision takes place as soon as ideas for drafting occur, even among third grade children. Children's writing cycles appear to be almost simultaneous rather than recursive or linear. Calkins described Andrea's early willingness to revise as "a guiding act," a way of looking at writing as a revisable medium.

Graves (1983) has listed eight different ways children use oral language while they compose:

1. The child composes aloud and translates from speech to writing rather than from thought to writing as adults might.
2. Beyond meaning, the aesthetic qualities of language appeal to the child who experiments with prosodics—rhythm, intonation, and other voice qualities—while composing aloud.
3. The child may say a word, dividing and exaggerating the parts to spell better.
4. The child may spell the letters in an attempt to recall the correct spelling.
5. The child may read aloud from the beginning to remember what he or she has said and to decide what will come next.
6. The child "consults a drawing or makes a procedural comment" to decide the next step in writing.
7. The child tries to determine how much more is left to be done, often counting pages or writing "The End" on the last page before finishing.
8. The child tries the book out for effect on other children, often by talking about the picture.

As the children mature, they spend less time composing aloud. They compose silently and are likely to vocalize only when trouble solving new problems emerges. To borrow Vygotsky's term for the shift from thinking aloud to thinking silently, the process "'goes underground'" (1962, p. 18).

Graves (1979b) has pointed out that revision often occurs spontaneously in media other than writing before a child is able to write. Children repair their speech spontaneously and revise their dramatic play, block structures, and drawings. However, the children's investment in their writing as a representation of a personal experience and the prospects of publication made children more receptive to suggestions to revise than they might have been if their only audience had been the teacher. Teachers discussed revision with the children rather than leave it to chance. They made revision procedures limited and available, and children who revised shared their procedures in conferences. A closer approximation to the original story or a reconceptualized version rewarded the writers. There was no mystique associated with revision. It was simply the last kind of work to do before writing the final copy.

Calkins (1980a) found among third grade children several distinct patterns in revision that characterized the least to the most mature. First, random drafting appeared when children wrote one draft, put it away, and wrote another without reference to the first. They seemed to have no direction or intentions to carry out other than to "make" a second draft. Second, refining was a process of making small, almost cosmetic changes in the first draft. Calkins says this is not a process of discovery, but a backward referral to the first draft. Third, transition revisers employed a variety of strategies, sometimes random drafting, sometimes refining. Calkins believes these children demonstrated a productive restlessness and dissatisfaction with the earlier draft that would soon impel them into the next category. Finally, interacting drafters were adept at changing their focus as they revised. They reconsidered their relationship to the audience, to the language they used, and to the experience that prompted the piece. They were quite agile in changing their perspectives and making substantive changes in drafts.

Given a situation in which children are expected to revise by recopying a draft with intended changes, no matter how short the piece, these divisions among children are quite marked. The difference in tools for writing in the third grade—loose sheets of paper for older children instead of pages stapled in a book, which make substantial changes on the facing page easy for younger children—has made these stages highly visible. The stages may be artifacts of instructional tools. Instruction and closely supervised follow-up in earlier grades minimize differences among children's capacities to revise in earlier grades. Perhaps random and refining revisers would have been interactive revisers sooner if they stapled their pages together in books.

Other Issues in Writing Development

The children's concepts of writing changed over time and with instruction. In conference, children were asked to evaluate their work and to tell why a particular piece was worthy of publication. These were instructional questions they asked each other. Researchers asked them what a good writer must do. Among the earliest answers from one boy, the least ready to write among the case study children, was this response, "First you got to hold the pencil." The mechanical difficulties reflected in his answer usually gave way to a reflection that it was important to write neatly, to make the page look nice. Another early response was that a piece of writing was good because it was *about* something the author enjoyed. There was little separation of the piece of writing from the experience that prompted it. Writing did not merely represent; it was an extension, an integral part of the event, just as children consider the name of an object or person to be an attribute of that object or person.

Children gradually acquired an understanding of the concept of information, and they used it often to justify a piece as good writing. They also cited their peers' reactions and liking for it. Some wanted a piece published because it represented a great deal of work on their part. They might say, "I went over it again and again. I did a lot of work on it." Still more mature articulations of qualities of good writing involved not so much the quantity of work or information, but a careful selection of details to convey the meaning the author intended. Not any experience a writer had, but a significant experience often justified a piece of writing. A frightening visit to an elderly relative in a nursing home; the loss of a favorite birch tree which sheltered the author when s/he felt alone and reflective; comforting domestic routines such as curling up beside one's father; and recounting a memorable experience at the age of 2 that foreshadowed 8-year-old bravery or assertiveness—these were significant to the children.

The children not only acquired a vocabulary for criteria for good writing, but also acquired a procedural vocabulary. They used terms such as draft, lead, revise, edit, conference, focus, details, and many others to help them identify in what part of the writing cycle they were working. Use of writing terminology helped them plan, anticipate, and interpret their activity.

Teachers limited the children's forms of writing in grades three and four, but not in grades one and two. Children began first grade by writing many "all about" books, that is, lists of attributes of a subject. Published books early in first grade showed the "all about" books outnumbered the chronologically-ordered narratives by 2 to 1. By the end of the first grade, published chronologies outnumbered "all about" books by the same proportion. Children who had not written previously often began second grade with "all about" books. The form was an elaborated list with a central topic, such as swamps, boats, or my pet mouse. These inventories perhaps gave children a feeling of control not only over the medium of writing, but over their knowledge as well. A primitive kind of exposition, the listing sentences recall the beginnings more mature writers make in a piece. They are their notes before chronological or expository writing begins (Sowers, 1979b).

The Atkinson children failed to coordinate attainments in writing into patterns of levels or stages. The order in their achievements can best be described as reaching milestones in their performances of aspects of writing. Children's invented spelling improved in a predictable manner, for example, but independent of growth in revision, handwriting, or rehearsal for writing. Instruction was, no doubt, responsible for the order of some learning. Nor was reaching a milestone, such as the correct use of periods or a sufficient number and quality of details to convey a message with conviction, a permanent achievement. Circumstances in the composition of the next piece of writing might appear to wipe out all the gains, and without social support the piece might suffer the effects of cognitive overload or insufficient enthusiasm on the writer's part.

CONCLUSION

Levi-Strauss's model of the *bricoleur* (1966), the tinker who constructs with whatever materials come to hand for ends that may be altered as new and interesting components come into view, perhaps best conveys the spirit and style of the activities in which children's growth in writing was visible.

Given time, attention, and a few lessons in the craft of writing, children tinkered with a piece more attentively and longer than was necessary. They surprised adults by imposing writing problems on themselves—representing with clarity the confusion of a squirrel that seemed to meow, the challenge of an extensive piece of writing such as one first grader's 50-page journal of his team's baseball season, and the techical problems Mark set for himself in describing milk flying and his body sprawled on the stairs. Problem finding, according to Getzels and Csikszentmihalyi's study of art students (1976), is the hallmark of creativity, not problem solving. In *The Having of Wonderful Ideas,* Duckworth (1972) reported that children who had participated in the African Primary Science Program behaved differently in relation to materials offered them for exploration than the children who had not participated. In one phase of the program's evaluation, the participants settled down to work alone or in groups, displayed more ideas for using the materials, and spent more time on one problem. Children who had not participated in the program more often followed a leader and ran out of ways to use the materials. Duckworth hypothesized that one outcome of the African Primary Science Program was increased alertness. The child who formulated intentions and experiments with the means to achieve them was engaged in the process of *bricolage* that students of art, science, and writing seemed to share. Through writing, the children became authorities, the authors of their intentions, and, in Barb's words, the mothers of their writing.

REFERENCES

Bruner, J. (1981). *Vygotsky and language acquisition.* Address given at Harvard Graduate School of Education.

Calkins, L. (1979). Andrea learns to make writing hard. *Language Arts, 56,* 569–576.

Calkins, L. (1980a). Children's rewriting strategies. *Research in the Teaching of English, 14,* 331–341.

Calkins, L. (1980b). When children want to punctuate: Basic skills belong in context. *Language Arts, 57,* 567–573.

Cazden, C. (1982). Adult assistance to language development: Scaffolds, models, and direct instruction. In R. Parker & F. Davis (Eds.), *Developing literacy: Young children's use of language.* Newark, DE: International Reading Association.

Cook-Gumperz, J. (1975). The child as practical reasoner. In M. Sanches & B. C. Blount (Eds.), *Socio-cultural dimensions of language use.* New York: Academic Press.

Duckworth, E. (1972). On the having of wonderful ideas. *Harvard Educational Review, 42,* 217–231.

Flavell, J. H. (1963). *The developmental psychology of Jean Piaget.* New York: D. Van Nostrand Co.

Getzels, J. & Csikszentmihalyi, M. (1976). *The creative vision: A longitudinal study of problem finding in art.* New York: Wiley.

Graves, D. (1973). *Children's writing: Research hypotheses based upon an examination of the writing processes of seven year old children.* Unpublished doctoral dissertation, State University of New York at Buffalo.

Graves, D. (1975). An examination of the writing processes of seven year old children. *Research in the Teaching of English, 9,* 227–241.

Graves, D. (1977). *A two year case study observing the development of primary children's composing, spelling and motor behaviors during the writing process.* Proposal to the National Institute of Education.

Graves, D. (1979a). Let children show us how to help them write. *Visible Language, 13,* 16–28.

Graves, D. (1979b). What children show us about revision. *Language Arts, 56,* 312–318.

Graves, D. (1983). The growth and development of first grade writers. In A. Freedman, I. Pringle, & J. Yalden (Eds.), *Learning to write: First language/second language.* New York: Longmans.

Kamler, B. (1980). One child, one teacher, one classroom: The story of one piece of writing. *Language Arts, 57,* 680–693.

Levi-Strauss, C. (1966). *The savage mind.* Chicago, IL: The University of Chicago Press.

Marshall, S. (1963). An experiment in education. Cambridge, England: Cambridge University Press.

McDermott, R. (1980). Profile: Ray L. Birdwhistell. *The Kinesis Report, 2,* 1–16.

Mead, G. H. (1934). *Mind, self and society from the standpoint of a social behaviorist.* Chicago, IL: University of Chicago Press.

Murray, D. (1982). *Learning by teaching: Selected articles on writing and teaching.* Montclair, NJ: Boynton/Cook Publishers.

Perl, S. (1979). The composing processes of unskilled college writers. *Research in the Teaching of English, 13,* 319–336.

Piaget, J. (1928). *Judgment and reasoning in the child.* New York: Basic Books.

Piaget, J. (1965). *The moral judgment of the child.* New York: The Free Press.

Piaget, J., & Inhelder, B. (1969). *The psychology of the child*. New York: Basic Books.

Ratner, N. & Bruner, J. (1978). Games, social exchanges and the acquisition of language. *Journal of Child Language, 5,* 391–401.

Read, C. (1975). *Children's categorization of speech sounds in English*. Urbana, IL: National Council of Teachers of English.

Sowers, S. (1979a). A six-year-old's writing process: The first half of first grade. *Language Arts, 56,* 829–835.

Sowers, S. (1979b). *Young writers' preference for non-narrative modes of composing*. Paper presented at the Boston University Conference on Language Development, October.

Statistical Update, Center for Field Services. (1980). *Is it fair to you? Data on New Hampshire's school districts: Ability to pay, effort, and state foundation aid*. Durham, New Hampshire.

Vygotsky, L. (1962). *Thought and language*. Cambridge, MA: Massachusetts Institute of Technology Press.

Vygotsky, L. S. (1978). *Mind in society: The development of higher psychological processes*. Cambridge, MA: Harvard University Press.

Wood, D., Bruner, J., & Ross, G. (1976). The role of tutoring in problem solving. *Journal of Child Psychology and Psychiatry, 17,* 89–100.

Author Index

Subject Index

A

Adapt, adaptation, 130, 166–169, 172, 181, 183
Alphabetic system, 129
Asides, 181, 193
"Ask" us "tell," 287
Attitude toward writing, 201, 295
Audience, 135–136, 148–162, 172–173, 195
Author, 129, 148, 162, 171, 195
Autonomous, 147

B

Basal readers, 128
Bottom-up (*see* Theories, theoretical)

C

Categories of correspondence, 263ff
  acknowledging receipt of a letter, 273, 278
  corresponding with continuous discourse, 278–288
  sequential corresponding without continuous discourse, 269, 273
  simultaneous corresponding, 264–269
Children's purposes for writing letters, 207, 208ff, 256, 261
Classroom organization, 300–309
Communicative (intent, function), 148, 192
Community of readers and writers, 53–55
Competency, 136–139
Composing, composer, composition, 128–129, 150, 158–161, 164, 167, 169, 176, 177, 181, 191–192, 194
Comprehension, 131, 147
Conceptual systems, conceptualization, 150
Conferences, 305, 307, 309–325
Context, contextualization, contextualized, 6, 19, 145, 148, 166, 169, 171–173, 184, 187, 211
Conventions, conventional, 128, 130, 139, 142, 147–150, 155, 162, 166, 180, 192–196, 330

Conversation, 129–130, 134, 136, 147, 153, 155, 166, 168, 171, 182
Copying, 17, 82, 85–86, 92–93, 105, 113
Correspondence in letters, 203, 262ff
Culture, cultural, 38, 129, 140, 176–177, 193
Cursive writing, 138–139, 149

D

Decoding, decontextualized, decontextualization, 130, 145, 162, 177, 183
Development, 127, 131, 143, 166, 169, 192, 194–196
Developmental sequences, 130, 149–150
Diagnostic, 182
Dialect, 87, 102
Dialogue journals, 202
Dictating, dictation, 128–130, 133, 145–147, 150, 158, 161–164, 166–168, 170, 173, 176–177, 180–181, 189–190, 194
Dramatic play, 62, 80, 88–91, 98–99, 100, 119, 120
Drawing (and writing), 14, 15, 31–33, 62, 80, 88, 102–103, 118, 120, 149, 153, 193

E

Elaboration, 228
Elements (*see* Name elements, Well-learned elements)
Emergent literacy (emergence of literacy, emergent reading, emergent writing), 128, 130, 133, 148, 163–164, 166, 168, 177, 189, 190–191, 193–196
Ethnography, 129
Experimental, 127, 129, 158

F

Formal instruction, schooling, 132, 192, 196
Functional writing, 202